AWAKENED CHINA

The Country Americans
Don't Know

FELIX GREENE

AWAKENED ☆ CHINA

The Country Americans Don't Know

DOUBLEDAY & COMPANY, INC.
Garden City, New York
1961

For Elena

ACKNOWLEDGMENT

It would be impossible for me to list by name all those in Asia, England, and America who have in one way or another contributed to this book, whether by assisting me in preparation of the manuscript, or by deepening my knowledge and understanding of events in China.

To all of them, I remain enormously indebted.

Especially, I would not wish this book to leave my hands without an expression of gratitude to the scores—the hundreds, actually—of individuals in China who extended to me hospitality, courtesy, and hours upon hours of time. These included peasants and scientists, laborers and engineers, bellboys and cabinet ministers. Among them were many in official positions, but by far the larger number were ordinary citizens.

They were as eager to tell me about their country as I was to learn. Otherwise, this book could not have been written.

TABLE OF CONTENTS

PREFACE

In the past ten years hardly a dozen residents of the United States have set foot on the mainland of China with U.S. government approval. Only three were reporters. I was one of them and the only one who has been there twice.

I went to China first in 1957, taking with me all the prevailing assumptions and apprehensions generally prevalent in the United States. I expected to find a country of vast impoverishment and dreadful squalor and disease. I prepared myself to see a people embittered by the rigid coercions of a police state. I expected to see fear as I had seen it in Russia in the early thirties and later in Germany and Italy. That was the China I expected but it was not the China that I found.

The discrepancy between what I had been led to expect and what I actually saw was at first bewildering and disturbing. No one can be in China for more than a few hours without sensing an almost tangible vitality and an enormous optimism. I saw in the people a buoyancy and confidence which was utterly unlike my expectations.

I had already traveled, either as a staff member of the British Broadcasting Corporation or, later, on my own as a businessman and free-lance correspondent, to most of the countries of the world. I thought of myself as a hardened traveler. I was rather blasé. I did not think that seeing a new country could ever really stir or excite me again. But I was wrong. No experience in my life shook me so deeply as this first visit to China. I was not blind to the mistakes that were being made or the extent of the poverty that still existed. I knew something, too, of the suffering and bloodshed that had accompanied the birth of this new China. But all this took on a new meaning in the light of the accomplishments that I could see around me wherever I went. I came away certain that, whatever our view of it might be, what was taking place in China was one of the great historical events of our era.

But how was it possible that a journalist like myself, presumably well-informed on world events, could have gone to China so totally unprepared? The reason is simple. Not only has the United States been cut off diplomatically from China but it is cut off also from any serious information about a country that is moving very quickly to the forefront of political and economic power. I am convinced that this ignorance is dangerous and detrimental to our interests.

In 1959 I went to Asia again—not to China, but to broadcast political commentaries from several of China's continental neighbors. I interviewed a number of Asian leaders. Among these were Mohammed Naim, Foreign Minister of Afghanistan; Prasad Koirala, Prime Minister of Nepal; the Dalai Lama; Dr. Subandrio, Foreign Minister of Indonesia. I spent an evening of discussion with Mr. Nehru. I also visited Burma, Thailand, Laos, Singapore, and Japan. As a result of these talks, one thing became clear to me: that with a variety of hostile, friendly, or ambivalent feelings, Asian leaders are watching the transformation of China into a world power and are wondering when America will understand and come to terms with this reality.

In the summer of 1960 I went to China for the second time, under contract to write this book. And here I should make a personal explanation. I write as an Anglo-American. By this I mean that I am both, and could never again be either one alone. Born and educated in England, I have spent twenty-five years of my adult life in the United States. My legal residence is in America; but my mixed activities of correspondent and businessman take me to England at least twice a year. Technically I am a British subject (and I traveled to China on a British passport). Practically, countless associations of business and friendship and family bind me to

America. Much of my work is here; my home is here; I married here; my child, Anne, goes to school here.

Only those who have lived in both Britain and America as I have can know how both countries can be *home*: how it is possible to feel loyalty to both with no essential conflict. I suppose it is the similarity of national values which makes this possible. I explain this to avoid what might otherwise seem confusing: for though I went to China on a British passport (and could not have gone on an American), the "we" used in this book refers (by long habit of affectionate identification) to "us" Americans.

A journey to Communist China, which so few Westerners have visited, immediately gives rise to a host of questions: Was I free to travel where I wished? Were places prettied up for my benefit? What restrictions were placed on my photography? Did I ever travel alone or was someone always accompanying me? Was I able to meet anybody opposed to the regime? And could they talk freely? Not all these questions can be answered with a simple yes or no, but I believe they are all answered in the course of this book.

I have relied a great deal on my journal—the notes taken while I traveled; and I have also made use of letters which I sent from China to my wife Elena and others. My own fluctuating moods appear in these notes and letters, and that perhaps is as it should be. No one can travel in China without feeling enchanted, angry, overwhelmed, frustrated, touched, saddened, optimistic, puzzled—everything but bored. I do not think that anyone with a grain of human curiosity could feel bored in China today.

I have tried to cover some of the more important facets of Chinese life. There are serious and obvious gaps. Factual information is not easy to come by in China. There are no standard reference books such as one could expect to find on America or even on Russia. There are no resident correspondents who have lived in China for years and who could fill one in on the background. The Western diplomatic corps, while friendly and helpful, are themselves able to see less of China than a traveling correspondent like myself. And, of course, with statistics you can never win. If you quote them, they will be "unreliable." If you do not, your report will not be "factual" enough. I have included some essential data which I believe to be true and which British industrial experts, Western economists, and others have accepted as accurate.

What I have tried most of all to convey is the *feel* of China, what the people are like, how they live, what they think, how the country functions. There are many inconsistencies in my report, because China is a very inconsistent country. There's too much going on. The country is in full spate of experimentation. And it's changing all the time. No one reporter can do anything but touch the fringe of all this. China is in the middle of a gigantic social and industrial explosion, and explosions are not always ruled by consistency.

One important element in the whole China picture is her feelings about us. China is deeply *involved* with America. The intensity of her hostility colors her world perspective and profoundly influences her policies. It is altogether too frivolous to brush this hostility aside as being deliberately engineered to maintain an otherwise uncertain unity at home. The causes have far deeper origins than that. Many Chinese (and especially those who have been educated in America) spelled out to me with considerable cogency and a wealth of documentation why they feel so bitterly toward the United States. I have assembled my notes of these talks and have compiled from them what I have called "the Chinese case." This may not make comfortable reading; but if we hope to understand China we better know why she feels about American policies as she does.

There is another reason why China is difficult to write about: the intense partisanship which China evokes, especially among Americans, and the partisanship evoked by America among the Chinese. Out of this mutual distrust has come a tragic and almost total breakdown of communications. Yet one country is the most powerful industrial nation on earth, the other comprises one-quarter of the entire human race. We in America are now beginning to realize that vast changes are taking place in China, and that we know almost nothing about them. The "biggest story in the world," and we have no reporters there to cover it!

This lack of information and the fears which it evokes have in turn intensified a curious rigidity in our thinking. Nothing today, it seems, can be written about China which is not controversial. Even to *discuss* China seems perverse to some people; and to question our present policies, to analyze the structure of the Chinese government, to try to learn what it is that is moving the Chinese people to such extraordinary efforts is, to many, positively subversive. But, of course, ignoring facts does not make them disappear.

I went back to China with many questions in mind. I had been impressed and surprised by much of what I saw in 1957, but what changes had taken place since then? Were the people still as solidly behind the government? Was their revolutionary enthusiasm beginning to flag? What new developments had taken place in education, in medicine? I wanted to know more about the basic structure of China's economy and more about law and how it was being applied. What about prisons? What about Sino-Russian relations? And above all there were the communes about which we had read such dire reports and which were not even heard of when I was there before.

To find answers to these and many other questions I spent nearly five months traveling over 10,000 miles. I talked with cabinet ministers and pedicab drivers, with heads of government departments and writers. I visited schools, factories, prisons, hospitals. I went to many communes, spent days with the peasants, and ate with them in their communal dining halls. Before I left China I had a long talk with Premier Chou En-lai.

This book describes what I saw and what I learned.

AWAKENED
CHINA

The Country Americans
Don't Know

PART ONE ☆

Hong Kong *1*

May 23

My last day in Hong Kong. The usual rush. All the things I had put off or forgotten, and a hundred others never before thought of. Fountain pen, extra notebook paper, color filters, extra batteries for the new tape recorder. Every store in town, of course, claiming the rock-bottom cut rates. I studied one of the new Bolex 16-mm. cameras, rapidly weakening. Would they ever permit taking movies of the communes? Probably not. But they might, they just might—I broke down: Bolex, zoom lens, all the gadgets, complete with the lightweight tripod which I think weighs half a ton. Sweating and encumbered, I dodged through the crowded streets of this summer city.

On my fourth trip to the China Travel Agency, bad news for the fourth time. Still no visa . . .

"It will be all right," said the agent.

"But they definitely promised the confirmation from Canton."

"It will be all right."

I gave up. In any case the whole business was now out of my hands. And I wanted to look up Kwai-ling before I left. . . . Hailing a cab, I rode to the grocery store where she worked . . . where she *had* worked when I had last seen her the year before.

"Gone," said the proprietor.

"Gone? Where?"

A shrug of the shoulders.

I went to the tenement she had lived in, across the bay in Kowloon. It was gone too. I mean the whole building was gone; they had pulled it down. Nothing was there at all, no one to ask: a gaping hole in that ghastly row of structures. Disappointed, I found myself searching for her along the crowded street as if she might still be somewhere near. One face among three million; what a hope!

Late this afternoon I returned to my hotel. At the desk was a phone message, an invitation for cocktails at six to one of the grand houses on the Peak. I made it there by seven and found a larger crowd than I had expected. I remembered a few faces from before . . . some of the government people, several correspondents. Hong Kong is infested with correspondents. All hoping to get into China, all suspicious of those who do. But I am going *in*. I'm no longer part of this . . . provided the visa comes through. I was too anxious, too excited, too close to China, to care very much what went on at a cocktail party.

Drink in hand, I stepped out onto the terrace.

Below in its myriad winking lights, lay the city of Hong Kong and the harbor with its ships; and lights glimmering in the black water, and beyond the harbor the lights of Kowloon. Farther, off behind the dark hills, was China. I thought again of Kwai-ling, who had come from China, and wondered where she was now; and I thought for a moment of all the other Kwai-lings . . . all these trim, twinkling, tragic, undaunted little Chinese girls of Hong Kong. How many thousands had traced out their lives through the darkness of those fantastic lights?

I had been introduced to Kwai-ling by mutual friends, distant relatives of hers, I believe, when I had been in Hong Kong on a reporting job the year before. She was a refugee . . . nineteen, quick and slim, with a shy laugh. I took her out to dinner once or twice and she told me something about living conditions of the refugees in Hong Kong. One day I went to the grocery store where she worked.

"Kwai-ling," I said, "when you're through work, let me see where you live."

"Oh no, *no!*" she exclaimed. "You wouldn't like it at all. It's a very bad home."

"That's why I want to see it."

She considered this for a moment. "All right you come. Then you must tell other people how girls in Hong Kong have to live."

That afternoon, after work, we rode the ferry across to Kowloon. Kwai-ling's home was in a seven-story tenement off one of the main streets. We climbed flights of creaking stairs, dark, stinking of urine. I remember that she took my hand to lead me down a black corridor. She knew the way as a blind person knows, with her feet. Opening a door, she switched on a light.

"This is where I live."

The room was no larger than a closet.

The bed was a plank on brackets with mattress and the room was exactly long enough for the bed and there was space beside to stand. That was all. No window. The only light came from the bare bulb in the ceiling.

"How long have you lived here?" I asked.

"Three years."

The walls were flimsy wallboard, one wall was made of cardboard. As we stood silent, I heard the stirrings and movements around us, footsteps. The room, I remember, was meticulously clean, but everything, the air, the walls themselves, smelled of decay. One tiny cupboard held Kwai-ling's possessions. And there was a box too, the size of a shoe box, upon which she had propped a photograph. It seemed inconceivable that this young girl, so precise and neat in her blue dress, could find only a hole like this to live in.

As there was no chair—there wasn't room for one—we sat on the bed.

She explained that this was a great improvement over the first place she had lived because here at least she was alone.

I picked up the photograph. It showed a large family group in a garden, posed rather formally.

"That's my father and that's my mother," Kwai-ling told me. "And that little girl is me." She pointed out her sisters, her aunts and uncles. "The picture was taken in Canton before the trouble began. My father is dead now and my mother is back in Canton, though I don't know where. I have a brother in Taiwan, a sister in America. . . ."

A very usual Chinese story . . .

She took the photograph from me, held it in both her hands and looked at it as if she hoped that by gazing at it long enough she could will herself into that garden.

"Would you like to go back?" I asked.

She said nothing for quite a long time. "I think we all want to go back. It's our country. More and more of us are going back. But I'm frightened. What would it be like? What would they do to me? And if I couldn't stand it . . . could I get out again? There are still some who get out and come here to Hong Kong . . . and they tell us such different stories . . . and why doesn't my mother write? I don't know. I can't stay here but I don't know where to go. The American quota is closed or I might be able to join my sister there. I just don't know. And now that you've seen where I live, you'd better leave."

"Come along. Let's go find some place to eat."

But she was still looking at the photograph and shook her head.

I said good-by, and found my own way down the dark staircase. That was a year ago.

And where was she? Back in China? Or still fleeing it, still somewhere in the city below?

I heard a burst of music from inside as someone fiddled with the record player. A man I didn't know, an American, joined me on the terrace with a glass in his hand.

We stood looking over the harbor of Hong Kong and the lights of Kowloon, at the distant hills.

"I hear you're off to the promised land."

"Yes. Tomorrow."

"How in hell did you manage a visa? Special pull?"

"No. I've been waiting a long time. Of course," I added, "it helps to have chosen a British father."

He fingered his glass. "Never mind," he said. "Hong Kong has its compensations . . . no slogans, no communes, no production statistics . . . and the girls! I bet you'll be mighty happy to see Hong Kong again when you're through getting led around those communes. And just bear this in mind. You're jail meat if you so much as wink at a girl. China? You can have it!"

Going In 2

Far too early, I arrived at Kowloon station.

The confirmation had not yet come. "But it will be all right," the travel representative once more assured me. "It will be at the border." But will it? Who can tell? I already imagined the border official, polite, smiling: "So sorry, Mr. Greene, it will not, after all, be quite convenient for you to enter China just now. . . ." It had happened to others—the last-minute change of mind in Peking. But at least I was not afraid today, as I had been three years before. I was actually half hoping, then, that I *would* be turned back at the border. There had been so many warnings from Hong Kong friends. "You're a damn fool to be going in," they had told me. "They know you live in America. They'll trump up some spy charge against you. Then you've had it." Another had said, "Everybody is followed continuously, of course, and your letters will be opened and phone calls monitored. Watch your step, man!" Worst of all was the dapper little Chinese who had approached me in the hotel lobby the night before I left. (Who *was* he, anyway?) Slipping an innocuous picture postcard into my hand, he had said matter-of-factly, in perfect English, "If you get into trouble, Mr. Greene, or if you think they are about to arrest you, mail this and we will see what we can do." He had disappeared before I could even say "Hey, wait a minute!" I tore the postcard up.

Despite the frightful warnings, I had gone into China, spent four or five weeks, and lived to see Hong Kong again. So I knew better this time, my only real anxiety now was that damned confirmation from Canton.

At 10:20, on schedule, the train pulled out of Kowloon headed for the border. We meandered past vegetable plots and paddies, among the low hills, the lakes and inlets of the New Territories. At each stop a few more passengers left our first-class coach. None got on. At last there were only three of us left. Nothing could have conveyed to me more eloquently how cut off China is from the Western world. There are two ways by which Westerners can enter China: from Russia (there's a jet plane service twice a week from Moscow to Peking), and this daily 10:20 A.M. train out of Hong Kong. Into England more than four thousand travelers come every day. New York alone receives at least a thousand daily by ship and by air. Here, going into China (which has almost three times the population of the United States and England combined), just three of us.

My two fellow travelers, I learned, were Australians on their way to Peking to sell wool. Friends, but representing different companies. One was tall, distinguished, of English background; he would have fitted my mental image of a Director of the Bank of England. The other was short and tough, humorous in an American style (and originally was American). He introduced himself as Hank. The Director had never been to China before and didn't want to go. He seemed as nervous as I had been three years earlier. He believed, I think, that his chances of ever coming out hung by the slenderest of threads. Hank, who had been on regular circuit to Peking for the last five years, kept up a running patter which did nothing to cheer his friend.

Fifty minutes after leaving Kowloon the train clanked to a halt. We were at the border.

Instantly, from other carriages, hundreds of Chinese swarmed down and scurried off toward the insignificant iron bridge that links China with British territory. They were families returning from visits to friends and relatives in Hong Kong, or people from Hong Kong going on visits to China; or students home for the holidays; or small businessmen, merchants, peddlers—all struggling with bundles and baskets, nets of fruit, chickens, boxes, suitcases, great bundles of bedding; and everyone laughing and chattering as if it were a great spree. They all seemed to know where to go. The three of us did not. We stood, self-conscious and uncertain, till we were ushered to a small waiting room by a Travel Service man.

"We have sent your passports across," he told us. "When your visas are stamped, they will send them back and you can go."

We waited twenty, thirty minutes. Some hitch, I thought. The Director closed his eyes, pressing his fingertips to his forehead. Hank was telling me about a deal he had made last week in Cairo—but I wasn't listening. There's been a hitch, I told myself. There's been some hitch.

Our turn came at last. A Chinese official in spotless white jacket came to us and said, "I have your visas—will you please come?"

As we trudged across the bridge toward Shumchun, the railway station on the Chinese side, I recalled my 1957 trek and made some mental comparisons. There were still guard towers on each side, but this time I caught no glint of bayonets. I saw no machine guns, no barbed wire, no officers peering through field glasses. On the Chinese side only one somewhat bored khaki-clad soldier leaned on his rifle.

Most of our bags had already been carried across the bridge by porters—the last time I had had to carry them myself. And there was solid wood planking to walk on rather than tiptoeing on the sleepers. Precisely at the center of this undramatic iron bridge the three of us walked into China. I glanced at my companions. The Director, tall, erect, and pale, advanced to his doom. Hank, irrepressible, was trying his handful of Chinese words on the official beside him. All I could think was, My God, I'm really in!

All borders are a separation. And this trivial, almost unguarded bridge much more than most. To some this bridge has represented hope, to some disenchantment and despair. To all of us it has become a wall of ignorance and fear. But walls have two sides, and I have breached it, and now my work is ahead of me, difficult and defined: to see and report as fairly as I can what it looks like here on the other side.

Peking Express 3

Slung with Bolex, exposure meters, gadget bags, my Zeiss cameras, and that "lightweight" half-ton tripod, I staggered after the others. Health certificates first. In another waiting room, another long form to fill—border stations are the same all over the world—camera numbers? quantity of unexposed film? the usual questions.

Next, to the examination of baggage.

My miniature tape recorder intrigued the examiner.

"It's very small," he said.

I nodded. He was, I think, an electronics engineer at heart. He fingered the recorder affectionately. "Nickel cadmium batteries?"

"Yes."

"Does it have a wide frequency range?"

"No, but good enough for speech." I knew what he wanted and waited for him to ask.

"May I switch it on?" He was like a small boy.

"Of course."

The night before, in my hotel room, to test the thing, I had picked up an old copy of an American magazine, I have forgotten which, and read from the first page that fell open. What was it I had read? Panic as it came to me—too late. From the tiny machine, my own voice spoke, clear, distinct: "With the use of modern infra-red film and stereo lenses wide areas of territory can today be photographed from high altitudes——"

Why had I chosen *that*, of all pieces to read? Why not a symphony review or the latest dope on the New York Yankees? Why in the name of heaven had I not washed the thing off? The customs man, expressionless, was listening intently. I saw my China trip ending here . . . held for investigation . . . tape sent to Peking for analysis . . . an international incident . . . British spy . . . American saboteur . . . *idiot!*

The voice finally petered out.

The customs inspector switched the machine off and gently closed the lid. "Thank you," he said, "thank you very much. Very interesting. Very good voice reproduction." He held out his hand. "We hope you have a pleasant stay in China, Mr. Greene. The train to Canton will leave in an hour. There is a restaurant upstairs."

"Good-by," I said. "And thank *you* very much."

Upstairs, I found my two Australians studying the luncheon menu. The restaurant looked clean and bright with white tablecloths and flowers. The Director was a man reprieved but not yet altogether out of the shadows. No firing squad, just life imprisonment. "I must admit," he said, with admirable Anglo-Saxon sportsmanship, "that these officials couldn't have treated us with greater courtesy." But he added, "We have to realize, of course, it's all part of the plan to create a good first impression."

The Canton train was in by the time we finished lunch. Passengers with bundles, chickens, babies, boxes, children, stood waiting to board. Soldiers were in the line too—there was no priority. And no one shoving or pushing, but everyone talking at a great rate. We were led to an observation car at the end of the train—our bags were already aboard. Soon after, to a great blast of music from loudspeakers on the lamp poles, and another loud blast (with a different tune) from speakers on the train, the train rolled out of the station.

This was a fancy car, better than anything I had seen three years before. Leather chairs faced each other, set far enough apart for plenty of leg-room. At the rear was a potted tree, and several smaller shrubs, like a conservatory; and there were flowers and ferns on the tables between the chairs. Two rosy-cheeked, pigtailed girls, looking astonishingly young, in gray-blue skirts and white blouses, kept dusting and cleaning and fetched us tea at frequent intervals. The car was not full. There were perhaps ten others, aside from the Australians and myself. All were young men in T shirts. When I opened my Bolex and threaded a reel of film, they gathered around to watch. Everything was very informal. Catch a Chinese eye and it invariably responds with a smile.

The view from the train windows was like a scene from a Sung painting, even more Chinese than I had remembered. Old clustered villages with their curved roofs among the terraced rice fields. Tiny silver waterfalls sparkled from terrace to terrace, an irrigation system two thousand years old and still working. Peasants in the fields in their wide cone hats, at work, or walking languidly with rake or hoe over their shoulders. And water buffalo. And brakes of bamboo and banana trees; everything green and lush.

There were young trees everywhere, I noted, especially along the sides of the railroad track, five, eight, ten rows deep. Acacia, pine, eucalyptus. Trees—miles and miles of them. I remembered them as just twigs three years ago. Now they are eight and ten feet tall. There are almost no large trees visible. China must have been a treeless land. Now, looking back from the observation car, the track runs endlessly between groves of young trees, their branches wildly waving with the rush of wind from the train.

We rolled into Canton late in the afternoon; there would be a two-hour wait for the train to Peking. I had asked at the border for an interpreter to meet me in Canton and the Travel Agency had wired ahead. Mr. Chin was waiting on the platform. He was friendly, eager to help. He slung some of my cameras over his shoulders and arranged for a porter to carry the other luggage. We went to a large waiting room, cool, with white slip covers on the furniture and a large fan spinning silently overhead. A young woman in braids and trousers brought us tea.

Mr. Chin said, "How long did you work with the BBC, Mr. Greene?"

I glanced up, surprised.

"Oh, I remember you well from your last visit," he told me. We talked then about some of the other foreigners he had helped on their way through Canton. His comments were witty and perceptive. I asked what had become of my Australian companions and learned that arrangements had been made for them to go on to Peking by air.

It was very hot. Obviously Mr. Chin was sleepy and I was too, but I wanted to see something of the town. I suggested he stay while I went out for a stroll. At this he looked dubious. "You might get lost," he warned. But the thought of a short nap in the cool waiting room must have appealed to him. "Be sure to come back in plenty of time," he called, and settled himself into one of the armchairs.

Historically, Canton has long been a city of insurrection—it was here the Opium War started, and the Sun Yat-sen revolution; this is where the Communist movement in the twenties reached its greatest ferment and where it was ruthlessly crushed by Chiang Kai-shek. It was a city of secret societies and dark assassinations. It was from here that the Chinese traveled to make new homes in Southeast Asia, in Hawaii, in America. Today, the largest industrial city of south China, it seems the least touched by the great cleanup, the least refurbished, of any Chinese city. Gray and sprawling, crowded and dirty, Canton spans the Pearl River and here the tugs hoot and push their way among the thousands of sampans and junks with patched and tattered sails, on which Chinese still are born, and live and die.

In the streets I walked into the throbbing life of a Chinese city. The poverty hit me like a blow! I had forgotten how poor the Chinese are. But it's not a sullen poverty, or apathetic; not like India—not a sitting-around-waiting-for-something-to-happen kind of poverty. Here, in spite of squalid surroundings, a general atmosphere of vitality. Children playing lustily everywhere—some followed me, giggling.

At a lumber yard, tiny, slight men, stripped to the waist, backs glistening with sweat, were carrying waterlogged tree trunks from a river—each one fifteen feet long and at least six inches or more thick, a load for four or six men at home. Staggering, they carried these immense weights up a slope, then across a busy street to the sawmills. Unbelievable that these thin bodies could bear so heavy a load. I also stopped to watch some small-scale iron-casting—men hauling tremendous buckets of molten iron drawn from a kiln and pouring it into sand molds. Four men to a load. Rough ground. A single stumble and the bucket would have spilled, with dreadful consequences.

Vitality and poverty. Children and laughter. Shrill music from loudspeakers. Women sitting on doorsteps chattering, men calling to each other across the street. The noise, the children, the squalor, the buoyancy—I knew I was really back in China.

On the Train to Peking

I said good-by to Mr. Chin at Canton. I'm on my own and have just finished a splendid dinner—pressed duck, fish fried in batter with sweet-sour sauce, shredded onions, small peas, and rice, topped off with a huge bowl of soup. Soup ends the meal in China. All this with beer cost $1.20 American.

The dining car is clean and continually swept and dusted. I watched them dusting even around picture frames and over the moldings. The tables bear white cloths and covers of transparent plastic, easy to wipe off. General atmosphere informal and relaxed. I realize again that China is a worker's country. The ordinary people have taken over. It's their show. The men wear T shirts. Easygoing, a good deal of joking. No one pays much attention to me—except the children, of course, who always think foreigners are funny. There is no menu. The waiter tells people what's available and they order by word of mouth. Service is quick. Among the diners I could spot, here and there, serious young men in glasses, obviously intellectuals. Schoolteachers perhaps, or scientists. They wear the same clothes, but seem a little quieter than the others, though they join easily enough in the general talk.

I see no pictures of Mao on the train. The dining car has garish prints of some of China's beauty spots. Also one of Lenin and Stalin shaking hands.

I think I am the only foreigner on this twelve-coach train. The train is not at all crowded. I have the compartment to myself, so far. My books, cameras, typewriter are scattered on the other beds. Nearly every hour the girl knocks and fills my tea mug from a huge can of steaming water. We try and talk together. Pointing, she tells me the Chinese for "tea," for "mug," for "bed," for "book," (*cha, bei, chuang, shu*). Then she points to her hot-water can to indicate that she must be off on her rounds.

I get down at most station stops, partly for exercise, partly to sniff the atmosphere. As in America, an attendant stands at the coach entrance wiping off the handles. The passenger trains here are all colored green with yellow stripes, except for a very plush-looking "Peace Train" we passed which is painted blue. The "Peace Train" I am told is a slightly more luxurious special which runs four times a week. I happen to have hit a day it doesn't run.

The train staff has a passion for cleanliness. At several of the longer stops girls with long-handled brooms and buckets of water wash down the outside of the coaches.

The coach I am traveling in was made in China in 1957. It isn't sleek. No air-conditioning, no vista-dome, no chairs that tilt back at the touch of a button. Simple, utilitarian. There are two classes. I'm traveling first class, which means a compartment with four berths, each berth with sheets, a blanket, and one not very soft pillow. There are double windows—the lower half of the outside pane is a fine screen, which dims the view and holds back the larger lumps of soot (all trains are coal burners) but allows the fine dust to get in. The Chinese have built several diesel-electric locomotives but they are not yet on regular runs.

Above the window is a loudspeaker; a strident woman's voice and the piercing wail of Chinese music, with now and again a more melodic tune that reminds me of a Scots lament. The perpetual music and running commentary was driving me mad till I discovered a control knob under the table, by which the volume could be lowered or the loudspeaker turned off altogether.

Cost of Travel: Canton–Peking, forty hours, more than a thousand miles, with sleeper for two nights—117 yuan, or $46.80. Air fare: 159 yuan, or $64.00.

Meals: Western breakfast of three fried eggs with ham, tea, toast, butter, and jam, usually around fifty cents U.S.; Chinese dinner and lunch (quite lavish, with beer or wine) around $1.20.

Hints to Travelers: Take your interpreter to the dining car before the train starts and he leaves you to your own devices. Let the chef know you like Chinese food and leave the choice to him. Ask when they would like you to come for meals. He will then do his best—some of the tastiest meals I have had in China are on the railroads. There's no tipping in China, *anywhere*. Don't even *try* to tip, it will be as embarrassing as if you tried to tip an airline hostess in the States. Receipts are given for everything, even the two cents you pay for the tea and hot water, which are brought continuously to your compartment.

Before you go to China, try and learn a *few* Chinese characters and words. It pays off in the appreciation that is apparent everywhere. A little book put out by Foreign Language Press in Peking, *English-Chinese Conversation*, is quite helpful. With the help of this book I was able to tell the waiter in the dining car, *"Fan hen hao chih!"* (the food is excellent). I was not quite certain he understood, but a few moments later the chef popped his head round from the kitchen and gave me a wave—my message had reached its destination.

Leave everything in your compartment. Nothing is stolen. Beer is all in *large* bottles and very good. Today I tried some red wine, which is good too, though rather sweet. Take your own towels. They *do* provide toilet paper but it's like sandpaper. Toilets on the trains are not clean by U.S. standards, but I have seen worse in Britain and France.

Just accept the fact that you will get black. Don't wear white clothing. There's a choice—open your window and let the fine dust through the screening and *breathe*, or close the window, keep clean, and *suffocate*. I chose the dirt and air.

At one station during a ten-minute stop a crowd of interested young men gathered round me as I was making a recording of some station sounds. A policeman shooed them away—thought they were worrying me, and I couldn't get him to understand that I didn't mind. They moved off sullenly. When the policeman had gone I waved them back and they came grinning.

At another stop I saw the conductor was looking impatiently at his watch while the engine took on water. I checked my watch with his—saw it was an Ingersoll "Triumph." Made in the U.S.A.

We are moving north across the Yangtze Valley and soon will be crossing the Yangtze River. From the train window, mile upon mile of rice terraces, in all shades of green, many with water standing on them. These terraced fields are so old, so gently conform to the contour of the land, that they seem to have become part of the natural landscape. Rice apparently has no season. I saw some being planted—girls with rolled-up trousers calf-deep in water, bending, with swift, deft movements planting the green tufts. Elsewhere peasants were harvesting. In some villages I saw them tossing the rice into the air, letting the wind do the winnowing, in the ancient way.

Almost all of this main line is now double-tracked. The new track, especially, appears well ditched and ballasted. Kilometers, in quarters, marked off along the track. I watched the locomotive being oiled last night under floodlights. A swarm of oilers were at work while the engineer stood with list in hand and checked off the bearings as the oilers reported to him. Only when the list was fully checked did he signal that the locomotive was ready to go.

At all stops of ten minutes or longer, wheel tappers went down both sides of the train inspecting the wheels, lifting journal-box covers, feeling for the heat of the bearings. I watched a maintenance man check the adjoining track, both for level and for gauge. He could read on a rotating dial the amount of any deviation. I walked with him for a few moments and watched him closely as he moved down the line. The tolerance permitted seemed a narrow one. Each deviation beyond this tolerance he carefully recorded in a book. Trains in China ride astonishingly smoothly, even at high speeds.

At Canton I had walked up to the locomotive before we started. In the cab was a round-faced girl engineer. She wore a peaked cap stuck jauntily on the back of her head. By her confident looks and gestures one felt how proud she was at having stepped into this man's world. There was an engineer, a man, with her. Both wore white cotton gloves.

At 7:30 this morning, while we stopped briefly, I watched the railway staff lined up on the platform doing their setting-up exercises to music and instructions from loudspeakers. Not much zip.

Last night, at one of the stops, there was a gaily covered booth with curved roof selling toilet articles. I bought a plastic soap box and a washcloth (fifty cents for the two, which seemed rather high). Lots of business. I lined up with the rest waiting my turn. When the girl looked up and saw it was a foreigner, she broke into a delighted grin.

A security policeman travels with the train. He seems to be always putting on his jacket, which is never properly buttoned up. I prefer this to the overcorrect. Before we come into a station he hastily buttons up and puts on a belt. I often see him in the dining car chatting with the train crew over a cigarette. Old-timers in China later told me that security police who rode the trains in Chiang Kai-shek's time were quite tough.

May 26

As we approached Peking, the excitement grew. I was summoned to lunch very early and I understood why later, when I saw the tables in the dining car being scrubbed, chairs piled high, soy-sauce bottles emptied and washed. In the sleeping car, carpets were lifted and the floors mopped down. During the forty-hour journey from Canton I estimated the outsides of the coaches must have been squeegeed at least ten times. The train arrived as bright and shiny as when it left Canton.

I went into the kitchen after my last meal to shake hands with the four cooks and thank them. "*Shieh-shieh ni.*" They were delighted. "*Hen hao, hen hao,*" they said: very good, very good. When I got back to my compartment, the train was slowing down; we passed the city wall and slid slowly into a brand-new station. Potted plants stood in rows along the platform; and from the inevitable loudspeakers came the blare of a Sousa-type march, "Socialism Is Good."

We arrived two minutes ahead of schedule.

A Banquet 4

The Intourist representative was waiting for me at the station. An intense young man, apparently just on the boil under the surface, with unexpressed feelings and wordless passions. He was somewhat brusque. He conveyed that I was not to expect any little insincere speech of welcome from him, and I liked him for it. Whisking me through the ticket barrier, he said, "This is our new station, you can see it all later"; and with that, we were into a taxi and off through the wide and tree-lined streets of Peking to the Shin Chiao Hotel. (The Chinese spell it *Hsin Chiao*. Throughout the book I have, except in the spelling of well-known names, translated Chinese words to the closest English phonetic equivalent.)

The Shin Chiao is a large gray structure, built in 1954 for returning Overseas Chinese, now one of the main centers for foreign visitors. The much grander Peking Hotel is known as "The Mausoleum," and I was glad not to be there. Accommodations at the Shin Chiao are unpretentious but adequate. Each room has a private bath, telephone, desk, and two easy chairs, but, curiously, no chest of drawers. A message awaiting me at the desk requested me to call at the Information Office of the Ministry of Foreign Affairs at my earliest convenience.

I unpacked, sent my "good" suit to be pressed and set off by taxi for the Ministry. I would, I supposed, very shortly learn something of what was in store for me. Would the government be helpful? Would they be suspicious or friendly? What facilities would be given me to photograph? To travel? To interview those I wanted to see? There was also the question of extending my visa, which had been issued for only a month. I would need much longer than that to gather material for my book. I felt I would soon know the answer to these questions. But in China such matters are not decided so quickly.

I learned that I was at liberty to photograph whatever I wished excepting military installations. As to motion pictures, that was a different story. I could put my request in writing. Extension of the visa? Maybe so, maybe not; perhaps best to leave that till a little later on, Mr. Greene. Meanwhile, would I submit a list of things I wished to see while in Peking? I agreed that I would; and as I took my departure, I was presented with an invitation to a banquet being given by Premier Chou En-lai that evening for the visiting guest-of-state, Field Marshal Montgomery.

It was after six thirty when I got back to my hotel. The banquet was to start within forty-five minutes. No suit! "Sorry," said the floor boy. "Pressing department is close. Suit ready tomorrow morning."

"But I'm invited to a banquet with Mr. Chou En-lai!"

"Excuse—we shall see." He took off down the corridor at a dead run. Fifteen, twenty minutes went by; time to leave. I hurried downstairs, found no one who spoke English. I tried the telephone. "Sorry," said the phone girl. "Laundry and pressing room are close."

Where's that floor boy? Had he gone home? I waited, and there at last he was, like a relay runner, the suit on its hanger extended at arm's length. And beautifully pressed!

Cars were drawing up when I arrived at the great curved ramp at the northern entrance to the Great Hall of the People. Police, in white jackets, were directing the flow of traffic. There was no confusion. An immaculately uniformed soldier stood motionless on each side of the wide doors. No one asked to see my invitation or checked my credentials. Under the crystal chandeliers the new arrivals were moving slowly up a lane of heavy carpet laid across a vast foyer toward a magnificent flight of stairs. I glanced around at my fellow guests. Many looked like senior government officials; there were military officers, some young men in workers' uniform, girls—some in skirts, others in trousers. Here and there were members of China's many minorities in vivid national costumes.

I knew no one.

At the head of the stairs we were directed to a reception room where the official whom I had met earlier at the Ministry of Foreign Affairs at once came forward to greet me and to introduce me to others. Here I met Ron Farquhar, of Reuters. Only two Western news agencies have permanent representatives in China— Reuters and Agence France Presse. I talked to some officials from the British Embassy. Strictly speaking, there is no British Embassy in Peking (as there is no Chinese Embassy in London), for the two countries have not yet exchanged ambassadors. It is officially "The Office of the British Chargé d'Affaires." Britain is represented there by a Minister. I was also introduced to Madame Kung Peng, Director of the Information Department at the Foreign Ministry. I was immensely glad to meet her. Madame Kung has become something of a legend among foreign writers who have visited China. I first heard of her from James Cameron of the London *News Chronicle*. Sooner or later her name crops up in any conversation among journalists dealing with China news.

Madame Kung was dressed in black. Her manner was quiet.

She spoke in a low voice, pausing for a moment's reflection before answering my questions. I had been warned that she was somewhat "formidable." Certainly she appeared composed and self-possessed, and I judged not much would escape that level and slightly ironic gaze. She was a person, I felt sure, not much interested in the minor social flatteries, but once her interest was engaged on a serious level the sense of formality vanished. I found her not at all formidable.

Madame Kung Peng pointed out several of the guests who were seated in a central group of chairs. There was Henry Pu-yi, last of the Chinese Emperors, who had been released from confinement only eight months ago. (Henry Pu-yi had "ruled" China from the age of two until he was six. The Japanese brought him back in 1932 as Emperor of their puppet state of Manchukuo. He was then called K'ang Te.) Not far from the former Emperor sat Marshal Chen Yi, now Foreign Minister, the Communist general whose forces captured Shanghai in 1949. Beyond Chen Yi were several other generals who had fought under Chiang Kai-shek against the Communists. One of these, Tu Yu-ming, had at one time been Chiang's commander-in-chief in Manchuria. He had led the Kuomintang forces in one of the last decisive battles of the civil war, in which he had been routed by the Communist armies under General Chen Yi. Later Tu had been condemned as a war criminal, and like the one-time Emperor, had only recently emerged from prison. Here they all were, chatting pleasantly together at an official banquet!

The Prime Minister, Chou En-lai himself, now came in with the guest of honor, Field Marshal Montgomery. Monty looked trim and alert, though rather older than I had expected. Chou En-lai, apparently ageless (he is now in his early sixties) appeared dapper, suave, thoroughly at ease in a simple gray Chinese jacket and trousers. I watched this man, fascinated by his gestures, and by the rapid alternation of his expressions. An extraordinarily mobile face —now ironical, now jesting, now, at some comment from Montgomery, instantly alert and attentive.

Here, without doubt, was one of the most outstanding figures of modern history. He had been in the thick of it from the very start; a founder of the Chinese Communist Party in 1921, a soldier on the Long March, a leader throughout more than twenty

years of civil war and a decade of war against the Japanese. He
had led a life of miraculous escapes. Captured and imprisoned by
Chiang's forces, he had slipped out of their fingers. A quarter of
a million dollars on his head, he had walked unguarded among
the peasants. Several times he had survived what for most human
beings must have been total and annihilating defeat—and now he
is Prime Minister, chief executive officer of the People's Republic
of China. Hero to millions, devil to millions of others. What was
one to read in such a face? Tenacity, a lively humor, the keenest
intelligence, certainly; a man fully committed without divisions
within himself; yet also, perhaps, able to stand outside, watching,
cool, detached, thoughtful. . . .

I was quite close as Chou introduced Monty to Henry Pu-yi.
Monty asked if he was happy. The last of the Manchu Emperors
replied:

"I am a gardener now and I have never been happier in my life.
It is much better to be a gardener than to sit on the throne of the
Imperial Palace doing just what you're told to do."

Chou laughed. Monty looked bewildered. I wondered if he knew
who Pu-yi was. The Prime Minister now turned to the generals
who had risen from their chairs and were waiting to be introduced.
Pointing to Tu Yu-ming and Chen Yi, the Prime Minister said,
"These two fought each other. This one lost."

"How many men did you have?" Montgomery asked Tu.

"A million."

"Why did you lose if you had a million men?"

"They all ran over to his side," said Tu, nodding toward Chen
Yi.

Chou En-lai threw back his head and laughed.

We moved on to the banquet hall for dinner. This chamber, I
was told, can seat five thousand guests at five hundred round tables. Tonight there were only a hundred or hundred and fifty people, but the room had been skillfully reduced in size by screens
of potted plants. At one end was a stage hung with curtains of
heavy gold brocade. Between courses, the curtains were drawn back
and a program of Chinese singing and dancing was presented, both
classical and modern, ending with a professional performance of
Western classics by the Central Philharmonic Symphony Orches-

tra. The entire program was magnificent. And the food! Well, here were some of the items (among a good many others) on the menu:

> Jasmine chicken soup
> Three-colored shark's fins
> Green peas in chicken oil
> Steamed shad
> Roast-pork slices
> Duck with tea flavor
> Strawberries with cream

There were also red and white wines, Chinese brandy, and *mao tai*, a distilled liquor rather like a fierce vodka. We were served by young women who moved about with so little fuss and clatter that you scarcely noticed the constant reappearance of steaming platters in front of you.

Chou En-lai made a short speech of welcome to the visiting Field Marshal. He offered a toast to the British people. We all stood. Chou walked from table to table—he came to ours and I tipped glasses with him—while the band played God Save the King. Monty, glass in hand, then made his reply:

"I would like very much to extend to Prime Minister Chou En-lai a very warm invitation to visit me personally as my private guest at my home in England so that I can show him my country and I hope very much that he will come."

This was translated and brought a burst of applause from the guests.

Monty continued: "Old China suffered many years of external aggression in which perhaps we British were not completely blameless, and suffered internal oppression of a feudal nature. You have swept away emperors, war lords, absentee landlords, and foreign devils. All have gone.

"There is a new China under a new leadership which is determined to be master in its land and to plan its own destiny in its own way without any outside interference. From what I have seen, I like the new China better than the old.

"Now there are great misconceptions in the Western world about the new China. I find the Chinese people to be happy and cheerful, whereas in the Western world it is considered that the Chinese people are very depressed and unhappy. . . ."

(When General A. C. Wedemeyer, U.S. Army, retired, read this speech, he challenged the British Field Marshal in a letter to the Washington *Star,—see Kaleidoscope 2.*)

I walk home alone.

The night is warm. Everywhere about me I see the changes that have taken place since my previous visit. Tien An Men (Gate of Heavenly Peace) Square has been enormously enlarged. Old buildings are gone, walls gone, streetcar lines gone. There are new buildings, new trees. Tien An Men itself, the main gate to what once were the Imperial Palaces, softly lighted, its roofs curved like a tent, still broods majestically over the capital of China.

Shi Chang An Chieh, the main boulevard which crosses the city from east to west, is ablaze with lights. But there are not many people out this late. A few young men, nearly all in white open-collar shirts, and women in trousers and colored blouses, stroll homeward along the sidewalks. The last cars from the banquet hall go speeding by; and a late pedicab trundles down the wide avenue carrying a prodigious load of furniture. I walk past Peking Hotel, then along Tai Chi Chang to what I still can only think of as "Legation Street." The Shin Chiao only a few blocks beyond.

I am tired; but the long suspense is over. I am *here.* Back in Peking. I feel again the enchantment, the strange and subtle spell that this extraordinary city casts on all who come here. I sniff the night air and am deeply content. I feel confident that all will go well with my undertakings. . . .

PART TWO

Peking,
the Old and the New 5

In 1949 when the Communists marched into Peking, the city, with a population of not much more than a million and a half, was wholly enclosed within its walls. As in the days of the Emperors the gates of the city were shut at night. Immediately beyond the walls were the rice fields and vegetable gardens. Today, eleven years later with a population that has soared to four million, seven and a half million if the whole municipal area is included, Peking has burst through its walled enclosure and has burgeoned outward in every direction. The forty-foot-thick walls have been pierced to allow new boulevards to radiate from the city and the walls are now not much more than picturesque reminders of a legendary past.

Peking continues to be the heart, the mind, the controlling center of China.

It is a very ancient city; its origins are buried in the far past. Records show that over four thousand years ago there was already a settlement at the spot where the present city stands. By the twelfth century, known then as Chungtu, the city was playing an important role as a commercial center and as headquarters for the forces protecting the country from the encroachments of nomadic tribes from the north. When Genghis Khan swooped down from beyond the northern deserts he captured Chungtu. A hundred years later his grandson Kublai Khan, having conquered the whole of China, rebuilt the city and renamed it Tau—the Great Capital. Called Peiping (Northern Peace) in the Ming dynasty, its name was changed in 1420 to Peking (Northern Capital), which it retained until 1928 when Chiang Kai-shek moved his capital south to Nanking and it was known again as Peiping.

Laid out when London was still a village, Peking has been burned, rebuilt, sacked, demolished by earthquakes, and rebuilt again; for six centuries it has been the city in which China's learning and wealth, culture and politics found their national focus.

In October 1949, when the Chinese People's Republic was established, its position as the national capital and its name were restored and it is today known as Peking throughout the world—except in the United States, in deference to the myth that Chiang Kai-shek still is the ruler of China. (To call it Peking would imply that the capital of China is there and not in Taipei on the island of Taiwan.)

Peking is a city built on an ancient Chinese pattern, a series of rectangles enclosed by walls. Its primary purpose was to enshrine the Imperial Palace. Peking, though its avenues are wide and straight, is a city of walls, of walls within walls. There is the wall of the Chinese City and the wall of the Tartar City; within the walls of the Tartar City are the walls of the Imperial City; and finally within these, are the rust-red walls of the Imperial Palace, the Forbidden City itself. In this inmost sanctuary are the golden-roofed palaces, the courtyards, the gardens from which successive Emperors held sway over the vast expanses of China—*Chung Kuo*, the Middle Kingdom. The architecture is massive but of flawless proportion. One feels that these buildings, like China herself, will be here forever. Never before, not even in Greece and Rome, have I felt so powerful a sense of the continuity of human history as I have in these palaces of Peking. Walking through the courtyards it is not difficult to imagine their past glory and their almost total isolation from the teeming, hungry life of the ordinary mortals who lived beyond the walls.

The Forbidden City is no longer forbidden. It is open—free to children, and to anyone else who can raise the equivalent of two cents for admission. The halls, the temples, the living quarters of the Emperors, most painstakingly and beautifully restored, are now national museums. Days can be spent here strolling through palaces with absurd and poetic names—the Hall of Supreme Harmony, the Palace of Heavenly Peace, the Hall of Mental Cultivation, the Palace of Earthly Tranquillity. Crossing the Golden Water on bridges of white marble you mingle with the crowds of visitors—soldiers walking hand in hand, Tibetans in derby hats, Africans slung with cameras, schoolchildren with bright-red scarves, babies hauled piggyback by brothers and sisters scarcely older than themselves. Pools reflect the drooping willow trees, butterflies hover over silent lotus ponds; and on a stool, watched by wide-eyed children sucking frozen sugar-water sticks, a man sits carving the sayings of Confucius on a single grain of rice.

Today, the city in no sense seems enclosed, but rather of limitless physical expansion. To this capital come visitors from almost every country on the globe. To millions of Asians, Latin Americans, Africans, Peking has become the new Mecca.

Walking through Peking one is given a strong impression of living in two eras. Peking is a big, clean, well-functioning modern city; it is also—one is reminded of this everywhere—a city that has just stepped out of the Middle Ages. From my hotel window I can see the Great Hall of the People completed in 1958, and almost in the same glance my eye catches one of Peking's ancient gates—the Chien Men. Everywhere the old, the new. In the street below me a caravan of pedicab drivers will, on their makeshift and dilapidated tricycles, be transporting delicate apparatus from an electronics plant.

There are more theaters in Peking today than in New York. Most of the fifty-five cinemas—some have wide-screen projectors—were built in the last ten years. There are sixteen main hotels, nearly all have gone up since 1950; they are up-to-date with private bathrooms and telephones in every room. Unlike Moscow, everything —plumbing, hot water, room service—really *works*.

The postal service with 350 post offices in the city and suburbs is efficient and deliveries are rapid. China is a member of the International Postal Union and letters can be sent from here to anywhere in the world, including the United States. For reasons unknown I discovered that mail to America arrived much sooner if Hong Kong could be avoided. This could be done by writing "via Moscow" on the envelope.

Officially there is no censorship of mail in China and I have no reason to suspect that any of my letters were read, but other West-erners, permanently resident in Peking, feel certain that some of their letters are opened. But *where* they are opened (in China or somewhere else along the line) is anybody's guess. When I questioned the head of the incoming foreign-mail department at the Peking central post office, he swore, of course, that mail was never tampered with in China.

You can cable from Peking to any country in the world. I received many cables from the United States and sent many, and they all went through without a hitch. One cable sent from California reached me in Peking in two hours. The domestic telegraph service is cheap and fast—there is a flat rate, regardless of distance, of the equivalent of 13 cents for ten words, with an additional 1.3 cents for each additional word. Documents or other written material can be sent by facsimile to most of the main cities of China for 70 cents a sheet.

You can telephone from Peking to almost every country in the world *except* the United States. Telephone communication with Canada is possible and I tried once to telephone to my wife in California *through* Canada. The Chinese accepted my call and said they would do their best to set it up but came back later and told me that the United States would not accept this arrangement. Long-distance calls to cities within China are subject to delays and often the circuits are poor. In Peking itself there is a dial system a great deal more efficient than the London service, which, I admit, is not saying much. Again unlike Moscow, there are plenty of telephone directories, though unless you are an advanced scholar in Chinese, to try and find a number is a hopeless proposition. Local calls cost the equivalent of two cents from a booth, but hotels make no charge for calls. If you dial 07 you will be given the time; if you dial 05 you can ask for a weather report, learn what's playing at the theaters, or subscribe to a newspaper or magazine.

Other developments that have brought Peking into the twentieth century are the hospitals—at least thirty large new ones have been built and some of these are as up-to-date as any in the West; more about these later—a modern sewage system, and water which is safe to drink. The Chinese have become very "public-hygiene conscious"; people with colds are expected to wear surgical masks—this is a common sight. The streets—even those in the small lanes which are still of tamped earth—are swept and sprinkled down every day. Big water trucks are constantly washing down the wider streets. Peking is as clean or cleaner than many of the cities of England or America. No piles of garbage, no refuse, no smells, no cigarette stubs—and (it's true) almost no flies. China is now so clean that I broke what is otherwise one of my iron rules of traveling—namely, never to eat uncooked vegetables or salads. In China I did both for nearly five months, including meals on the train, and suffered neither anxiety nor ill effects. I know of no other country in Asia where this is even thinkable.

The sheer volume of building construction going on in China—and I found this to be true in all the cities I visited—is overwhelming. New offices, hotels, museums, schools, apartment houses, colleges, technical institutes, stadiums, gymnasiums, swimming pools, are going up in such numbers and at such a speed that it has to be seen to be believed. The construction—I have had some experience in the building line—is without question superior in technical quality to the buildings I have watched being erected in the Soviet Union, where the engineering is frequently inferior.

In speed of construction the Chinese have far out-Americanized America. By 1954 they had mastered the problems of smooth organization, a steady supply of materials to the building sites, and round-the-clock continuous operation. James Cameron of the London *News Chronicle*, who was in China that year, reported in his book, *Mandarin Red*, how even then the pace of building was, unless you watched it yourself, unbelievable; how four new hospitals, six factories, and eleven full-scale Ministerial blocks had been laid out, started, completed, and inhabited in a matter of weeks. The hotel I stayed in in Nanking in 1957—a four-hundred-room hotel with tiled bathroom to every room, telephones, elevators, all equipment—was (I was assured by a British resident who had watched it) completed in seventeen weeks, including the landscaping with almost full-grown trees brought in. James Cameron saw the Chinese genius for rapid construction in 1954; I saw it first in 1957; and now in 1960 they were outdoing even these earlier efforts.

To celebrate the *tenth* anniversary of the regime (1959), the government determined in 1958 that Peking would undertake *ten* major building projects and complete them in *ten* months. (The Chinese are fond of this kind of play with numbers. The Chinese

Revolution was celebrated as Double Ten [October 10] and still is on Taiwan. Double Seven [July 7, 1937] signified the Japanese invasion of China proper.) Two of these projects were the construction of the Museum of Chinese History and the Great Hall of the People. These vast buildings stand each side of Tien An Men Square. The Square itself was enlarged from twenty-seven to nearly one hundred acres in extent, five times the size of St. Peter's in Rome, and it is now the largest, and I think perhaps one of the most pleasing, squares in the world.

On the east of the Square is the new Museum of Chinese History. Here you can trace the history of China through its art from its earliest beginnings to the modern era. This is now the repository of China's finest artistic treasures. Air-conditioned, beautifully lighted, and with its displays presented with the taste one would expect from these artistic people, this will take its place as one of the great museums of the world.

Facing it across the square—the square is five hundred yards wide —stands another new building, the one that takes pride of place in the hearts of all Peking—the Great Hall of the People. Size and taste don't often go together. Here they do. The size of this building is staggering, its proportions and simplicity are noble. Eleven hundred feet long, fronted by ten columns, this building contains within it not only the five-thousand-seat banqueting hall where the dinner to Montgomery was held, and twenty-odd reception rooms each as big as a normal ballroom, but the Great Hall, itself. With two sweeping, unsupported balconies, this auditorium holds ten thousand people and it is here that the National People's Congress meets, and all the other great political meetings and rallies, as well as the large concerts, are held.

There are several novel features about this hall. Its design breaks every known rule of acoustics, but you can, in spite of its size, hear distinctly in every part of it. Unknown to you, the sound from the stage is reaching you from ten thousand small loudspeakers—one is installed at the back of every chair. All seats on the ground floor are equipped with earphones through which you can hear a simultaneous translation of a speech in any one of twelve different dialects or languages. Russian and English are invariably among these. Another interesting fact about this hall is that while fourteen thousand workers were employed in its construction, citizens of Peking could give whatever volunteer help they wanted, and many thousands did so at weekends, in the evenings, or during vacation times. One of my interpreters, a girl, once pointed to the building as we passed it in a car and said, "I helped build that hall!"

If this hall (even with the help of volunteers) had been built in ten years, it would still have been an architectural triumph. Designed, built, equipped, landscaped, and fully completed in ten months, it is a miracle.

The ugly gray Shin Chiao Hotel, ten minutes' walk from Tien An Men Square at the end of Sungcheng Street, is my home base. It is from here that I set out every morning for the day's activities. Soon after my arrival in Peking I was asked by the Information Department at the Ministry of Foreign Affairs for my list of what I wanted to do in Peking and the people I wanted to see. I spent my first weekend preparing my list, which filled fifteen typewritten sheets. (As I handed this formidable document to an official, he blanched and for a moment I felt he was about to lose his composure. "It is a very long list . . . we cannot promise . . . we will do our best. . . .") And now, working heroically through this list, Mr. Shen Shou-yuan is on the phone every morning at eight o'clock to check with me the arrangements for the day.

It is from the Shin Chiao that I step out strong, fresh, rested, eager for whatever the day may bring; new film in my cameras, lenses cleaned, and a semi-Western breakfast under my belt. And it is back to the Shin Chiao that I limp in the evening, dirty, sweaty, tired, my eyes red with coal dust from a visit to a factory or boots muddy from a five-mile trudge across the fields of a commune. Or I may come back clean, but with my head spinning with facts and figures and analyses presented at some long briefing at a government department—and knowing that it will take six more hours of work to make sense of all this information and record it in my journal before I am deluged with yet more material the next day. I have worked on other reporting jobs under much more trying conditions; I have never worked harder than in those first few weeks in Peking; and I've never enjoyed a job more.

From time to time when the pressure was too great I would phone Mr. Shen and, after the necessary courteous formalities of inquiring after each other's health, tell him that this day I wanted to look around on my own.

It was on these "off" days when, in the soft Peking light, I strolled alone through the streets that I came gradually to terms with this amazing city. I began to learn what trolley buses would take me where. I was (at times) even understood when I ventured to ask my way. Peking still held me in a magic spell (and I think it always will) but I began to wake up in the mornings without the sense of stupefaction just at the thought of being there. I learned my way around the labyrinth of little lanes, the *hutungs*; how to reach the Street of Beautiful Objects to browse among antiques, or the Street of Silks, where I fingered the rich fabrics which I could admire but could not buy, since nothing made in China can be imported into the United States. I would idle for an hour watching the children play among themselves; I stood to listen to the traffic policeman calling to pedestrians through his megaphone, telling them they must hurry please across the road before the light changed or shouting at the boy on a bicycle that he would most certainly meet his death if he didn't stop wobbling all over the street. On these days I would stroll to the parks, join the easygoing holiday-makers on the pleasure boats, and watch the children career down slides or, like children everywhere, play with endless fascination in the sand. I explored the restaurants. I began to know where to go for Peking Duck; where to find "Instant Boiled Mutton" Mongolian style or the hot spicy food of Szechwan province. And when thirsty I would sit on the sidewalk with a row of others sipping pale tea which I had bought from a vendor for just one fen. Always something new. One day it's the tinker who comes by, tools balanced on his head, beating a little wooden drum; or boys carrying slogans which I cannot read; or a women's militia brigade trying to look earnest and efficient but not quite managing to keep in step.

And the tree planting. Trees everywhere. Nine million trees (they tell me) have been planted in Peking alone, and I believe it. Trees line every street—and not just a sober row or two along each avenue but eight rows or ten or twelve. Down one new avenue beyond the walls I counted trees *twenty* rows deep on either side. Around Tien An Men they have not planted small trees and waited for them to grow but brought in grown ones, pines and evergreens, roots carefully boxed. Not just a few but hundreds. One day I watched several more coming in on a truck and a giant crane lifting them each in turn, and lowering them gently, almost lovingly, into the waiting cavity below. Peking that was once treeless is now a city of trees.

Up before five today and off for a walk. The hotel was quiet, everyone asleep except the man at the desk. He appeared undismayed at seeing a guest out so early and paid me no attention as I went by.

I walked in the cool daybreak past Chungwenmen (which old China hands used to call Hatamen). The first sun was just touching the top of this great gate and thousands of swallows swooped in the pale sky. The streets were almost deserted. I passed a few old men walking in great dignity with hands tucked in their sleeves. After strolling along Chungwenmen Tachieh, I turned off into the maze of little gray alleys—the *hutungs*.

Here and there a rooster crowed; smoke curled up from breakfast fires. Householders sprinkled down the dust in front of their doorways. At one corner a group had collected around a vendor of brown, fried bean curd; a father was feeding his little son. Little by little the sidewalks became crowded. I heard the motors start up in a small machine shop, the rasp and pull of a handsaw from a cabinet shop.

Men and women, buttoning their jackets, hurried along to the bus stops. No one appeared to notice me as a foreigner, no one bothered to look my way—a big difference from three years ago. It was a good walk. It reminded me that the great Tien An Men Square and the Imperial Palaces and the Hall of the People, where I had been a guest at the banquet for Monty, are staging—they provide the necessary heroic form to these stirring times. But the people of Peking were going about their daily, commonplace routines, as were the people of all other great cities of the globe this morning.

Back at the hotel for breakfast I share a table with a young Dutchman. We have met several times already. He is a businessman, here to sign a big contract. He is alert, sharp, likable, and impatient. When fully three or four minutes have passed since he sat down and no waitress has taken his order, he snaps his fingers. The waitresses look across but don't hurry. "They're impossible," he said. He has been here six weeks dickering over the contract, always on the verge of agreement; I think it will be another six weeks before he's finished. Snapping one's fingers doesn't produce results in China today.

Mr. Shen was on the phone at eight o'clock. What will it be to-day? A children's hospital? a commune? a museum? an interview with a cabinet minister? Today it's steel. "May I photograph?" "Of course."

Yen Chao-hua, my interpreter, was waiting for me in the lobby. Tall, loose-limbed, casual, Yen reminds me of an American college boy. His blue jacket is usually unbuttoned. He is always pleasantly at ease. He talks to a steelworker or a pedicab driver in exactly the same tone as he does a cabinet minister—he's invariably polite, never servile, never ruffled. And he enjoys his work. And because he enjoys it he is a rattling good interpreter. If he knows I am to visit a lawyer, he will study up on legal terms; or before a visit to a hospital he will have spent the night before with a medical dictionary. A bad interpreter can ruin an interview; a good one can almost make one forget that the conversation is being interpreted at all. Yen is one of the best. He tells me nothing about his own life—the Chinese feel more than we do that that is their own affair —but in the course of time I learn that he is twenty-six years old and is married, and that's about all I ever learned about him.

China is a country of infinite and bewildering variety; but these official visits—whether it is to a government department, a com-mune, a school, or a prison—seem to follow a standardized pro-cedure. So on this day I knew ahead of time that the director of the steel mill would be waiting to greet me as I stepped out of the car. How long, I have sometimes wondered, have I kept these busy people waiting? Friends of mine who have visited Mao Tse-tung were astonished to find him standing waiting to greet them as they alighted from their car. Great stress is placed on this act of courtesy; which, of course, makes punctuality enormously important. Our first stop will not be the blast furnaces or rolling mills, but a quiet reception room where over tea and cigarettes I will be given a de-tailed briefing and have a chance to ask my questions.

The director of a large steel plant must obviously be a very busy man. Yet, however much work he has piled on his desk, however many urgent telephone calls his secretaries may be receiving for him, he will not by the least gesture show impatience. If an interview is once granted, there is no time limit. It was not unusual for my talks to last four hours; I caught nobody surreptitiously looking at a watch. No secretary ever breaks in. Tea is poured, cigarettes are passed, and the talk continues. Almost always there will be one or two others in the room who take no part in the conversation. I am never introduced to them. They take notes assiduously. I am never told who they are. Probably members of the Party, which keeps an eye on everything that goes on, anywhere, everywhere, in China. However, I learned from visitors who were not journalists that no one took notes of their discussions. This procedure may be followed only when there might be need to check over the accuracy of a published report.

"This factory," the director was saying, "was started in 1918 by the war lord Tuan Chi-jui. Those were times of great strife and during the next three years only 36,000 tons of pig iron were produced. . . .

"During 1959 the plant turned out 740,000 tons of iron and 170,000 tons of steel. We have just opened a new blast furnace with an annual capacity of 500,000 tons. . . ."

This, too, is the pattern of all such discussions: *growth*—over the cups of tea the facts and figures of a fantastic expansion. And whether or not one cared to question the figures, the *fact*, in broad outline, was indisputable. I needed only to glance out of the window to see it: the chimneys, the columns of yellow smoke slanting across the blue sky.

"We employ fifty-one thousand workers today! Two years ago it was only twelve thousand! We are leaping forward year by year and the lives of the workers are improving every day!" Everything was exclamatory. The director rocked forward on the edge of his chair, cigarette in hand, ejecting puffs of smoke like a forced-draft engine. I never found out whether he was married or got along well with children, or what sort of problems he was having with his mother-in-law. But this man was enjoying life. He was tough and hard and vital, like a successful Texas oilman. He was, one felt, an individual functioning to capacity. His work was his life.

"To what," I asked, "do you attribute your advances?"

I was pitching him my slow ball. And back it came, as I expected, without a second's hesitation. "The reasons? First: the correct leadership of the Party and Chairman Mao. Second: the unselfish assistance of our brother countries, especially the Soviet Union. Third: the growing political awareness of the workers. . . ."

Imagine, I thought, a General Motors plant manager in Detroit telling a visitor that the success of his assembly line was due to the correct Free Enterprise policies of the National Association of Manufacturers! And yet, come to think of it, he just *might* if the visitor were Russian! And my director here, I felt sure, would find he had more in common with an American manager than he would have expected, if political concepts could be set aside and *management* and *technique* were the subjects of their discussion.

After two hours of background briefing and questions we went on a tour of the plant. I have been through steel plants in Pittsburgh and Sheffield, and this one looked exactly the same—the same roar of machinery, the screech of switch engines from the shunting yard, the hiss of steam; the same huge cranes moving through the same kind of fiery glare and the same perpetual rain of soot.

The new welded steel tube plant was half a mile away. It was almost completely automated. In an enormous, cheerfully lighted building, a handful of workers, several of them women, were minding sets of electric relay switches. Rolls of steel plate, fed in at one end, emerged at the other as completed tubes, cut to length, counted, bundled, tied, and were whisked away to be loaded on flatcars. This monster was of Russian construction, and I actually saw one Russian there keeping a rather casual eye on the operations.

While we watched, one of the relays went out of whack and the whole show came to a halt. A girl on the control platform with a smear of oil across her cheek, and her cap on the back of her head, flicked open one of the switch panels, but obviously didn't know what to do next. The Russian, though he was standing nearby, made no effort to intervene. The girl called to another man (Chinese), who strolled over (there was, in all this, no sense of pressure, although the entire assembly line was now waiting), produced a screwdriver from a pocket of his coveralls, diddled with something inside, and closed the cover. The girl then pressed the warning signal and the line began to move again. But she had forgotten to switch on the high-voltage welder. There was a good deal of joshing, which I took to be the equivalent of, "Hey there, wake up! Why don't you do your sleeping at night?"

She seemed not in the least abashed—she tripped the switch and shouted some answer which set all the others laughing.

"*We Clap Our Hands We Are So Happy*" 6

I received an invitation yesterday to a children's party. June 1 in China is "Children's Day." So I set out that evening for Chungshan Park, and at the gate met a French correspondent who seemed rather an unlikely candidate for a children's party. I think he considered Peking rather dusty, the Chinese tiresome, the regime appalling.

The park was like a fairyland. Thousands of tiny colored lights had been strung between the trees, and beneath them some fifteen to twenty thousand children were playing, dancing, laughing. Troupes of jugglers, clowns, actors, acrobats, performed to audiences that shrieked and applauded with delight. It was an amazing spectacle.

"It is all so *organized*," said the French correspondent. "*C'est si regimental.*"

Regimental or not, I thought, if New York could put on a carnival like this in Central Park, or Paris in the Bois de Boulogne, we would have reason to be pleased with ourselves. These kids were having the time of their lives.

Yet they never forgot to be polite. We couldn't stop at any show without a dozen little boys and girls leaping up to offer us their seats. In a way this was all part of the fun. Wherever we went, the children clapped us (as foreign friends, I think, not foreign devils). And then we had to clap back—that is the custom here; and the kids would clap in rhythm simply exploding with merriment, sometimes bringing the shows to a halt. Then the performers clapped too, everybody clapped, till we waved and moved along.

I noticed the Frenchman fingering the palms of his hands as if they were getting rather tender, and he raised his eyebrows, shook his head. This was, after all, a sufficiently tedious affair. . . .

I went out the other day to visit a kindergarten near Peihai Park. There was, of course, the usual briefing on general background, over cups of tea; the same emphasis on growth ("We started our kindergarten in 1949 with thirty children; today we have four hundred"). And here too, 1958, the "Year of the Great Leap Forward," had been decisive, because that was the year in which perhaps tens of thousands of mothers went out to work for the first time in industry. There was also the same sense of boundless optimism, the same conviction that human happiness would be achieved through solution of immediate tasks. It would have been senseless, here, to have raised a question as to the *purpose* of education. The purpose was to produce citizens each of whom would carry his fair share of the burden of socialist society—just as the purpose of the steel mill was to produce those structural members which would support the roofs and bridges of socialism.

My hostess, Miss Chiang, was the director. She sat very trim and neat in a blue skirt and rose-colored blouse. Rather "correct"—like schoolteachers all over the world. Her voice was gentle, but I suspected this concealed a very determined and efficient nature. The room we sat in was full of sunlight and we could hear the children at play outside. "Our children," Miss Chiang said, "when they grow up, will take their place in the country's work—they will be children trained in Communist ideals. They will love labor. They will respect people."

"How can you teach them proletarian politics at four?" I inquired.

"The principles of the education of children," said Miss Chiang, "are expressed in the *Five Loves:*

"1. Love of Motherland,

"2. Love for People,

"3. Love of Work,

"4. Love for Knowledge,

"5. Respect for Public Property."

"How . . ." I began.

"These principles," Miss Chiang continued, "are taught according to age levels, in conversation, songs, nursery rhymes, art, and games."

I went with her into several of the classrooms. In some the children ran up to me, catching me by the hands and tugging me this way and that to see the things in their room. (How much, I wondered, was all this really spontaneous?) They seemed not at all disturbed by the arrival of a stranger, and a foreigner at that. In one room I found the class gathered in a circle around the teacher, all singing together while the children took turns acting the parts of the song. They performed their parts with much gusto. One little boy, when his turn came, leaped to his feet and shouted his lines at the top of his lungs. I asked what the song was and learned it was about the pig-breeding campaign on the farms and a man who raised a pig that weighed five hundred kilos.

Here are the words of other songs they were singing, as they were translated to me word for word:

> I have a good mother,
> She works in the fields;
> She works so hard that the commune
> Has presented her with a red flower.
> Our mothers are all good.
> All are working
> For the benefit of our new country.
>
> We clap our hands we are so happy!
> The communes are so powerful!
> My father works in a factory!
> Our country is led by the Communist Party!
> My brother drives the tractor,
> My sister works the loom,
> The electric light lights every household.

As I walked back to the reception room with Miss Chiang, I learned more about the kindergarten.

Many of the children go home every evening, some stay from Monday through Saturday. The school keeps close contact with parents, and parents may visit whenever they wish. Some children, having lived happy-go-lucky lives at home, find it difficult to adjust, at first, to the ordered routine, and particularly in the all-week group, children get homesick when they first arrive. For this, there is a period of "full-time looking after"—which means that a single nurse or one of the younger teachers is in constant contact with the child, and becomes (though this was not the term Miss Chiang used) a mother-substitute. The child looks to this person for comfort and help, and the teacher or nurse, by watching the child closely, learns what his problems are: eating and sleeping habits, likes and dislikes. In this way the child learns quite quickly to adjust to the community life of the school.

Personal possessions are not allowed. Everything is *ours*, nothing is *mine*. Toys brought by the children are put into the common pool.

I asked about the signs one looks for in emotionally disturbed children. About bed wetting. Very infrequent. Nurses on duty at night know the ones who need to be wakened during the night. Thumb sucking? Only a few suck their thumbs when they first come—but it doesn't last long. Night terrors? Never more than a few weeks.

"None of the teachers are permitted to tell gruesome or frightening stories," Miss Chiang told me quite severely. "If you walk around the bedrooms at night, you might hear children laughing in their sleep. Fears are very rare."

"Temper tantrums?" I had to describe the symptoms.

"No, we never see children in that condition," Miss Chiang said. "We have naughty children, of course. But we always believe that these naughty children are the clever, specially-gifted ones—we just have to direct their energies. So we let a naughty child be captain of a ship, or locomotive driver. We let him use his talents and he ceases to be the naughty one."

"Do you teach them," I asked, "about American imperialism?"

"Yes, we do, as far as they can understand it. We tell them that American imperialism is the greatest enemy of the world. But the ordinary people of the world, even the ordinary workers and farmers of America, are their friends. The teachers here, for example, took part in the great anti-American rally a few weeks ago and they told the children about it."

Miss Chiang filled the teacups. We were now back in the reception room bright with chintz slip covers and sunlight. There was a fragrance of incense in the room, and from outside, the sound of the children calling to each other on the playground. Flowering quince brushed the open window and beyond I could see the shadow of a willow tree against a wall. A Chinese miniature.

"Do you not think," I asked Miss Chiang, "that these international enmities will have been resolved by the time these little children grow up? And what can a child of four or five understand about these affairs so far removed from their young lives? What can they possibly *mean* to them?"

Miss Chiang replied, "We are socialists and proletarians. Imperialism exists. It is a fact. And we believe it to be the greatest single danger to our world. Even children must know these realities. We tell them about China's past, too. These children were born after liberation, but they must know something of conditions before that. They ask, 'Did you have kindergarten then?' No, we were so poor we could hardly keep ourselves alive, we tell them; and many of us died of hunger. You from the West can have no concept of our poverty and hopelessness in those days. But our children must understand this. They must know of our past, our present, and our future—and the dangers that lie ahead from imperialism.

"We have a Chinese proverb: 'Think of its source when you drink water.' We want our children to think of the source of their improved lives when they enjoy playing and eating and singing at a nursery school like this. The source is the socialist state which we are building. . . ."

And with steady hand Miss Chiang refilled our cups.

*

A *Letter to a Friend, a child*
psychologist in California   June 18

Dear Isabel

Hardly a day goes by without my wishing you were here so we could talk. There's so much going on—this country is in full creative ferment, but much of it remains a puzzle to me. The *outside* stuff is reasonably easy to follow—the material progress since I was here before: the schools, the new hospitals (hundreds of them), factories, kindergartens. Vitality and confidence in the future are apparent everywhere—you should just see the young gals stepping down the street with pigtails swinging, as if the wide world belonged to them. And the kindness they show to each other and to strangers! That's fine; one can make some sense of all this. But what goes on *inside*—especially what goes on inside children? It's just here I am most baffled. . . .

I have spent a lot of time watching children playing in the streets—little tots all on their own. They are endlessly inventive in their games —a piece of wood or a bit of string will keep them happy for hours. *They never fight.* Why don't they? They never snatch—never "that's *mine!*" They seem to have almost no *personal* achievement motive, no combativeness; another child coming along will immediately be included in the group (no exclusive "gang" feeling); and no apparent anxiety about absence of adults. They not only never fight but they *never cry.* The only child I have heard crying was one who was physically hurt. *What's* going on?

Some of this can be explained by the almost total permissiveness in the handling of children. I saw a small boy piddle in the middle of a big department store. *He* didn't mind, his *mother* didn't mind, other people didn't mind; the department-store man who came to mop up smiled as if it were his special pleasure to mop up little boys' messes. I have seen a child squat outside a store-front, and the storekeeper came out with brush and pan and stood courteously waiting till the boy had finished. A small child can do no wrong, and is surrounded by people who look after him. If he is traveling alone in a bus, an adult gives him a seat. To him *all* adults are "uncles" and "aunts" and so the need for the presence of his *own* parents seems less important. His assurance comes from the adult world in general, not his own parents in particular. All this must have a very profound effect on a child and his feelings about himself.

But that's too simple and too pat. Because from our point of view these Chinese children are all *too good.* It seems as if total permissiveness leads to total docility—and a docility that continues into adulthood. I have never known a people who all think so much alike—and they *really* do, it isn't put on for reasons of political security. I am quite convinced that if there was an absolutely free vote in this country, an overwhelming majority—way up in the 90 per cent bracket—would vote the same way. It is a monolithic structure, *not* based on external coercions but on what is much more powerful—a psychological unity. This in the end may have its profound weaknesses, too.

I have tried to make some cross-checks about children in the kindergartens and hospitals—places where young children would be away from home. Bed wetting? Very rare. Only in three- and four-year-olds. At the big kindergarten I visited today, the director could recall only one instance of persistent bed wetting at the six-year level—and this turned out to be a girl with a physical bladder ailment. Homesickness? A little at first. Easily handled. Crying at night? No known cases. Temper tantrums? Lying on the back, kicking the heels, screaming? They look at one another in amazement. No they have not had any problems like *that!* Fights? Very rare. Their idea of genuinely *naughty* behavior seemed to be for one child to push another. At the kindergarten I visited, and in several nursery schools, I have asked, "Do they own anything of their *own?* A doll? A toy?" And the answer is *no.* If the child brings something from home, it is put in with all the other toys.

Here they have a great many toys that belong to all of them, was what the teacher at the kindergarten told me. *They don't want anything of their own.*

But *don't* they? If they *do,* and are angry about having to give up their own particular thing, where does the anger go? Where is the aggression going? What's happening to the normal childhood hatreds? I haven't the faintest idea, and I can find no clue. The collective, *national* aggression finds outlet through hatred of an externalized enemy, *America;* but this cannot be an adequate channel for individual frustration among the young.

Here are some other facts to throw into the melting pot: Young children take on responsibility very early. You see a child of four caring for a baby of one—feeding it, playing with it, keeping it warm, carrying the baby for blocks, staggering under the weight. Also helping with family chores, cutting up vegetables—really tiny children.

Adult docility. I went to Peking's only prison a few days ago, having been interested in penal reform in England, and here I found the Chinese doing what we had been trying to get the English authorities to do for years without success. Mainly, of course, to get the stigma, the moral stigma, out of imprisonment. Peking has a total prison population of 1800—an incredibly low figure in a municipal area of seven and a half million. Forty per cent of these are political cases, but all mixed up, no segregation. The "security" is minimal. There is one guard at the gate with a rifle (the gates are open) and there is one guard in a tower. No one else is armed. The walls are low. No locks anywhere. The window bars have been replaced by large casement windows. In one workshop of about fifty prisoners I asked where the guard was and was introduced to a smiling youngster in a T shirt who was showing a prisoner how to fix a machine—he was the only warder in this room. If these were American prisoners they would all be out of that place inside three minutes. Why don't they escape? (Very occasionally a prisoner walks out—one every two years or so; they are ready to take that risk, for the benefits that an "open" prison confers.) Here is docility taken to an extreme. They have great re-education sessions—"reform through education" is the slogan.

Now to my point . . . Can it be that the Chinese child, having had a total sense of *belonging* when young, has a permanent, built-in dread of being "outside," of *not* belonging? A Chinese child, unlike ours, has never had to learn to be on his own bucking opinion around him, has never learned to stand on his own rock. So that the worst possible psychological pain to a Chinese adult might be to be socially outcast. Is this at the back of their "re-education" process? Is it the permissiveness, the total security for the Chinese child, that makes possible the monolithic quality of their social structure? In other words, that dissent becomes a psychological impossibility?

Or is the structure of the unconscious itself different? After all, the Chinese developed their society for four thousand years uninfluenced by Western concepts and behavior patterns. Is it possible that the highly separate, individuated consciousness which some of our psychological historians believe developed in Western man only at the time of the Renaissance, has never had to evolve here? In other words, that the consciousness of *I* being separate from *you* is not so sharp here as it is with us? *Me* and *not-me* tend to merge in the collective *we*?

If we are to understand the Chinese (who are rapidly moving to a position of world influence) we simply cannot go on taking for granted some of our own psychological assumptions. We must escape our own cultural conditioning sufficiently to see them in terms of *their* assumptions. I stand here baffled at behavior which seems to turn some of our neat conclusions upside down—behavior which cannot adequately be explained by any of our accepted theories but which to them, of course, appears commonplace. . . .

Peking Incidents *7*

"What do you take me for—an imbecile? Do you think I've flown six thousand kilometers from Paris in the utmost discomfort to see an old railroad station?" Her voice was shrill and contemptuous; she was a free-lance journalist on an assignment from a French left-wing magazine.

"It isn't an old station" (it was Hsu doing his best), "it's really quite new." She didn't want to hear.

"I come to China to see communism, I come to see Mao Tse-tung, I come to see the rebirth of a great and glorious people—and you say go to a railroad station!" and out of Mr. Hsu's little office she flounced.

"What's this all about, Hsu?"

Hsu, my original Intourist greeter to Peking, had become something of a friend. We shared a mutual dislike for Peking opera and a mutual attachment to ballet and some of the new dance-dramas that are being developed in China today. He seemed to have a miraculous ability to get seats at the last minute for most of the shows I wanted to see—on one occasion (I only learned this afterward) giving up his own long-awaited chance to see a particular play so that I could go. I liked him enormously, especially his capacity for anger.

One day in his office in the Shin Chiao, I sat, fascinated, listening to him conduct a fifteen-minute uninterrupted high-speed high-temper tirade on the telephone which even with my ignorance of the Chinese language I knew was making the wires sizzle, and then at the end, having slammed the receiver down, he turned to me without a second's pause, flourishing a ticket in the air. "Mr. Greene, Mr. Greene, I have a seat for you for *Swan Lake* tonight!"

"What's all this about, Hsu?"

"It's our new station—she didn't want to see it."

"Is it worth seeing? What's special about it?"

"Go to it—you'll see."

And Hsu being Hsu, I went.

Hsu had phoned ahead, so Mr. Wang, the vice-director of the station, was waiting to greet me. He took me across the huge central concourse (the ceiling is 120 feet high!) to one of the six VIP waiting rooms—this was as large as a ballroom—for the tea and briefing and then for a tour.

This station is impressive. There are four main escalators (made in Shanghai) to take passengers to an upper floor where there are seventeen waiting rooms, seating in all 17,000 people. There are several interesting features. Platform entrances and exits are arranged so that *incoming* passengers and *outgoing* never intermingle though using the same platform; each long-distance train has its own waiting room, so that when the train is ready all (except mothers and children who go ahead of the others) can board at the same time. It was fascinating to see the gay national costumes of the people waiting to board the train, which follows the old silk route, to Urumchi in Sinkiang; and in another waiting room those, again many in national costume, about to start on their long journey to Munankwan on the Vietnam border in the south. The restaurant (open day and night) seats seven hundred people at a time—a bright clean place with a fountain bubbling at one end. There are four rooms reserved for children, and two nurseries for infants, where mothers can leave their children under the care of young trained nurses. In one of the nurseries I saw rows of little tots fast asleep in their cots.

Tickets can be ordered by telephone from anywhere in the Peking area and will be delivered by messenger promptly. Eighty-five per cent of all long-distance tickets are sold before the date of departure and no more tickets are sold than the number of seats in the train. For incoming passengers there are service bureaus for those who haven't made hotel reservations, need to find their relatives, or arrive without money; interpreters in all dialects and for Russian and English are available. There are reading rooms and TV rooms for those who have a long wait between trains. Everything is spotlessly clean. I watched the sweepers with mops on rollers six feet wide mop down the immense areas of terrazzo and marble flooring.

Every waiting room has telephones connected with a central inquiry booth, and—this was the feature that most intrigued me—dotted here and there were closed-circuit TV inquiry stations. Standing in front of one of these gadgets the inquirer is immediately seen by the young ladies in the central inquiry bureau. I watched a child, not more than ten years old, come on to one of the screens to inquire anxiously about her train. She was afraid she had missed it. As it turned out she still had another half hour to wait. She was asked whether she was traveling alone, and when she said yes, one of the other clerks picked up a phone and spoke to an attendant in the child's waiting room suggesting that the child should be given special attention. With this explained, the little girl's face gradually changed from anxiety to a broad grin. "Have a happy journey," the clerk said through the TV circuit.

There's probably not another station like this in China; nor perhaps, anywhere else. Mr. Hsu was right, the French journalist should have come.

A *Letter to Elena* June 21

Almost a month here already . . . the days go fluttering by like leaves in the wind. I try to wring the fullest meaning out of every moment but am horribly conscious of how much I'm misreading, how much I'm not even *seeing*. . . .

Last night, partly impelled by loneliness, partly because I have so far refused every other invitation from the Embassy, I went for a while to the "club" (at the British Embassy) for a dance they hold there every few weeks for the Western community. Germans, Swedes, Finns, Indians, Dutch—they were all there, but it was unmistakably a *British* party. The tasteless music blaring too loudly from a loudspeaker, the "bar" around which most of the men clustered leaving the women stranded like islands in a receding sea; nothing—not a flower, not an ornament—to give the rather drab room a little gaiety or beauty. It could have been a Saturday-night dance at a second-class commercial hotel in Bristol. In America they do these things better, always with greater taste and flair.

I shouldn't have gone. It's the problem of the exiled foreigners. I have seen this all over the world. But the "enclave" mentality is always most acute in the countries "behind the curtain." The small group of outsiders huddle together, not because they specially like each other, but because there are so few, and it's difficult to make adequate social contacts with those among whom they live. It's difficult enough to become friends with Russians in Moscow; I think it is even more difficult for the Westerners here ever to really strike up friendships with the Chinese. But because one can explain it, it doesn't make the consequences any more happy. Unavoidably, it seems, this isolation leads to an "us" and "they" attitude, and "they" are always "quite impossible!"

But what I, as a visitor, find especially trying is the tacit assumption among my compatriots that I also think in terms of "us" and "they"—in fact, that if I don't it's disloyal, that in some obscure way I'm letting the side down; and that, of course, I also feel that "they" are really "quite impossible." But I reject this assumption, and I don't feel "they" (in this case the Chinese) are any more "impossible" than we are. If I remain silent, their assumption is strengthened; if I say what I think, there is an argument and nothing is gained either.

That's why I shouldn't have gone.

Then the giant judgments based on the tiniest personal grievances! I had a fine example of this at the dance last night. I was dancing with a Swiss woman—she's been here three years. "Have you *ever*, in all your life, seen such *lazy* people!" (Of course she was referring to "them.") I stopped dead in my tracks. I thought I had heard the Chinese people called everything under the sun—but never *lazy!*

"Yes, downright lazy," she went on. "This morning I went up to a rickshaw driver [that's what she called him—there haven't been any rickshaws in Peking for years] and told him to take me home—and they know perfectly well we Europeans always have to pay them more than the Chinese do [she's wrong]. And do you know what the man said? He said, 'I can't because I'm just going to have my lunch.' See what I mean? Lazy!"

I looked at her. She was youngish and rather pretty. We were still standing at one side of the dance floor. "Lady," I said, "I think you have missed the meaning of this small event. The pedicab man wasn't lazy. But this is the first time a pedicab driver can say 'no' to a foreigner, and it's the first time for 2000 years that he can say 'no' because he has a lunch to go to." She looked at me strangely and walked away. I wasn't living up to the rules.

The evening ended with my being asked to convey a drunken businessman back to the Shin Chiao. He's here to sell steel. We were driven back in a bouncy embassy jeep. The businessman was telling me how he had been shown the Great Hall of the People that day. "And do you know what I did there?" he asked, and he heaved with laughter at the memory. "Told my beads, that's what I did! Didn't let on of course—hah, hah—had my rosary in my jacket pocket—told my beads all the time they were talking . . . and [very confidentially] I think that was *historical* . . . yes, really historical . . . because I bet you ten pounds that no one ever has told beads in that hall before."

He was very drunk. At the hotel I propped him up on my shoulder and we weaved our way to his bedroom. He clung to me. ". . . C'mon in . . . just one last little one. . . ." I pushed him onto his bed and went along to my room.

PART THREE ☆

Assembly Lines 8

The Northeast (formerly known as Manchuria) is historically the oldest industrialized area of China and contains enormous deposits of coal and iron ore. Foundaries and steel mills were established in Mukden and Anshan by the Japanese early in this century.

Until 1880 entry into the land of the Manchus was forbidden by decree of the Emperors. By 1900, however, land-hungry peasants from North China—Shantung province in particular—were encouraged to immigrate. This sprawling area of some half a million square miles then had a population density of only seventy persons per square mile compared to more than five hundred in some areas of China proper.

The Northeast, despite its severe winters, has rich farmlands as well as great mineral wealth. Principal crops are kaoliang, soybeans, wheat, millet, flax, beets, rice, and in the hot summers cotton can be grown.

The Russians had for many years claimed a vague suzerainty over large areas of Manchuria; and after the completion of the Trans-Siberian railway and the suppression of the Boxer Rebellion in 1901 they pushed southward to the warm-water ports of Port Arthur and Dairen. But after Russia's defeat by the Japanese in 1905, Japan took possession of the richer part of Manchuria, the south; the Russians continued to occupy the northern half until the Russian Revolution, when they formally withdrew. In 1931 the Japanese drove the Chinese out of Mukden and took over all Manchuria.

The Japanese exploited the area's rich resources. They built roads, railroads, and factories and set up a typically colonial regime which shipped raw materials and semifinished products to Japan. In 1932 the puppet state of Manchukuo was established and the Northeast's resources and manpower were utilized as cogs in the machinery of Japan's growing industrial and military empire.

After Japan's defeat in 1945 there followed a period of almost indescribable chaos and destruction; the Russian army moved in and stripped many plants that fell under their control, as did Chiang Kai-shek's officials. The Chinese today refuse to acknowledge any Russian looting, but the removal of great quantities of machinery from the factories in the Northeast and its shipment to Russia is well documented. Most of the larger cities were taken over by Kuomintang troops while Mao Tse-tung's army controlled almost all of the countryside.

It is interesting to recall that at this time the Russians were still helping Chiang. While the Communists were taking over the countryside, the Russian army, which had smashed the crack Japanese Kwantung Army in August 1945, was helping to install Kuomintang officials in the cities. The Russians were even asked to remain longer than originally requested in order to give Chiang more time for the Americans to transport his troops from south China.

Nearly 200,000 Kuomintang troops were rushed to the Northeast by American naval vessels and planes immediately following VJ Day. After the Russians evacuated Harbin and other cities in the north, Chiang, with five American-equipped armies, began a drive from the south against the Communist forces.

The Kuomintang, however, military and civil administration alike, was already far advanced into that state of decay which was to ensure its defeat. Officials were, for the most part, more interested in looting industrial properties and selling on the black market than they were in getting factories and mines into operation. The great open-pit coal mines of Fushun, for example, which under the Japanese had been turning out 25,000 tons a day, was reduced to 2000 tons a day. The Anshan steel mills, which produced 840,-000 tons for the Japanese in 1943, yielded less than 9000 tons during twenty-two months of Kuomintang control. At one time this steel center had 100,000 workers in its mills. In 1948 there were less than 10,000.

With the renewal of open civil war in 1947 Chiang was soon thrown back onto the defensive in the Northeast. The Communists controlled most of the region, two-thirds of the railways, and the majority of the food-producing land. The Kuomintang controlled the big cities and industry. By the end of the year, a good part of seven Kuomintang armies, trained and equipped by Americans, had been shattered by Communist General Lin Piao. Moreover, as in the case of the Formosans, the good will of the people had been lost; however, instead of revolting as the Formosans did in 1947, the people of the Northeast went over to the Communists. (See Part Six, page 273, for an account of the Formosan revolt.)

In the early autumn of 1948 the Communist armies, for the first time, launched an offensive aimed at taking major cities. The fall of Changchun and Mukden in October signaled the complete collapse of the Kuomintang in the Northeast, and heralded the final victory of the revolution in all of China. Within fifteen months Chiang Kai-shek had fled to Taiwan.

Thus, it was not until 1949 that a stable Chinese government controlled the Northeast. Slowly the new regime set about picking up the pieces, straightening out the frightful shambles which was all that remained of this once important industrial center.

After more than a month in and around Peking I set out on a swing through this industrial Northeast.

From My Journal. July 1—Harbin

Up at four, and boarded the airline bus at the terminal near the Peking Hotel. The driver couldn't get it to start. Some of us jumped out and tried pushing. No use, something was really jammed. Another bus towed us—a huge racket and the wheels locked when the bus was put into gear. It sounded as though every gear would be stripped. This went on for a couple of miles when suddenly our engine turned over and we proceeded to the airport without further mishap.

The new Peking airport seems spacious enough for present needs. Quiet (almost hushed), very orderly, and with a good restaurant. Visitors who arrive here by jet from Russia invariably compare it with the noise and unutterable confusion of the Moscow airport.

Only fifteen kilos (thirty-three pounds) are allowed for domestic baggage. Flight designation is not by flight number but by plane number, which is stamped on your ticket when you buy it. Each plane has a number, printed large, on its sides. Thus, if several planes are lined up, the passenger knows which one to board. There is no checking at the gate, but loudspeaker announcements are made every few minutes. As I couldn't understand these I just wandered out when the time was near and boarded the plane with the right number.

The plane was a Russian version of a DC-3—twin engines and unpressurized. Pilots and crew were Chinese. The plane was half full of wooden crates, rolls of linoleum, and a rough wooden crate containing a radio transmitting tube suspended on delicate springs to absorb shocks.

As in Russia there were no seat belts. The stewardess, minus insignia, dressed in white blouse and blue skirt, brought us tea in glasses and sweets, but only after we had gained altitude and our ears had already popped. A large clock in front with two dials, one indicating air speed, the other altitude. The girl noticed that my chair would not tip back because of the tightly-wedged mail bags in the seat behind. She had these rearranged without my mentioning it.

At the second stop I wandered into the airport building. I didn't realize it was Harbin and the end of my journey until the stewardess appeared carrying my bags, books, typewriter, and cameras, which I had left on the plane. There was no one to meet me. No one spoke English. Long conversations on the phone. An Intourist man finally got on the phone and told me he'd be right over. The reason he wasn't there? The plane had arrived an hour ahead of schedule.

Letter to Elena   July 2

. . . I flew up here from Peking yesterday. I was pleasantly surprised at this city. I expected a vast, dreary, smoke-laden industrial town like

Pittsburgh or Manchester; but instead I find it a city of trees and green lawns and girls in bright skirts. There are lots of parks. There's an absolutely delightful one running for two miles or more along the edge of the river. Here couples were sitting under trees, little boys with nets were trying to catch fish, a man with a concertina was entrancing a dozen eager-eyed children. Hundreds of people strolling at leisure eating ice cream; and a group of Buddhist monks—shaved heads and all—stroll by. At one end of the park there is a restaurant (at one time a Japanese officers' club which now belongs to the Railway Union). It's open to the public every night for dancing. Along the river, boats are for rent and there they bob up and down in the waves with laughing youngsters getting their oars all mixed up. This city seems so relaxed after Peking. No one walks fast, just strolls along as if they have all the time in the world, often arm-in-arm. . . .

And under this almost casual swagger a tremendous sense of pride at accomplishments. I stopped to talk to this group or that—each person bursting to tell me what he's doing.

But it is an industrial city for all that. I have spent today, this morning, going through a city commune—a huge one: 162,000 people, eighteen large factories, dozens of small neighborhood workshops, 356 public dining rooms, 433 nurseries for children, 184 kindergartens—the figures make one's head reel. The size, the scope, the liveliness, the sheer volume of production, the new apartment houses, the range and variety of experimentation—who will believe me when I get home? Everyone doing something, no one idle, all find a place in this vast resurgence. In Peking I studied the theory and the figures—now I am seeing it function in reality. The impact is overwhelming. . . .

Later

. . . Small workshops and factories are scattered everywhere. You pass what looks like an old adobe cowshed—roof patched, one wall propped up, plaster peeling—and you look inside to find 150 young women in overalls tending precision lathes turning out some part for a larger factory, or making electric motors or radio sets or what have you. Most of these girls were illiterate three years ago; now they go to schools and technical colleges; they have language courses, drama groups, music lessons. A whole country in creative ferment—it has to be seen to be even faintly believed . . . and the production potentials that have been revealed!

They took me off to lunch, the director of a commune at Harbin and some of his officials. All young. The director, about thirty, the others younger. I asked about the industrial production in this commune. More figures. In 1958 (the year the commune started) industrial production 10 million yuan (about $4 million); last year this had jumped to 22 million yuan; and in the first five months of this year, 30 million. The commune now owns one hundred small factories. "The large state-owned factories in our area form the core of our industrial work," the director said; and he described how all the commune factories and workshops were integrated with these larger manufacturing plants. Until recently these large plants would get their parts made all over China; now the idea is to get everything they need locally made, with a tremendous saving in transportation costs. What is more, these parent plants can supervise production, train the workers, and adjust supply quickly to production changes.

After lunch I went round to some of these small commune factories. One—now an electrical instrument factory—was started a year and a half ago by three men (two watch repairers and a seal engraver) who had the idea of making things out of scrap and leftovers too small to be of use elsewhere. In a lean-to shed they began making miniature apparatus, out of brass filings, end-runs of plastic tape, steel shavings from lathes. Like so many of these commune factories this one mushroomed—it now employs 512 people and otherwise unusable scrap is brought to their newly built plant from all over Harbin.

There was a small plant in this neighborhood which was employing thirty-five women—all unskilled peasants—to make rope from twisted straw. A nearby state-owned fork-lift-hoist factory was looking for a local source for its ball bearings. They moved into the straw-rope plant, set up the necessary equipment, trained the women, and began to turn out ball bearings. The factory, greatly enlarged of course, now employs 678 people, and supplies ball bearings to many other local factories. I found one of the original straw-rope makers—she was in the quality-control department checking ball bearings on a precision machine. Other plants that I went to that had been established since 1958 were turning out saws, heavy-duty electric motors, soft-drink bottles, and furniture.

"Where do people get their hair cut?" I asked.

"Come along and see . . ." and they took me to the barber shop serving a new housing development. It was in a wooden hut, neat as a pin. About eighteen girls in spotless white coats. Clippers, combs, and towels sterilized in a home-made steam contraption. Special sterilization for Mohammedans, who mustn't use the instruments and towels used by non-Mohammedans!

"May I have a shave?" (I hadn't shaved this morning.) They grinned, terribly pleased. I waited until a chair was free, and a girl who looked about sixteen (but was really twenty-four), with two white ribbons set jauntily on each side of her head, set to work. I got a "Chinese shave," not only my whiskers, but everywhere— over my forehead, over my nose, round the back of my neck, every inch which wasn't actually my hair. Lots of hot towels. They wouldn't let me pay—normal cost is sixteen cents for haircut, shampoo, and shave. The barber shop runs on a no-profit, no-loss basis.

One more surprise. As I was leaving, my eye caught sight of a wooden box from which protruded a mass of wires. "What's *that*?" I asked. "That's a portable, home-made permanent waver. It's portable because some of the women can't get here and we go and do their hair in their homes. And look—in the box is a small radio, so that while the women are having their hair done they can listen to music!"

Then across a football (soccer) field to a huge, new housing project. The exterior was depressing. No trees, no grass—just these giant structures. I knocked at one or two doors and was answered with an immediate smile and a "please come in." Neat and clean, all of them, but really terribly poor. Usually two huge beds in one room, on which the whole family sleep. In one a crib suspended over the bed for the small baby. The pattern in each was about the same—each apartment has two rooms, a small kitchen and sink, and a private toilet. No bathroom—there are communal bathhouses quite near. In nearly all of them there was a radio, thermos flask, sheets and blankets piled neatly on the bed; most of them had rather garish pictures on the wall. Some had vivid imitation flowers on the table. I took photographs and they didn't seem to mind. These people's welcome was so spontaneous that had I not chosen these apartments at random myself, I would have felt sure that these families had been specially told to be ready to meet a foreign guest.

The rent? Some three yuan, others four yuan a month (twelve cents and sixteen cents) *including light and water!*

Who is given these flats? The street committee decides who needs the housing most urgently—usually those with children are given first choice. There's still a terrible housing shortage.

The hotel here reminds me of Russian hotels—a huge room, old-fashioned and Edwardian; plush furniture, easy chairs covered with white slip covers. The eternal thermos on the table. The bed is hard, but good, covered with an enormous eiderdown as in Switzerland. Either roast or freeze here. Nothing working too well in the bathroom—again like Moscow.

Rates are cheaper than in Peking, eight yuan a day. Food is cheaper, too. I had an excellent dinner last night: black caviar, a locally made vodka, a meat dish, soup, and sour milk all for 1.60 yuan (sixty-four cents)—the caviar was 80 fen (thirty-two cents) by itself.

Signs of Harbin's former large Russian colony are everywhere (there once were almost 50,000 White Russian refugees here)—the wide streets, shops, buildings, and even in some of the dress. My hunch is there are still more than three or four thousand, the figure given me by my guide. He said most Russians went back to the Soviet Union after this area was "liberated" by the Soviet armies in 1945. Those still here are referred to as Soviet overseas citizens. Quite a few have become Chinese citizens.

Notices, menus, signs in Chinese and Russian. I seem to be a rarity here, for few English-speaking visitors turn up. There should be more, since it is an impressive city.

Writing This in the Train

We are leaving behind a great city, chimneys pouring smoke, dark, rain-swept buildings, power pylons, coal heaps, more and more smokestacks; the jagged angles of factories. Then newer and pleasanter-looking houses, not yet smoke-grimed, with red roofs and young fruit trees and patches of garden like English "allotments."

A young man with a red armband interrupts my typing. He sits down and we have a long, uncomprehending conversation. I think he's asking me what time I want to eat lunch. But he may be the security guard, or just someone who wants to try his easily exhaustible English vocabulary on me.

"*Yi dien tzoong*" (one o'clock), I say. He seems to understand. I try some more: "*Pi jiou*" (beer), and he nods. He must be from the dining car. So I rattle off, "*Tzoong gwo tsai—tzu row, bai tsai*" (Chinese food—pork, cabbage). I revert to English: "Stewed fruit." He shakes his head no. Rice (my mind gropes), bread and butter—hell, I don't really want that. We sit silently for a few moments, he gazing at my portable typewriter. A few minutes later he gets up, smiles, says "please," and vanishes down the aisle.

I never did find out who he was; but at one o'clock I went into the dining car and the food, as usual on Chinese trains, was delicious.

Changchun: Facts, Figures, and Slogans

I suppose the Changchun truck-factory visit was jinxed from the start. That incredible man who turned up as my interpreter! I should have taken that as an omen. I am as irritable as most people, and this fellow annoyed me from the moment he met me at the station. "You have arrived late, and you shouldn't have come on a Sunday morning—everything is closed." (He sounded as if I were responsible.) These were his first words. Dressed in white shirt and white trousers, he made me feel underdressed in my blue polo shirt and baggy flannel pants. He ordered a porter to take my heavy bag but didn't offer to help with the two I was carrying. "Unreconstructed Shanghai type," I thought. He told me his name was —well it *sounded* like Nng, and that was the nearest I ever got to it. Definitely, we didn't get off to a good start!

The next morning began badly, too. I was about to take a photograph of the largest, shiniest automobile made in China today— the Red Flag (like a slightly enlarged Lincoln)—which was standing outside the hotel. "You must get permission to photograph that car"; it was Mr. Nng at my side, "it is a private car and we should get the permission of the owner." Hell! I didn't even trouble to reply.

Arriving at the truck factory, because time was so limited I suggested to the officials who met us that we leave the "background" briefing until afterward and get straight into my questions. I hoped to eliminate the political stuff and get some facts if I could. This insistence on reversing usual procedure may well have touched off the difficulties.

Our conversation, according to my notes, went as follows:

QUESTION: What are the principal products of this factory?
ANSWER: Heavy-duty trucks, the new Red Flag sedan, some variations on the basic design for trucks for special use, engines for combine harvesters, motors for pumping, for irrigation. . . .

Q.   How many units in each category did you make during the last three years?
A.   The factory was designed to make 30,000 trucks a year.
Q.   Have you achieved that?
A.   Due to leadership of the Party, Mao Tse-tung . . . etc., workers showing tremendous enthusiasm for increasing production, technical innovation, the Great Leap Forward, etc., etc., etc. . . .
Q.   (breaking in) How many trucks did you make in 1959?
A.   There was a slight shortage of material last year so we just about filled the capacity of the plant.
Q.   You mean you produced 30,000 trucks in 1959?
A.   I do not know the exact figure. . . .
Q.   What about 1958 . . . it must have been in the neighborhood of 30,000?
A.   But the figures are controlled by another department, I really couldn't be certain.
Q.   (trying another tack) How many people do you employ here?
A.   I'm not sure, I don't have the figures. I think the number of women is increasing. The Soviet government gave us all-round and unstinted help in setting up this factory—a large number of our technicians, as well as the administrative staff, went to the USSR to study their methods; a great many Russians came here.
Q.   How can I get the figures of production and of personnel?
A.   A great many of the technical innovations were initiated by the workers, especially since 1958 when the general line was laid down and the Communist Party of this district . . .
Q.   Who can give me the figures? May I see the Director—could he give me them?
A.   We didn't know when you came which figures you would

> want so that we were not able to gather the right facts together.
>
> Q. Look! I have been to a number of factories since coming to China—they have always known exactly what their production figures were. As for not knowing what questions would be asked, it's surely obvious when one goes to *any* factory, it doesn't matter *what* it is—shoes or toothbrushes—one of the *first* questions is "How many of these things do you make?"
>
> I am here to write a book about China. I want to write a fair and honest book. How can I if I can't get any facts?
>
> You say you don't have figures about the number of trucks you make or people you employ. Let's be frank. Every factory knows how many people it employs—at least approximately—and how many units it manufactures. . . .
>
> A. But this factory is so much larger than others—it's difficult to assemble the facts . . . if we had known this is the sort of information you require . . .
>
> Q. (I just had to!) I have been round automobile plants twenty times the size of this one and they know how many people they employ.

At this a huddled, whispered conversation between the chief and one of the "silent men" (Party members?) who always sit in. The chief then says that the production figures would be difficult to get unless the chief of the planning department is available. However, the number of employees is available and his colleague would go to phone the personnel department.

While waiting I tell them that I understand that *every* country has certain figures which it doesn't make public for security and other reasons. If their production figures are not given out for such reasons I would understand and respect that. But I think we ought to be frank and say so.

That's about as far as the conversation went. We were not too friendly, though on the surface things were all right. I didn't like being told untruths and they didn't like my pressing them and making them admit it.

Eventually the man came and said that as far as he could determine the round figure of employees was about 23,000.

As time was growing short, I broke off the questioning and asked to see the plant itself. We walked quickly through nearly all the main construction departments, hurrying, not because they set the pace but because of the enormous size of the factory.

Designed and equipped by the Russians, the plant began operations in August 1956. It is self-contained; it has its own foundry, forging plant, motor-tools and assembly unit, body works, and main assembly lines.

Because this was the first factory in China to turn out motor vehicles, the Chinese are immensely proud of it. To them it represents a step into the age of mass production. Perhaps it may stack up well by Russian standards; by our standards it has a long way to go.

I listed in my notes nine weak points in this factory. 1) An array of parts lying about between the buildings, many of them rusting. 2) Too many people not doing anything, a general lack of drive and precision. 3) Too much being carried by hand; a single part would be tugged along by a couple of men while other parts are moved on electric carts. All of this through a good deal of disordered rubbish. 4) Where there is good equipment it isn't being properly used. For example, main body frames are pressed out on a 3500-ton press. The press itself is fine; but a lot of time has to be spent prying the part loose from the press, by hand with levers. The pressing takes five seconds while removing the part takes half a minute. A few well-placed automatic punches from inside could eject each part instantaneously. 5) Too much single-occupation work: a man fixes one part with a welder and turns to do something else. 6) Poor lighting—even though it *was* a rainy day. 7) Assembly line moved so slowly it was difficult to see if it was moving at all. I timed it: a foot every twenty seconds. Trucks were spaced twenty-five feet apart so this means that maximum output would be only 115 per sixteen-hour shift, or 34,500 per three-hundred-day year. Even this is more than estimated. 8) Sloppy assembly-line techniques include passing tools from one side to another—not enough tools—and lack of testing, no checking anywhere. Lights were not adjusted for alignment, brakes not tested, and it took a long time to work gas into carburetor; I saw water leaking from a hose pipe insecurely fastened. 9) Lack of minimum safety precautions, e.g., there was no fire extinguisher visible near the gas supply.

I stood for ten minutes watching trucks being driven off. If this general carelessness was the case at this final stage, it can be assumed that a general lack of precision is true all along. The appearance of the factory supports this.

In general I would say from what I saw that the equipment in the factory is at least fair, if not good, but is not being used to best advantage. Given some technical planning advice and know-how by a crew from Detroit or France, a general cleaning-up of the factory, and a rearrangement of feed-ins, etc., my layman's guess is that with existing equipment plus some minor auxiliary stuff which could be made in China, and given an adequate and continuous supply of raw materials, this factory could turn out several times its present production, which is probably only one-third of the total capacity.

The trip to the Changchun truck factory was a useful reminder. The industries in the communes, the developments in heavy and light industry, the colossal human effort going into production all over China still do not add up to a thoroughly industrialized nation.

If the Chinese believe this plant shows that they are ready to turn out all the trucks needed, they are simply deceiving themselves. With tremendous muddle and waste they are producing in a year what Detroit could run off in a single day without turning a hair.

As to the product itself, by examining the truck, bouncing on it, listening to the motor, seeing it in operation under all kinds of loads, I would say it is a sturdy, no-nonsense vehicle without frills to go wrong; rather rough in the engine. I imagine it could stand a great deal of abuse and poor driving, bad gas and overloading. Probably what is most suited to China's present needs.

About a month after I was there, in August, another correspondent visited the factory. He told me afterward that it was operating much more efficiently than when I had seen it. He said they were expanding production and now expected to turn out 70,000 trucks a year. I think our diverging experiences proved to some extent the variability and inconsistency of so much of Chinese industry at this stage of development. Considering the lack of technological experience the Chinese had ten years ago, progress has not been inconsiderable.

Shenyang:
Pittsburgh of China

The final stage of the train journey to Shenyang—once known as Mukden—the largest city in the Northeast. Population nearly three million. As the train nears the city new factories, new blast furnaces, poke up through the rice paddies and kaoliang fields; then the scene becomes a jumble of industrial plants, smoking chimneys, and endless gray streets.

Shenyang is the main rail center for the southern part of the industrial Northeast, and is the focus of nearly a dozen major cities. In 1952, on the eve of the first Five-Year Plan, more than 50 per cent of China's industrial production came out of the Northeast. In terms of sheer industry, Shenyang makes Harbin and Changchun seem small-scale. There is simply no comparison. One could spend weeks here going through factories. I went through many—some as muddled as the Changchun truck plant; some in a curious state of transition, factories in which age-old hand methods were combined with modern streamlined techniques ("walking on two legs" the Chinese call this); and some that I think could, as smooth-running operations, compare with any in the Western world.

The Shenyang Number 1 Machine Tool Factory presents a sharp contrast to the truck factory I saw a few days ago. It took a bit of doing to discover the number of lathes being manufactured. I had hardly sat down when Mr. Nieh Tseng-kuo, deputy-director of the factory, confronted me with a base of 100 for 1956 and then proceeded to rattle off yearly increases to 180 per cent, 280, 350, etc. I shook my head, and asked him for something more concrete. After all, percentages based on a hypothetical 100 base are quite meaningless. I came right to the point and asked Mr. Nieh how many lathes were being turned out.

The first response to this was, "Our objective this year will be overfulfilled," and so forth.

"You must understand my difficulty," I broke in. "You give me a base of 100 for 1956 and then tell me that production has increased and you expect to overfulfill your plan. Really, that means very little. Supposing your production one year was five lathes, and the next year you made ten. Production would have gone up 100 per cent. It might sound good, but you still would only have produced ten lathes!"

We were sitting (a refreshing change) in his office, not in the usual reception room. A secretary sat at another desk and occasionally answered a phone call, but was otherwise busily engaged, and paid no attention to what went on. No one else here this time taking notes. In a bowl on the table before us two goldfish were swimming inexhaustibly round the Temple of Heaven.

Mr. Nieh was looking at me steadily.

"You are right. We are not revealing our annual figures, but I can tell you this. Our factory at present is turning out more than a thousand lathes of all sizes in our standard patterns each month (and he here listed the dimensions and capacities; the smallest of the standard lathes was five tons in weight). We hope to continue to increase this number during the rest of the year, provided supplies of raw materials continue to be made available. I can also tell you that a thousand lathes a month is 50 per cent more than our average production in 1959."

I felt like a winner of an international chess match who gains an unexpected victory. I had been given an actual figure—and I believed it to be a true one. This man was an engineer, not a propagandist.

"Is this the largest factory of this kind in China?" I asked.

"No, no. There are many far larger. This is not a large factory. It is listed as a medium-sized factory. I have seen many much larger than this."

I liked Mr. Nieh. He was direct. He hardly mentioned "the correct line" or the "inspiring leadership of the Communist Party." He answered my questions promptly and always to the point. Here are some of the facts I was given as I jotted them down in my notebook:

Twelve per cent of the six thousand workers are women, and they get the same pay as men. There is no piecework at all in this factory. The wage scale is comparable to other factories—the average wage for the entire factory is 70 yuan ($28) a month, the lowest wage for unskilled beginning workers who are being trained is a little over 30 yuan ($12), and the highest-paid technicians get something over 100 yuan ($40). The director gets less than his chief engineer, the highest-paid individual in the plant, who gets 200 yuan ($80). There are the usual welfare schemes—free medical aid, eight weeks' maternity leave on full pay, etc., as in other factories.

The educational facilities provided by the factory are extensive —there are spare-time schools for adults who missed schooling, from primary-grade level through college, and technically more advanced courses for those who want to go further. Writers from the Shenyang Writers' Union hold classes for creative writing; there is an amateur drama group; a sports and recreation club, and a documentary-film unit for those interested in making films. Ninety-five per cent of the workers make use of the educational facilities. There are the usual nurseries and kindergartens.

"Percentage of illiterates?" I asked.

Mr. Nieh (with a grin): "In this factory now—none. The last group passed their literacy test two or three weeks ago. We have very few old people and the young are very eager. Of course 'literacy' is a vague term. Our standard here is not especially high— I believe we have set it at fifteen hundred characters."

The factory itself is almost fully self-contained. Some smaller components and some electric motors are made by the commune workshops in the neighborhood, supervised by the factory technicians, who set rigid quality standards. Rejects from the commune workshops were high at first. "After all," Mr. Nieh said, "the workers were almost all women who had never handled a machine before, but now rejects are comparatively rare."

Before starting our tour of the factory I asked whether I could take photographs. "Take whatever you like," Mr. Nieh answered.

I expected that the quality of directness and competence that Mr. Nieh showed would be reflected in the factory itself, and I was not disappointed. If nothing else, my journey to this factory has revived my belief that the Chinese are capable of efficient large-scale organization. Watching the lathes roll off the line, the special train backed onto a siding for easy handling, and the general efficiency here, I feel that this factory really is producing lathes in considerable numbers. My guess is that the plant is working at 80 to 85 per cent of capacity. There were very few machines idle, and an absolute minimum of people just standing about.

The Chinese are not just talking when they talk about workers' innovations. Many were pointed out to me. There were automatic grinders which can now be attended to by one man instead of four, a bit clamp which can be tightened by one twist instead of being locked by tightening three clamps. A huge multiple plane was shown me as being a "technical innovation." I didn't understand, since it was of Russian manufacture. The answer was that the design was based on suggestions made by Chinese workers.

Quality and finish seemed excellent. The assembly line moved smoothly, seemingly without much pressure on those working the line. Every part was individually checked before assembly, checked after attachment to the main frame, and the completed machine is tested in a special room after coming off the assembly line. After this it is painted, greased, wrapped, and crated for shipment. Some of the lathes being crated were going to India.

There was a noticeable air of intense concentration on the faces of many of the workers. Each one seemed to pay close attention to the job at hand, with an eager look almost like students who have just mastered some new skill. I watched many at close range. They handled their tools well, seemed to know what they were doing—always with this eager quality. Perhaps this is just Chinese!

Letter to Elena July 5

I've just had dinner and feel comfortable and expansive, having had some excellent caviar and half a bottle of Shenyang wine. It's hot—95 degrees. I am sitting by the open window and from the street comes the sound of children at play. Far too sticky for them to go to bed yet and so there they are down there in the dark, inventive as always, playing their wonderful games, shouting and laughing.

Yesterday the truck works at Changchun—very evasive about figures, and in a way I don't blame them, for the figures would have revealed too much what a mixed-up place it was. Ford à la Russia in Chinese style . . .

Here I have a room in a hotel built by the Japanese, although German designed. Huge, ornate, but with remarkably pleasant rooms. This could be a rather good New York hotel. From the foyer is the door to a tiled bathroom, also American in style. There's a lace curtain between the foyer and the bedroom (they *had* to bring the lace in somewhere) which isn't Western, but otherwise this bedroom could be anywhere. The bed beautifully comfortable.

I have four nights in this capitalistic and unregenerate hotel. It's not too wildly unregenerate, of course. There's a bar, which never opens, and a billiard room which closes at nine. Earlier this evening I walked around the city to learn what was going on—I had a choice of a circus, movies, Peking opera, and the hotel billiard room. I decided to have a good dinner and write up my notes—which I better get to right now. . . .

En route to Anshan, which is about seventy-five miles south of Shenyang, accompanied by Chang Yung-tse, one of the very nicest and most intelligent of interpreters. I've seen so many factories in the past week or so that I'm beginning to feel like Chaplin in *Modern Times*. Anshan is the last stop on this Northeast swing.

Over the train loudspeakers the strains of the current hit, "Socialism Is Good," as we pull out of Shenyang station. Then the girl's voice (she really throws herself into it): "Now with the start of the train our life of travel begins . . . we are moving across the face of our beloved motherland . . . we all have different destinations but we all have one aim, to reconstruct our country quickly. . . ." More music.

After a while I dropped into the broadcasting booth in the middle of the train—the girl looked about fifteen. She told me she hadn't been doing this for very long. She apologized because the phonograph was an old one and had to be wound by hand and sometimes when the train joggled it would send the needle off the groove. As an old radio hand I complimented her on the way she faded the music and brought her voice in over it. "I think it's fun," she said. "Excuse me a moment," and while fading the music with one hand she announced through the microphone, "We will be arriving at . . . [the train seemed to stop at every town between Shenyang and Anshan] in two minutes. If this is your stop, please get ready and get off quickly since we are staying there only two minutes. Do not rush or you may have an accident. Be sure you take all your things and help anyone who needs help."

Later, when I was back in my seat, I heard her make the following announcement: "On behalf of the railway administration and the train crew we wish to apologize for the fact that the train is very crowded today and some passengers are standing. Many soldiers have had to travel with us unexpectedly and we were unable to add more coaches on short notice. Will the younger people please give their seats to the older ones, and everyone please see that no woman with a child has to stand. When unexpected difficulties such as these occur we must all help each other as much as we can. We promise you that all of us who serve on this train will have a serious discussion when this trip is over to see how we can avoid the mistake of not having enough seats in the future."

There is a real network of train tracks in this part of the country. From my window, at times, I can count as many as seven tracks, with many feeder lines going off on both sides. We pass long freight trains carrying coal. There is also a network of power lines. And, again, new factories everywhere rising out of the fields.

At one stop, looking out on a gray and drizzly landscape of tracks and coal cars, I thought how tediously like all other shunting yards these in China were. This could be Chicago, London. . . . Just then a locomotive puffed by, and riding on its boiler was a magnificently fierce, brightly painted dragon!

After one stop about a dozen soldiers came and sat down in the empty seats directly across the aisle from myself and Chang. They were traveling "soft"—coaches in China have two classes, "soft seats," first class, and "hard seats," second class.

Their loose-fitting khaki pants and jackets were unpressed, and all but one wore the usual sneakers. These men were officers, but except for the collar tabs which denote rank, they wear the same clothes as a private. Each wore a wrist watch and had a fountain pen clipped to the upper pocket of his jacket.

After a bit of eavesdropping I leaned across the aisle trying to strike up a conversation. They took me at first, I think, for a Russian. When one of them asked what country I was from, I replied quickly before Chang could answer, "Wo *shih Meigworen*" (I'm an American), to see what the response would be.

There was no particular show of interest. "Are you traveling alone?" And then we went on to other things. This is an example of the astonishing lack of curiosity about the United States which I have noticed everywhere. What a contrast to Russia! Or even China three years ago. Here was a lively bunch of officers and not a question about America!

I learned that the soldiers were an army basketball team on the way to a game in Anshan. I also discovered that there is no compulsory military service in China because the number who want to join is far more than the army can absorb. Any able-bodied man can apply, but only a certain number are selected after physical and mental examinations. Length of service is three years.

But at this point, to exhortations from our girl in the radio booth to be careful and to help each other, we arrived at Anshan station.

Anshan: Steel City 10

A Mr. Liu Tien-yi, an official of the steel company, met us at the station. "Let's have lunch," he said. I thought this an admirable beginning to a trip round a steelworks.

Liu was affable. Driving to one of the company's dining rooms he said, "I'll tell you the background, then you ask me questions." Swaying along through streets crowded with workers, bicycles, donkey carts, trucks, I jotted down some reminders.

"All this," Liu said with a grand sweep of his arm, "is part of the Anshan Iron and Steel Company. We have forty mines, mills, and fabricating plants—all under the same management—and we employ 170,000 people. The highest production before liberation was in 1943—840,000 tons—then it dropped almost to nothing. But by 1949 Russian technical experts were helping us to rebuild. It was a fearful mess. We didn't finish reconstruction of these plants until 1953. We've opened up some new open-hearth furnaces, several rolling mills, an automated seamless-steel-tube factory. By the end of 1957 we were turning out nearly three million tons and this year we will be topping six million—almost one-third of the national total."

We swung off the street to the company's head office. Lunch had already been ordered. We sat in our shirt sleeves in a room to ourselves. Good food, good beer. Chang, Liu, and I forgot about steel for a while. These young men were clearly of college-graduate level. They had never met before. I asked them about themselves.

Chang Yung-tse's family came to Shenyang from Shantung province. He had been a studious boy and his family, who owned a hardware shop, were able to send him to college.

In the early summer of 1948 Chang was one of a group of students from the Northeast who made their way down to Peking to petition the Kuomintang authorities for promised school funds. This was at a time when Peking's students were protesting arbitrary arrests in the schools. One night—Chang's group was camped in an old Buddhist temple—the secret police rounded them up and took them all off to jail.

"How'd you get out?" I asked.

"My father got word of what had happened, and after a few months enough money was raised in Peking to buy me out of jail."

Chang remained in Peking—some of his friends crossed the lines into Communist territory—and after liberation he entered the Foreign Language Institute in Peking.

All this was said rather hesitatingly and seriously.

Liu Tien-yi was a blunter type. His family had been connected with the steel companies in this area. The father worked here under the Japanese, for a pittance.

"Sometimes my father brought back so little at the end of a week's work that we didn't eat. I mean my mother and the children didn't eat. Mother made my father eat, because if he lost his health and lost his job we would all have starved."

After the Japanese were defeated the works was taken over by the Kuomintang and things got worse. Many of the mills closed. There was no work. "My father was ingenious and became a street hawker selling small necessities which he often made himself out of metal scrap that he would go out and steal—things like small pots and frying pans.

"After liberation, of course, things picked up. As many as possible were put to work clearing the rubble and cleaning up the destroyed factories. At first for little wages, but just to be doing something again was a help. When the Metallurgical Institute was opened here, I applied, passed the examinations, and got a four-year training course—then was taken on almost automatically by the steel company. My father is still working here—he's too old to be in the furnace plants, he works in the tube mill."

We had more beer. The room was full of smoke, and the relating of these stories (so unusual for Chinese to be so outspoken about themselves) had brought a certain atmosphere of intimacy between us.

We were silent for a few moments. Why wouldn't young men like this be behind the regime, I thought. But such musings could wait. I wanted to make the most of the present atmosphere to ask questions that had always somehow been evaded.

"If a boy sees a girl that he takes a fancy to, how does he get to know her?"

They both smile at this sudden switch in conversation. Apparently he does what young men all over the world do—he might wait for her outside the factory gate, make some excuse for talking to her, ask her out to a movie.

"And if he wants to marry her?"

"I don't think he would ask her himself," Liu said. "A few might, but not most. Not right out like that. He would first get a friend to ask her if it would be all right for him to ask her to marry him . . . and in that way he wouldn't make it embarrassing for her to say 'no' if she didn't want to or embarrassing to himself to be rejected. Then, of course, there might be a good deal of discussion between the two families—but the decision is entirely up to the couple. If everything is all right, then they must both get a health certificate. Then they can get married."

"What ceremony is performed?"

"Usually none at all, except, of course, the families will come together to celebrate with a small dinner. Then the couple are given a three-day holiday with pay by way of a honeymoon."

"Of course," added the serious Chang, "the boy and girl would ask each other about their political views in order to be sure to marry someone who is politically mature."

And now an even more delicate question.

"What about boys and girls sleeping together before they are married? Does it happen often?"

"Oh yes, of course it does happen," Chang said. "But it's against the law."

"No, no," said Liu, "it's not against the law, but it's frowned on. Not that we mind about people sleeping together from any old-fashioned moralistic ideas or religious notions—nothing of that kind; but if they sleep together they might have children, and anyway, isn't it better to get married?"

Mr. Liu, looking at his watch: "We better get going if we are to see the steel mills."

For the rest of the afternoon I went round the steel plant. It seemed in full production. There were no idle men, nothing that gave any sense of inefficiency or lack of direction. A constant pouring of metals, men sweating, steam, coal dust—a nightmare vision of what hell must be like.

The rolling mills seemed to be working full speed. Tremendous chunks of bright-red steel were being pushed around, flattened, squeezed through giant rollers till they went leaping, one hundred and fifty feet long, back and forth between the rollers like red serpents.

High above was the control room. The driving mechanisms below were operated by three men seated at the electric switches. Even here the heat was overwhelming, and the nineteen-year-old at the center controls was unable to prevent sweat running down his face. Over his head was a large mirror in which he could observe the incandescent snakes as they lashed out beneath him.

Below, the circular saws with a screech and a shower of sparks parted the snake into five rails. Seventy kilometers a day, enough for thirty-five kilometers of track. I timed the cutting and figured out the equation. It came to almost what Mr. Liu had claimed. If one were to discount half that amount for replacement use, the availability of even seventeen and a half kilometers of track per day from this plant seems quite good.

At this point Liu said he wanted to run me out to one of the smaller steel plants which the mother-company operates on the outskirts of Anshan. I said fine, anything to get away from the dust, the glare, the crash of cranes. . . .

We drove thirty miles. On the way I asked Liu to tell me what had happened to the small back-yard furnaces I had heard so much about. He said that in the summer of 1958 there were hundreds of thousands of these small furnaces all over China. "Everyone was making steel in home-made furnaces, some of them just a meter or a meter-and-a-half capacity. Foreigners laughed at us about these furnaces, and of course they were very inefficient. But they missed the point. The iron and steel that these furnaces turned out were never included in the national production figures, the iron wasn't good enough for industrial use."

(In a thirty-five-page report, the United States Department of the Interior, referring to the period of back-yard furnaces, stated: "As many as sixty million people were taken off the farms to look for minerals, work in coal mines and smelt iron. Although this program dislocated the country's economy as a whole . . . it served a useful purpose to the mineral industry with regard to the accumulation of information on resources and training a large number of persons in the fundamentals of mineral extraction. The by-product of this program was another great increase in mineral production, coal and steel output being respectively more than 100 per cent and 50 per cent greater in 1958 than in 1957. The back-yard program has since been junked, but it set the stage for many small and medium semi-modern industries."

This revealing report, which makes some of my conclusions about China's industry seem almost conservative, appears in Special Supplement No. 59, March 1960, Mineral Trade Notes of the Bureau of Mines, United States Department of the Interior, and is available to the public without cost.)

"It wasn't production that these furnaces accomplished," Liu went on, "it was education. Our people, especially our peasants, have never been around machines like your people have been. They were completely unmechanically minded. Many of them were in awe of technological processes. But now they were encouraged to make their own simple tools—wheelbarrow wheels, gate hinges, even their own ball bearings in a pestle and mortar—and out of iron they themselves had smelted! In one summer's hectic activity, our peasants learned not to be afraid of 'technique.' It lost its mystery. People who have actually poured their own steel and made things with it feel they can do anything. I don't know if that was really the reason why these furnaces were started—but the effect has been just what I said. In six months it was all over.

"There were other side benefits. The peasants discovered many unsuspected sources of ore and coal, which we can now exploit. Now integrated plants—medium-sized furnaces—have taken the place of the back-yard furnaces, and these are now dotted all over China. The steel they produce is as good as anything we turn out at Anshan. What we are going to see is one of the integrated plants which developed out of the little furnaces."

This enterprise (rising out of the rice fields) consisted of fourteen furnaces, each with capacity of fifty-five cubic meters.

The entire plant was set up in three months. Of the sixteen hundred workers—four hundred are women—almost all were peasants a few years ago, only eight men have any advanced technical skill. To construct these furnaces and produce steel with such an unskilled work force, my guides told me, would have been impossible except for the experiment with the back-yard furnaces. These provided a cram-course in applied metallurgy. Millions of peasants who had never conceived of making steel learned enough of the rudimentary principles so that they could now come into a medium-sized operation like this integrated plant almost without technical direction from above.

In the Train Going Back to Shenyang

Exhausted, Chang and I made it to the railroad station on time, with Liu to see us off. Late evening and a slow trip back to Shenyang. A tremendous crowd on the station—a new one is being built and this temporary one has no cover. The train is late and in the darkening light a fine drizzle begins. Men turn up their coats, women pull scarves over their heads.

A message comes down to us: Would the foreigner not prefer to go to the station office to keep dry? I say, no thanks; but Liu and Chang say, of course. The station office is a tiny room, full of

banners and paintings by workers. Innumerable telephones keep
ringing and no one answers. One wall is covered with pieces of
colored paper with black Chinese characters on them. I asked what
they were—I should have known. "They are suggestions from the
railway workers as to how we can do our work better."

The train finally steams in. It is dark now, and we have difficulty
in finding the "soft" seat compartment and when we do we discover
it is an old coach, musty, with an unused, shabby look.

As the train pulls out, a delegation of three wait on us—two
pretty girls and the head of the train crew. They stand looking very
serious. Very formally the head man begins. "We have come," he
says, "on behalf of the railway administration, to offer our apologies for the state of the coach in which you will have to sit on your
journey. Our own coach unexpectedly had to go in for repairs this
morning and we borrowed this old one from the Dairen headquarters." A deep breath. He is steeling himself to tell the worst.
"We do not have any way of making you tea. We ask you to for-
give us."

There they stood, the three of them, in such charming and obvious distress, that I laughed and readily forgave them, and they
went off in better spirits, but still, I am sure, feeling that in some
terrible way they had brought disgrace to the People's Republic.

Within a few minutes, Chang on one seat, I on the other, are fast
asleep.

I woke at one stop and peered out through the rain. My window
by chance was opposite a signal and switch-control tower. It was
well lighted and I watched, fascinated. It was a fully automatic
control system; on a panel rows of illuminated push buttons; above
the operator's head was a complete visual layout of his section of
the track and the station yards showing, by indicator lights, the location of each train, and each switch and signal light. I have never
seen anything more up-to-date. It was worthy of the New York
Central.

The train moved on and I settled down again to sleep.

China an Industrial Power 11

Chinese technical and industrial advances, hitherto (in the words of the *New York Times*) "only a rumble as far as most Americans are concerned," are now coming through "with thundering reality." This is no place to make a detailed and definitive assessment of China's industrial and commercial potential, and any such attempt would be rich in error. The technological revolution in China is too vast, is changing too rapidly, is too new for a single reporter to cover. It would require an army of experts, production managers, statisticians, economists, geologists, agronomists to visit China and interpret their findings for us; but by the time their reports were written their information would be out of date.

There are, nevertheless, some broad questions which can be asked and answered: How much credence can be given to Chinese statistics? Does China have adequate mineral resources to enable her to become a first-class industrial power? Does she have the technical know-how? We acknowledge that China is advancing industrially, but what is the pace of this advance? To what extent has she developed her international commerce? What particular technological problems does China face in the future?

Chinese figures—can we believe them?

A number of distinguished economists and industrialists from European and Asian countries have in the past few years visited China, and I am impressed with the fact that they make much use of Chinese figures in their reports. These men would quickly detect any sustained and deliberate attempts to mislead. No centrally planned economy can function without reasonably accurate statistics, and a nation consistently cooking its accounts would soon land itself into the most appalling troubles. Nor could it do so for long without its published figures revealing obvious contradictions. This does not mean that all Chinese statistics are accurate—they clearly are not; or that we have anything like full information—for there is much that is still hidden. In some cases (notably the 1958 agricultural returns) the original figures were grossly inflated. Statistical skills grow with experience. Great mistakes have been made; but the Chinese authorities appear to be following the practice of publicly correcting figures which are found to have been inaccurate.

There are innumerable government agencies and academic institutions in the United States which scrutinize, sift, and analyze every available Chinese document. In England there are commercial and industrial research organizations which do the same; and in their case, findings can often be verified by personal visits to China. All these reports provide a useful, interlocking cross-check of Chinese statistical data. After studying them one is impressed with the general unanimity of their conclusions.

In December 1960 the American Association for the Advancement of Science held a two-day symposium in New York designed to assess China's progress in science and technology—we shall be referring to this meeting several times. The *Christian Science Monitor* for December 29 wrote of the reports given at this symposium: "They were based mainly on published Chinese Communist literature. But in the few cases where experts had also first-hand experience, conclusions based on the literature jibed reasonably well with what they had seen."

We have learned to scoff no longer at Russian statistical claims —they have too often been found to be of very sobering accuracy. I think that we will learn that this is true of China also.

Does China have adequate natural resources?

The chief resources needed for large-scale industrialization are iron, coal, and petroleum. For many years, largely because no one had looked for them, it was assumed that China lacked adequate reserves of these minerals. That assumption must now be corrected.

The *New York Times* of December 27, 1960 reported:

"Intensive geological prospecting on the Chinese mainland in the last decade has disclosed mineral resources so extensive that they appear to make China one of the world's chief reservoirs of raw material. . . . Discoveries of raw material were described by Edward C. T. Chao of the United States Geological Survey. After World War II he said there were fewer than 200 active geologists in China. . . . Now there are 21,000 'geological workers.' . . . Also 400 foreign geologists have been brought in mostly from the Soviet Union and Eastern Europe. Discovered in the exploration of the hinterlands, was an unsuspected reservoir of 7,000,000,000 tons of iron ore in the Shansi area of Central China. Another deposit estimated at 3,000,000,000 tons has been found in Honan province. It assays at more than 50% iron oxide."

As a measure of comparison and to appreciate the magnitude of these figures the *New York Times* in this report said: "One pillar of industrial growth in the United States has been the Mesabi range in Minnesota. From 1892 to 1950 some 1,500,000,000 tons of ore were removed from it."

As for coal, all reports indicate that China has large reserves. In its report, the U.S. Bureau of Mines in March 1960, China's supply of both coal and coking coal are listed as being in the "first rank." A British book (*The Economic Development of Communist China, 1949–1958* by T. J. Hughes and D. E. T. Luard) states: "China has much greater coal resources than any other country in Asia. They are probably inferior only to those of the Soviet Union and the United States." Another British report (*Chinese Trade and Economic News Letter,* London, June 1958) said that China's known coal reserves are adequate for centuries and are well-distributed over the country.

China's chief weakness appeared, until recently, to be in petroleum. The fields in operation in Kansu, Sinkiang, Szechwan, and elsewhere were not able to keep up with China's growing demands and much oil has had to be imported from the Soviet Union.

However, the picture has altered radically. Very intensive surveys have apparently met with success. I met an East-European in China, an oil expert, who was convinced that recent new discoveries will in time make China "one of the great oil-producing countries of the world." It will take some years to bring these new fields into production. The U.S. Bureau of Mines report (already referred to) appears to confirm this: "Petroleum is inadequate but extensive exploration in recent years shows that the country will be prominent in this field five to ten years from now. . . . The country should no longer be considered poor in oil."

As to other minerals, China's position is exceptionally strong in tin, tungsten, molybdenum, and mercury (in all of which she has the largest reserves in the world); and in chromium, nickel, asbestos, and diamonds.

To sum up: There appears no doubt whatever that China, in the words of the U.S. report, "has a sufficiently diversified mineral base to become a first rank industrial power."

Is China developing the technical knowledge and skill to develop these resources?

"The Communist regime fully realizes," says the same report, "that the key to China's industrial progress lies in the uncovering and efficient utilization of its mineral wealth. . . . Geological, mining, and metallurgical techniques are constantly being improved. It is a fallacy to assume that the Chinese Communists are not cost-conscious and do not believe in efficient practices. Great strides have also been made in training technicians and industrial workers to supply the manpower needed in mineral development. . . . If energy can be considered a good gauge of gross national product for a country, it is pertinent to mention that the 1959 output of coal, which is the main source of energy in mainland China, was about five times that of the pre-1949 peak year. . . . Many other minerals industries are undergoing rapid expansion. . . . The so-called modern operations which produce most of the mineral products in the country, are fairly up-to-date from the engineering point of view, but, while comparing favorably with European and Japanese practices are much lower in productivity than U.S. operations. The reason again is that in any Asiatic country 'poor man's engineering' must be applied, which is good in quality but not in productivity. Generally speaking, the overall level of mineral technology in Communist China has advanced rapidly in the past decade; the technological gap between the Orient and the West is narrowing. In fact some practices in Communist China compare with the best in the world. . . . The fact that Communist China will soon have approximately a 100,000,000-ton-per-annum capacity in coal cleaning facilities . . . speaks well for technological process in controlling coal quality. Developments in mine construction and coal extraction are equally impressive; productivity is approaching European standards and advanced techniques like cutter-loader and underground hydraulic operations are employed at all large mines."

It would be a mistake to think that the technological advances in China have been limited to the development of mineral resources, or that scientific training has in any way been neglected. The advance has been a *general* one.

Dr. J. Tuzo Wilson, an eminent Canadian scientist from the University of Toronto, traveled to China in 1958 as President of the International Union of Geodesy and Geophysics. He has described what is going on in China as a scientific "renaissance." "The government clearly believes in, and supports, education and science," he told the Council of Scientific Societies of the Dallas–Fort Worth area on December 1, 1960. "Many scientists from the old regime, old universities and old institutes, are flourishing. They have never had so much support before. . . . I was impressed by the many new buildings and universities. The equipment was simple but far better and more abundant than I would have expected. . . . Some people have expressed a fear that scientific training in communist countries will produce nations of evil robots. I think this is balderdash. I saw no evidence of it."

Dr. Wilson, in the same lecture, mentioned conditions in the universities in Taiwan: "One thing which I found particularly sad on Taiwan was that although Taiwan is often called "free" China, the universities there have had less support and fewer new buildings in recent years than those on the mainland; the libraries were poorer and the scientific equipment was less good than that which I had seen during the previous month in Peking, Sian, Lanchow and Canton."

Sir Cyril Hinshelwood, who as President of the Royal Society—Britain's top-ranking scientific organization—visited China in 1959, reported on the Chinese scientific effort in *The New Scientist* (London):

"My Western prejudices against highly centralized organizations were very much mitigated by the open-minded and experimental view which I found prevalent. . . . I received the general impression of something rather more flexible than I had normally read of and would judge that even here the experimental method is rather widely understood and appreciated. . . .

"Laboratories and equipment are good . . . the vast and well-equipped workshops I found a revelation. Library facilities, both in books and journals are admirable. I have seldom, if ever, seen such extensive collections of scientific journals in all languages as I saw in several universities and Academic Institutes. . . . Students now learn both Russian and English, and many seemed to be making practical use of their knowledge in the libraries. . . . Although there is no question whatever of neglecting the basic sciences, there is much more conscious effort to mix fundamentals with practical applications at an early stage. . . . Among the students and the young research workers in the Institutes there seemed to be an atmosphere of enthusiasm. . . .

". . . In some places, especially in Shanghai, there are well-established research schools of very high quality. The topics of investigation and the methods of approach do not differ much from those met with in Western laboratories. . . .

"I would not say that any of the research is influenced by ideology. . . ."

Further evidence that Chinese technological skills were advancing rapidly was given in the New York symposium already referred to (*New York Times*, December 27, 28, 1960, and San Francisco *Chronicle*, December 27, 1960). T. C. Tsao of Columbia University reported that China had installed four nuclear reactors, and said that in view of China's rapid technological advances it would not be surprising if that country produced a nuclear explosion "in the near future." The per capita consumption of electric power, he said, has increased by 800 per cent since 1952.

In regard to technical literature available in China, Dr. John M. H. Lindbeck of Harvard reported that between 1956 and 1957 the Chinese spent $9 million in British sterling to purchase scientific literature from non-Communist countries. Dr. Robert T. Beyer, a Brown University physicist, pointed out that "about one-third of the scientific papers originating at the nuclear research center at Dubna, near Moscow, have Chinese names attached to them."

The rapidity of developments in the last decade was attributed, according to the *New York Times* reports, to such factors as: "the existence for the first time in many decades of a strong central government; the allocation by that government of extensive funds for science; and a sudden release of enthusiasm and interest in a scientifically-minded population."

I think enough has been said to indicate that there is no reason to doubt that the Chinese possess the scientific genius and talent to meet the technological demands of a modern industrialized state.

How fast is China's industry advancing?

To evaluate China's industrial progress a differentiation must be made between the absolute quantitative production, which reflects the nation's over-all strength, and the per capita production that reflects living standards. It is, I think, an accurate generalization to say that while China as a nation is rapidly approaching world-power status, the living standard of her people will remain relatively low for a long time.

China in 1949, even by Indian standards, was industrially an extremely backward country. So another warning must be given. Percentage increases may seem phenomenal because China started with so little. A workshop that formerly made ten bicycles in a given time and now makes a hundred has increased its production by 900 per cent, but it may have little significance in absolute terms.

Nevertheless, bearing these factors in mind, the *pace* of China's industrial development has outstripped all anticipations and is unprecedented in history. Dr. Charles Bettelheim of the Sorbonne, who was one of a group of French economists who visited China in 1958, reported (in *The Economic Weekly*, Bombay, November 22, 1958): "But above all, the feeling prevailing with my economist colleagues and myself is that of finding ourselves in a country that goes ahead at an unbelievable speed and which, in this respect, outdoes all the performances that could have been achieved elsewhere."

Dr. Bettelheim compares China's progress with the progress made by the USSR at equivalent stages of her industrial expansion. During China's First Five-Year Plan (1953–57) her expansion was approximately of the same rate as Russia's during its First Five-Year Plan (1927–28 to 1932). Both expanded at about 19.2 per cent annually. The new factor in China was the enormous acceleration of China's industrial growth that began in 1958. Within one year, Dr. Bettelheim says, Chinese production was raised from a lower level than that of the USSR in 1932 to a level not reached by the Soviet Union until after the Second World War, thirteen or fourteen years later.

The rapidity of expansion reported by Dr. Bettelheim in 1958 has not appreciably declined since then. For example, steel production for 1960 reached a total of 18,450,000 tons. This is a net increase of more than five million tons over 1959 and over 50 per cent more than the production originally set as the target for 1962, the end of the Second Five-Year Plan. In other words, steel production increased by nearly 350 per cent in three years, i.e., from 5,350,000 tons in 1957 to 18,450,000 in 1960, an average increase of 4,300,000 tons. (The average annual increase in the First Five-Year Plan was only 800,000 tons.)

In almost all sections of industrial production, increases of an unprecedented character have been reported. In February 1961 a British economic report, *China Trade and Economic News Letter*, stated: "It may be conservatively estimated that gross industrial output rose by not less than one-fifth, and perhaps as much as one-quarter in 1960 [over 1959]." And this same report states that the increase in steel itself will almost *equal the total 1957 output*.

China's advance in absolute terms is indicated by the fact that in production of coal she is now the second largest producer in the world; in machine tools she has surpassed Britain and Germany; in iron and steel she will quite soon be surpassing all but the United States and the Soviet Union. In cotton production she has already surpassed the United States. In textiles the city of Shanghai alone is outproducing Britain. In September 1958, British experts who keep close touch with developments in China stated that:

The pace of expansion is now such that within less than a decade China should become the third leading industrial power in the world, ranking only after the United States and Russia.

Will China be able to sustain this rapid advance?

In a radio broadcast after my return from China in 1957 I predicted that China was moving too fast, had attempted too much with too few resources, had greatly overextended herself in capital construction on too narrow a base of technological experience and a gross shortage of qualified personnel, and that for these very cogent reasons there would be a period of slowing up and consolidation. I might say that I felt fairly safe in this prediction because it was shared by almost every reputable economist who was in touch with Chinese developments. It was also shared by Western embassy experts stationed in Peking.

I could not have been more wrong.

A few months after my radio talk, the "great leap forward" began; the communes were started, the mass line was announced. Within three years China had *trebled* the gross value of her industrial product.

I shall now risk another prediction.

There are many indications that the period of industrial consolidation, which I had expected three years ago, will now take place. The Chinese government has announced an "appropriate reduction" in the scope of capital construction; the greater emphasis on agriculture will, I think, be bound to deflect resources which would otherwise have added yet further productive capacity to industry. If China is to compete successfully in world markets, the quality of some of her products must be improved; with an increase of general wage levels, demand for consumer goods will mean a further deflection from heavy industry. China needs to establish unified accountancy systems and standardized production procedures; she needs to increase her per capita productivity through further mechanization of her factories; she needs to develop her output of high-grade steel and special alloys. All this requires a breathing space, a period of consolidation.

But what will happen after this period (if there is one) is anybody's guess. My own is that in the next upward swing of China's industry, she will fulfill the British experts' prediction mentioned above. She will outstrip all countries except the United States and the Soviet Union.

This general technological advance is reflected throughout Chinese life today.

Though still far from being able to manufacture in sufficient volume to meet her own needs, there is almost nothing that China requires that she is not making herself, whether it is diesel-electric locomotives for her railways, jet fighters for her air force, heavy tanks for her army, ships of 16,000-ton displacement, or advanced electronic computers.

Having seen China three years earlier, I can attest to the marked increase in the range and variety of products that are today being offered for sale in the stores of the larger cities; and China's mastery of technological skills is even more dramatically shown in the permanent exhibitions (such as the Industrial Exhibition at Shanghai) which are primarily intended for overseas buyers. Here is a list, jotted down at random in my notebook, of some of the things I saw at these exhibitions:

Stainless-steel blades for steam turbines, TV cameras and transmitting apparatus, TV sets, a forty-five-ton press for the making of tissue paper, a machine for making 100,000 medicinal tablets per hour, automatic double-end grinding wheels, valve testers, automatic chemical analysis machines, record players, watches, clocks, cameras, grand pianos, motorcycles (and racing motorcycles, too), precision balances accurate to 0.0001 mg., and toilet fixtures in three different sizes and five different shades!

As far as consumer goods are concerned, though it will be a long time before the average Chinese will even remotely approach the living standards of Europe, the knowledge of manufacture is there, the skills are being learned. Already, it would be difficult to find in a Sears Roebuck catalog anything that China is now incapable of making.

How about international trade?

This was the question I asked Dr. Chi Chao-ting as we sat one evening at dinner in Peking.

A graduate student in the United States in the late thirties, Dr. Chi had traveled widely abroad and before 1948 had been a leading figure in Nationalist China's financial circles. His extensive knowledge of international trade and finance is widely acknowledged in the West. Today Dr. Chi is in the upper echelons of the regime, holding high positions both in the China Council for the Promotion of Foreign Trade and in the People's Bank of China. An inquiring reporter could not go much higher for information regarding China's foreign-trade policies.

Dr. Chi replied by giving me a wide survey of China's foreign-trade position. Her foreign trade had tripled, he told me, between 1950 and 1958 and this rate had been maintained with a slight increase since then. This, he emphasized, has been achieved in spite of the embargo imposed by the United States and American pressure on her allies to keep trade with China to a minimum. The embargo, he thought, had largely hurt Western businessmen because China was quite soon able to switch the trade she had lost to the socialist countries.

Today 80 per cent of China's foreign trade is with the socialist countries. There is little trade with Japan, and none at all with the United States.

"The pattern of our foreign trade has altered," Dr. Chi said, "for we are increasingly exporting things we never exported before—industrial products and minerals and processed agricultural products such as canned goods and frozen foods. Food exports do not greatly affect what is available for home consumption, they represent only 1.5 per cent of our total agricultural production." He thought the trend of China's exports will be increasingly toward mineral and industrial items. Fifty per cent of China's exports consist of items formerly not even made in China. As far as imports go, China is today independent of cotton imports, though she does import some long-fibered cotton from Egypt. China's main trade is with Russia.

China now takes 20 per cent of Russia's foreign exports, and 50 per cent of China's foreign exports go to Russia.

I asked Dr. Chi if he thought, granted trade were free, that America and China would find themselves natural trading partners. What does each produce that the other might need?

Dr. Chi answered my question by saying that China welcomes foreign trade but will never become dependent on it. China's primary policy is self-dependence, which does not mean the same as self-sufficiency; but China is determined never to reach the point where she cannot survive without foreign trade. "Some people in the West," he said, "think that the Soviet Union has provided much help for which we haven't paid. That is not so. The Russians have helped us (and are helping us greatly) by providing blueprints, allowing use of her patents, and so on; but otherwise we pay in full for all our imports from the Soviet Union. That reflects our wish to trade on a mutual basis—it must be to a common advantage and be honestly reciprocal. But this kind of trade can only flourish in a friendly atmosphere, it cannot thrive in an atmosphere of mistrust or enmity."

He went on to say that he felt, if these requirements were present, that substantial trade between America and China could develop to mutual advantage. "The United States and Britain make the same things, but that doesn't mean they don't trade together. As countries develop industrially they will naturally buy more and more from other industrialized nations. I have no doubt at all," he repeated, "that trade between the United States and China could develop very well if there were a friendly atmosphere, a mutual trust, and a real desire to base all trade on an absolutely fair and reciprocal basis.

"It must be remembered that China does not *have* to trade abroad," Dr. Chi went on. "We do not have a surplus productive capacity. We could consume all our produce. We export today to buy imports which we need or to help countries, such as Ceylon, which need some economic assistance. But that is very different from having to export to get rid of things which we have produced and cannot ourselves consume. That is America's predicament, not ours.

"Westerners are full of unfounded fears about China. Some people fear, for instance, that we will try to force our trade upon other countries. That is not so. . . . Of course, socialism being a superior economic system, our goods will be able to compete successfully with those of capitalistic countries, but that is not the point I am making. Our home needs are so vast that if a surplus did appear in this or that item we could then very quickly change the pattern of our production. That is one real advantage of a socialist system. Some people fear that we will disrupt the economy of other Asian nations by becoming a great exporter of grain. If ever a time (which would be very distant) did come when we had to face this problem, then we could switch even our agricultural production to other items which our people or others in the world would still be needing."

Industry Is People

Sustaining all these gigantic endeavors are the minds, the muscles, and the sinews of the largest population on earth. It is on the long-term readiness of the people of China to support these great plans that the country's success or failure will depend.

There is a prevailing opinion in America that the Chinese are being threatened, brainwashed, or bludgeoned into this work of national industrialization; that a small group of power-hungry Communist leaders have fastened themselves onto an unwilling and resentful population and are driving them fiercely forward against their will. Indeed, for nearly a decade our national policy was based on the openly expressed hope that sooner or later the people of China would rise against their "oppressors."

I believe this picture is the very opposite of the truth.

And so do others who have seen the country for themselves. On his return from China in 1958 Mr. James Muir, President of the Royal Bank of Canada, reported to his shareholders (in the *Royal Bank Magazine*, October 1958) as follows:

"The growth in industry, the change in living standards, the modernization of everything and anything, the feats of human effort and colossal impact of human labor are not within our power to describe and still give a worthwhile picture of the scene. All I can say is that it must be seen to be believed. It is truly stupendous.

. . . We think the vast majority of the people of China have a government they want, a government which is improving their lot, a government in which they have confidence, a government which stands no chance of being supplanted."

Mr. Muir, in a letter to me, expressed his view that America's policy toward China was "one of the greatest diplomatic tragedies of the century."

Another, more recent, visitor to China was Mr. Kurt Mendelssohn of Oxford University. An author of several books on physics, Mr. Mendelssohn was invited on his return by the BBC to discuss the impact of technology on the Chinese people, and his words were published in *The Listener*, February 9, 1961:

"Technology is not only based on machines but also on people: people with emotions, people who can be hostile to a program, or indifferent, or enthusiastic. . . . For the worker in the West . . . industrialization always savours of enslavement and exploitation. The industrial revolution has left a bitter taste. Things are different for the Chinese. There, the Communists are not, as with us, a force which tries to destroy a well-established pattern of society. On the contrary they have brought order and peace to a country which was torn by civil war. When the Chinese speak of liberation, they mean it; liberation from a nightmare which lasted half a century. . . . Technology is a great and joyful experience, an adventure into which they have thrown themselves with enormous enthusiasm. Anyone watching them at work will be struck by this enthusiasm which, to me at least, appears the most significant feature of their technological advance. . . .

". . . It [is] said that being told constantly what to do is the price which the Chinese have to pay for development. We might consider being ordered about as tiresome, but I am fairly certain that the average Chinese does not feel like that at all. There is this exciting development going on in which they are all interested, and they expect—and enjoy—being given a lead and advice and hearing all about it. Contrary to the old days of Mandarin rule, the government now addresses the common people directly and they feel that they are being taken into their rulers' confidence. . . . What may appear as boring indoctrination to us is likely to be of absorbing interest for them. . . .

"In Moscow my colleagues told me that the Chinese students coming to work in the Soviet Union are gifted and incredibly hardworking, and that they are often at the top of their classes . . . when they enter the field of industrial competition in earnest, they are likely to do so in their own right and not merely as imitators of Western methods. Discussing scientific or technological problems with the Chinese, one becomes acutely aware of many centuries of mental schooling. Their arguments are clever, shrewd, and to the point, and one feels that the minds which for more than a thousand years have been sharpened by classical training find little difficulty in making the change to science. . . .

"One of the many slogans which has caught on particularly well is 'Learn while you work.' . . . I was told that at the building of the great Yangtze Bridge they started with a fairly small number of skilled crews. The others watched. Soon many more could do the skilled work, and so it went on in a chain reaction of learning. . . . The workers of China have this immense desire to learn because they enjoy it and not just because they want better jobs. In terms of industrial production this means that the Chinese scientists and engineers will be backed by a good supply of eager and enthusiastic technicians, a grade in which our own industry is lamentably short.

"It is a sad reflection that the East should have succeeded where we seem to have failed. . . . The great advances which we have achieved in man's domination of the forces of nature . . . have been met in the West with nothing better than apathy or even revulsion. The Chinese . . . take these same things as exciting new developments, destined to enrich the life of human society. . . .

"However modern the political and economic views of one's Chinese friends may be, subconsciously they are backed by the past greatness of China. When the mind of China now turns to technology, it does so with the moral strength of historical successes. . . . Wherever one goes and whoever one may talk to in the new China, these 2,000 years of unbroken civilization are in evidence. The buildings and monuments of the old China are receiving the same love and care as the new machines. One is made to feel that to the Chinese technology is not an aim in itself or a copy from the West, but simply another chapter in their long and glorious history: if you like, a new mandate of heaven."

China ☆
Kaleidoscope 1

Notes from My Journal and Letters

Are things specially arranged for foreigners?

Yes and no. No in any significant sense of changing things to impress a visitor. Often the foreigner is alone, as I am. Are they going to disrupt a factory employing 25,000 just so one person will be pleasantly surprised by what he sees? I have often at the last minute changed my plans and decided to see *this* instead of *that*. Are they going to go to much trouble for a plan that might be changed by a visitor's whim?

Secondly: They simply don't care! They are not overly concerned with what we think. They are enormously busy—as a nation at war is busy. We don't care in the middle of a war whether some foreign journalist gets the "right" impression or not. It is part of our self-importance to think that our opinion matters so much to them.

But *yes* in a different sense. Preparations are made; a hotel room is booked; certain plans are arranged for, the picnic lunch is prepared. The most "casual" day, you can see afterward, was most carefully thought out—mostly for your own comfort. The Chinese have a rare sensitivity about a traveler's needs. They seem to know exactly when he's had enough, when he wants to be alone, when he needs a nap, when he needs a beer. Chinese are among the best hosts in the world, and the least formal. You can have a good time and laugh with them. Or be silent with them. Silences are not uncomfortable socially as they are with us.

At Anshan, after a beer or two with Mr. Liu, who had been showing us around, we became rather cheerfully friendly and he told me some of the difficulties from their side. "You know," he said, "we Chinese like to be hospitable, but we often don't know how to be. We haven't traveled, we don't know your customs and we often don't have the faintest idea of what you really want to do. We try our best but we are never quite sure, especially as you come from so many different countries all with different customs. We never feel certain as to whether we are doing the right things for our guests."

Sense of Equality

This is an important aspect of Chinese life. I remember my surprise when I first came to America from England to see a senior surgeon in a hospital lining up at the cafeteria with nurses and orderlies—this simply couldn't have happened in prewar England—and, another time, seeing the head of a company having to wait for an elevator because the office boy got in first. China is like this, but more so.

It runs through their entire life. Yen, my current interpreter, feels perfectly at ease with cabinet ministers when I go for interviews. He shows respect, of course, but speaks as an equal. I have been told by one of the diplomatic people here that when Mao visits a farm or a factory people are eager to talk to him and do so at will, not fluttery and nervous. The judge at the court, the conductor on a train, the head of a factory, the senior engineer on a hydroelectric dam project, all of them I have noticed, walk around among the workers but never as "bosses." No one is obsequious. No one makes way specially for them—they aren't even noticed very much. They are another kind of worker doing their job.

Letter to Elena   June 15

. . . This afternoon I saw the floor boys in a huddle in the private dining room opposite the elevator. The double doors were open and I stood and watched six or seven of them around a table talking. Later I asked one of them if it had been their regular political meeting. He said, no, it was a meeting to discuss how they could become better floor boys, manage things better, be of better service to the guests.

Once more this passion for improvement! I believe that hotel boys in England or America would not meet like this; or if they did they would be talking about how to get more money or how to wangle a better job.

But perhaps it's not so much the desire for money that drives us as much as the need to feel *important*. We all have need to be somebody. The personal-importance motive doesn't seem to operate here in the same way, or possibly it's submerged in a collective drive for mass advance. Our corporations often secure the allegiance of an employee, not by more money, but by giving him more importance—a new title, a carpet, his name on the door, etc. I don't believe that would work here.

I have come to believe that the Chinese derive their deepest emotional satisfactions not from a sense of personal importance but from sharing in activities which have aims beyond the individual. The government here has been extremely skillful in giving nearly everyone a sense that his work fits in somewhere, is part of the whole. A floor boy in this hotel feels that he is participating in the rebirth of China every bit as much as a big shot in the government. All of them, down to those who do the most menial jobs—pedicab drivers, say—are made to feel they are an essential part of the whole show.

Item for Stamp Collectors

A recent stamp issue contained paintings of about a dozen different varieties of goldfish. Others are of animals and birds, some are of children running and skipping. During the "grow more pigs" drive a series came out with pictures of fat porkers. Domestic postage rates are four yen, less than one cent in our money.

One of China's less sticky problems comes up almost daily. They have no adhesive on their stamps. Post offices provide small paste pots and you do your best with both stamps and envelopes. It is quite a tedious business, and if one has a pile of letters it not only takes some time, but the letters tend to stick together because the paste always oozes onto the back of the envelope. The reason given for continuing this absurdity (it started long before 1949) is that licking stamps is "unhygienic."

Here at the hotel post office a damp handcloth is supplied to wipe the paste off one's hands.

Letter to Elena   June 24

. . . Another appallingly frustrating day. I phoned the Ministry again today, but couldn't get anywhere; no answer, not even "no." The Chinese have a highly developed sense of *timing*. They will wait until *they* think it is time to act. And then, if need be, they can act quickly. But they *won't* be *pushed!*

I have never in my entire life come up against this in quite the form it takes here. It is like being pitted against a solid wall of rock. There is no way to climb it or push it, or to get around the ends. It is just there; a colossal disregard for anything but that which they consider important. There is tremendous strength in this and it creates havoc with anyone who cannot bend a bit.

This is what the early Europeans found when dealing with the Emperors. This is what the Americans found when negotiating with the Chinese in Korea. This is what has been going on for more than five years of ambassadorial meetings in Warsaw. The Chinese are ready to meet, ready to talk, but not ready to compromise a single basic principle.

It has been a difficult lesson for me. I'm usually impatient, as you know, to get things *done*. But the Chinese refuse to be hurried or made to do something in a way that is not right to *them*. One sees it, too, in the ordinary people everywhere. They are never rushed, never petulant, never impatient; they go their own way and at their own speed.

Sex and Rumors of Sex

China is going through a period of intense sexual morality. They are determined not to have foreigners make sexual liaisons with Chinese girls. This is less likely to happen with Russian and East European technicians who come for a year or more with their wives and families. The problem is with foreign students. There's a rumor (I distrust rumors) that seven or eight foreign students are now in jail in Peking awaiting transportation back to their own countries because of illicit sexual relations with local girls.

A Hungarian technician (this is another story that's going the rounds) who was here fell in love with a Chinese girl and wanted to sleep with her. She said she had to get permission from her organization first. The next thing the man knew was that his visa had been cancelled, and he's now on his way to Budapest.

An African student (this I think is a true story) who traveled to school every day on the bus was attracted by a girl conductor. He made sure he caught the same bus every day. An after-work meeting was arranged and he invited the girl to his hotel room.

The girl arrived accompanied by a friend, whom she hoped to leave downstairs. However, the hotel management wouldn't allow a single woman in a foreigner's room, so both went up. They all had a pleasant time—but perhaps not the kind the man had hoped for.

The incident got back to the girl's superiors and she was reprimanded. She didn't lose her job, but was transferred to another route. The student soon discovered that his studies were being rather mysteriously curtailed and his visa was not extended. He sent the girl a letter and a small gift, offering his apologies. The gift was returned and the letter remained unanswered.

Burial Mounds

From the windows of trains I frequently see burial mounds scattered over fields; they take up valuable space and make mechanical cultivation difficult. The government rule apparently is strictly adhered to—no removal of graves without permission of the families. The government knows its people too well to interfere in a matter which touches them so deeply. And it is only a matter of time, they think, before the younger, less superstitious, generation will give the necessary permission. All grave removals are done with the family present and at government expense. Ancestral remains are removed with appropriate ceremony to new cemeteries.

Sunday Church

Up early and caught the Number 10 trolley to the Catholic church near Peking's East Wall. I wanted to check the attendance and what sort of people they are. Was astonished to find this large church better than half filled. More women than men. Children everywhere, allowed to laugh and run around. Two confession boxes in operation. My guess was that half the congregation was under forty; about 20 per cent of *these* were in their teens or early twenties. The priest was young, assisted by a man in his working clothes—the priest in a robe of the most lovely apple green. The singing was fervent—chanting rather than singing. This church is *alive*. There was no national flag here as I had seen at the Protestant church last week. Dodged out early to count the people coming out—540. Outside the church people stood around chatting—gave me the "after-church" feeling as in England.

Chinese Puzzle

When I first went to Russia in 1931, the government was using the churches in Moscow for anti-God museums, for birth-control clinics, and even for stables. But here things are done more deftly. A few days ago I learned from the Reverend Chao Fu-san (he's a Protestant pastor and a teacher at the Peking Theological Seminary) that while the government gives the Christian organization no moral support at all, it does give them some material help. He said that all church property is tax-exempt and that repairs are paid for by the government. Also, when the various religions hold their national conventions the government gives delegates free rail transportation and helps them get hotel accommodation. (I learned from a priest today that this is true for Catholic churches too.) When I asked Reverend Chao "Why?"—he said (this country is really full of paradoxes!), "Oh, because they have to—the constitution guarantees freedom of religion!"

Shuo Fu

Today, near the covered market on Wang Fu Ching, a pedicab, loaded with bolts of cotton from the textile factory, went through a red light. These Peking pedicab drivers are humorously contemptuous of the traffic police—like the cockneys in London. The police carry small megaphones and yell through them, but pedicab drivers seem to make a point of never paying the slightest attention and usually get away with it. But today the policeman ran after the driver and made him pull over and stop. We were standing nearby, so I waited to see what would happen. The policeman talked and talked while the pedicab driver, an old hand at this, said nothing but kept mopping his sweaty face. I asked my guide what the policeman was saying. Apparently he was delivering the man a lecture on what socialism means, the responsibility all have for the safety of everyone, and what would happen if everyone disobeyed the lights, and that if China was to become great, her people must be socially conscious. It went on and on—a long lecture, nothing more. No ticket. This is an example of what the Chinese call *shuo fu* (to convince by talk). The idea that explanation, talk, discussion will eventually convince, runs through Chinese society today.

The incident today reminded me of another example of *shuo fu* when I was in China three years ago. October 1 was the day of the big national parade in Peking and the people got up early to get good positions along the route. I got up early, too, to see how they handled the crowds. By eight o'clock, two hours before starting time, I was standing under the trees not far from Tien An Men. Thousands of people were already lining the wide street. But apparently a mistake had been made; this section was supposed to have been kept clear. An officer with a megaphone was shouting at the crowd, insisting they move along—the space was reserved for the army.

But the people had already been there for several hours and

damned if they were going to move. The officer shouted and
gesticulated, but there was no response whatever. Presently several
truckloads of white-jacketed police arrived. They linked hands and
began to push. The crowd wasn't having any of this and stood its
ground. More police arrived. They began to push those already
pushing and the pressure on the crowd was now quite tremendous.
Yet it was all surprisingly good-humored, with lots of joshing between the police and the people. It reminded me of bobbies and a
London crowd.

The crowd was now losing ground and was just about to be
pushed into the street, when—the idea must have occurred to them
all simultaneously—they all sat down! That did it. The police were
left with nothing to push. Kids, running in and out under the
linked arms of the police, made it all appear quite ridiculous. I was
watching the officer. He gave some new orders; the police piled into
their trucks and off they went. The officer too. Good for the crowd,
I thought. They've won.

But I had forgotten *shuo fu*, the appeal to reason. In about fifteen
minutes, a small flatbed truck arrived and parked in front of the
crowd. Out of the cab jumped a young man who hung up a couple
of loudspeakers, climbed on the flatbed, and began talking. He
didn't yell, he just talked. And he talked and talked. No one seemed
to be listening. They sat there on the ground, looking anywhere but
at the speaker. This went on for more than thirty minutes. Then all
at once the crowd got up, laughing and clapping, and he laughed
and clapped at them; and they streamed away down the street. Yell-
ing hadn't done it; pushing hadn't done it; but *shuo fu* did the
trick.

PART FOUR

How the
Communes Started   12

It was in the autumn of 1958 that the word *commune* first began to appear in the American press. There were rumors of something big developing in China—some new, ominous upheaval. Details were lacking (at first) but the word itself held sinister connotations: and in any case, nothing good could be happening in mainland China. If it weren't good, clearly it was the duty of honest statesmen—not to mention news analysts—to say so.

They did. On November 14, Secretary of State Dulles informed representatives of the Colombo Plan nations assembled in Seattle that the Chinese were "imposing mass slavery on 650 million people." They had "degraded the dignity of the human individual." They had created "a vast slave state."

Scripps-Howard newspapers featured a series of articles entitled "Chain Gang Empire." I recall one of the cartoons illuminating this series offered a row of skulls above a blood-spattered wall, upon which was written (in words of blood) "Family destruction," "bestiality," "slave labor." And *Life* magazine presented pictures (artists' drawings, that is) of burning villages and weeping women.

I was in America when the commune movement began. I felt I knew enough about the Chinese people (and by this time enough about how the press was treating news from China) to discount most of the stories about "breaking up the families" and about men and women being segregated and herded into barracks. What is more, some European reports were presenting a rather different version of events in China. But the horrible accounts of the communes must, I felt, be based on something. So I was looking forward with the keenest curiosity, and also a little apprehension, to learn for myself what the communes really were. I pass along what I was able to learn pretty much as it came to me in discussions with European agrarian specialists, through talks with staff members of the Peking Agricultural College and, later, through a careful personal study of about fifteen different communes.

How It Began

Professor Keith M. Buchanan, of the University of Wellington in New Zealand, who was making a study of agriculture in the Chinese countryside in October 1958, has stated: "We must keep in our minds a picture of old China—not the China of exquisite jade carvings and golden roof pagodas and elegant scholarship, but a country of poverty and exploitation. A country where children with swollen bellies died by the wayside and peasants ate roots and grass."

Only one-ninth of China's land area has, until recently, been arable. But 80 per cent of the Chinese people are peasants—at present more than 550 million of them.

For the past three thousand years the chronic semistarvation of this vast mass of human beings has broken the "exquisite" surface of Chinese history like a great barrier reef.

A feudal system of land tenure, a pyramided landlord-serf relationship, had been fastened upon the peasantry at least ten centuries before the beginnings of feudalism in western Europe. Buttressed by religious beliefs and superstitions which demanded unconditional respect for tradition, patriarchal, isolated, each village hardly in touch with the next, the system maintained itself with amazing durability into the fourth decade of the present century.

Nine hundred years ago a Sung dynasty writer, Su Shiun, said:

The soil has ceased to belong to those who till it, and they who have the owning thereof toil not in the fields. Of their yield the landlord takes one half; for every ten farmers there numbers but one proprietor and thus it is that, daily laying his share aside, he fattens in prosperity whilst the others, exhausting theirs in order to keep every day alive, sink into poverty and hunger. And there is naught they can do.

And as recently as 1946, only three years before Chiang Kai-shek was driven from the mainland to Taiwan, Theodore H. White commented in *Thunder out of China:*

The ancient trinity of landlord, loanshark and merchant is a symbol hated throughout Chinese history. It represents a system that has shackled China's development for five centuries. During the last century, however, the system has tightened about the Chinese peasant as never before because of the impact of the West, by commerce and violence, on its time-worn apparatus. . . .

The plight of the Chinese peasantry has been documented in countless studies by Western writers and scholars. The need for reform was recognized, theoretically at least, by the Chiang Kai-shek government. In fact, a land reform program was projected in 1948, by Americans working with the Kuomintang, which included a five-year plan for transforming all tenants into independent proprietors.

Like most other reforms under the Chiang regime, this land program came too late and was never implemented.

It was, fundamentally, the explosion of the peasantry which destroyed the Kuomintang on mainland China. The Communists gave leadership to the long overdue agrarian revolution. This was their "secret weapon," against which Chiang, with all his American equipment, remained powerless. In every district where the Communists came to power, there followed a confiscation of all landlords' land (above a certain minimum, which the landlord could stay and work for himself if he cared to) and division of the land among the landless peasants. After the Communists took over the national government in 1949, a redistribution (or "land reform" as it was called) spread rapidly and by 1952 had been carried through the entire country with the exception of certain remote areas.

The leaders of the new government, however, did not regard this as a final solution. As early as 1943 Mao Tse-tung had stated that:

"the one way in which the peasants can overthrow their poverty is progressively collectivizing; and according to Lenin, the one way to collectivization is via co-operatives." Article 34 of China's provisional constitution, the Common Program, in force from 1949 to 1954, admonished the government to ". . . gradually lead the peasants into organizing various forms of mutual aid in work and of co-operation in production."

Distribution of land, the wiping out of feudal landlordism, was a first step, but small-scale farming by individual owners could not meet the need for basic modernization and mechanization of agriculture. Without this, China's chronic food shortage must continue. The peasants had become proprietors. They were free of the enormous burden of rent and debt, but this didn't help them much. The plots were too small; most peasants had no tools; land improvement, the making of ditches and repairing of dikes, had to be done together. The farmers were persuaded, and in some cases bullied, into forming mutual-aid teams, to pool resources to work together, to learn how to co-operate. The pressures on them were great but they didn't have to join these mutual-aid teams, and some didn't. And when mutual aid later developed into co-operatives, some rugged individualists stayed out of those, too—I met a few of them in 1957. But as the years passed and the advantages of co-operative farming became more evident in terms of the equipment and per capita production compared with private farming, most farmers joined them.

Thus, the mutual-aid team was the first step toward collectivization. By 1955 many of these small mutual-aid groups had joined together in voluntary co-operatives. At this stage the co-operatives were of a simple kind; land was still owned individually but worked collectively as one big farm; then from this there developed the "advanced type" of co-operative in which land and farm implements were held in common and at harvest time profits were divided among the families in proportion to the days of labor each family had contributed. By the end of 1957, 97 per cent of China's peasants were in advanced co-operatives.

However, even these co-operatives, averaging less than two hundred families, were still too small. No real modernization plans could be based on these small units. And what is more, they were incapable of solving the chronic underemployment of the Chinese peasantry. No underdeveloped country that was hoping, as China was, to move quickly into the modern world could afford to have four-fifths of her people working less than half time. The situation was ripe for the next stage.

During the winter of 1957–58 the government initiated a nation-wide water-conservation and irrigation program. Considerable attention had already been given to irrigation as a means of raising the country's food production, some four and a half million acres having been brought under irrigation since 1950. The winter projects, however, dwarfed everything that had gone before. Tens of millions of peasants, together with volunteers from the cities, turned out to build dams, dredge canals and ditches, dig water-storage ponds, and drill wells. During these months of massive effort nearly fourteen million additional acres were brought under irrigation, which made possible the large agricultural yields of the following summer.

But the irrigation drive had outstripped the capabilities of the co-ops. They were too small. For the large dams and canals necessary for effective irrigation, many co-operatives, often the people of an entire county, had to pool their labor, machinery, and materials. The same was true of tree planting. One village had plenty of barren land in need of forestation, but no extra labor power. Another might have the manpower but no land. The same for mining. Also, at this time the government was pushing mechanization of agriculture, but farm machinery was too expensive for many individual co-ops to finance on their own.

For these compelling reasons, informal mergers of co-ops began taking place in various parts of the country. Such mergers were called *ta shê,* "co-op federations" or "enlarged co-operatives." They were an indication that the co-operatives were no longer able to meet the demands being made upon them.

Apparently the commune movement as such really got under way first in Honan province. In Sueiping County in that province twenty-seven co-ops merged in April 1958—a combination of 9,300 families (more than 40,000 persons). Following the usual procedures, leaders were elected and the peasants divided themselves into work groups. With a larger pool of manpower to draw from, nurseries were set up for mothers working in the fields. Some of the women banded together to start a kitchen to bring food out to the field gangs during the spring harvest. After a period of trial and error, and the usual group discussions, the merger of these twenty-seven co-ops was formalized and a set of bylaws adopted. They called themselves the *Weihsing* (Sputnik) Enlarged Co-operative. There was nothing very unusual about all this. These peasants in Honan were concerned only with their own affairs and probably had no idea that they were sparking a movement which was soon to sweep the entire country.

One can assume from a reading of his earlier works that Mao Tse-tung had for some time had some such system as the communes in mind. In *Socialist Upsurge in China's Countryside,* published in 1957, he said:

Most of our present semisocialist co-ops have only twenty or thirty families in them, because co-operatives of that size are easy to run and they give the administrative staff and the members an opportunity to gain experience quickly. They cannot operate on a large scale or use machinery. The development of their forces of production is still hampered. They should not stay in this position too long, but should go on to combine with other co-operatives.

Mao apparently concluded from these first mergers that the time was ready; and gave them the official support which sent the movement off to a flying start. The Chinese attribute the use of the word *commune* for the enlarged co-ops to Mao, himself.

From that moment on the Chinese press was filled with reports of co-operatives throughout China merging with their neighbors. Details of the Sputnik were publicized and it is said that 85,000 people visited it to see how it worked. Within a few months the movement had swept through the country. By the end of the year almost every farm family in China was in a people's commune.

Chinese rural life had been reorganized three times within a decade—land reform, the co-operatives, and now the communes. This three-stage development, the Chinese believe, has taken one of the earth's most atomized and least productive farm systems to the threshold of becoming one of the world's most consolidated and potentially most productive systems.

Basic Structure
and Finances 13

Returning to China in 1960, I brought with me a host of preconceived ideas—as well as apprehensions—about the communes. Many of these centered around the significance of the word *voluntary* and the accusations of forcible breakup of families, both of which I will touch on later. As for the communes themselves, I suppose I must have imagined some sort of physical structure into which one could walk and say, "Now I am in a commune." The fact is that wherever you are in the countryside in China today, you are "in a commune"—just as in America, in the country, you are always in some particular county or township. At first you might have walked through hundreds of villages without noticing anything new, because the change is primarily administrative and social. Today, however, you would see changes in the form of new buildings: commune schools, canteens, kindergartens, factories, and workshops.

In extent, the commune equals roughly the basic political division of the Chinese countryside—the *shiang,* equivalent to an American township. Ordinarily a *shiang* comprises several villages with a total of from five to ten thousand families, although it can be considerably larger. And some of the really large communes cover several *shiangs.*

The commune took over responsibility not only for agricultural work in its area but for all those functions usually assigned to local government, or (in the United States) to small business. Primary and middle schools, nurseries, kindergartens, "spare-time" (adult-education) schools, canteens, industries, clinics and hospitals, banking, housing, barber shops, repairs, markets, libraries, theaters, sports, vital statistics, the care of those "senior citizens" who had no families—all these, and many others, are today administered by the communes.

Communes are self-financing. Their products, over and above what is consumed by the commune members, are sold either through government purchasing agencies, or directly, to national or provincial factories. Prices are fixed by the government on the basis of a national average of production costs. They seem to have remained stable. Comparing prices for staples such as wheat and rice, in town and country, with my past visit, I noted they had not varied.

Commune expenditures fall into the following main categories: production costs, depreciation of public property, state taxes, free food distribution, basic wages and bonus awards, public welfare funds, and an accumulation fund for capital investment. In 1960 communes were taxed 6 per cent of their total production value. This, nationally, amounted to 4.1 billion yuan and represented 5.9 per cent of the total national budget revenue.

The bonus payments (if a profit remains after other expenses have been met) are awarded, after public discussion, to the work brigades that have done especially well. Sometimes these bonus payments take the form of small presents—notebooks, the works of Mao Tse-tung, ball pens, or a citation to be hung on a wall. The accumulation fund provides the financial resources for school and hospital buildings, tractors and machinery for the workshops, capital improvement of the land by dams, electric pumps, irrigation projects, etc. Tractors and industrial machinery can be bought from the factories on an installment plan without interest charges. It is not lack of money, but the shortage of industrial output that prevents the communes from mechanizing as fast as they would wish. The welfare fund provides the cost of free education, medical care, maternity benefits, entertainment, burial allowance, pensions, and a home for old people who have no family, as well as a reserve fund to help any family through an emergency.

The method of setting money wages varies from commune to commune and comparisons are difficult. Broadly speaking, however, one can say that a worker in a commune will earn 7 to 12 yuan a month as a basic wage ($2.80–$4.80). This is, of course, in addition to the free food. Wages are paid monthly and are not (as formerly) paid only to the husband, but to the individuals—including wives or children—who have actually earned it. Most families have several wage-earning members.

To the Western observer, these payments appear pitifully low, as indeed they are. But it must be remembered that cash wages form only a minor part of the commune member's real income. One of the first demands in nearly all communes was for a comprehensive system of social security and the greatest security for the Chinese peasant is food. To him, money—for the first time the peasant is receiving a wage—is less important than the assurance of food. Thus, from the very beginning, communes have undertaken to provide "free" food to all (some give only grain, some furnish all foods). In addition, there is housing, education, medical care, and all the rest. Wages may be low, food at times scarce, and the work extremely hard. But to the Chinese peasant, life on the commune represents a real improvement over the conditions of the yet-very-recent past.

Visible signs of the upswing of living standards (with the exception of food, which was in short supply in 1960 because of recent poor harvests) struck me forcibly after an absence of three years. Many peasants now were blossoming out in "Sunday clothes" on the holidays. There were more bicycles. Inside the cottages I sometimes noticed radios and clocks. I frequently saw piles of new blankets.

One would not have imagined that wages of less than five dollars a month would leave much to spare for savings. But the fact is that in all the communes I visited, an appreciable number of peasants had opened savings accounts on which they were earning from 3 to 8 per cent interest. Many savings were on a very modest scale. In a commune I visited in Honan province—a poor area—total personal savings averaged only 6 yuan ($2.40). In the "Green for Four Seasons" commune in Hopei province, on the other hand, 57 per cent of all families held savings accounts with an average value of 97 yuan ($40.00) per family. A decade ago bank savings of any kind were unheard of among the peasants. (A friend of mine who lived in China for many years exclaimed, upon reading the above paragraph: "Impossible! I know a great many things have changed, but I simply can't believe that peasants have bank accounts, let alone radios and clocks!")

A major objective of the commune movement, along with increasing national agricultural production, was to develop the industrial potential of the countryside and to use much more fully the huge underemployed resources of manpower. To do this, tens of thousands—perhaps even hundreds of thousands—of small factories or workshops were built in villages and towns throughout China. I will later describe several of the workshops which I visited.

Here let me point out that beyond these aims having to do with production, appear others of a less tangible nature. There is, for example, the growing wish in China to lessen the gap between city and country life—to give country people the cultural opportunities and the technical conveniences enjoyed by those living in cities; and, closely linked to this, the hope that gradually the differences between workers and intellectuals can be reduced. Behind this is a concept that workers should also be thinkers, and that intellectuals should also be able to work—that is, that the range of man's experience in life can be widened, once these arbitrary classifications are removed.

"We want to release the buried talents in ourselves and others" is a phrase I heard in various forms from many people active in the commune movement. In more strictly Chinese Marxist terms, the objective of the communes is to move the country forward to the time when full communism can be established—that is, a classless society governed by the principle, "From everyone according to his ability, to everyone according to his needs."

During the first hectic months these long-range objectives had to take a second place. Organizing elections, working out details of management, new construction, the building of clinics and hospitals, the starting of schools, the establishing of communal kitchens, the equipping of workshops, the setting up of kindergartens and nurseries, and the training of young people to look after the children —these and a thousand other activities kept everyone at full stretch; and all this at a time when the work in the fields and the normal routines of harvesting, plowing, and sowing had to be sustained! Exhausting as those months must have been, I found that many of the people I talked to looked back on 1958 as a climactic point in their lives—a "great time to have lived"—very much as the British still look back on the blitz, or the French on their resistance.

But to return to the basic structure of the communes: Article 24 of the constitution of Sputnik Commune says:

A vigorous, regular democratic life must be ensured in the commune, and in all its production contingents—production brigades, factories, mines, timber yards, livestock farms, tractor teams, schools, hospitals, shops, banks, canteens, and military units. All organizations which keep their own accounts must publish their balance sheets . . . all administrative staff must take part in productive labor. . . .

The Commune Congress is the chief governing body. Representatives are elected by members through the work brigades and serve two years. The congress, in turn, elects a "management committee" which handles day-to-day affairs. The executive leader and deputy leader are chosen from among the management committee members. (I found that in most of the communes I visited, the deputy directors were women.)

The management committee sets up departments to take care of agriculture, industry, water conservation, finance, schools, hospitals, and so on. Heads of these departments are nominated by the management committee but must be approved by the Commune Congress. Directors and deputy directors are usually elected for a term of one year, but can be dismissed by the Commune Congress at any time for neglect of work or inefficiency.

As a check on the management committee, the Commune Congress appoints a supervisory committee which has the power to investigate its actions and see that Congress decisions are carried out rather in the way that American co-ops and credit unions elect an independent supervisory committee.

Financial accounts are supposed to be public and kept open for inspection at any time. Council members and other officials receive the same pay as ordinary workers, but the director and deputy usually receive a small additional wage. Most, but not all the commune directors I met were Communist Party members.

Actual work of the commune is carried out by work brigades, each of which is responsible for some special sector of production. The brigade elects a council of its own and the councils of the various brigades comprise the Commune Congress, referred to above. Thus, the work brigade forms the basic electoral unit of the commune.

Anyone over sixteen is eligible for membership in the commune, to vote, and to be elected. The only exceptions are "former land-

lords, rich peasants, counter-revolutionaries, and other people deprived of political rights," who "may be accepted as unofficial members of the commune and when granted political rights according
to law, may be accepted as full members." Although these people
do not have the right to vote, they may "enjoy the same economic
treatment as full members."

Westerners, reading this description of what the Chinese call
"democratic management," may wonder how much of it is window
dressing and how much, if any, is ever put into practice. They might
also inquire to what extent Chinese and Westerners can mean the
same thing in speaking of democracy. Such questions are legitimate and perhaps impossible to answer. However, I am convinced
that the key to much of what is taking place in China is group discussion and co-operation. Without an appreciation of this element
it is impossible, I believe, for us to comprehend the power of the
mass movements which have swept the country during the past
decade—and which will, I feel certain, continue to do so.

By whatever name one wishes to speak of it (the Chinese call it
democracy), an outstanding feature of life in China today is mass
participation by means of meetings and group discussions. Such discussions invariably are led by members of the Communist Party
who will report what the people think. It is through these meetings
that the Chinese leadership keeps closely in touch with public sentiment and has often been able to correct errors before they create
too serious a problem. Undoubtedly the Party advances predetermined decisions which they wish the people to acquiesce in. This
is a technique of education and persuasion developed in the early
days of the Chinese Communist Party and is closely connected with
Mao Tse-tung's theories of leadership. Every traveler like myself
soon becomes conscious that China is a country where discussions,
talks, meetings, debates, take place everywhere on every conceivable subject.

The London *Times* once referred to China's government as:
"government by endless conversation."

From a British friend who was touring China in 1958 just after
Mao Tse-tung had requested permission to resign his position as
Chairman of the People's Republic of China, I obtained this rather
quaint example of "discussion by the masses." Visiting a primary
school, he listened to five-year-olds gravely weighing Mao's request.

They decided that he should *not* be allowed to resign, and their decision was duly recorded and dispatched to Peking. Several days later, in another school, my friend followed a similar debate by teen-agers. They came to an opposite conclusion. Chairman Mao should be allowed to resign, "provided he kept in touch with things." Evidence as to how far Mao was influenced by these recommendations is not conclusive.

But the political wisdom of holding such discussions is obvious. Mao is the national father figure—the Abraham Lincoln of China—a symbol of protection, continuity, and strength. An unheralded resignation would have come as a real shock. But being made the subject of discussion in every community and by every group, the shock was avoided and the discussions themselves gave the people a sense of having (however remotely) actually participated in the decision.

The National Picture 14

The reasons why the national government determined to press forward with the commune movement become obvious when one moves from an examination of the individual commune to an assessment of the effects on the nation as a whole.

In any underdeveloped economy one of the chronic problems is agrarian underemployment. At peak times, as during harvesting, there may be work for all, but mostly there is a severe shortage of work opportunity. This has been a centuries-old riddle for China as it still is in more than half the world. The peasants of China represented a huge surplus labor force. A prewar survey covering seventeen provinces by Professor J. R. Buck showed that the average days (or day equivalents) worked per year by men was 133. Thus, for almost two-thirds of his life the average peasant was without employment and without earnings. (The above appeared in an article by Shigeru Ishikawa of the Institute of Economic Research, Hitotsubashi University, Japan, in the *Far Eastern Economic Review*, September 29, 1960. I am much indebted to Professor Ishikawa for his lucid discussion of this aspect of the communes.)

Even by the mid-fifties this condition had not fundamentally changed. A survey undertaken in 1955 estimated the working year for men and women in a "lower co-operative" as totaling only 130 days (the figure would have been higher for men alone). Although the survey related to a single province, Anwhei, the editor of the report notes it as reflecting a general situation. By 1957 (the last year before the communes) men working in "higher co-operatives" were still only working the equivalent of 161 days a year.

Governments of most countries in the world, confronted by the underemployment of their rural population, have looked for a solution to the expansion of urban industry and the gradual movement of surplus rural population into the cities. This pattern has been seen in the USSR, Japan, and many other countries. The process has been at best a slow and costly one, and offers a somewhat questionable "solution," since the mushrooming of industrial cities (as many nations have learned to their cost) tends to create as many new problems as it solves old ones. In Soviet Russia the rural population began to decrease from the thirties onward and it was expected that a similar trend, sooner or later, must appear in China. China's difficulties were aggravated by unemployment already existing in her cities—the whole problem being further compounded by the rate of population increase. Any real solution to rural unemployment in China, therefore, was remote.

The commune movement appears to have struck directly at this problem. Surplus labor in the country has found employment without migration to the cities. A survey taken in China in 1959, the first year after the communes, indicated that peasant working days had risen to 300 per year. This tremendous increase from the figure of 161 days only two years earlier reflects the results of establishing small rural industrial plants in the communes and of the use of labor surplus for agricultural capital construction (soil conservation, forestation, dams, irrigation). China thus appears to be approaching what no other underdeveloped country has yet achieved

—a solution to the riddle of underemployment. I was informed, and I believe correctly, that today in a number of areas there is actually a labor shortage—astonishing as this may seem for a country of such enormous population.

I met, while in Peking, an Indian active in trade-union work. He told me that of all that he had seen in China, the absence of unemployment was, in his view, the single most impressive achievement. I experienced in a personal way what this means. I carried with me in China a good deal of photographic equipment—movie camera, tripod, still cameras, etc. I asked if I could hire a man to help carry this stuff. Invariably the reply came back, "We are very sorry, it would mean taking someone off his regular work." Anyone who has been to India, of course, knows that if you so much as whisper the fact that you might need a carrier, several dozen applicants would within minutes be waiting on your doorstep.

One of the most significant features, economically, of the commune system is that it enables the country to finance agriculture improvements and to establish rural industries with almost no help from central funds. Large sums are being plowed back into capital investment rather than being used to increase the standard of living. The productivity of the Chinese peasant today is rising far more steeply than is the increase of his individual purchasing power, the difference representing commune investment in capital equipment and capital improvement of the land.

This idea of holding down the rate of increase of wages is explicitly spelled out, and in discussions with the peasants I found they were well aware of its significance. The pitifully low wages referred to in the previous chapter are, in part at least, voluntary. In the constitution of the Sputnik Commune, Article 22 declares:

When the average wages (including grain supply) of members of the commune rise to a level that guarantees a living standard equivalent to that of the well-to-do middle peasant, the rate of increase in wages should be reduced to insure the rapid growth of industry, the mechanization of farming, and the electrification of rural areas in the shortest possible time.

Wages, of course, *are* increasing, but not as fast as productivity.

Still other benefits, nationally, are accruing from the commune movement. Larger units of cultivation make possible more advanced technique. (How rapidly, one wonders, could American agriculture have advanced had it been limited to the old-fashioned units of single-family-size farms?) Mechanization, spread of scientific information, proper use of fertilizer, pest control, experiments in hybridization of seed corn—all become vastly easier.

Meanwhile the rural workshops in the communes not only are adding to national output, but are converting a peasantry innocent of any previous contact with machines into a labor force with considerable mechanical know-how. Millions of men and women, who until a few years ago were unable to read or write, are now interpreting blueprints, operating precision lathes, turning out work to decimal-point tolerance. This is not likely to be a disadvantage for a nation driving, as China is, toward industrialization.

One further national asset growing out of the communes should be mentioned, and that is a kind of strategic invulnerability. Decentralization of governmental functions and administrative apparatus and the scattering of industry provides a security not enjoyed by other industrial nations. Add to this the plans for regional self-sufficiency, the growing capability of local industry to meet local needs, and it becomes conceivable that a third or a half of China might be destroyed or overrun without too severe a dislocation in the remainder. The survival capacity of such a nation is enormous.

Clearly Chinese agriculture still has a long way to go, as the inadequate harvests of 1959–60 indicate. The Chinese themselves are more than ready to admit that by comparison with advanced Western countries, their methods remain extraordinarily primitive. They point out, however, that their very successes are responsible for many of the strains on their resources.

For example, a study completed in the autumn of 1960 demonstrated that the change from partial employment to full employment involved a greater consumption of food. Women who yesterday were puttering around their small houses, today are out in the fields and the workshops. They eat more. The government estimates that with the establishment of community dining rooms in the communes, grain consumption by former poor peasants and lower-middle peasants has risen to the level of middle peasants. During land reform the Communists divided the peasantry into rough categories. "Poor peasants" were peasants who had no land and worked entirely for others; "lower-middle peasants" owned some land but not enough to support themselves and so worked part-time as hired hands; "middle peasants" owned enough land and could support themselves without employing others; "rich peasants" not only owned land and worked on it themselves but could employ other peasants to help them; and "landlords" referred to those who owned land and were rich enough to enjoy its benefits without working themselves and could lease land to others.

The great improvement in the clothing everywhere (one of the first things I noticed on my return in 1960) keeps cotton in short supply, despite the fact that cotton production is reported to have more than quadrupled in the past ten years. By mid-1960 the Minister of Agriculture, Liao Lu-yen, summed up the situation as follows:

With the development of industry . . . the amount of grain to be supplied to the cities has increased. . . . The amount of grain to be supplied to the cities in 1960 is estimated to be nearly twice as much as in 1953, the first year of the Five-Year Plan. . . . Ours is a country where industry is not well developed. . . . It needs to import a certain amount of machinery and equipment which it cannot produce as yet or of which its output still fails to meet the demand. In order to import we have to export. In 1959 China's total exports nearly quadrupled compared with 1950. Of the exports more than 70 per cent were farm produce or processed farm produce. . . .

The average annual rate of increase in China's grain output for the last ten years has reached 9.6 per cent . . . but its per capita grain output is still comparatively low. . . .

It is not difficult to solve the question of providing the productive equipment for the development of light industry; the question is where to get the necessary raw materials, especially the supply of farm products which are the main raw materials for light industry. For instance . . . there is no difficulty to build in a year ten or even more textile mills each with 100,000 spindles. But to provide the raw materials needed by ten mills in a year . . . we will probably have to build up cotton-production bases with an area of several million or even up to ten million mu (a mu equals one-sixth of an acre). . . .

Agricultural production in our country is still done almost entirely by manual labor. Most of the semimechanized farm implements are also operated by animal traction and manpower. . . . The present task is to equip the people's communes with modern farm machines so as to carry through the mechanization and modernization of our agriculture. . . .

The switchover to the people's communes and the level already attained in industrialization have prepared the necessary conditions for the mechanization of agriculture. . . . The areas cultivated by farm machinery [most production is manual] in 1959 constituted only about 5 per cent of the country's cultivated land.

This statement by the Minister of Agriculture indicates that leadership is under no illusions about the backward state of Chinese agriculture.

If their agriculture is backward, the Chinese still believe that the communes give the best prospect for advance. Progressively greater national resources will be deflected to help them. Steel allocation for agricultural mechanization in 1960 was double the allocation for 1959, and in 1961 may well be doubled again. Confidence in the system itself remains unshaken; the communes will continue to be the basic unit of Chinese rural life. And it must be admitted that the results have been impressive. The "disasters" prophesied by Western writers in the early days simply haven't happened. Even the reasoned doubts expressed by some responsible economists and agronomists have not been fulfilled. Professor Shigeru Ishikawa, whom I have quoted before, frankly admits this. "About two years ago, when Agricultural Producers' Co-operatives were abruptly being reorganized into Rural Communes, I entertained a doubt about the stability of the new organization and its contemplated effect on production. . . . However, my fears have not materialized. . . . On the contrary, the organization of Rural Communes has persisted and played a crucial role in promoting changes in the economic structure of Mainland China which may have far-reaching implications in the future. . . ."

Some Key
Questions Answered 15

Since returning to the United States I have lectured extensively on my experiences in China. There are certain questions about the communes which I am asked by almost every audience: Wasn't it a system ruthlessly imposed by the government? Were there not terrible blunders committed by the Communists? Hasn't the family system been destroyed? These are key questions; and unless we understand the answers we can make no meaningful appraisal of the communes. These questions I believe have been inadequately dealt with in the press, and I am therefore attempting in this chapter to give what seem to me the answers as I see them.

1. *Were the communes imposed ruthlessly from above?*

I believe the answer is no.

No comment, prediction, exhortation by Chinese officialdom before the summer of 1958 gives so much as a hint that something new was imminent. Yet it would be completely out of character for the leadership to have embarked on such a program (had they known they were going to do so) without a long, careful "discussion and education" period ahead of time.

Nothing important happens in China without the direction of the Communist Party, and it is a party that keeps its ear very close to the ground. But after talking to many Westerners who watched this sudden, rural eruption in 1958 I have come to believe that the government was taken by surprise, if not by the movement itself, by the extent to which the peasants seized the initiative. A rereading of the Chinese press of that time confirms the reports that local initiative was consistently outrunning government expectations, and that one of the government's primary concerns was how to control popular enthusiasm without diminishing the energies that had been released.

The first public comment by the Communist Party was not made till the end of August 1958, after a number of communes had already been established. The Communist Party Resolution of August 29 urged the peasants not to carry out mergers too hurriedly, to be sure "to adapt their plans to local conditions," and to take steps "only after full discussion." Decisions about private plots of land need not be dealt with hurriedly; "clear-cut decisions" could be postponed. It further urged that no change of ownership be made "beyond the desires of the owner."

On September 1 an editorial in *Hongqi* (*Red Flag*), the fortnightly publication of the Central Committee, followed this up:

> Only through a full airing of views and debates, only when the people in a locality are willing to go in for it entirely of their own accord, should the agricultural producer's co-operatives be transformed into people's communes.

On September 3, the Peking *Renmin Ribao* (*People's Daily*) said:

> People's communes must be set up on the basis of full discussion by the people concerned and it must be a matter of the people's own choice. No rash, impetuous, or domineering attitude should be taken, especially on the question concerning change in the ownership of the means of production.

All this has the sound of brakes being applied.

But once mass support for the communes had become evident, government and Party both gave full support.

2. *Have there not been disastrous psychological and economic blunders in the commune movement?*

From all I could learn there were at first plenty of mistakes.

The gravest apparently arose from overenthusiasm. The promised day had arrived: the Kitchen God was smiling; free food—

who had ever heard of free food in China before? So why not free clothes, free shoes, free everything? Even some Party cadres were, it seems, caught up in the general fiesta and began to force the pace too hard. It must have been a rousing sight to see the new production brigades on their way to work with their flags and drums (how the Chinese love a good show!), and difficult to keep a cool head amid such general excitement. Everything seemed to be going right. Even the harvest was a bumper one—the largest in China's history. Throughout the country there was talk of how communism was "just around the corner, if only we could work a little harder yet."

The initial mistakes, the bungling, the overwork, are admitted today, but in the light of the total advances are accepted as inevitable, rather than serious.

"Research" became a magic word. As communes pooled their resources, they found they had extra funds and with these began to build "experimental" and "research" centers long before they had adequate technical knowledge. In some communes the excitement and novelty of starting industrial workshops (this was the first time many young peasants had ever been around machines) led to neglect of the farm work. In others a drive to pile up record grain production meant that not enough attention was given to pig-breeding or poultry-raising. When the communal dining halls were established, women in their relief at not having to cook any more turned in their pots and pans for the "steel drive" and later, when they wanted to do some cooking at home, found they had nothing to cook in.

In nothing did the Western press so widely miss the mark as in its attacks on the communal dining halls. Although I heard scattered complaints about the cooking, I found no woman who looked at the dining halls as anything but a blessed innovation. The virtues of Chinese food are well appreciated by Westerners, but anyone who has seen women bent over the crude charcoal or wood stoves in the country cottages, fanning the flames, or figured the time and effort that go into cutting vegetables for a single dish, will appreciate the collective sigh of feminine relief that must have gone up when the communal dining rooms were started. While I was in China I visited the elderly mother of a Chinese friend, a professor in an American university, and asked her what special message she would like me to take back to her son. Her first words were, "Since the beginning of the communal dining rooms my life has become much happier. . . ." She went on to describe how, being elderly, if she found it difficult to walk to the cafeteria, especially in rainy weather, some young person would bring the food to her at home. "Of course," she added, "we cook at home when we have friends in or at festival times."

There were more serious breakdowns. The rise of the communes coincided with a sudden astonishing increase in industrial production. This combined to create an enormous strain on an inadequate transportation system. Food grown in one area could not be shipped to another because the railroads were clogged with freight trains handling industrial shipments. On-the-spot shortages were common. Deliveries, even those for export, were delayed for weeks at a time. Statistical surveys broke down. No uniform system of estimating, or even of measuring, grain yields had yet been established. Storage capacity was inadequate for the unprecedented harvest. Even when grain was properly measured, some of it was lost by rotting before it could be used.

The government failed to realize the extent to which the agricultural figures pouring in from the countryside were wildly optimistic. All China, during this hectic summer and fall, was in a state, it seems, of national euphoria. Before long, however, the practical quality of the Chinese people reasserted itself, and they began, with cooler heads, to tackle stubborn agricultural problems which do not easily yield to sudden onslaughts.

Mistakes were remedied. Hours of work were normalized. Collectivized vegetable plots, pigs, chickens, fruit trees were turned back to their original owners. Bicycles were "decommunized." Undoubtedly new problems will arise and adjustments will continue to be made.

That the communes had overextended themselves is now generally conceded. As a result, some of the authority taken on by the commune organization was whittled down and handed over to the smaller units: the production teams (the work unit) and the production brigade (about two hundred households), which usually takes in the whole village. While I was still in China the orders were sent out that temporary helpers and government cadres from the cities were there to help the teams and brigades, rather than to order and direct policy.

The commune will retain its over-all administrative responsibility and will supervise the industrial workshops and the varied aspects of the people's welfare; but the individual peasant will once more feel himself working as part of a smaller group—his neighbors and friends—rather than the more impersonal "commune" with its tens of thousands. Rather larger opportunities are now being given the individual household to earn a little money on the side, and (this was true even while I was there) peasants are being encouraged once more to develop small private plots of ground for their own family use.

Some interpreters of China in the West have seen these moves as a backing off and a turning away from the original aim of the communes. Less restrained quarters have even proclaimed that the communes have been "abolished." The Chinese take a different view, claiming that it is an attempt to give the peasant more of a say in how things will be run. Time will tell who is correct.

In my judgment these adjustments, in relation to the whole, are relatively small. They indicate, of course, that mistakes were made, but when one considers the magnitude of the changes that took place—that the whole management of local government, agriculture, welfare, education, and industry was being taken over by half a billion peasants most of whom could not read a few years ago —I remain astonished, not that mistakes were made, but that the movement did not collapse in one colossal confusion.

The first effervescent phase of the commune movement is now over. The next, I suspect, will be a period of consolidation. Looking back over this first period the Chinese would say that the mistakes and muddles arose from "positive" causes, that in great measure they came from unexpectedly high production, from enthusiasm, in short from success, rather than from conflict or failure. They were growing pains. The Chinese, who are fond of catchy phrases, talk about this period as a period of "dynamic unbalance." "When things are static," an economist said to me, "they are dead. We would rather have things unbalanced but moving forward, than have things balanced and nothing much happening. Mistakes we can always rectify." And he finished with a phrase which I had heard before: "*Yo kwun nan, yo ban fa*"—where there are difficulties there is a way.

By the beginning of 1961, a few months after I returned from China, new ways of meeting difficulties were being found. Changes in the administration of the communes were announced, continuations of adjustments which were getting under way before I left China.

Emphasis was placed on the recognition that in farming the long experience of the peasants themselves is often more valuable than theory, so the major change was a yet greater measure of freedom for the small production brigade to decide on the nature of the crops to be raised and the time and manner of cultivation. Encouragement was also given to spare-time cultivation of private plots, and in addition, brigade members, actively engaged in food growing, are no longer to be at the beck and call of the commune for other temporary tasks.

According to the Chinese press the small production brigade is to have "the right of reforming cultivation methods" as well as "the number of the labor force and the right of managing animals and implements. . . . Members' activity in raising livestock and the carrying on of domestic industries and tilling their own land should be encouraged. The state still allows the existence of village markets."

Once again the Chinese government has shown extraordinary flexibility when confronted with problems or actual mistakes, and responsiveness to the actual needs of the farmers themselves. There is, apparently, to be less administrative control of the communes by the party cadres, for—in the words of the government—the "masses must be daringly trusted."

3. *Have the communes destroyed family life?*

It is my opinion that they have not and that they were not intended to.

I have, I suppose, discussed developments in China with at least fifty trained observers—Canadians, British, New Zealanders, Australians, French, Indians, and others. Some of these have known China for years and speak Chinese fluently; all have traveled extensively and visited many communes. I have yet to meet one who has seen any evidence of the forcible separation of husbands and wives; or of children being taken from mothers.

The only "barracks" that I (or any of the others I spoke to) have seen, are temporary structures at some large construction project far from any city. Since women as well as men work on these projects, there are of necessity separate barracks. All the new housing I saw in the communes had obviously been planned for families.

This does not mean that family life in China has not undergone some profound changes. The old, enclosed, "feudal" family system has all but vanished. Men can no longer treat their wives as property. Today women have equal rights before the law; they receive equal pay for equal work and their wages are paid directly to them. Women have equal rights concerning marriage and divorce. (See the Chinese Marriage Law in the Appendix.) The sociological and psychological changes that this has involved have been considerable. Professor Chao Kuo-chun, visiting professor at the Indian School of International Studies, in New Delhi, who was in China in 1960, describes the impact of the communes as follows (*Far Eastern Economic Review*, Hong Kong, September 29, 1960):

The people's communes are affecting not only many social institutions (such as the ways of family life) but also values and even personal relationships. It is true from what I observed during my visit to more than a dozen cities in China, I found no evidence that the nucleus family was being broken up by the commune movement or any wholesale transfer of residents from one place to another occurring. However, the husband-wife relationship or the status of the housewife in a joint family could never be the same once she joins work at the commune. Not only her independent source of income but also her new, broader social contacts enable her to foster a new sense of self-confidence and personal dignity. Many city women, now relieved of the bulk of household chores, develop a higher spirit and are readier to enjoy recreational and cultural activities . . . many ceased to be idle gossipers or quarrelsome over trivial matters. Their husbands are the first to benefit from such changes.

Before leaving this question it might be well to see what the Communist Party itself has to say on the matter. I quote from the official text of the "Party Resolution on Questions concerning People's Communes," dated December 10, 1958 (the italics are mine):

Nurseries and kindergartens should be run well so that every child can live better and receive a better education there than at home, and so that the children are willing to stay there and the parents are willing to put them there. *The parents may decide* whether their children need to board there, *and may take them back at any time they wish.* The old existing houses must be reconstructed step by step; new, picturesque townships and village settlements must be built by stages and in groups; these will include residential quarters, community dining rooms, nurseries, kindergartens, the Homes to Honor the Aged . . . schools, hospitals, clubs, cinemas, sports grounds, baths, and latrines. The construction plans of townships and village settlements should be thoroughly discussed by the masses. We stand for the abolition of the irrational, patriarchal system inherited from the past and for the development of family life in which there is democracy and unity. . . . Therefore in building residential quarters, attention must be paid to making the houses suited to the *living together* of men and women, the aged and young of each family.

It is true that the Chinese people have broken the feudal patriarchal [family] system. It must be known that this patriarchal system has long since ceased to exist in capitalist society and this is a matter of capitalist progress.

It would be unwise of us, I think, to dismiss this merely as Communist propaganda. It is an official pronouncement on family life in the communes which has been nationally publicized, read and reread by the people whom it concerns, all 550 million of them. It forms the official policy instructions to be followed by all members of the Communist Party.

I certainly am not in a position to say that these instructions have in every case been carried out; but from everything I saw and learned while in China, the pronouncement by the government does reflect the general sentiment of the Chinese who live in the communes; the new home construction that I saw was invariably based on families living together (and in China "families" always means three generations). Any Chinese government that tried to "break up the family" would, I think, meet insurmountable popular opposition.

Press Coverage 16

Developments in China since the revolution have been most inadequately reported by the American press, and much of what is written has been tendentious. It is through newspaper stories and wire-service reports on radio and TV that the American public forms its opinions. Whether or not the American people are correctly informed may have a considerable bearing upon the survival of Western democracy, and perhaps upon the survival of mankind itself. I am not one who believes that any vigorous people need be shielded from the facts.

Unable to send its own reporters to China, the American press seems to have abandoned all attempts at any serious analysis of what is actually happening there. China's economic achievements have now (belatedly) been conceded, though sometimes skeptically. Reports trickling in from British and Canadian travelers, the accounts given by responsible international scientists of the tremendous advances made in Chinese science, and some blunt warnings from British and other industrialists that China may be the third largest industrial power within a decade, have made it impossible to conceal that some very rapid and striking advances have indeed taken place there. These advances have been explained in the American press by what one might call the "slave-labor" theory. According to this, the Chinese government has dragooned their population. By driving the half-billion Chinese peasants into communes, by uprooting traditional family patterns and working the entire population fantastically long hours, enormous resources of manpower have been made available for agriculture and industry. In other words, material gains have been achieved by what Joseph

C. Harsch in the *Christian Science Monitor* (December 24, 1958)
described as "the greatest mass sacrifice of human heritage, human
comfort and human effort in all time."

I submit here some examples of how the press in general dealt
with the communes.

NEW YORK TIMES (October 17, 1958)

Communes in Red China Raze Homes to Make Way for Crops

[A story date-lined Hong Kong reports that Chinese abroad are]
beginning to realize with dismay the profound change coming over
life . . . under the new system of communes. [They] have gone
to visit their homes in China . . . have found that they no longer
exist. Under the new communes . . . individual homes are often
eliminated and members live in communal houses and eat in mess
halls.

Older houses, especially those that obstruct efficient use of
farmlands, and sometimes whole villages are being torn down. Ancestral graveyards are being razed . . . so that the earth above
them can be cultivated. The collective farm system left peasants
their homes and small plots for vegetables, pigs and poultry. The
communes are beginning to do away with these private prerogatives.

NEW YORK HERALD-TRIBUNE (November 25, 1958)

REDS' REGIMENTATION IN CHINA TOPS RUSSIA. *Peasants Like an
Army March from Barracks to the Fields*

. . . Regimentation . . . finds women "liberated" from their
homes and placed in barracks separated from their husbands and
everyone from teenage youth to oldster trained to put gun worship
over ancestor worship—and commune life also requires them to
march off to assigned tasks in preassembled squads; to eat, sleep,
according to plan worked out by somebody else.

The peasants were severed from the small amount of acreage
they had. . . . Their homes were either torn down or made
into supply depots and they and their families were placed in
barracks. . . .

CHRISTIAN SCIENCE MONITOR (December 17, 1958 headline)

Red China Packs Peasants into Communes

[A news story two days later, by staff writer Takashi Oka, begins:] Now that almost all of mainland China's 500 million peasants have been herded into "people's communes" . . .

UNITED PRESS INTERNATIONAL

[A story date-lined Tokyo appeared on December 18, 1959, reporting that in the communes:] . . . normal family life is wiped out by this latest Chinese Communist instrument.

. . . Some quarters on the outside are speculating that the love-every-two-weeks policy established within the communes actually may be a birth control technique conceived by Peiping to halt population growth.

To control and push their millions of commune workers, the Communists are reported to be sending more and more arms to distant areas. As more and more arms are sent out to control the restless masses, the greater become the chances of these arms falling into the hands of revolutionaries. Western intelligence sources have reported there is reason to believe the people within Communist China would give considerable support to a Nationalist China landing force, if they thought it had a fair chance of success. . . .

SCRIPPS-HOWARD

[A series of four articles entitled "Chain Gang Empire" by staff writer R. H. Shackford is introduced on December 17, 1958, with the following editorial note:] *The Chinese have always been devoted to their family life. What is happening in Red China today as the regime tries to weld its teeming millions into a faceless mass existing only for service to the state? The following article tells the grim story.*

[Mr. Shackford himself begins in the following words:]

Abolition of the family is an avowed, primary sociological objective of Red China's new commune system—the first serious effort in history to put a whole nation on what amounts to a prison chain gang. [And later:] The regime does not hide its determination to abolish the family. In fact, it callously boasts of it. Segregated barracks for men and women are replacing cottages.

LIFE (January 5, 1959)

MISERY, OPPRESSION, FEAR INSIDE CHINA'S COMMUNES . . .

Two Chinese who escaped tell of Reds' harsh regimentation which tears families apart, puts children in barracks, even regulates sex—by James Bell.

All over China the family-centered, individualistic Chinese are being reduced to 653 million indistinguishable and interchangeable parts in a vast, inhuman machine. This machine is the commune, the most frightful form of regimentation in history.

The newspapers and periodicals cited above represent some of the more distinguished organs of American journalism. Their coverage represents a fair sampling of how the rise and the development of a highly significant aspect of Chinese life was purveyed to the American public. One need only thumb through back files and it will reveal a high degree of uniformity in all the newspapers. There were variations, of course, but the central theme was the same—the Chinese people were the helpless slaves in the grip of a ruthless and malevolent leadership.

My two trips to China have given rise to the serious belief that much of our information has been woefully inaccurate and that many of the conclusions we have drawn are erroneous. Civil wars are always among the most cruel of human conflicts. No one can claim that either side in China did not inflict the most enormous suffering on the other. None of the great historic revolts of a people against unendurable suffering and injustice has ever been a picnic and the contemporary world always recoils aghast at the violence that accompanies them. This was true of the French and American revolutions; it was equally true of the Chinese revolution.

While in Peking I had access to the ambassadors and staffs of most of the Western neutral embassies. I also had discussions with many well-informed Europeans who have lived in China for many years. Their reports on the present leadership in China were impressively similar in substance. China is not being led by a group of men hungry for personal power who have fastened themselves on a resentful population. It is, rather, a leadership that has shown itself genuinely concerned with the welfare of the people. Though changes in the leadership take place from time to time, there is no evidence of that jockeying for power or of personal rivalry that we have so often seen in the Kremlin.

I have come to believe that Mao Tse-tung is not surrounded by yes-men fearful of arousing his displeasure. We are not dealing with a Hitler or Mussolini, or a latter-day Stalin whose moral judgments were poisoned by a paranoic mistrust of those around him. China is being led by historically conscious, strong, and enormously competent men who as far back as the 1920's identified themselves with the people and knew their needs. They won their revolution because they carried out the demands of a people driven to extremities of suffering, and who were determined to end the disease, hunger, and corruption which had held them in subjugation for centuries. If ever in history there was a people's revolution, this was it.

Clearly the original ban by the State Department on trips by American journalists, and now the reluctance of the Chinese government to come to an understanding on this matter, has posed a serious handicap for our press, and I, for one, hope sincerely that a free flow of information in both directions will soon become possible.

But this is only half the problem.

As matters now stand I doubt that allowing American newspapers to send correspondents to China will by itself insure an accurate picture of events. The disturbing element is that before and during the same period when the news stories quoted above were being published in the United States, a growing body of factual material—the firsthand observations of many reporters and reputable Western scientists—was available to people in Western Europe, in Canada, in India, in Australia, but was hardly ever mentioned by the American press.

I have already referred to some of this material in earlier chapters. Let me offer some further samples, the italics being mine:

LE MONDE (Paris, October 12, 1958)

René Dumont, Professor of Comparative Agriculture at the Agronomic Institute, Paris, in an article entitled "Chinese Agriculture":

Without the *active and voluntary participation of the majority,*
the mountains would not have been terraced nor would the terraces have been held in place by gravel, nor would the gravel have
been humped, basket by basket, from the river beds. It is my impression that the Chinese Party has succeeded in marrying its
authority to the peasant's consent after due deliberation, a consent obtained by protracted explanations.

MACLEAN'S MAGAZINE (Canada, November 22, 1958)

Edward B. Joliffe, lawyer, leader of the Cooperative Commonwealth
Federation of Ontario:

Having visited such communities this year—and having entered
many a peasant home forty years ago—I am amused by the story,
zealously spread by certain writers from their posts in Hong Kong
and Formosa, that the peasants (five hundred million of them)
are kept in the co-ops by coercion and terror.

ECONOMIC WEEKLY (Bombay, November 22, 1958)

An article by Professor Charles Bettelheim of the Sorbonne in Paris,
entitled "China's Economic Growth," states:

I think that one must first of all recognize that the manner in
which Chinese economy and society are developing presupposes
an essentially energetic direction which can be neither of a bureau-
cratic nor of an administrative nature, nor, still less, come in the
shape of pressure from the police (as some people imagine). Such
growth implies great clearness of thought, a lucid vision of all the
possibilities of development, of the manner in which these possibilities are interconnected, of the effort which each and every one
is prepared to make in order to transform these possibilities into
reality. This development also implies that this lucid vision does
not remain the privilege of some people who keep aloof from the
masses, but on the contrary, is shared by the masses. . . . Once
the masses understand that technique has nothing mysterious
about it, one witnesses the extraordinary development of enterprises run by local authorities and co-operatives, one witnesses a
real technical revolution coming from the masses themselves.

NEW STATESMAN (London, December 20, 1958)

Dr. Joseph Needham of Cambridge University, eminent historian of Chinese science and Sinologist, who served during World War II as scientific attaché to the British embassy in Chungking, writing of a trip made to China at the start of the commune movement in 1958:

> I traveled some 12,000 miles within the country . . . meeting hundreds not only of scientists and scholars but all sorts and conditions of men. My most outstanding impression of China this year was of the unreality of ideas so cherished in the West that the population is dragooned to perform its tasks. On the contrary, everywhere one sees spontaneity (sometimes overrunning government planning), enthusiasm for increasing production and modernization, pride in an ancient culture equipping itself to take its rightful place in the modern world. What has been done in public health, social services, industrial development, and advancing amenities of all kinds and what one sees going on under one's own eyes would be absolutely impossible without the *willing and convinced cooperation* of all types of workers, manual and intellectual.

NEW STATESMAN (January 10, 1959)

R. H. S. Crossman, British M.P., generally a sharp critic of developments in China, writes of a visit to several communes:

> On each visit I was able to select a village for inspection. . . . Every village I visited was equipped with a creche, a kindergarten, a primary school and canteens—with the result that women were out at work and the labour force had been doubled. Of course, a foreigner who knows no Chinese must be wary on this subject, but I saw no signs that family life was being destroyed. Families were sleeping, as usual, in one bed; and I do not believe that communal feeding will destroy a relation with children as tenacious and affectionate as any I have seen. . . .
>
> I am inclined to conclude . . . that the movement for the People's Communes did indeed come not from a remote official stratosphere but from that hard puritan elite of Peasant Communists. . . . If I am right, this episode confirms that Chinese Communism still remains a dynamic mass movement and that its leaders still respond to pressures from below.

THE SUNDAY TIMES (London, June 19, 1960)

An article by Field Marshal Viscount Montgomery:

> For China today the Commune system seems to be necessary; indeed it is essential if the problems of a poor and backward nation are to be solved. . . . One hears it said that children in the Communes are removed from their parents. I investigated this and found it to be totally untrue.
>
> There are great misconceptions in the Western world about this new China, particularly in the United States . . . and that cannot be stated too clearly.

THE OXFORD MAGAZINE (Oxford, England, November 5, 1960)

"A Visit to China" by Sir Cyril Hinshelwood, President of the Royal Society:

> There is much that is tremendously impressive and admirable in the New China: there is, of course, no doubt that an upheaval of a far-reaching kind has taken place: there are some aspects of the socialist state which are uncongenial to a Westerner: but most of the things for which, at a distance, I had admired and loved the Old China, seemed to me to be intact, and some indeed appeared to be fostered more sedulously than ever. China possesses, of course, a communist organization with what most of us here regard as the inevitable restrictions associated with it. But the Chinese people never had much personal liberty and it is quite likely that many of them are now freer in some ways than they have ever been. And certainly the constructive achievements are very impressive indeed. . . .
>
> The total picture was warmer and more human than I had been led to expect. . . .
>
> The [commune] I visited, I must confess, did not seem an unhappy sort of place.

The sources from which I have drawn the foregoing extracts contain a wealth of reliable information on what is actually happening in China. There are other reports too—medical reports from British doctors, articles by British industrialists and scientists, technical papers by French, British, and Canadian economists, reports by Indians on advances made in Chinese village life; all this has been available to any newspaper.

In all fairness it should be noted that there have been times when unslanted reports have appeared in the press, originating from inside China. The British news agency Reuters has been operating in China for several years. On occasion some of the larger papers, the *New York Times*, the *Christian Science Monitor*, and a few others, have used its reports. Nevertheless, the over-all image of China in the public mind has been similar to that conveyed by the press coverage of the communes.

The present phase of reporting about China is strongly reminiscent of what happened after the Russian Revolution in 1917. For the first four years there were no competent American correspondents in Moscow or anywhere else in the USSR. Nearly all Russian news came from violently anti-Russian sources at Riga (then not under Russian control). The result was a mass of material very similar to what we are getting today about China, mostly from Hong Kong. Families in Russia also were reported as being deliberately "broken up"; Lenin and Trotsky had quarreled; Lenin had Trotsky shot; Trotsky had shot Lenin; both had killed themselves in a suicide pact; women had been nationalized (which meant that all women were public prostitutes operating without fees), etc., etc. The public believed these stories because they had nothing else to go on.

In 1920 Charles Merz, who was later to become an editor of the *New York Times*, and Walter Lippmann wrote a famous supplement to *The New Republic*, "A Test of the News" (August 4), analyzing press coverage of the early years of the then new Russian government.

In this famous article, Lippmann and Merz wrote:

From the point of view of professional journalism the reporting of the Russian Revolution is nothing short of disaster.
. . . On the essential questions the net effect was almost always misleading, and misleading news is worse than none at all.

And that, I believe, goes for our reporting on China today.

Visit to a
Rural Commune 17

Chengchow, Honan Province

Today I went to a rural commune near this city, which lies in the Yellow River Valley.

Honan province has always been one of the poorest areas of China. Last night, when they asked me what kind of commune I wanted to see, I said, "Your worst." They didn't seem to resent this. The commune I saw today was, they said, the poorest within driving distance, and after seeing it I can believe it. So much for the story that visitors see only the show places.

We left at eight. They had a Russian car for me today, small but brand-new, and we drove out of Chengchow over a reasonably good dirt road. (They drive with more zip here and without that maddening habit of rushing ahead and then coasting, which the Peking drivers are convinced saves gas.) After half an hour we branched off and for another thirty minutes we bounced along a wagon track. It was already hot. The sky was pale blue; there were no clouds.

Groups of peasants in wide straw hats were in the fields at work with hoes and rakes. Some were resting. The land here reminds me of parts of northern Spain, arid and barren, and the crops of wheat and millet looked sparse. The whole area has been badly hit by drought.

My interpreter told me this was the first time he had been in this part of China. It seems that there was no Intourist interpreter in Chengchow and he had been sent from Wuhan to meet me. A foot infection held me up in Peking and he's been hanging around for ten days waiting for me. He told me all this while we were lurching and bumping over the cart track, I wildly clutching my precious Zeiss cameras and praying for the Bolex in the trunk.

Behind us we left a cloud of dust.

We came finally to a small village, with a faded banner strung across the street, and the car turned into a courtyard enclosed by low whitewashed buildings. More flags and pictures and slogans painted across the walls. Mr. Chiao, the director of the commune, was waiting to greet us and he invited us in for the usual preliminary talk over a cup of tea. The room he took us into was long and narrow with a table and benches running the full length. This was the meeting room of the commune management committee. From the wall at one end Mao Tse-tung smiled benignly down at us; at the other were portraits of Liu Shao-chi, Chou En-lai, Chu Teh— the four heroes of the revolution. With Mr. Chiao were two others who accompanied us all day, but they left the talking to Mr. Chiao. Occasionally one or the other would bring out a notebook and record some question and answer. I never did learn quite what their function was; but I have become accustomed by now to these silent observers at my interviews.

As we sipped our tea Mr. Chiao gave me the background picture. The basic problem of this commune was poor land and difficult climate. There was constant alternation between flood and drought. Five rivers, all flowing finally into the Yellow River, cross the commune land. Before liberation no one bothered to tend the dikes or clean out the canals which were constantly silting up. Only a small rise brought the rivers to flood stage. Two hundred millimeters rainfall in a season meant certain inundation.

Crop yields had almost always been poor. A high grain harvest for the region would be 60 catties per mu.—approximately 6.5 bushels per acre. More prosperous communes I visited were harvesting as much as 1000 catties per mu (17 bushels an acre). By way of comparison, according to the *Statistical Abstract of the United States, 1960,* American output in 1959 was 21.3 bushels of wheat an acre.

Some years there had been no crop at all. In 1942, for instance —a year which the peasants still look back on with horror—during an autumn, winter, summer, and succeeding autumn no grain grew. More than two thousand families left the area to go and beg. Three hundred and twenty-seven people died of starvation in this immediate vicinity. Two hundred children were sold by families unable to feed them. People were eating the dry roots of grass and the bark of trees.

Most of the land was tenant farmed. The Communists arrived in October 1948 and plans for land reform were started almost immediately. This area went through the same general stages as most other sections of China—mutual-aid teams, early co-operative period, advanced co-operatives, and now, the people's commune. Even the advanced co-ops, Mr. Chiao felt, had been incapable of meeting basic agricultural needs. In the matter of water conservation, for example, those higher up the river might take too much, leaving those farther down with not enough. Or in floodtime some ill-considered action upstream could increase the flood level lower down. Also, the co-ops were too small to mechanize effectively. Tractors were scarce and as they were under the control of central tractor stations, the co-ops had to apply in advance for them. In rush seasons tractors would arrive too early or too late.

When news of the Sputnik Commune spread across the country, peasants here at once began debating whether to form one of "these new communes." Everyone seemed in favor, representatives were sent to the county government to apply. The county approved and the commune was formally organized on August 17, 1958.

The first thing they did was to tackle water conservation. Armed with picks and shovels, and carrying-baskets, thousands of men and women, working after the fall harvest and before spring sowing, had constructed five new reservoirs with storage capacity for 2.3 million cubic meters, as well as a network of drainage and irrigation canals. As much as three hundred millimeters rainfall now would not cause flooding, Mr. Chiao thought; and despite the serious drought conditions for the past two years, some crops have been saved.

"What is your current crop yield?" I asked.

"Poor. The drought now is just as bad as 1942. The last two hundred days of last year there was no real rain at all, just a few sprinkles, and this year [1960] not a single drop. The water level is really low. The irrigation ditches helped our crop last fall, but this year we have had to replant some of our fields four times and each planting has dried up. We are carrying water by hand and we have laid temporary piping. The crop will be far below normal, much less than we had hoped for. But, we will have something. No one will starve. There will be no 1942."

I watched Mr. Chiao as he recited these facts. He was, I judged, about thirty-five. He had muscular arms and calloused hands. In shirt sleeves, elbows on the table, he looked straight across at me out of a tanned, weather-beaten face. Here was no city commissar. This man was from the land and part of the land. I could well understand why he had been elected to direct the commune.

"Come," he said. "I'd like to show you what we're doing."

We stepped out, shielding our eyes, into the blaze of midmorning sunlight. Our driver had pulled the car into the shade of a nearby tree and was fast asleep. We woke him, piled in, and headed for the tractor station. Tractors, clearly, were one of Mr. Chiao's favorite topics. He told me the commune now owned thirty-five, in addition to four combine harvesters and fifty-one power machines, including some large pumps. At the tractor station we saw a repair shop equipped with several lathes, and mechanics at work on some disassembled machines. The tractors were lined up outside. I counted thirty-eight plus five combines. Mr. Chiao apologized. He said he had given me last year's figures; recently they had bought three more tractors and another combine.

One of the tractors here was of Chinese manufacture, from the nearby works at Loyang. The rest were Czech or Bulgarian. When I asked about performance, Mr. Chiao said the Loyang and Czech were the best. The Chinese tractors have most power and can draw two combines while the others draw one.

Into the car again and as we drove Mr. Chiao continued to bombard me with information about the many activities of his commune. They manufacture paper and chemical fertilizer; bottle wine and vinegar; raise fish which they sell to nearby markets; they have several assembly shops associated with large state factories. They also have a brickworks and are under contract to supply two million bricks this year to the city of Chengchow. The commune owns 6000 pigs. (There is a national "pig drive" this year, I learned, aimed at doubling China's pig population.) As to livestock, Mr. Chiao told me, the commune has 160 horses, 4000 chickens, and 1500 ducks. When I said this seemed a surprisingly low figure (one chicken to every ten people) the director explained that *privately* owned animals and poultry were not included in the figures he had given.

I asked if the members were allowed to keep their own chickens and ducks and to cultivate vegetable patches.

"They are not only allowed," he replied, "but encouraged. We have another drive on right now. [I had lost count of the drives.] We call it *'Use-the-ten-edges campaign.' Use every little strip of land around you. The edge of the road, the edge of the river, the edge of the orchard . . .*"

At this point the car came to a halt in front of a new brick building—the ball-bearing plant—and we climbed out. Actually this was an assembly shop rather than a factory, the parts themselves being sent out from Chengchow. We saw some two hundred girls in blue overalls, seated at benches, and assembling various types of bearings to the accompaniment of music from a loudspeaker. I stopped by one bench where a girl—the prettiest of the lot—was bending over her work. She was so absorbed that she did not notice me till she heard the click of the camera. Then she looked up and broke into a delightful half-shy grin.

I asked her name.

"Shu Shao-yen," she said. (Shao-yen, the interpreter told me, means swallow.)

"How old are you, Shu Shao-yen?"

"Eighteen."

"Can you read and write?"

"Yes—but I am still going to spare-time school to learn more characters."

"Do you like your work?"

"I like it. And that we can help, too."

"Help? How do you mean?"

"It helps our country," she said, "to build socialism."

The ball-bearing shop seemed quite up-to-date and efficient, which was not the case with the other industries we visited that day. Nevertheless, the one that fascinated me most was not the ball-bearing plant but a paper mill, because of its Robinson Crusoe, do-it-yourself quality. Here was a series of home-made wooden machines booming and thumping away like the big wheel and little wheel in the spiritual, which ran by faith and the grace of God. But they *were* running and while straw and leaves were pushed into a primitive pulping machine (powered by a donkey) at one end of the shed, out from the other end between two rollers made of logs jerked a ribbon of wet paper, the coarsest I had ever laid eyes on. However, intended for packaging, it was quite adequate.

No problem of modern mechanics, I thought, would long resist the ingenuity that turned this collection of barrel staves and tree trunks into a paper mill.

On the way back to commune headquarters I asked Mr. Chiao how much members were earning. He gave the figures for the commune's single complete year, 1959. The average cash wage was 6.80 yuan a month. Food, education, medical care, housing are free. The food distribution, he estimated as 53 per cent of the total payment.

"Are you building new housing?" I asked.

Mr. Chiao said they were, but not very fast. During 1959 they had added eight hundred new rooms, a total of 13,000 square meters. (This would represent approximately 120 two-bedroom-size American tract homes, and there are 8000 families in the commune, most of them still living in small huts and cottages.)

"There are so many things that have to come first," Mr. Chiao said.

It was good to pause for a while in the committee room, good to get out of the glare. We were parched, dehydrated, and soaked with sweat. As we sat down again at the long table a girl brought in tea, and cold wet towels with which we mopped our faces. For a few minutes we silently sipped our tea. I dusted the camera lenses and put another hundred feet of film into the Bolex. Then, back to work.

"Tell me about education," I said.

"To start with the little ones," Mr. Chiao replied, "we run 120 nurseries and 89 kindergartens." I interrupted to ask if all small children went to these. "Oh no," he said, "we couldn't take care of them if they did. Only about 40 per cent of the children go—the rest stay at home with the grandparents. Then, in this commune we have 44 primary schools, 16 of which are run by the state."

"Why doesn't the state run them all?" I asked. "Isn't it the national policy to give primary schooling to every child?"

"Yes, but it would be impossible at this stage for the central government to set up schools in all our scattered villages. Besides, we like to run our own affairs. It makes good sense, too. We have the houses and we now have young people with enough training to be teachers, or we can get them from the colleges in the city.

"We provide spare-time education for adults too. Not only for the illiterate but for anyone who feels he hasn't had enough schooling. The majority of our members had no education at all when they were children. Now they can get it later in life. It doesn't matter what age they are, they can start as low as first grade if they want to and go through the schooling that they missed."

"How many are still illiterate? And what is your definition of 'literacy'?"

"There are a good many people who are just too old to learn to read and write. We don't press them. Spare-time education is only useful for those who really want it—and we have thousands of our adults enrolled in classes. But about 20 per cent will never become literate. By literate we mean knowing how to read and write about twelve hundred characters—that's enough to be able to read a newspaper. In cities the test is usually higher—two thousand characters or more. But here in the country . . ." He wiped his face again on the towel. "In the country we have to take things as they are. And it's quite an event when one of our people passes the literacy test. We make a little celebration for them. Do you know what they nearly all want to do first? Write to Chairman Mao to tell him they have learned to write! He must get thousands of letters like that every day.

"You must understand, the communes have three purposes. They are to develop agriculture, to build local industry, and to advance education and culture. We want eventually to give people in the country the same opportunities as city people. One day the communes will have colleges and technical schools, their own theaters and schools of music, drama schools. . . ." His voice trailed off and he leaned back, looking through half-closed eyes at the ceiling.

This seemed like a good time to ask a question, one I asked in every commune I visited. "Have you ever," I asked Mr. Chiao, "found it necessary, perhaps for a short period, to house husbands and wives in separate buildings?" Mr. Chiao asked the interpreter to repeat the question and the interpreter turned back to me. I repeated it.

The interpreter began to laugh and the director and the other members joined in. Mr. Chiao, still laughing, said something and the interpreter said, "Mr. Chiao wants to know if that's what they do in England." The widely publicized Party Resolution of December 1958 had ridiculed Mr. Dulles' speech in Seattle in which he had informed the world that Chinese families were being broken up. Cartoons of Dulles and Eisenhower were often painted on commune and factory wall boards. In all communes my question about family separation provoked mirth, except in one where the director said with a certain contempt, "You have been reading Mr. Dulles!"

"What do you do," I asked, "about a boy and girl who fall in love and have a child before they are married? Or before legal marriage age?"

The interpreter's translation of this question was followed by a rather lengthy silence. It was obviously an unusual question. The others at the table became very busy readjusting their notebooks and examining the points of their ballpoint pens. The girl who was picking up the wet towels paused to listen.

"There is no problem now about marriage," said Mr. Chiao. "Formerly, many could not afford to marry. But that is no hindrance now. Formerly also, the low level of education made some fall into wrong habits. That does not happen any more."

"But human nature is human nature," I insisted. "You just can't expect me to believe that babies are never born to unwed parents."

Mr. Chiao shook his head.

I pressed the point as far as I felt the traffic would bear. It would hardly do to dispute the director's accuracy; I could not go out, after all, and count the babies as I had counted the tractors in the tractor yard. And who knows?—he may have been right. I told him that officials in Peking and elsewhere, people at the university and in the health office, discussed these problems as a matter of reality. . . .

Mr. Chiao, however, stood his ground. "You may not believe me," he said, "but we really have none of these problems now."

I nodded and changed the subject.

China is today an intensely, almost compulsively "moral" society. Of the many communes I visited, all except one denied any knowledge of any children born out of wedlock. In the one exception, two cases were cited, both involving parents who were under the legal marriage age (twenty for boys and eighteen for girls). Both cases were resolved in the same way: by court orders permitting early marriage, "in the interest of the child."

I had by this time formed a high opinion of Mr. Chiao. Despite his official position, he was neither servile nor overbearing in his manner. I noted that he spoke to those who were "under" him in the same tone that he used to me, or to my interpreter. Besides that, I liked him for his obvious enjoyment of his job. He must be working like mad most of the time to keep up with this three-ring circus, and loving every moment of it.

I asked him to tell me about himself.

He shrugged the question aside, but as I persisted, he finally told me he had been born in a nearby village, not in what was now this commune, but in a neighboring county. His father was a lower-middle peasant. The family owned a plot of land, too small to live off, and worked for a landlord and rented an extra field from him too. They never got out of debt. After liberation the family received eight mu of land, still inadequate for a living; but with mutual aid they began for the first time to move ahead.

"When did you learn to read and write?" I asked.

"At the spare-time school, six years ago."

In these few and rather unwillingly spoken words, it seemed to me, lay a large part of the secret of the Chinese Revolution: the release of buried creative potential.

Ten years earlier Mr. Chiao was grubbing out his life on half an acre. Today he is dreaming of power stations, technical colleges, schools of music. And not only Mr. Chiao, but the girls in the ball-bearing factory, the youngsters who had dreamed up the fantastic "paper mill," the nurses in the kindergarten, the men installing a new (commune-made) electric irrigation pump. Just in this one morning's visit I had seen hundreds who were using talents that would previously have remained immobilized. I remembered a slogan I had seen some days before painted in bold, red characters across a commune building: *Don't be frightened of the experts— compete with them!* They appear to be learning that technique has nothing mysterious about it; they are not waiting for the state to tell them how. . . .

Mr. Chiao brought me back. "There's time to show you the hospital before lunch," he said. "I'd like you to see the hospital."

Three Buns for Lunch

I was glad the hospital was only a short walk from headquarters. It was a simple structure of whitewashed brick, less than a year old, with clean earth floors and a little tiling. On each side of a central corridor were small single rooms—thirty in all—with a nurse's office at the middle. There were ten patients at the time and two neatly dressed nurses were on duty.

A doctor arrived while I was there and I had a brief talk with him. He told me there were twelve doctors attached to this commune, and they spend most of their time on rounds in the villages. Six doctors are trained in Western, and six in traditional Chinese medicine. Only two of the Western doctors are fully qualified.

In addition to this small hospital, which he regarded as inadequate, they have set up sixteen hygiene stations serving groups of villages (there are ninety villages altogether). These are clinics which can handle simple first-aid and immunization. They try to see that every infant gets BCG at ten days and is later vaccinated against smallpox, diphtheria, and epidemic encephalitis (Japanese B).

The commune medical staff is still too small, 120 in all, including doctors, nurses, and technicians. They conduct continual programs on health matters among the peasants by means of posters, movies, and lectures. This, and the immunization program, are paying off. There have been no cases of smallpox since the commune started, no cholera, no venereal disease, which used to be one of the worst problems here. They have been burning off the banks of the rivers and have virtually eliminated schistosomiasis, a disease caused by ova of a blood fluke to which a small water snail plays host. The ova develop into minute, free-swimming cercariae which can penetrate the skin of a human being who wades in the water or even wets his hand while filling a pail. Elimination of the snail is the most direct step to break the cycle. Symptoms of the disease are severe and include enormous extension of the stomach and progressive enfeeblement of the victim. This remains one of the most serious medical problems of China. There are still an estimated ten million cases.

In this commune bacillary dysentery is the most stubborn problem. Midwives are now trained and the days when umbilical cords were cut with unsterilized scissors and bleeding stopped by dirt are past. Infant mortality has dropped, though the hospital was unable to give me the figures as the records were kept in the hygiene stations.

I asked whether the hospital was sufficiently equipped to perform an appendectomy. One of the doctors said they are treating most cases of appendicitis by traditional methods, not by surgery. (They tried to tell me the same story in Peking and claimed a number of cures. See the chapter on medicine for a further discussion of this question.) But on being pressed the doctor admitted that all advanced cases were operated. Most surgical cases from this commune would be taken to one of the modern, fully equipped hospitals I had seen in Chengchow.

After the hospital Mr. Chiao, on behalf of the commune, extended me an invitation to lunch.

I would stay, I said, provided I could eat in one of the canteens exactly as the commune members were eating. They agreed to this. But on our return to headquarters the meal was already spread out on the table in the meeting chamber. I argued and begged. So did Mr. Chiao. This would be so much more convenient, we could talk more easily, and particularly now the table was set. . . .

But I insisted.

The canteen, one of 119 in the commune, was a pleasant airy room, fifty or sixty feet long. Straw matting hung under the slope of the tile roof and there was a portrait of Mao.

By this time it was well past two o'clock and most of the members had already eaten. But a few were still drifting in from the fields. The only table at which there were chopsticks was obviously ours: the five of us and the driver of the car sat down. Three or four dishes of vegetables and a platter piled high with steamed dough buns were brought in. There were no bowls or plates; nothing to drink; we pitched in out of the common platters. When I looked to see what was being served at the other tables, I understood their reluctance to bring me to the canteen. The workers were eating nothing but the dough buns (*man tow*). I tried one. These buns were about the size of a woman's fist, of dark wheat flour. Inside were about two teaspoonsful of chopped cabbage. This was the entire meal. Each worker had three; the children one.

I have seen poverty in many countries—in Mexico, in South America, in India—and I have always found it difficult to understand how a human body could go on day after day with so little nourishment. Here then was the bare truth. The people of this commune were desperately poor. I could hardly bear to watch these men coming in tired after working in the fields since daybreak; stopping at the kitchen to pick up their three buns; sitting down quietly to eat them. And the children, munching without a word!

Chalked on a blackboard I noted what looked like a menu for the week. I asked for a translation. Tonight, noodles. Anything else? No, just noodles. Tomorrow for breakfast, these same *man tow* but without the vegetable filling. Lunch, the same, but with something else inside. Tomorrow night, soup; and so it went.

"How often do you eat meat?" I asked.

Chiao hedged. "Not very often."

"How often?"

"On festival days we have meat, and sometimes fish. On three festival days we eat meat, and on three days fish. But this will improve as time goes on. . . ."

"You mean three days in the whole year?"

"Yes, in the year."

"And that's all the meat or fish you eat?"

"For the present, yes."

What of those six thousand pigs I had heard about, I wondered. Or the fish-breeding pools from which they sent fish to the Chengchow market. There was a contradiction here I could not understand.

"May I see your fish-breeding ponds?" I asked.

And into the car we piled again to go bouncing over some very rough roads for twenty minutes or half an hour. The fish project, Mr. Chiao explained, was the second task to which the new commune had turned its energies after water-conservation problems had been taken care of. Fish breeding, it seemed, was completely new in this area. They had reclaimed some otherwise useless swampland, and in the first complete year of operation (1959) bred 29 million fish of which they sold 313,000 pounds on the Chengchow market.

I was impressed by the figures.

I was even more impressed by the fisheries themselves. These were, I think, one of the most remarkable features of the entire commune. Over many acres of low-lying ground between two rivers, shallow ponds had been made with well-banked divisions. Each division had its own generation of fish. Each was neatly labeled as to date and type. Mostly silver carp. Young men, wading thigh deep in the ponds, swung their nets over their heads, letting them balloon out in a wide circle before falling into the water. A universal method this, always fascinating to watch. Slowly the nets would be gathered in and every throw would collect thirty or forty slithering, fighting silver fish, all of uniform size, probably four or five pounds each.

After I had photographed these young fish catchers, some of them walked back with me to the car. The sun was horribly hot. I suggested we sit for a while under a tree. One of the young men went off and brought back an armful of small melons—I don't know what kind they were, but they were juicy and ripe and we sat under the tree eating them, spitting out the seeds.

Then I raised the question which had been troubling me.

"You eat fish in your communal dining rooms only three times a year. To judge by your menu you are not eating very well. You are not getting enough protein. Sooner or later your health will suffer. Why don't you eat the fish you raise in your own commune?"

There was a general outburst of talk, everyone saying something at once. Finally I sorted out what they were trying to tell me. This question of eating the fish from their own fisheries had been a matter of considerable controversy in the commune. They had had several meetings, mass discussions, special sessions of the management committee.

"But what are the objections?" I asked. "Why *not* eat the fish?"

"Money," they said. "We need to earn more money."

"Money for what?"

"Listen," one young man told me, "we only have one rather poor hospital. We should have a properly equipped one—and the instruments and the buildings and the X-ray equipment and all that costs money. Point one. Point two: look at some of our primary schools—housed in old sheds. A disgrace. Point three: we need libraries. We've seen them in other communes. We don't have any. Oh yes, we have so-called reading rooms, but they are mostly for kids. We need a place where we can stock books and read, and have rooms in the different villages and the books can go from one village to another. Point four: we want some decent movie equipment. You should see the old projector we have—well we have two, but only one works. It goes the rounds of the villages, but that means we only see a show once every week or so. We need at least ten good projectors. All this costs money. Point five: the old people's homes. Go and see them. We have two that are all right—the others, well they are nothing to be proud of."

The young fellow paused long enough to spit out some seeds, and continued, "What we have to understand is that we are a very poor commune. Other communes can do all these things because their land and conditions are better. So some of us think, 'let's put off eating more fish until we get ahead and have done these things which need doing.' Of course, others think that food is more important. But they don't understand that we are building a socialist country [he spoke scornfully], they are not politically aware and mature."

"But what about health—isn't that important, too?"

"Look at us," they said, laughing, "do we look weak?" and they flexed their arms and showed their muscles. "And the women and children who need more food get it."

Perhaps here, sitting under the tree with these young men, I had hit on one element that, above all else, was enabling China to move forward so rapidly—the sense of self-restraint, the awareness that sacrifices now were necessary to lay the foundation of future prosperity. The almost unbelievable fact is that they are doing it, and to a great extent, voluntarily. Of course, the peasant cadres, the dedicated, professional, hard core of Communist youth, are giving the lead. I'm sure they do a lot of the talking at these public meetings and discussion circles and their powers of persuasion are great. But the people are let in—they can say what they feel, just as these young men under the tree were saying what they felt. The fish are sold to the city, but not "by decree," which would leave a sullen and resentful peasantry who would do their best to sabotage the plan as soon as the leaders' backs were turned. The sacrifices, the self-restraint are not being imposed by young men with machine guns, but by young men who talk—and there's a world of difference.

All this went through my mind as we drove back to the central village. But *had* there been an improvement? I wondered. How far was I being strung a line about the bad old days? How much worse than this could it really have been? I made the suggestion that I would be interested in talking to some of the commune members in their own homes. Mr. Chiao agreed; and even offered no objection for me to see them on my own—on my own, that is, with the interpreter. As we climbed out of the car in front of headquarters, he waved us down the street and called, "See who you can find at home," and disappeared inside.

Personal Histories

Half a block farther along I pointed to a door at random, in a row of newish houses. The interpreter knocked and the door was opened by a woman with two children at her side who at once asked us in. Her name was Mrs. Chang. The house consisted of two rooms and a small kitchen. Along one side of the living room was a wide brick ledge (*kang*) upon which the entire family would sleep at night.

The room was not much larger, I think, than ten feet by twelve. The floor was tamped earth. There were four children in all, the two who had come to the door and a four-month-old baby in the lap of a five-year-old who was squatting on the floor. The baby had a dark area on its head, like a burn or some fungus. Mrs. Chang was pert and eager. She wore a blue blouse shirt with bright-green plastic buttons and the usual work trousers. I asked her later how old she was and she said thirty-two, but she looked older than that. She was self-possessed, not at all put out by having two strangers burst in on her, and one a foreigner. Her face was serious, but pleasantly so, and she showed occasional flashes of humor. Her hands were delicate and clean. (I have often noticed how well the Chinese, even the very poorest, keep their hands.)

As we talked her story came out little by little, hesitatingly at first, then more readily; and sometimes, as memories stirred her feelings, the story came with great fluency. I took it down precisely as she gave it to me:

"I was born in this very village. My father was already fairly old when I was born, and my mother was blind, from an illness that she had had some years earlier. I was the eldest child of three—a brother and a sister. We had no land and my father worked for a landowner. The hut we lived in was very tumbled down, grass on the roof and so on. As my mother was blind, we depended entirely on my father's work, but as he was already fairly old, however hard he worked he could never get enough to support my mother and three children.

"I was the biggest, so when I was eight my mother and I would go out regularly every day to beg. I was still fairly small when we began this, so we were limited—we could just go about five li a day. Nineteen forty-two was especially bad for us. It was a drought year, my father was ill. We had nothing we could sell and couldn't send my father to be cared for. He was very thin from lack of food and his illness, but he kept on trying to go out. On the second of July in that year he went out, but he fell in the street and died there—it was really half due to his illness and half due to not having eaten anything for so long.

"His death was a disaster for us. My mother couldn't work, I was thirteen, my brother was eleven and my little sister was five. It was really a bad year. It later rained a great deal and one day there was a tremendous storm—it was still summertime I remember—and the roof of our house fell in. We got out our bedding and took them to the temple. That winter, too, was cold. My mother and I would go out begging every day and sometimes our young brother would come too. One day, I remember, he fell into a deep hole full of snow. It was cold and we didn't have any clothes for that kind of weather. Nothing happened to my brother, we fished him out.

"The next really bad year was 1944—another snowstorm. My sister was very ill and we had just nothing at all to feed her. By this time we had moved from the temple to a kind of shack where we lived. It was just when my sister was so ill that the big snowstorm began—it lasted for three days and my mother and I couldn't get out at all. Only seven, sister was terribly ill and terribly undernourished. She died, during those three days of storm.

"After the death of my sister there were only three of us left to feed, which made it a little easier, but even so we never seemed to have enough. My brother and I used to go to the fields and pick up grains of rice or wheat which had dropped after harvesting, grain by grain. We would sometimes go to the market and pick up the little bits that were dropped on the ground. This sounds as if we were in an extra bad position, but we were not. This was the normal way of living for many people around us those years. There were some actually much worse off than we were.

"This area was liberated in 1948. The Japanese never actually occupied this area—they were north of the Yellow River—and the fighting between the KMT [Kuomintang, Chiang Kai-shek's Nationalist Party] and the PLA [People's Liberation Army] took place about twenty kilometers from here so we didn't see any actual fighting. The first time I saw the PLA men come here I was very frightened. The PLA sent some officials to us to explain things and tell us not to be frightened, but most of us were; we didn't believe them. They tried to organize us into an agricultural district and asked our family to join, but we were not sure what they were really after and we didn't join. We were only convinced when we were actually given some land under the land reform and when we really got rid of the landlords. That convinced us.

"At land-reform time my brother and I were old enough to till the land. The family got nine mu of land. The landlord pretended to be willing to distribute his land but in his heart he wasn't satisfied. So we held big speaking-bitterness meetings to tell the landlord what we thought of him and to calculate how much he had exploited the peasants on his land. We held several meetings to speak our bitterness to him. Sometimes at the big meetings there was only one landlord, sometimes several. We finally convinced this landlord that he had done the worst things to the peasants and he was ready to hand over his land. He was given his share of land—he is now somewhere in this commune but not in this section of it.

"I never went to school as a child, but in 1950 I went to a spare-time school and now I know enough characters to write letters and to read the newspaper. I'm working in the fields most of the time now, but also do work with pregnant women, especially to see when they should stop working. I got married in 1949 and have four children—these two go to kindergarten, the girl of two goes to nursery, and this baby as well, when I am busy and can't look after him."

From Mrs. Chang's we crossed the street to another house which turned out to belong to a cheerful-looking chap with bad teeth by the name of Yang Chin-li. His hair was cut very short and there

were many crinkles around his eyes as if he laughed a great deal.
His ears were slightly pointed and the skin drawn up, which gave
him a bit of a puckish look. During our conversation he seemed to
be always on the verge of bursting out laughing, as if all this business of recounting events out of the past was a great joke, another
example of how odd foreigners could be.

Here is Mr. Yang's story as he told it:

"My father worked as a poor peasant for a landlord. I went to
school when I was seven, but only stayed one year as my parents
didn't have enough money to pay for me. There were six of us—my
parents and four children. I have one sister older than I am and the
rest are younger. My father rented eight mu of land—but rented
land is always the worst, for the landlord kept the best land for
himself, and usually for about eight months of the year we never
had enough to live on. We kept on trying different crops and filled
every corner, but we never made enough to pay the landlord and
our debts to him kept growing. We did have a donkey and during
the idle season when we didn't need him we rented him out to
others and made a little that way.

"Our debt to the landlord was not money—it was in crops. The
actual rent was paid for in wheat and sorghum. But that wasn't all.
Before harvest time when we had no food my father would borrow
from the landlord—but for every twenty kilos of grain we borrowed
we would have to pay back double after the harvest. We sometimes
could pay off a little of the debt by working—one day's work was the
equivalent of five kilos of grain. We never got out of debt.

"We were always in trouble until I was sixteen years old. At that
time we planted nearly thirty mu of land—the landlord lent us the
additional land. But this land was paid for by an arrangement where
we gave 80 per cent of the crop to the landlord and kept 20 ourselves. We had to work very hard. Our living—our food—was better at this time but our debts never got smaller. We never did
get out of this trouble until liberation when under the land reform
we got eighteen mu of land. It was fairly good land, too, and we
could get a living off it, but we had some economic difficulties too,
due to the climate—some harvests were good, others were bad. The
government subsidized us when we had serious difficulties.

"At the bitterness meetings we all calculated how much the landowners had exploited us, charging us too much rent and too much

interest, and we showed how the landlord owed *us* debts rather than that we owed *him* debts. He had complete control over my family for years. The landlord ran away after one of these big meetings, but I believe he came back later.

"I can read and write now. I started in the spare-time school in 1953, and by 1956 had learned to read. It was difficult but I always wanted to finish school and this was too good a chance to miss.

"When land reform changed to mutual aid and then to the co-op period, it meant that we had to give up this land that had been given us. It was difficult for many peasants to see the advantages of this and some wouldn't. I could already see that we would never really get ahead just working our own land, so I was ready to join the co-op, but a lot of the others weren't. What we did then was to give them time. The co-ops were voluntary, so those of us who wanted to joined up, those who didn't stayed out. But little by little they saw that we were doing better than they were and most of them joined up when they saw it worked.

"I think all the changes have worked out pretty well. This commune idea is working. It's ten thousand times better now than when I was a child! Look, I have five children—a girl in middle school, a boy and a girl in primary school, a girl in kindergarten, and another girl in the nursery—*and with no money worry!* My mother is living with us—she's very old—but she's taken care of, too. Five children being taken care of—and my parents couldn't keep just one child at school!"

Out once more into the heat. The sun was lower now and its sting had gone, but the gray earth had absorbed the heat all day and was now reflecting it like a furnace. A few peasants were beginning to straggle back from the fields in twos and threes, men and women, and the dust whirled up in little puffs from under their feet. They looked tired and walked tired, saying very little. A few dropped into the general store to make some purchases. One man was walking alone and I greeted him as he went by. He stopped immediately, and with a show of courtesy took off his wide straw hat. His face was withered and his clothes were patched, and he, like the child I had seen earlier, had a blue mottled stain over one side of his face. I asked him his name and what work he had been doing. "Hoeing," he said. (He told me his name but I made no record of it.)

"What were you doing before liberation?" I asked him. He glanced at me with a wry grin: "Me? Oh, I was a landlord." "How much land did you own?" Waving his hat vaguely around, he said, "All this . . ." I asked him to tell me about it, and he did, but before he began we walked across to the shady side of the street and sat, leaning our backs against the mud walls of a house. He didn't speak as fluently as the others I had questioned. Perhaps there were too many painful memories involved. Perhaps the presence of my interpreter restrained him. But this is the story as it came out little by little:

When the Communist army came through in 1948 he tried to escape, but the village was surrounded and there was no way out. His land was not immediately confiscated though he realized that there was no chance of his keeping it if the Communists won the civil war. There was no formal trial, but the villagers organized "speaking-bitterness" meetings in which he was put on a platform and all those who had rented land from him could come and speak their mind.

"These meetings," he said, "were very difficult. Sometimes I was alone and the people would be shouting at me all the things they thought I had done wrong; sometimes they would have several of us at these meetings and the crowd would then be larger. Anyone who had any grievance against us could come to these meetings and speak their mind. The people were sometimes very angry. I didn't understand any of it at first; I didn't know they had any special grievance against me. They then added up all the money they thought I owed them, so they said that the land I owned was really theirs now, for they had worked it for years for too little. I was, they said, a rich landlord, because I didn't have to do work myself; but I don't think I was nearly as rich as they thought I was and I had plenty of economic troubles too.

"When the village committee was established to settle how my land was to be divided up, there was some argument among the peasants themselves, but they got it settled. All my land was taken from me."

"All?" I asked.

"All except a small piece which they said was my share. It was very poor land, the poorest, but I was allowed to build a small house on it and that is where I and my family lived. The first few years were very hard. No one would speak to us and we could hardly earn enough from the land to keep going. When mutual aid came in they did help me a little, but never as comrades; we were always shunned. I had to attend political-instruction meetings twice a week.

"When the co-ops came I thought I'd better go along with it and I asked that my piece of land should be included. They did this, and it helped me; but we were not real members of the co-op. We couldn't go to the public meetings, we couldn't vote, but they began to talk to us more freely in the fields."

"Are you now a member of the commune?"

"Yes. When the commune came in they had some meetings to decide which of the former landlords should be allowed in. As I had co-operated in the fields and because they felt I was beginning to understand what they were trying to do, they allowed me to join. Some of the others are not yet full members, they cannot vote or go to meetings. But I am a full member."

"They speak to you now?"

"Oh, yes. They accept me. I do my share of work."

"Looking back on all this," I asked, "do you think things were handled well or badly?"

"I was very bitter at first, because I couldn't understand what I had done wrong. But I think I understand it now. Yes, I suppose it was a necessary thing. Some of us have suffered, but things before were very bad for most people. There are some things to be grateful for. My grandchildren go to school. They learn to read and write. I was a landlord but I never learned how to read and write."

"Were any landlords in this area killed by the people, or by the courts?"

"Not here. Some ran away and disappeared and we don't know where they are. None of us who stayed were killed. There are many former landlords in the commune. Yes," he said, looking at my interpreter, "socialism is a fine thing."

And with that he cleared his throat and let loose a wad of spit.

Peasant Poets

As we turned back toward the main commune building to say good-by to Mr. Chiao and the others, we passed the main store, where there was also a barber shop, a small radio station, a post office, and a fix-it shop for clocks and radios. But what particularly interested me was the village notice board.

Notice boards play an altogether unique part in Chinese life today. I have never seen any to compare with them. Every factory, institution, school, or college has its notice board—sometimes a whole series of them. Their Chinese name describes them well— *ta tze-bao* (big-character news). Opinions, information, complaints, suggestions, are all publicized in this way. Every factory has a special *ta tze-bao* for workers' complaints. I have seen these complaint and suggestion boards a hundred feet long outside large factories.

And here was the commune *ta tze-bao*, in three large sections, covered with gaily colored paper fluttering a little in the warm air. One entire section, my interpreter told me, was the commune "writing board." Here were posted poems and stories which the peasants had written. I had already seen such boards at factories, but was fascinated to learn what the country people would be writing.

"Do please copy a dozen or so of the shorter poems," I said.

I later added many other samples from the *ta tze-bao*'s of other communes, and back in Peking I asked a friend to translate them —but with no "improvements." Here are several chosen almost at random:

> Outside the village, peach blossom
> opens out; now at this time
> commune members work their hardest.
> Furrows with the sod turning over
> like waves breaking along a beach.
> Then in the paddy fields, rows of wheat
> being planted out like long arrows,
> so swiftly. An eighty-year-old man

insists on coming to work, standing
at night in the middle of the field
holding the light for all to work by.

*

Lad and lass with two hearts
as one, treading together
at the windlass that brought up water
from the well below. At times
he pushes faster and then she
keeps pace—always the two
in harmony, the water flowing out
in a bright stream of silver.
And they in their day walking
together so many miles, yet never
leaving the place an inch. The water
in the well stays as deep as ever
but not so deep as their love
for each other.

*

Don't hurry little sister.
A great round moon, bathing
our village in its light,
and by her window, little sister
doing up her hair. So I ask
just where is she going, knowing well
it is off to night school.
Then asking her not to hurry
but to wait for me while I go home
to change, so that we two
may walk to class together,
perhaps on the road helping each other
to write a poem for our village
newspaper.

*

So lovely was she, standing there
under the trees, flowers all over her.
Though we have grown up together,
today, for the first time I seem
to really understand her; and though
I would speak to her, and try a thousand
times, yet somehow the words do not come

from my lips—simple words that say
"When will you marry me?" Any others
I say easily enough but somehow
only these I do not dare to ask.

*

Drought? but we have
plenty of sweat to spend.
Steep hills? but then
we have lithe legs.
Water too distant? See
how strong are our shoulders.
You old weather God,
what can you do to us?

And Above All, Hope

On the basis of studies made in fifteen communes in various parts
of China it would seem to me that the general plan of organization,
the pattern of daily life as I saw it in the Chengchow commune in
Honan province, is typical of the entire movement.

I visited other communes which were much more prosperous. For
example, in the dining halls of communes near Peking, and near
Shanghai, meat and fish were being served once a week instead of
six times a year. I observed a menu in one of these dining rooms
which offered a choice of fourteen different dishes. These were communes with more fertile soil, better climate, and favorable locations
close to large urban markets. I saw communes with modern, excellently equipped hospitals and laboratories. Buildings, housing,
schools, the variety of goods available in the commune stores—everything on a higher level. In Chengchow, to summarize the picture by one comparison, average accumulated savings per family
amounted to only six yuan; in some communes savings per family
were almost a hundred yuan.

The average level of rural existence in China lies somewhere between these two limits. The fact is that China's peasants are lifting
themselves by their own bootstraps out of an abyss inconceivable
to our imagination. It is clear that conditions have improved. Life is
tough; life is austere; yet I found it often lighted by a certain gaiety
and enthusiasm, and above all by *hope for the future*. Along with

the facts and figures I set down, let me quote several notes from my journal, which may be more revealing than any statistics.

Hopei Province

Met a teacher at one of the nurseries. The children were all out in the yard helping to wash down their little chairs in preparation for the October 1 festival. The walls had been newly whitewashed. This young girl—she looked twenty-two but was probably older—turned out to be a graduate nurse from Peking Medical College. She was doing her stint "in the country"—originally for four months but this has been extended and she doesn't know how long it will be. She said she was enjoying the work with the children and looked as if she meant it. She was definitely not of peasant background.

Kirin Province

We visited the old people's home. It is usually depressing to see people at the end of their usefulness just waiting their time out. But not here. Watched the men playing chess. The oldest is ninety. They seemed a cheerful enough bunch of old fellows. One of them whom I spoke to told me that in the old days he had owned one mu of land. He never married. He had lived with his nephew until the nephew died three months ago.

"What would you be doing today," I asked, "if you didn't have this home to come to?"

"Me?" he cried. "I wouldn't even be *here* on this earth!"

Honan Province

They showed me their "radio station"—a small bedroom in which three people slept, but which could also be used as a studio. This station is linked by land-line to all seventy-five villages in the commune. They use it for announcements, news bulletins, and music. Also they have "radio conferences" in which the six brigade leaders can confer without having to come in from their districts. Sometimes the commune committee meets in this room and the proceedings are broadcast.

Hupeh Province

Another "Home to Honor the Aged," described this time in a letter I sent to Elena.

I asked to be introduced to the oldest man in the home and they called him from his bedroom. A wrinkled, stooped old fellow of eighty-five. We sat at the table and talked while the others stood around listening and joining in with comments and sometimes jokes which I couldn't understand. I asked this old-timer where he had lived before the communes were set up. "Nowhere," he said. "But you must have lived somewhere." "No, I didn't have anywhere," he said. "But where did you *sleep?*" "I had a light handcart on wheels," he said, "and at night I would tip it over and lean it against a wall, and sleep under it."

Kiangsu Province

Each production brigade represents a village and in this commune there are six. I was taken to visit a fruit-picking brigade—they were picking things that looked like English medlars. When we arrived, the group was not working and we found them under a lean-to to keep out of the sun, singing. A young girl led the song by pointing out the words written in large black characters on sheets of newspaper. They all sang with gusto, paying no attention to me. "What's the song about?" I asked. The three marvels, I was told: the commune system, the mass line, the great leap forward! When I photographed the song leader, for some reason they all thought this terribly funny and the song broke down because of the laughter.

China ☆
Kaleidoscope 2

Notes from My Journal and Letters

Patterns of Thinking

Patterns of thinking are not easy to shake. The prevailing Chinese image of the United States is that of a country controlled by a few rich capitalists grinding down the poor. They refuse to listen when I try to correct that image and when I tell them that American society is far more varied, far more complex, far livelier than they imagine and that whatever fraudulence and exploitation does exist is more subtle, more hidden than their image would suggest.

When I tell the Chinese something that conflicts with their preconceived idea, they are bewildered but are too polite to tell me that they think I'm stringing them a line.

Examples of things they have had a hard time swallowing: that the Negro girl who comes once a week to help my wife with the housework comes in a car better than our own (Negroes are the most crushed of all the American poor); that I take the garbage to the dump and help with the washing up (a capitalist like myself, rich enough to travel, would have poor people laboring for him); that the unemployed are not lining up in the streets in New

York waiting for the soup kitchens to open, and that they often have enough funds to keep running their cars for a while.

The Czech football team had a big party on the top floor of the hotel a few nights ago, celebrating a victory. There was much singing and drinking—an outburst like this, I am sure, hadn't been seen at the Shin Chiao for many a year. This completely floored the Chinese. They watched in amazement. Americans get drunk and become boisterous, but not Communist friends!

Three years ago the Indians had a magnificent exhibition here in Peking and I went along with my guide to see it. The Indian guides and I got talking (they all spoke perfect English) and they invited me and my interpreter to have lunch. My interpreter declined. Afterward when I rejoined him I could see that something was disturbing him. "Mr. Greene," he finally said, "how is it possible that these Indians could invite you, an Englishman, to lunch?" "Why on earth not?" I asked. "But you represent the cruel colonial power that has been crushing India for years!" My lunching with them just didn't fit the image!

Cables on Credit

I've noted many times indications of the trust that runs through Chinese relationships with each other. Yen, my interpreter, has a monthly ticket for the Peking bus and trolley-bus service—it's a reduced-rate card that's good for unlimited travel. On leaving the bus I give up my ticket to the girl who stands at the door, but I have noticed that Yen merely says "monthly ticket" and she accepts this and has never, while I've been with him, asked to see it.

Another example took place at the Central Telegraph Office. Sending cables from China is fiendishly expensive and, on this occasion, I was cabling the BBC in London, CBC in Toronto, and NBC in New York. The messages were all very long.

When the girl totted the total up it came to more than 350 yuan ($140). I only had half the amount and so I told her I would go back to my hotel to fetch some more. "Pay tomorrow, or when you come this way again," the girl said.

"I can't do that," I replied, "these cables have to go immediately."

"Oh, we'll send them right away, but pay us when you come by next time."

There are those who will say, "They know where every foreigner lives, they would quickly catch up with him if he tried to get away without paying." And that is quite true. But I don't think this went through the girl's mind at all. Here, they go on the assumption that people are *not* cheats.

Censorship, Chinese Style

Recorded a fourteen-minute news commentary for the Canadian Broadcasting Corporation today at Radio Peking. Studios, wood-paneled and air-conditioned; equipment, first-rate. Studio rather more "live" than we have ours. Two technicians, a man and girl, took charge and afterward made duplicate tapes for me to send to the New Zealand radio network and the United States. The correspondents here had told me there was no censorship bureau—they file their cables through the regular telegraph office and they shoot right through.

I took my tapes to the Central Post Office to airmail them, wondering whether this freedom would apply to news tapes too, or whether they would hold them up to check them. The girl asked me for my press card (which I showed her) and then having unwrapped one of the tapes, to my alarm, she brought out a pair of scissors. From the end of it she snipped about an inch, tested it with a match to see if I was using safety tape or inflammable (it was safety), wrapped up the parcel for me again, and accepted them all without demur.

## Letter to Elena	July 20

The Chinese have a characteristic which is both charming and infuriating, a knack of making the simplest situation an *event* (and therefore complicated). Everything must yield its last ounce of amusement or drama or intrigue. At home, ordering a taxi, arranging a dinner, or buying a railroad ticket can be settled in a few moments by phone. But how dull! Here nothing like this is simple; it is developed into an "occasion," requiring talk, discussion, planning. There are always undertones, nuances, even intrigues, which baffle the newcomer. And if an element of *secrecy* can be worked in, so much the better. It lends color to life and an exciting uncertainty.

I have watched Western businessmen come bustling into Peking. "Everything is set—just came to sign things up. Be back in London by Monday." Three weeks later they are still here. "Business" to the Chinese is more than signing an agreement. I sometimes feel it is really an excuse for something much more important—the real interplay of personalities.

These thoughts come to me as a result of an encounter with an old man on a bus today. As always, someone had stood up for the foreigner when I could find no seat; but then farther along the way an old, bent, weather-beaten man climbed onto the bus. I was sitting near the door. No one had apparently noticed the old man, so I got up and offered him my seat. His clothes were dirty, his face lined, and his hands were clutching a small parcel. He was so stooped that he had to look up sideways at me, and when he saw that it was a foreigner who had offered him a seat, he looked utterly astonished. He then gave me a broad grin and with a small bow as dignified as that of any grand seigneur, he took the seat. It was perfect. Part real, part a superb bit of ironic acting. So much richer an encounter than if he had mumbled something about me keeping my seat.

This kind of wry, humorous interplay I notice everywhere. The Chinese make the most out of a situation. For us, to stand in line for half an hour waiting for a bus is a tedious waste of time. Not for the Chinese. They don't allow it to become a boring interlude with chilly strangers. They make contact, they acknowledge each other's presence, they are in touch with one another. They are never anonymous, never unresponsive. They may (rarely) be angry; they may be friendly; they may argue; but they are never indifferent or aloof.

I go around by bus whenever I can, rather than by taxi. Not only to save money. And not to be "close to the masses," as my interpreter says. Or rather, not in the way he means. I go by bus because something always *happens*, some oblique exchange between people who are themselves strangers, some humorous incident which makes us all laugh, and very often tiny acts of marvelous kindness. I feel I am among a large family who are communicating at a number of levels.

Hsinhua

We are quite cut off here from Western papers—you can't just go down to a newsstand and buy *Newsweek* or the air edition of the *New York Times*. Thanks to Clare McDermott I see Reuters' copy of the London *Times*—which if it connects with the jet from Moscow gets here within two days. But by-and-large it's the English edition of *Hsinhua* (the official Chinese news agency) that I have to digest with my breakfast every morning.

Hsinhua is both interesting and maddening. Interesting, because reading it you look at the world through quite a different kind of telescope and read things which you would never see in a Western newspaper. But its style is excruciatingly bad. It is high-sounding, boastful, repetitive, and boorish—in fact, all the things that the Chinese are *not*. It breaks every rule of competent journalism. As a result you could read *Hsinhua* a thousand years and never know that the Chinese are a highly perceptive people, of subtle and sensitive intelligence. To this extent, and in this way, *Hsinhua* does China a notable disservice. It would be a pity if *Hsinhua* ever became just another Western-type news service; it would be wonderful if it could become really Chinese.

Wages

It is impossible to come up with any worthwhile comparison between the wages here and in the United States. Some Intourist interpreters, for instance, earn the equivalent of twenty-five dollars a month, which seems little enough. But then, Mr. Ku (one of the interpreters) tells me, he only pays one yuan (forty cents) a month rent for his two-room apartment.

I could, with immense and tedious effort, come up with a chart showing how many hours a man would have to work in China in comparison to an American to earn enough to buy this, that, or the other. And all this would show would be something we know already without the help of charts—that the American workingman is prodigiously better off than his Chinese counterpart.

To the Chinese the only meaningful chart is one comparing today with ten years ago, and this year with last.

Grasshopper in a Hospital

In Chengchow I went to one of the hospitals to have my foot dressed. It was built in 1953, I was told. It was much less crowded than the P.U.M.C. Hospital in Peking and with an even more informal atmosphere.

I was taken at once to the out-patient surgical department where a young doctor (slender, capable hands, and the look of an intellectual) showed me into a room where I lay on a surgical bed. Everything very neat and trim. The door was open and several people wandered in to see what was going on. They were just friendly and curious. The doctor was quite at home with these people and didn't shoo them out as I was afraid he might.

While the doctor and nurse, both in surgical masks, were fixing my foot, I tried to chat with some of the people but they couldn't understand my Chinese and just giggled. A raggedy boy of about ten came and stood quite close staring at me. His hands were cupped; he was holding something in them. After a few moments he opened his hands so that I could see what he was holding—it was a bright-green grasshopper. It was his pet, I think, for he looked at it affectionately and stroked it from time to time. Then he handed me the grasshopper to hold. I held it by the hind leg and stroked it too and then gave it back to the boy. He went off smiling.

Passion for Improvement

The train yesterday taking me to Wuhan from Loyang was a long-distance one—it had started several days earlier from the far Northwest. I had Chin with me so could get to talk with the girl who sweeps up the sleeper and brings the incessant rounds of tea.

I asked her if she would have a few days off before her next trip.

"Yes," she said, "but first we must have our meeting."

I thought she meant a political study meeting, but she said no, it was a meeting to discuss the journey. Apparently after these long-distance trains reach their destination the entire train crew get together to see what went wrong, and how they can do things better next time. It's also a way of letting out any gripes. If there wasn't enough bed linen or if the beer ran out—these are the sort of things that come up.

"Also," the girl said, "if we have complaints against each other, we discuss them at these meetings. For instance, if the locomotive driver should stop too quickly and things in the dining car get spilled, the dining-car attendants will ask him about this and he will either explain why he had to brake so fast or he might apologize and say it was a mistake. In ways like this we can learn how to run our trains better."

"A *Deeply Disappointed Man*"

For the people, life is not all production quotas, political meetings, and slogans. I feel that I am in a country breaking through on all fronts into a new world.

Last night I had tickets to a concert in a big semiopen-air theater that has been built in one of Peking's parks. The entrance fee is a few fen. I arrived early and sat on the grass near a rose garden watching the audience as they drifted in. Old men and women, students, soldiers, youngsters of ten and eleven, even of five and six, young men and their girls.

Not far away I could see the colored lights above the dance area and hear the orchestra tuning up for those who wanted to dance Western style. A small moon was coming up through the trees.

Sitting there, among these lively unhurried people all having a good time, a phrase from a supposedly profound analysis of China in the *Atlantic Monthly* flashed through my mind. Envisioning his country today, Mao Tse-tung, said the writer, "is probably a deeply disappointed man."

And *that*, I think, must be the silliest remark in the history of highbrow journalism.

Diplomatic Gallup Poll

In the past few weeks I have been invited to most of the West
European and Asian embassies. I have taken the opportunity of
conducting a one-man poll. I have been posing a hypothetical question: If the people of China could, entirely freely and secretly, record their approval or disapproval of the present regime, how many
would record their approval?

The *lowest* figure that anyone has yet given me is 80 per cent.
Some have put it higher than 90 per cent.

Tonight I was again at one of the embassies. Someone had
brought along a copy of a Hong Kong paper which had quoted
General Wedemeyer's letter to the Washington *Star* of June 24.
The General was incensed at Montgomery's remarks at the banquet here in Peking. "Obviously he is unaware," the General wrote,
"of ample evidence concerning the massive famine in China of recent date and the official police action required to crush ruthlessly
the dissident elements rioting for food. . . ." And ". . . Naïvely
Lord Montgomery accepted Mao Tse-tung's statement that there
is widespread hatred of the United States throughout China. . . ."

When part of this letter was read aloud there was a kind of em-
barrassed laughter. Someone said, "If that's representative of the
information about China in Washington, then Lord help us all!"

The Psychological Revolution

The longer I'm here, the more fundamental the changes that are
taking place appear to me. The new developments in education,
the advances in medicine and industry, are only the outward mani-
festations of inner, psychological changes and it is *these* which in
the end may be more important than anything else. The changes
going on inside people really intrigue me more than production
statistics.

For example, the relationship to possessions. The Chinese, it appears to me, are significantly changing their attitude to property, to
ownership. Men's activities in the past have very largely been domi-

nated by a search for security, and to possess things is one way to secure a small foothold on a life full of uncertainties. But this drive to possess seems always to run to excess. Above our basic biological necessities we in the West have constructed an immense and ever-expanding pyramid of supposed necessities which are not necessities at all but psychological wants, or luxuries.

The Chinese recognize that every human being needs an adequate standard of food, shelter, and clothing. But they are aware, I think, that ownership above these minimal real needs leads to competitiveness and rivalry and that everything above the simplest personal possessions can much more happily be held in common. The result is that the element of *personal* acquisitiveness here appears to be reduced almost to a vanishing point. This is no "me first" economy; it is a "we" economy that is growing here. They are *really* not interested in making more money for themselves.

We must all wonder whether this isn't too good to last. Perhaps the personal-possessiveness drive is inherent in human nature and will eventually emerge here as it has elsewhere. It might be that China is like a country at war which must for sheer survival bury individual rivalry until the crisis is over. Of course China needs to raise its general level of life and will want to go on raising it. But will she avoid falling into the same old trap that the rest of us have been caught in—I mean making the "standard of living" the end all and be all of life, with everyone wanting to possess more and more of everything regardless of whether it makes us happier or not?

No one can tell. They seem to be fully aware of the problem and that's half the battle. Economically, they are already looking (though it is still a long way off) for the day when the work week will be very greatly reduced and are in a thousand different ways encouraging the development of personal creativity. But on a deeper level the Chinese have long been aware (without expressing it in psychological or religious terms) that personal rivalry and personal protectiveness both lead to alienation. The Chinese appear to be finding their basic psychological security not in the search for personal possessions, but in the quality of their relationship with each other, and the implications of this are enormous.

PART FIVE ☆

On Chinese Law   18

At whatever level one views the China scene today, it is a nation on the move, in a state of flux. Law in China is no exception.

The nation has many laws, but no codification of laws. It is impossible in China to refer to any legal abstracts or résumés. Even the structure of the courts, the definition of crimes, the procedures of handling criminal and civil cases are changing almost from day to day. Chinese law is in a trial-and-error period.

"A time of rapid social change is not the time to codify laws," I was told by one of China's top legal authorities, Mr. Wu Teh-peng, vice-president of the Chinese Political Science and Law Association, and a member of the Committee of Judiciary of the National People's Congress. "We are now in a period of transition from one kind of society to another, moving toward socialism," Mr. Wu said. "Law is the armor of the social system and it must change as the system changes. If, for example, laws pertaining to property had been codified during the co-operative stage of agriculture, they would now be quite out of date, since the commune movement has altered the whole basis of ownership." Mr. Wu, vigorous, with a bristly mustache, was, I felt, a very able scholar-politician. He looked at me over his glasses. "Besides," he added, "we prefer a gradually evolving system. Law must always remain in harmony with the realities of human nature. . . ."

This last comment struck me as being very much in the Chinese tradition. It reminded me of all that I had read of earlier Chinese legal procedures; it would have been a remark, I feel sure, that would have been approved of by Kuan Tzu in the sixth century B.C.

We tend to forget, sometimes, that China has had a long and remarkable legal tradition, though based on principles quite different from our own. As early as the sixteenth century Portuguese travelers were bringing back accounts about the care which was taken by Chinese magistrates to see that the people's rights were protected; and they reported that life was held much less cheap in China than it was in the Europe of those days.

The Chinese mind has never thought comfortably in terms of absolutes. Just as the sense of "sin" (the breaking of extrahuman, divine rules) never played much part in their religious life, so in their law the sense of an abstract right and wrong was largely missing. The Chinese never considered that an illegal act could be judged just on its own; it must always be seen in the light of the circumstances which surrounded it. To prescribe a fixed punishment for a given crime would, in their eyes, lead more often than not to injustice. In civil law, disputes were not seen so much in terms of one party being right and the other wrong, as in terms of a disharmony that needed to be resolved. The Chinese have always been a pragmatic, unsentimental people and they recognized that there are two sides to every question, that human motives are always mixed and often dubious.

Abstract law appeared to the Chinese mind as too rigid, not sufficiently in harmony with the ebb and flow of human nature, and therefore likely to be destructive of human relationships. Professional legal sophistry was avoided, for the aim was not to see that the niceties of justice were imposed but that equity was achieved. It was tradition, rather than "respect for law," that held Chinese society together through the centuries.

Criminal law was the only law that concerned the state, and it was often severe and cruel. It applied only to the common people, for the scholars and the aristocracy (except where treason to the throne was concerned) were usually unrestricted by any law at all. For the ordinary people all other disputes—civil, commercial, religious—were discussed by the elders of a village or the leaders of the guilds and associations of which a citizen might be a member. It was by discussion that the real balance was found and harmony was restored—and always, if possible, without one side or the other feeling injured or resentful. Such discussions were usually held in public so that friends and neighbors could follow and see that neither side was unfairly treated; and they would participate too. Problems were talked out and neighbors helped to build a bridge between opponents.

But a system of behavior enforced by tradition is highly vulnerable at moments when tradition itself is foundering. With the disruption of Chinese society that began with the "opening up" of China by the Western powers, ancient rules and unwritten restraints broke down. In the final agonizing decades the ordinary Chinese learned that he had neither custom nor law to look to for his protection.

All this passed through my mind as I sat with Mr. Wu Teh-peng, who was telling me about the new legal structure that was being built in China today. . . .

"We are attempting," Mr. Wu said, "to develop a system of law that can combine the needs of a modern industrial society and yet remain in harmony with the best of our ancient Chinese precepts." He went on to explain that they want their law to "grow" out of actual practice and real needs, "just as your English common law has grown," he said. "But we expect it to grow much more rapidly because the rate of social change is much more rapid."

Despite this emphasis by the Chinese on *experimentation* and *movement*, it is clear that the broad lines of a legal apparatus have already been marked out. There are at present some three thousand civil and criminal statutes adopted by the National People's Congress. As China is a *unified*, rather than a *federated* state, these laws have nationwide application (with certain exceptions in the cases of autonomous nationalities), and this is true also of the hierarchy of courts. The court system comprises three main levels:

> The Supreme People's Court
> Special People's Courts
> Basic People's Courts

The last-named are courts of first instance. Article 19 of the "Organic Law of the People's Courts," adopted in 1954, states that in addition to trying cases, these courts will "settle civil disputes and minor criminal cases which do not need a trial"; and "direct the work of people's conciliation committees." Higher courts can act either as courts of first instance or of appeal. Judges in China are appointed by the legislative bodies corresponding to the level of the courts and may be removed by the same bodies. There are thirty thousand of them.

But the number of cases that come into court is small, Mr. Wu told me; and the number reaching trial smaller yet. (This was confirmed everywhere I went.) This is partly because property of a personal kind plays a far smaller part in the life of the Chinese today than it does in ours; and this is especially true since the development of the co-operatives (and later the communes) in which property is held in common. A very high percentage of the cases that come before the U.S. courts are concerned, in one way or another, with property rights. Many minor disputes (which would otherwise come to court) are disposed of by the Conciliation Committees described later in this chapter.

In all China today there are, according to Mr. Wu, only two thousand lawyers, and these so underemployed that it causes the government serious concern. The government is anxious to maintain law as a subject of study and is recruiting students to enter the several law colleges. Lawyers frequently take jobs as teachers. As for the judges, most of whom do not have enough court cases to occupy their full time, and who are not permitted to accept other employment, the government encourages them to help in legal educational work—teaching the background and the importance of law through lectures and seminars in communes, factories, and colleges.

One reason for the small number of lawyers is that China is what could be described as a nonlegalistic country. "Contracts" play only a small role in Chinese business relationships; the given word is still a binding sanction. Even insurance is often a matter of a word promise rather than a contract requiring lawyers. Basically one might say that China developed as a highly homogeneous population whose closely-knit social life had to depend on a mutual trust.

I asked Mr. Wu whether the death penalty was still applied in China. He said, "Yes—for murder, rape causing the death of another person, for rape of a girl under fourteen years of age, and for certain anti-revolutionary crimes. But the law requires that all death sentences be reviewed by a higher court whether there is an appeal or not; and, further, that the penalty in every case be suspended for two years before it is carried out. Some Westerners have told us they think this a cruel provision. We think of it otherwise. Our aim is to get a man to reform during those two years—and what chance does a man have to reform if we kill him? Only on very rare occasions do we now carry out the death sentence."

When I asked Mr. Wu how many executions there were in a year, he said that he was unable to give me the number, as it was a state secret. "We are Marxist-Leninists," Mr. Wu continued, "we do not believe a *class* can ever be reformed; but we think *individuals* can be. In the ten years since liberation there have been a number of people condemned to death who are now living useful and productive lives."

Like the European systems based upon the Napoleonic Code, Chinese law makes no provision for jury trial. However, a somewhat analogous function is performed by the People's Assessors. Trial courts at first-instance level are composed of one judge and two assessors who serve, in a sense, as lay representatives of the public interest. Assessors must be citizens, twenty-three or older, and are elected, Mr. Wu said, by popular vote for a term of two years. Judges, in all cases, are persons who have had several years' legal training. People's Assessors receive some legal training while serving their terms of office; and they may be re-elected.

Discussing the role of the assessors, Mr. Wu continued, "There are usually forty to a hundred assessors elected in each county. When a case comes into a district, the county is asked to send two assessors. They are paid only the equivalent of their loss in salary plus a modest travel and expense account. In court they share equal rights with the judge. Two assessors can outvote the judge.

"Assessors are not used in appeals since these usually revolve around legal points. The *facts* are presumed to have been determined in the indictment and trial of first instance. Appeals are heard before three judges.

"At a level below the regular courts we have what we call the Neighborhood People's Conciliation Committee," Mr. Wu went on. "These committees are composed of residents in a local community who are well liked and trusted by the people, and their function is to try to settle personal disputes, minor infringements, and domestic conflicts. Parties in a dispute come before their neighborhood committee only if they wish to—it is entirely voluntary. The committee cannot compel anyone to appear—citizens can take their grievance to a formal court if they prefer. The findings of the conciliation committee are not binding, although the public gives them its moral support and they manage to settle a great number of small grievances which would otherwise have to be heard by the courts. As in the old days," Mr. Wu continued, "the neighbors and friends are present and take part in meetings of the conciliation committees."

So much for Mr. Wu's outline of the general structure of the courts. I was, of course, particularly interested to find out what protections are provided by law for the rights of accused persons. I was glad to have made available to me a report by a Canadian attorney, Mr. Kenneth Woodsworth, entitled *Notes on the Legal System of the People's Republic of China*, which he prepared after his return from China in 1960.

Mr. Woodsworth reported:

. . . There seems to be a considerable degree of protection against arbitrary arrest and imprisonment, and the impression is that the direction is towards greater safeguards in this respect. . . . Before a person may be arrested on suspicion of a crime, a full investigation must be made and evidence sufficient to satisfy the court (i.e., judge and people's assessors) must be submitted in advance. . . . After charges are laid, the arrest must be made publicly, in daytime, and witnessed by neighbors, and the family must be notified. No inducement or compulsion may be used to secure a confession. The accused must be shown the full evidence at least three days before trial and he may choose his own counsel, or ask that counsel be appointed for him. Trials must be in public, except in cases involving public security. If a case is not heard and dealt with within one month of the time when charges were laid, the delay must be explained and approved by the court of next instance. After conviction, the court must explain to the prisoner his right of appeal. . . .

Mr. Woodsworth attended not only several criminal trials but also meetings of the conciliation committees. Discussing the work of the committees, Mr. Woodsworth wrote that "he was very much impressed with the judiciousness and common sense conduct." Mr. Woodsworth concluded his general discussion of Chinese law with these words: "The nation appears to have left behind it the comparative chaos of the immediate post civil war period. It would seem that a permanent structure of law is emerging that is providing certainty in the administration of justice. I was favorably impressed with the general appearance of public order everywhere and with the conduct of legal processes, as I had opportunity to see them."

In 1956 an outstanding British barrister and Member of Parliament, Mr. F. Elwyn Jones, Q.C., visited China to observe several major criminal trials. In a report over the BBC on his return (included in *The Listener*, July 19, 1956), Mr. Jones said:

My impression is that the stage has been reached where more attention is being given to the rights of the individual citizen. I felt a real concern for justice among the lawyers I met, and a desire to create an effective independent court system.

The difficulty I found in seeking to assess the quality of their justice is that their basic approach is different from ours. In our own history we have found that the independence of our judges from the Government and from political control is a vital safeguard of the liberty of the citizen. The Communist doctrine does not accept this. They claim that the government is the people and that the people does not need to be protected from itself.

I attended two criminal trials. The first was in the High Court at Peking. The accused, a peasant, was charged with murder and with being a Japanese agent in 1942. He was tried by a judge sitting with two "lay assessors," as they are called. There is no system of trial by jury in China. The accused was represented by a defending lawyer. Each year they are training more lawyers in the law schools. . . . I was glad to find that the Chinese accepted the principle that it is essential to the administration of justice that accused persons on serious charges should be represented by a professionally qualified lawyer.

The Peking trial ended in the conviction of the accused and a sentence of three years imprisonment. The trial was conducted with dignity and simplicity. There were no wigs or robes. But there was a real sense of gravity of the occasion. The accused in this case pleaded guilty and he had previously made a full confession of his guilt. After the trial was over, I asked his lawyer whether he had satisfied himself that there was independent proof of the accused's guilt apart from his confession. He assured me that he had. This prisoner had been in prison for four months before his trial. It appears that since 1951 the period of waiting between arrest and trial has been cut down a good deal.

In the second trial I attended, at Nanking, the accused was an electrician charged with causing malicious damage in a factory. The prosecution alleged that the accused had become bitter because the management had promoted someone junior over him and this had led him to commit the crime. The electrician denied the charges vigorously, as did his defending lawyer. I did not discover the result of this trial because it was adjourned for the calling of further evidence. I saw no press reporters in this or indeed any court I went to, and there is little, if any, crime reporting in the Chinese press. But there were relatives of the prisoner, students, and members of the public in all the courts I attended. . . .

The most interesting case I heard was an appeal in the Shanghai High Court of a prisoner who had been sentenced to death on a charge that he was a colonel in Chiang Kai-shek's army, who had been landed secretly from Formosa in 1954 in order to organize a counter-revolutionary group in the Shanghai area. He too had a lawyer to represent him. His appeal was successful and his death sentence was varied to one of eight years imprisonment.

These accounts (so largely favorable) by visiting experts do not mean justice is all-triumphant in China. China's civil conflict is not yet over; it is a nation still at war. And as in every country at moments of danger, so today in China normal legal procedures are subject to the overriding imperatives of survival. Civil war and extensive borders make it easy for spies and saboteurs to infiltrate. Chiang Kai-shek talks openly of the spies who are parachuted onto the mainland or put ashore from boats. And there must be many of the formerly privileged who, while outwardly going along with the present regime because they have to, are still bitterly resentful and antagonistic.

There are no signs of terror in China today and no sense of fear; but there is intense vigilance. With those who are accessible to discussion, to persuasion, the Chinese are often remarkably patient; but little mercy would be shown to those who remain determined to throw obstacles in the path of the social progress that is being attempted. I rather think appeal to "legal rights" would be of little help to them.

A Divorce Trial 19

During a tour of a heavy machinery plant in Shenyang, word reached me that a municipal court would be in session
at eleven o'clock. As I had not yet had a chance to see a court in
action, I at once called off the factory visit and drove back into the
city with Mr. Chang Ming-lun, one of the most efficient interpreters I ever met. His ability to give an instantaneous, running translation of the court proceedings enabled me to transcribe them
almost verbatim.

We arrived at the court early. I looked around. The courtroom
was a small, rather drab chamber, filled almost to capacity by about
thirty women. The wooden floor had been recently scrubbed. Between the benches for the public and the judge's platform was a
long table covered with a bright-red tablecloth. This was the only
splash of color in the room. No flags, no slogans, no pictures even
of Mao Tse-tung. While we waited for the judge to appear, I
learned from the court secretary that the case to be heard was a
divorce action, and the presiding judge would be one of the youngest on the bench—only twenty-three. This particular court, he told
me, heard thirty or forty such suits a year, and a smaller number of
criminal cases. To divulge the exact number was not permitted.
There were only six municipal courts of this kind in Shenyang, a
city of nearly three million. He told me the court was called in
session only when there was a case to be heard, usually only every
ten days or so.

A woman, whom my interpreter told me was the court recorder,
entered through a door behind the judge's table and loudly summoned the public to rise. As we did so, the judge and the two
assessors took their seats on the platform. One assessor was an
elderly, bespectacled man who might have been a shopkeeper or

small businessman. The other was a buxom woman, a housewife perhaps, with white ribbons binding her black hair. The judge himself, in his freshly-pressed cotton work suit, looked even younger than twenty-three. I would have taken him for a college student. His face was serious. From the moment he stepped into the court this young man was in complete control of the proceedings. He looked at us for a moment and then said:

"Please, everyone sit down."

He remained standing.

"Before this hearing begins," he said, "I wish to tell the members of the public what the regulations are. They are simple and I wish them strictly obeyed. There is to be no smoking. Do not clap or shout. Do not fidget. If any members of the public have questions to ask or suggestions to make, please do so at the end of the case. Do not interrupt during the hearing."

In addition to the judge, the two assessors, and the court recorder, another woman had taken a seat on the far side of the dais. She was to be a witness, I was told.

The judge then said, "Let the man and woman be brought in."

A young couple entered, side by side, and stood facing the judge, their backs to the public. On a gesture from the judge they sat down in two chairs which had been placed there for them, and remained seated throughout. The judge asked each in turn for name, age, occupation. The woman was a school teacher, twenty-four years old, her "cultural level" that of high-school graduate. The man was a doctor, twenty-seven, and a college graduate.

The judge then told them:

JUDGE: My name is Tao Wan-yi; the people's assessor on my right is Liu Shi-ying and on my left Li Shu-lan. The recorder's name is Chiang Ming-chin and the name of the woman's representative is Yie Rung-chin. She is the principal of the primary school where Chang Wen-hung works. Your rights are these—you can put forward your reason, Chang Wen-hung, for wanting to divorce this man; and then Chang Wei-man will have the right to tell this court why he opposes divorce. You have the right to call evidence and you have the right to appeal to the higher court if you are not satisfied. You have the right to call any friends you wish to speak for you. You have the right to have a lawyer if you wish to have one. You also have the right to read the record of today's hearing at any time during the next four days, and any members of the public can read it also. If either of you two have any reason not to be satisfied with this court, either as to myself or the two people's assessors, you have the right to withdraw the case now and take it before another judge and assessors.

Have you listened carefully to what I have said?

All three say yes.

Have any of you any question as to the membership of this court?

No.

We will then proceed. According to this woman's depositions she says she wants to divorce this man because there is no harmony in the home, that they often quarrel over quite minor things; that they have different temperaments and tastes and because he has a very bad temper. He says in his deposition that she pays too much attention to her family and not enough to him, that she is not tender and very rarely has a good word for him. He also admits that he has a bad temper but is trying to correct that. But he opposes the divorce because he still feels there is a basis of a good relationship.

That briefly is the situation. The law says that when two people agree on a divorce it is to be granted, provided adequate provision is made for the protection of the children's interests. If either party disagrees then a hearing must take place before a people's court. That is the position today.

JUDGE: (to the woman) When did you first get to know your husband?

WOMAN: In 1955.

JUDGE: When did you get married?

WOMAN: In May 1956.

JUDGE: How long did you love him before getting married?

WOMAN: For a year. But I didn't get to know him very well. He talked very well and pretended to be a good man. He often asked me to go to the park with him or to some movies and kept asking me to marry him.

JUDGE: How about your feelings after you got married?

WOMAN: Not very good. He began to be rude and my state of mind about him became clearer and clearer. Since 1958 I helped him with his work, so that though the feeling wasn't very good between us it was still possible. But his temper got worse and worse and he often beat me. I often spoke to him but it had no effect. We didn't seem to be the same family—we began to have nothing but quarrels and fights.

WOMAN ASSESSOR: Did he beat you?

WOMAN: Yes, and I couldn't stand his rude ways with me. His mother always supported him and that made things worse. We would often quarrel in the middle of the night. His mother didn't help at all, only made things worse.

MAN ASSESSOR: Why do you want a divorce now?

WOMAN: The work at my school is very heavy; I just cannot stand the strain any longer. If ever I come in late from school he would say, "Where have you been? What have you been up to?" For a long time I felt that though he beat me and slapped me things would improve. While he was a medical student at Shenyang Medical College I helped him with money and other things and gave him as much as I could.

MAN ASSESSOR: How did he treat you while you were helping him?

WOMAN: Not always very good but much better. His attitude wasn't always patient. But I decided to go on just as long as I thought the relationship had a chance of improving. I tried to discuss things with him, especially about the children, and all he would say was, "You gave birth to them, they aren't my responsibility!" How can one bear it when one's husband says that about his children?

JUDGE: What does he do with the money he earns?

WOMAN: Usually spends it on himself or on his mother, so I use my money to keep the children and for food and so on. I sometimes need books too, so there is often no money to hand over to him, though he thinks there should be.

JUDGE: What resources do his parents have?

WOMAN: They have enough to get by—there's no need for him to spend money on them.

MAN ASSESSOR: Do you ever have a discussion with him about how to spend the family money and how to arrange the economy of the family?

WOMAN: Oh, yes. Before he graduated we had many discussions as to how we would budget our money. But after he graduated these talks annoyed him. Sometimes when he saw what the children needed he would buy them something, but usually he left that to me and paid no attention to the children.

JUDGE: How did the quarrels begin? Who started them?

WOMAN: Sometimes he did, sometimes I did by trying to correct him.

JUDGE: Did you ever strike him?

WOMAN: No.

JUDGE: What did he strike you with?

WOMAN: His hands. Sometimes he would come home at midnight —a normal man doesn't come back at that time.

JUDGE: Do you often try to correct him?

WOMAN: Yes, and I asked friends to intervene. . . . Sometimes quarrels would last until midnight and neighbors would complain.

JUDGE: He said in his deposition you often swear and curse at him— is that true?

WOMAN: (Part of this reply couldn't be heard) . . . I was treated just like a stranger by his mother, who would also call me names.

JUDGE: Who did the housework?

WOMAN: His mother mostly, because I had to go to school; but I did all the children's laundry.

JUDGE: Who looked after the children's expenses?

WOMAN: I did.

JUDGE: How many children have you?

WOMAN: Two. One three years old; one, one year.

JUDGE: Are you pregnant now?

WOMAN: No.

JUDGE: (turning to the man) What about your feelings toward your wife?

MAN: After our marriage it was very good. We often did things together, cooked together, and we paid much care to each other.

JUDGE: Was this because she was supporting you while you were at college?

MAN: Yes.

JUDGE: How did you treat her?

MAN: Very well. I tried to study well.

JUDGE: Did you put your feelings of kindness into acts?

MAN: I wasn't much good at looking after the children. At that time I was living at the college and we would see each other on Saturdays and Sundays.

JUDGE: Why, after two years, did it get worse?

MAN: I think the trouble was largely because she wasn't on good terms with my mother. She had a weakness too, in that she couldn't stand anything that would distress her, anything unpleasant. Also we are very different temperamentally. She likes to lead a quiet life, I like to be active.

JUDGE: She says you often beat her—is that true?

MAN: We had frequent quarrels, but I didn't beat her frequently.

JUDGE: Why did you quarrel so often?

MAN: My irritation and temper. Also she looked down on me. I'm a doctor, but she would always know best.

JUDGE: Do you feel superior to her culturally?

MAN: Yes.

JUDGE: (bearing down on him) Don't you know there's a law that says couples should help each other? If you thought her cultural level was low you should have helped her to improve it. You think you are her cultural superior—is that a right way of thinking?

MAN: I think my thinking was wrong. I relied on her for money and help but when I got near to graduation I began to think "I'm better than a mere primary-school teacher"—that, I admit, was wrong.

JUDGE: Who do you think is responsible for the quarrels?

MAN: I think I am because I asked too much of her.

JUDGE: Has she tried to help you with your rudeness?

MAN: She has tried to improve me lots of times!

JUDGE: Why didn't you take her help and advice?

MAN: Because of loss of face; I couldn't admit my weak points.

WOMAN ASSESSOR: Why do you think you would lose face by accepting her advice?

MAN: Mainly because I looked down on her culturally and couldn't accept her as an equal.

JUDGE: Why did this all happen only after your graduation?

MAN: Because then I could support myself.

JUDGE: Is it your lack of feeling for her or her lack of feeling for you that is the real problem? When she paid such tender care for you, why were you unable to respond in the same way?

MAN: Because of my lack of knowledge of how to look after a family and a wife.

JUDGE: Do you know the marriage law?

MAN: Yes.

JUDGE: Since you know the marriage law you should know the husband's obligations toward his wife and children.

WOMAN ASSESSOR: Is it because you had different opinions, that you fought with your wife?

MAN: No. But because in the past, before liberation, I often saw my father beat my mother and I was brought up to think that men should be superior.

JUDGE: When did your father beat your mother?

MAN: In the old society.

JUDGE: And what does the present law say?

MAN: That men and women are equal. But I still think the wife should obey the husband.

JUDGE: But don't you know the law?

MAN: I don't think it matters if a man beats his wife—but he mustn't beat others. In the family it's all right.

JUDGE: What law allows the husband to beat the wife?

MAN: No law.

JUDGE: What was the reason you beat her the last time?

(Courtroom throughout all this very still. Everyone listening intently. No interruptions at all.)

MAN: Because she took the children to her mother's without consulting me. I also loved the children and my mother did too, and we didn't want them to be taken away.

JUDGE: But isn't it fair for her to see her parents and take the children there too? Who else did you beat?

MAN: I hit her mother once, but that was quite accidental—a slip of my hand. It happened in a struggle . . . and also I had had some wine.

JUDGE: On what have you been spending your own wages?

MAN: Sometimes on myself. I bought a bicycle.

JUDGE: Do you agree to the divorce?

MAN: I think it's been my fault and I think it's quite reasonable of her to ask for a divorce. But I hope she gives me a chance to correct myself. I'll try my best. If later on I again fail, then I won't object to the divorce.

JUDGE: What is your plan for the future?

MAN: I will certainly pay more attention to my wife and family.

JUDGE: (to the woman's representative, the principal of the school where the teacher worked) Do you want to say anything?

REPRESENTATIVE: I have made a thorough study of the case and all its aspects and made many inquiries. Though love was there at the start, there was never any real basis of a good relationship. He used fine words to start with.

You cannot see the realities of this marriage on the surface. The marriage on this basis cannot be consolidated. I believe the main trouble has been the man. The law says that marriage should be based on free-will and equality. Everyone has the right to freedom and to social life and a mutual life of shared obligations, and the shared duty to look after the children. But instead this man beat her —even when she was pregnant. As a doctor he should know very well that is a time when special care should be taken—and that is why she began to lose her health.

Bad treatment—those are the grounds for this application for divorce. This man has no real feelings for this woman and his actions show it. He has often promised to change, but hasn't. He often apologized but never changed. It is his feudal background that makes him treat his wife as an object to be possessed—it is a bourgeois view to look down on a wife as he has done. While he was dependent on her help, he never showed his real nature, but when he became independent his real attitude showed itself—a college graduate looking down on a mere primary-school teacher! No real relationship can ever be built on another's pains. When he says he doesn't know how to look after children he's only lying. Fancy! a doctor saying he doesn't know how to look after children! And the only reason why he doesn't want a divorce now is because of public opinion!

JUDGE: Anything more?

WOMAN: No.

JUDGE: Anything more?

MAN: No.

JUDGE: Do any of you have anything to say about the representative's statement?

(to the woman) Just now your husband said he would like to correct himself and pay tender regard for you and the children. What do you say to this?

WOMAN: This is not the first time he has said this. He will be quite different as soon as he gets back home. One moment he says that he looks down on me, the next he says he will be kind to me. I am firm.

My mind is made up. If this court does not grant me this divorce, I will take it to a higher court.

JUDGE: (to the man) What do you say to that?

The man was struggling to find words. The judge leaned forward, waiting. Finally the man began to speak. He was looking straight ahead, over the head of the judge, but seemed really to be addressing his wife.

MAN: I know the basis of our life has not been good. I have not been a good husband, nor a good father. But many people have educated me and today I have really woken up. I know in the past I have heard all these things, but I didn't ever realize them as I do today. I have loved you, but I have neglected you. I have really loved you. We have two children and I now really commit myself to look after you and our two children. I know I have said this before, but today it is true.

This is the last time, and in front of so many people, I tell you that you can trust me and I am asking you to give me one more opportunity. Let us try once more to make a happy home and in this way to contribute to our society. I still believe we can make a happy home for ourselves and the children. I will take tender care of you. I will never again think, as I have done in my bourgeois way, that the man is more important than the woman. I now see that is nothing but a feudal attitude which I have not shed from my past.

JUDGE: (to the woman) What do you think of giving him another opportunity?

WOMAN: It's not true that our relationship was ever all right. He has said all this before. He so often goes back on his words. . . .

MAN: (breaking in, his eyes still straight ahead) Please . . . please.

The room was absolutely silent and all eyes were fixed upon the woman. We could not see her face, but from the set of her shoulders, and the bitterness of her previous words, I felt certain her answer would be no. The judge also had been watching her closely and at the very moment she started to speak, he rose to his feet, interrupting her. A superb piece of timing. He said, "There will be a recess for fifteen minutes for this man and woman to talk things over in private. Then I ask that they come to see me personally. The court is recessed."

We waited for half an hour or forty minutes. Some of the people went out to smoke and talk on the steps. The court secretary, as before, announced the court's reassembly. The judge, the assessors, the secretary, the woman's representative came in; then the man and woman. The woman had been crying and was twisting her handkerchief in her hand.

JUDGE: (standing) Please sit down. The court is again in session.

Chang Wen-hung, teacher, and Chang Wei-man, doctor, have had an opportunity to talk together while the court was in recess and they have informed us of their discussion.

Chang Wei-man has declared several times this morning his determination to improve his behavior toward his wife, and she has told us that she agrees to give this marriage one more chance, but only on one condition. The condition is that if she finds that his behavior does not improve and that she feels it necessary to apply for a divorce again, that her husband will not oppose her. In that case the divorce would be granted without a court hearing. The court will now make its declaration.

As the judge said this, the two assessors and the court recorder also rose and stood while the judge gave the finding of the court.

This court declares that since Chang Wei-man has criticized himself in public here today and since his wife is ready to give him another chance, that her application for a divorce should be considered withdrawn on the condition she has made. The two people should now try to make every effort to consolidate their relationship in affection and understanding.

MAN: I would like to thank the judge and the assessors and all the comrades present who have consistently advised me.

JUDGE: (to the man) The court wishes to address these words to you. I think you have many problems which you must think over, many difficulties you have with your own character, especially your bad temper. You have shown a bourgeois attitude and this you must do your best to eradicate. You are hereby formally reprimanded by this court. We charge you to do your utmost to correct your behavior and erroneous attitudes and we charge you to see that you carry out in your actions what you have promised here in open court this morning.

(more gently) You are a doctor. As a doctor in a socialist state you have a great responsibility. Try in future to conduct yourself so that you can lead a happy family life with your wife and two children, and this will also help your country and comrades. While we reprimand you, we want you to know that we understand how difficult it is to shed old attitudes. Our whole country is in the process of changing from one set of values to another. That is a very difficult task. Changes of attitude can only come when we consciously become aware of the old values which have to be eradicated. We understand the difficulties, and ask you to do your best.

(to all of us) The court is now over. After we have left we wish the public to remain seated until Chang Wei-man and Chang Wen-hung have left the courtroom.

The man and woman, without looking at anyone, the man with slightly averted face, left by the public door. The audience rose and we drifted slowly outside.

As I went through the outer lobby to the street I saw the judge, a policeman, and some of the people who had been watching in the courtroom lighting cigarettes and chatting together.

Prisons:
Bad and Good 20

At the culminating end of any system of law stands the system of retribution or of reform. In the West both these ideas, retribution and reform, have become intertwined. We frequently call our prisons reformatories; we often declare that our aim is to rehabilitate the transgressor and send him out again as a functioning member of society. In practice, however, we still demand of the law that it exact revenge. The criminal must "pay his debt to society"; the violator must be made to suffer. The result, since retribution and reform are nearly always mutually exclusive, is that our penal institutions customarily fail of both aims.

I have always been deeply concerned with prison reform. I was for years a member of the Howard League for Penal Reform in England. I have visited prisons all over the world, lectured *in* prisons and *about* prisons. In general, my conviction has been that caging people can never cure them. There will always be some who are psychologically so injured that they must be kept out of society. But the vast majority of those we put behind bars should not be there. And when they are released, far from having been reformed, they are usually less capable of fitting into society, and more bent upon beating or outwitting society, than they were when they went in.

I was, therefore, keenly interested in learning how China approached this problem.

In theory, or at the verbal level, the main stress appears to be on *reform* rather than retribution.

Mr. Wu Teh-peng, the vice-president of the Chinese Political Science and Law Association, and member of what would correspond in the United States to the House Committee on Judiciary, had said to me, "The essence and spirit of our laws is not solely to punish the criminal or to give society powers of reprisal. Our aim is to prevent the criminal from continuing in his criminal ways and to transform him if amenable to education. Generally criminals are put in prison. Certain crimes are punishable by death, but even in these cases we give opportunity for reform."

Prison sentences, Mr. Wu told me, ranged from six months to twenty or twenty-five years. Six months is the minimum sentence. Misdemeanors and minor crimes are not handled by imprisonment. Sentences are always subject to reduction for good behavior, parole, and so forth.

Thus, with the exception of the two-year delay between imposition and execution of a death sentence there appears no great difference, at the theoretical level, between the Chinese and Western penal systems. When it came to actually visiting prisons, however, I found some striking differences, and also some notable similarities.

I was able to inspect two prisons, one a "good" prison in Peking, and the other a very "bad" one, not only in my view, but in the opinion of the Chinese as well, in Shanghai.

Let me start with the "bad" one.

My visit came about in a rather curious way. I had heard talk in Peking of the Nanking prison as being one of their very best—the most advanced, the "freest," the model which best illustrated their new attitude. In Peking I had been assured I would be able to visit the Nanking prison; and on my way to Shanghai from Wuhan I left the riverboat which was taking me down the Yangtze River at Nanking, largely for the sake of that visit. There, however, I learned that my visit to the prison would "not be convenient." They were very sorry. The directors were away. I said I didn't care whether the directors were there or not, I was more interested in the prisoners and the prison than I was in the directors. But in this I made no progress. It was clear they were saying "*No.*"

Later I was told that there is considerable local autonomy in these matters, and probably a certain guarding of prerogatives. Local officials don't like to feel themselves pushed by Peking; and perhaps if I had arrived in Nanking without any prior word from the capital, they might have been delighted to show me their prison. But who can tell?

Arriving in Shanghai the following morning, I mentioned my interest in prisons and my disappointment of the previous day. They immediately invited me to visit the Shanghai prison. This I had already heard of as being one of their very worst.

The Shanghai prison was of the fortress type, built, I am sorry but not surprised to say, by the British, sometime between 1913 and 1925 (the Kuomintang had lost the records). Known as the Ward Road Jail, it had been patterned, quite obviously, after late-nineteenth-century prisons in London. As we drove up, we came to an immense iron gate, guarded by a soldier with a tommy gun. The gate was opened, the car moved forward to an inner portcullis. Above us loomed a row of frightful brick structures, four stories high, with rows of barred windows.

The chief warden, however, seemed curiously out of place in this sinister pile. He was a young fellow, wearing a white short-sleeved shirt with open collar. An open face, firm but likable. They certainly *use* young people. His name was Wang Chi-hu.

The style of the prison, he told me, made it difficult to adapt to the new system of reform through labor. But they were not planning to build another prison because they thought that within a few years there would be no need for anything as large as this. The prison population has been steadily diminishing. They now have 2400 inmates. (According to the Department of Correction, the prison population of New York City as of March 1, 1961 was 9574.) The prison is less than half occupied. Several of the huge cell blocks are being used for storage, a fact I was able to confirm by my own observation, though I was not able to confirm Mr. Wang's even more interesting statement that this was the only prison in Shanghai, a city of more than six million population.

With respect to vital statistics and the general routine of this somber institution, Warden Wang gave me the following facts:

They have one hundred guards.

The guards are all armed.

There are no escapes.

Families normally visit once a month, but may come at any time if there is some special reason. Mail is unlimited but letters in and out are censored. Visitors are separated from the prisoners by barred grills.

Prisoners have the same rations as the people outside, in winter they eat meat here three times a week, fish more frequently in summer. There is a big library, unlimited reading material is permitted. Prisoners work eight hours a day in workshops: at printing, shoemaking, and other light industries. A large part of the cost of the prison is met by the profits made out of the production.

There is a spare-time program which offers classes in reading and writing and various technical skills, as well as current events and international relations. Movies are frequently shown and they have lectures by people brought in from factories, communes, steel mills. The purpose is to keep the inmates informed of the progress of their country, to make them want to get out and take part.

Every prisoner receives a very thorough medical examination on entrance and regular checkups. Mr. Wang said there had been no new case of venereal disease during the past three years. At the time of my visit the only cases were two men over fifty. The TB rate was fairly high, but he would not specify. A separate section of the prison is reserved as a sanatorium for tubercular prisoners.

Six months was the shortest sentence, Mr. Wang said; the longest was life. This did not exactly tally with the statement made to me by Mr. Wu Teh-peng, to the effect that the maximum sentence in China was twenty to twenty-five years. Perhaps, however, as in other countries, "life sentences" are all commuted after a prolonged imprisonment.

I inquired what percentage of prisoners were second offenders. "None," said Mr. Wang.

I record the remainder of this conversation exactly as I noted it down.

I asked, "What happens to the family of a prisoner if he had been the only wage earner?"

"Since the family has committed no crime it should not be punished. The family receives an allowance from the state."

Commonest crime, both for men and women, is theft. When I asked about prostitution, he said no, a girl arrested for prostitution would not be sent here; in fact, would probably not be arrested at all, but would be referred for medical care and rehabilitation counseling. At the time of liberation, he told me, Shanghai had many thousands of prostitutes; these were rounded up and sent to special centers for treatment and education.

"What are the means of rehabilitating, or reforming, prisoners?"

"Confession must be the first step. The prisoner must realize and fully accept that he has done wrong, or rehabilitation is impossible."

"Are life sentences ever remitted?"

"Many. The policy is to remit sentences for good behavior and upon evidence of a desire to take part in the country's efforts. The prisoner is then more useful outside than in. Some life-termers are released after only a few years." Paroles were not allowed for harvest work, he told me, as they frequently are in Russia; but in case of family illness or bereavement a prisoner could go and visit his family.

"Do you have many prisoners," I inquired, "who were under death sentence and are now serving out commuted sentences?"

"Several dozen."

"Prisoners sentenced to death," I said, "pending this two-year stay of execution—would you think the majority give satisfactory indications of reform?"

"There are exceptionally few who do not reform before the expiration of the stay."

That I could readily believe.

"What about society's attitude toward the ex-prisoner?" I inquired. "Does this make a problem in rehabilitation?"

He said he thought there were no such difficulties.

That night I wrote in my journal:

Prisons are appalling places; symbols of society's failure, or, more accurately, symbols of ignorance. Future generations will one day look back on our prisons—Shanghai, London, Alcatraz—with shocked wonder at our insensibility, just as we look back to the days (not so long ago) when children could be publicly flogged for stealing a penny or men could be hanged for stealing a sheep.

It was lunchtime as we passed through the great main cell block—the men were back from the workshops, locked in their cells. They sat on their haunches, hardly looking up as we went by, apathetic, lost. How it reminded me of those English jails—the locking and unlocking of every door as we passed through from one section to another! England has left a really bad part of her here in Shanghai as a legacy!

They must, of course, have been up against a far tougher type of prisoner here in this one-time "wickedest city in the world," than in any other part of China—this city which was a kind of mecca for every pimp, drug trafficker, and gangster in Asia.

But the most startling and, I would like to think, the most hopeful of today's impressions was the contrast between the old laggards, the leftovers, and the young chief warden. And the most impressive thing about him was not his level-headed, unsentimental approach to his job, or even his youth, but that to him these wretched creatures behind the bars were still men.

Peking prison stands at the end of Self-Renewal Street.

It too is an old structure, built about the turn of the century. The prevailing impression is one of drabness: old gray buildings, dusty courtyards, vegetable patches heavy with dust, and a few trees with drooping leaves in the inner courts. But compared to Shanghai, this prison is a gem. There are no guards in sight except a soldier at the gate with a rifle and another on a distant tower. Inside, I saw that the guards were unarmed and the doors unlocked. In fact, the old iron doors had been taken from the cells and replaced by glass doors and there were casement windows, many standing wide open, where obviously, at some earlier date, had been barred windows.

Even I could have escaped from this prison.

Over tea and cigarettes with Mr. Wang Chien, the vice-warden, I learned there were 1800 prisoners, 100 of whom were women. This, he said, was the only prison in the municipal area of Peking, which now includes seven and a half million people.

Commonest crime for both men and women is "corruption," which is defined as "converting public property to private use," and the familiar crimes against persons. Forty per cent are in for counter-revolutionary crimes (espionage, assassination, sabotage, etc.) but these prisoners are not regarded or treated differently from the others. "Counterrevolutionary," Wang explained, would mean those who have performed concrete acts against the state. For those who have merely spoken against the state, there is no punishment, though such people may be recommended for some sessions of political instruction. But an overt act is necessary before opposition becomes a criminal matter. Incitement of others *is* considered an overt act; but apart from this, voicing hostile views is not a matter for punishment. (Here is a subtle distinction upon which the United States Supreme Court has expended a good many hundreds of pages of argumentation. I did not press the point with Mr. Wang, but went on, as I had in Shanghai, to the problems of rehabilitation.)

Here, too, confession, the inner recognition of fault, was emphasized as the necessary first step.

"The prisoner must realize the dangers to his country resulting from his criminal action and must understand that his punishment is deserved. This lays the foundation for the prisoner to accept reform as a conscious process.

"The prisoner is educated in current affairs so that he can understand the significance of national and international developments, so that he can realize the strength of the socialist state. To help him perceive the great advances being made, to enable him to compare the old with the new, he is taken on field trips to communes and factories, he hears discussions by leaders and workers from outside.

"The purpose of this stage is to make the prisoner realize that labor is a glorious matter and can create a national wealth which he should be sharing, and in the building of which he should be taking part." Here Mr. Wang quoted Article 4 of the Labor Reform Code: "*To carry out a policy combining punishment and surveillance with ideological reform and to integrate productive labor with political education.'"*

He went on to explain that the prison routine, which requires each inmate to put in eight hours a day in one of the prison workshops, not only inculcates regular work habits, but guarantees that the prisoner, when he gets out, will have acquired some useful skill. Afterward there would be no problem of his getting employment. And because there was a general understanding of the policy of reform through labor, there would be no special stigma attached to his having been in prison. The manager of the factory or commune where he went to work would be informed of the prison term, but it would be up to the individual whether or not he informed his fellow workers. Most do, Mr. Wang thought. The prison keeps in touch with the progress of discharged prisoners.

"Not to look down on criminals is highly important," the vice-warden declared. "Reform is absolutely impossible if there is an atmosphere of moral condemnation and disapproval. It would only make it much more likely that he will become a criminal again."

The general routine here was similar to that of the Shanghai prison, but much more relaxed, much fuller. There are radios in the workshops and living quarters. The daily schedule for inmates would run something like this:

8 hours work
8 hours sleep
2 hours study
1 hour for cultural activities and recreation
5 hours for meals, washing, resting, letter writing, etc.

There are arrangements for spare-time hobbies, as well as spare-time education. The prisoners have an amateur theatrical group. Women are allowed to mix with men at evening socials, which may be dances, performances by the theater group, or movies.

Prisoners have one complete day off every two weeks which they can use in any way they wish.

Good behavior is rewarded by a bonus in money, or a present of some kind, or by a citation on the good-behavior bulletin board.

And, of course, parole or reduction of sentence by the court would be based on the behavior record.

Bad behavior may be punished by warnings or a citation on the bad-behavior bulletin board. Genuine bad-actors may be sent to "meditate on their misdeeds" in solitary for a few hours, or for as long as a week. No physical punishment is permitted.

Mr. Wang said, "We only very rarely meet here cases of prisoners who do not respond to education and reform. We can recommend to the courts that the sentences of such prisoners be lengthened. But this almost never occurs.

"After the confession stage," he continued, "and the understanding of the need to reform, they almost never try to escape. Those who do—well, nearly always they will be sent back by their own families."

I noted in my journal at the end of that day:

Given the ideological framework, and the emphasis on "re-education and reform through proper understanding of Marx-Leninism," the prison apparently is doing its job, with a real attempt at humane treatment. Obviously the thing to do if convicted is to *go along*, to become a model student and get the hell out. And perhaps this *going along*, even though begun for an ulterior motive, is the way they catch the individual within the collective assumptions on which everything is based. There would be tremendous relief, particularly for certain types of neurotics, in abandoning themselves to authority, as in the army. But what of those whose neurosis drives them to separateness, whose satisfactions derive from the need to be in rebellion? There must be a hard core of *unreformables*. What becomes of them?

And what about this "confession" business? It seems absurdly unreal to me (just ask an American or British prisoner to "confess" and hear him tell you where to put yourself!). What methods do they use to secure them? I'm probably falling into that old, old error of trying to understand the inner processes of another people in terms of my own. If my theory is right, that the greatest psychological pain for a Chinese is to feel himself outside the group, then "confession" perhaps is the door that is offered to reacceptance, reinclusion, an end to an intolerable isolation. Who knows?

So many questions remain unanswered. . . . Still, it is ironic, particularly for one who formerly put in as many hours as I did over the years agitating, with so many others, and with such notable lack of success, for the humane treatment of prisoners, for the removal of the moral stigma of imprisonment as a precondition for rehabilitation—ironic to find these very principles being extolled, and to some extent practiced, by prison authorities under the "inhumane" regime of Red China.

The Mass Line in Education 21

Within its boundaries, China includes one-quarter of the human race, probably more than a quarter of the world's children, and certainly more than a quarter of the educational problems of the world.

Consider the China of eleven years ago. A population of over half a billion people, 80 per cent or more illiterate; a land predominantly agricultural, but with almost no schools in its rural areas; a nation with virtually no industry, little technological or managerial experience; with skilled labor, teachers, professionals in desperately short supply. Consider further that this nation had been devastated by a prolonged civil war and a seven-year military occupation by Japan. Consider a country in which disease and illness were rampant and in which the number of trained doctors was so few that there was only one for every 25,000 people, and where a province, Sinkiang, twice as big as France, had only fifteen; consider a people so close to starvation that (foreign estimates) 20,000 bodies were picked up each year off the streets of Shanghai alone —adults and children who had gone under, who had lost the relentless struggle for survival.

And consider finally the determination of this country to shed this nightmare past and thrust forward, and fast, into the twentieth century.

That, in brief, was China's educational problem.

The segments of the problem interlocked. To support an expanding educational program, a higher national productivity was needed. But increasing national productivity depended on "raising the level," with respect to skills and technical training, of the labor force. And raising the level of the labor force depended on teaching workers to read and write. Here was a veritable Chinese puzzle.

The first segment of this closed circle against which the new regime launched a massive attack was, as might have been expected, illiteracy. Actually this campaign began in the Northwest and the border regions several years before the Communists captured Peking. By 1960, the year of my second visit to China, the spare-time schools for adults, tens of thousands of them, and the new network of schools for children were showing results. The Ministry of Education expected 130 million people (10 million more than the population of the United States in 1940!) to pass literacy tests during 1960; and estimated that by the end of that year illiteracy would be down to just over 30 per cent (mostly people too old to learn).

A factory manager in Harbin told me, with a sense of pride, and before he mentioned productivity figures or quality of his output, that his factory would be able to "liquidate illiteracy" among its employees that very month.

On hundreds of factory and commune bulletin boards I saw posted the poems and letters of men and women who had just passed their literacy tests.

I met a commune manager in the Yellow River Valley, running an enterprise which involved seventy-five hundred families and millions of dollars worth of plant and equipment who had, himself, learned to read and write only a few years previously at the age of thirty-two.

All this, of course, is at a primitive level. The literacy test, for urban areas, is generally based on knowledge of two thousand characters; for rural regions it varies between twelve hundred and fifteen hundred. With twelve hundred characters it is possible to read simple newspapers.

Literacy, the means of communication, is the essential tool which the people of China, or of any other country in the world, need for their advancement. With it, change is possible; without it, almost nothing is possible. China today can no longer be classed among the illiterate nations of the world. I noticed that even the pedicab drivers of Peking, formerly among the most ignorant people, today invariably were able to read instructions, directions I had had written out for me.

Next to "liquidation of illiteracy" in order of importance, comes the provision of universal primary-school education. Target date, according to Mr. Shiu Fang-chien of the Ministry of Education, with whom I spent a long evening going over these matters, is 1962; and he thinks they will make it. The target date for universal secondary education (that is, to college level) is 1967; and he rather doubts they can make that. "But if we don't get there by 1967," he said, "we will get there soon afterward."

I learned from Mr. Shiu that the total enrollment of primary-school students in the best year prior to 1950 was slightly more than twenty-three and a half million. Enrollment in 1960 was ninety-one million, an increase of almost 400 per cent. Secondary-school population during the same period has increased from something less than two million to thirteen and a half million (a 675 per cent increase). In spite of this advance, high-school education in China is still a privilege reserved for the more fortunate; but the "fortune" hinges not at all on financial affluence, but on ability and on geographical location. A large percentage of city children go through high school, but a very small percentage of rural children do, because of lack of teachers and schools. And as for enrollment in institutions of higher learning, it has risen from 110,000 to 810,-000—736 per cent increase. It is no longer one Chinese out of nine thousand, as it was fifteen years ago, who has the opportunity to go to college, but one in eight hundred. This figure is still very low. Entrance is determined by ability alone. Competition is usually stiff and the eagerness and quality of the students is correspondingly high.

It is probable that no country in the world is devoting so high a proportion of its national revenue to education as China. In 1960, 8620 million yuan ($3448 million), or 12.3 per cent of the national budget, was allocated to education and health, and of this 6,400 million yuan was for education. The proportion of the national budget in 1960 spent for education and health was 48 per cent *more* than that spent on China's military expenditure. And this is only *national* expenditure. More schools are run and paid for by local communities, communes and factories than by the Ministry of Education.

My own observations tended to confirm this. In almost every factory I visited I went through factory schools, which would be offering classes for adults all the way from ABC and first-grade arithmetic to college-level engineering. The same was even more true in the communes, though here the schools were generally of primary or secondary level. In Honan province I visited a large but quite poor commune, all of whose children were going to primary school. Sixteen of the schools were national; twenty-eight were run by the commune—and this meant providing the buildings and paying the teachers. Like others I met, the chairman told me he had learned to read and write only a few years ago.

"We believe that communes have a three-fold purpose: to develop agriculture, to develop industry, and to develop education. We have accepted education as part of our purpose."

What about the quality of education? Undoubtedly this varies enormously and is much more advanced in the cities than in the country. The primary schools I saw were lively, gay, and apparently a source of great enjoyment both for the children and for the teachers. Some of the secondary schools I visited, however, seemed to me rather stricter in their discipline than we would expect to see in America, and more on a par with English schools. In high-school science classes I saw in Peking and elsewhere the laboratory equipment and the quality of the experiments and demonstrations being conducted were also comparable to their English counterparts.

There is a strong trend toward science and technics. But at least one foreign language, and some art and literature, are required of secondary students. Most high schools offer both Russian and English as a foreign language and the child is free to make his own choice. I was told the proportion learning English a few years ago was higher than it is now but that it is still about the same number as are learning Russian. The Chinese fully realize their language is a difficult one for foreigners and the authorities hope that one day all Chinese children will be bilingual.

The standard high-school-level curriculum includes thirty-six weeks a year of classwork, four weeks for review and examination, and three weeks on some work project. There are eight weeks set aside for vacations. And one week is kept free—it may be granted as vacation or used for special study. The six-day week itself is divided into six or seven fifty-minute periods daily. Chinese school officials believe that children should never spend more than eight hours a day studying, and this includes homework.

From secondary level on, military training is included. All boys are taught drill and marksmanship. Propaganda and patriotism probably occupy a larger share of the school day than they do in the United States or Western Europe. In an earlier chapter I have described a kindergarten where the teachers discussed American imperialism with their four-year-olds. And Dr. T. F. Fox, in his article in *The Lancet* (see Part Seven, Chapter 27), expressed doubt as to the wisdom, for internes and doctors, of devoting as many hours a week to political studies as he found them doing.

It is not only a question of taking time away from other studies. The danger, it seems to me, is that an undue emphasis on patriotism, on understanding and adhering to the correct political line, will create an atmosphere where conformity will become more important than originality or independence.

This, I think, may constitute a serious danger for Chinese education, particularly in the years ahead.

On the other hand, it would be impossible to mistake the intellectual renaissance taking place today in China. It is nothing less than a cultural explosion. One of the problems I heard alluded to by every educator I talked with was that students, particularly at college level, studied too hard. They were not allowing time enough for sports and recreation, and this, in the view of school authorities, will hamper all-around development, and would, in the long run, lower intellectual achievement as well.

At Peking University the head librarian told me they were considering closing the library on Sundays in the effort to get the students out-of-doors. While it may be difficult for Americans to view this very seriously, the problem itself is intensely revealing. School for the Chinese does not mean football, or necking in the park, or ski trips. It means a chance to catch a grip on life. They throw themselves into the business of learning with a passion. And this is not propaganda from the Ministry of Education: I have watched it myself.

It is difficult for most of us even remotely to imagine the *hunger* that exists for education in countries in which until recently educational opportunities for most people were denied. This is not only true of China, but of Asia, Africa, and Latin America. Education, to millions of people, is the tool, the magic key that opens new worlds, new and undreamed-of opportunities. For an adult to learn to read is, as one Chinese said to me, "like a blind man being granted sight." The government of China, by providing the organization and leadership to make this expansion of education possible, has, in this respect alone, won the allegiance of tens of millions of people in China.

One aspect of China's educational program is the emphasis on productive work as part of the learning process. This applies at every level. On my visits to the communes I several times ran into classes of small children, with their teachers, busily engaged in "assisting" the communal farmers. These were children from city schools, having a whirl at pig-raising or poultry-breeding. Many secondary schools have established their own workshops which produce and market such things as fabrics, machine parts, condensers, preserved fruit.

Peking University is literally humming with such enterprises. In addition, the students are sent out for regular stints on the farms or in industry. At the Conservatory of Music I was told that these work periods provide an essential link between the art of the young musicians and the needs of the peasants and workers. On a visit to an Academy of Folk Opera in Kiangsu province, the director assured me that some of their richest discoveries in folk music were being made by students at work in back-country communes.

The concept of work-in-learning and learning-through-work is the present "mass line" of Chinese education.

It is not, it seems, a line that was easily arrived at. During the early fifties there took place a debate of long duration and considerable asperity among pedagogues and government officials over the general direction of education. One group favored a crash program which would turn out specialized technicians through cram courses (similar to the classes developed in England and the United States during the war, in which, for example, a student completely innocent of trigonometry, might learn celestial navigation in a couple of weeks). The other group favored a longer-range program aimed at "all-around" development of versatile individuals, capable (in the words of Engels) "of going over in sequence from one branch of production to another, depending on the requirements of society." According to this view, the student must not only learn how to wind the armature, but must understand Ohm's law and the theory of electromagnetic force.

By 1958, the "year of the great leap forward," the second group had carried the field and their position was made official in a report by Vice-Premier Lu Ting-yi, entitled, appropriately enough, "Education Must Be Combined with Productive Labor."

"We maintain," said the Vice-Premier, "that workers should be versatile in industrial production and peasants should be versatile in agricultural production; moreover that workers should at the same time be peasants and peasants should be workers. We maintain that civilians should take up military service and retired military men go back to production. We maintain that cadres should participate in physical labor and productive workers in administration. All these propositions are already being put into practice gradually. Measures such as these which involve both the division of labor and change of work conform to the needs of society. They are more reasonable than the division of labor under the capitalist system. They not only increase production but enable the state to carry out reasonable readjustment of the productive forces when this becomes socially necessary, without causing social upheaval."

We can catch a glimpse here of the virtuosity with which Chinese leadership has adapted a rather abstract program (that of Engels), formulated a hundred years ago in Western Europe, to the needs of China in 1960.

The "mass line," however, offers even greater advantages than mobility of personnel. It points a road, through education, to national unity.

For many centuries the curse of China has been its dual division, by geography and by caste. The geographic division separated north from south, east from west, rural from urban. The caste division separated the scholar from the landowner and the merchant, with their satellite bureaucracy, and the vast majority of the Chinese people, the peasants. But above all, it separated the hand from the brain.

Intellectual activity was the privilege of the upper caste. Work was the burden of the lower. Thus for a scholar to pick up a wrench or a screw driver was to demean himself; for a peasant to pick up a book was to overstep the laws of nature. Every feudal society has generated such a separation. The relics of it may still be found in Latin America, even in Western Europe. But in China the separation had acquired the rigidity of centuries.

When one bears this background in mind, the "mass line" in education acquires a new perspective. A great deal of criticism has been directed by Western writers to this mixing of education and physical work. Stanley Rich, as American Broadcasting Company correspondent in Hong Kong, for instance, wrote with horror at the Chinese attempts to wipe out the distinctions between mental work and manual work, between peasants and intellectuals. Mr. Rich (in the *New Republic*, January 5, 1959) draws the conclusion that "the worker . . . is stripped of his technical identity. He may be a teacher one day, a farmer the next, a steel-smelter the next."

But this, surely, is precisely what Western sociologists have so often called for, a move away from the increasing and deadening specialization of our way of life, which tends to limit human beings to an ever narrower range of experience.

Dr. Joseph Needham, of Cambridge University, takes a different view after seeing Chinese education for himself (in a letter to the *New Statesman*, London, January 31, 1959):

"In China in the olden days there was a great traditional aloofness of the scholars . . . from manual work—perhaps nowhere in the world was this more marked. Now the Chinese people are determined to overcome it. There may be exaggerations in particular times and places due to excessive enthusiasm, but the movement is fundamentally sound.

"All cultures and civilizations have suffered from this divorce of theory and practice. But the greatest thinkers, experimenters, and artists have always seen that only when the manual and the mental (or the intellectual) are combined in one individual's experience can mankind reach its highest stature. The combination not only brings true knowledge of Nature but also deeper sympathy with those members of society whose contribution must still for some time be primarily manual. . . . To think of manual work as a humiliating punishment is to misunderstand utterly what the Chinese are doing."

Peking University

Professor Wang Shê-chen, vice-dean of Peking University, and I were sitting in one of the smaller houses on the campus. The room smelled faintly of incense and the light filtered through the green foliage of the bamboo outside the window.

Founded in 1898, the university was, for many years, a hotbed of radical activity. It was sparks from on campus that kindled the May 4 literary renaissance just after the First World War. Mao Tse-tung was an assistant in the library. Founders of the Chinese Communist Party studied and taught here, and Lu Hsun, later known as the Chinese Gorki, was a professor of literature during the early twenties.

Since 1952, Peking has been graduating more technical and scientific personnel than any other university in China. There is a liberal-arts school, but more than 70 per cent of the nearly 11,000 students are in basic and theoretical science. The college of medicine and department of agriculture were transferred to Peking Medical College and Peking Agricultural College after the nationwide amalgamation in 1952.

The average age of entering students has gone down to eighteen, with the increase in secondary-school attendance. Students of the arts get a five-year course, science students, six—those who show special ability can stay on for three years of research.

Women make up 20 per cent of the student body, a lower percentage than in teacher-training and medical colleges. There are three hundred foreign students from thirty countries.

Tuition, rooms, books, and medical care are free. Those who are able to afford it pay 12 yuan ($4.80) a month for food, those unable receive a subsidy. Sixty per cent of the students get grants for food and clothing. The library they showed me contained over two million books—it is too small and a new library is about to be completed.

The top salary for teachers is more than that of the general manager of a steel mill. Depending on seniority, salaries range from 62 to more than 300 yuan a month; the average is about 200.

There is a two-month stint at "putting theory into practice" for students. Chemistry majors, for example, spend their time at a chemical plant; a physics student will work in metallurgy or electronics. The second month can be spread out over the school year, a few days at a time depending on the student's schedule. Professors go for one month, the ailing or aged being excused.

I talked to a number of students as I wandered with Professor Wang around campus, in the workshops, through the dormitories, and into the dining hall. We were joined by a young student who was an English major—he had studied English since secondary school and now he had a chance to make use of it.

In the women's dormitory I found four girls having a late lunch. Their room was extremely simple: four stacked bunks, one chair, and one table by the window. It was neat and clean. There were a few pictures, one of a film star, and on the table some bright artificial flowers. The girls were in their second year, studying Chinese language and literature. In another room a girl wearing glasses was reading at a table. She told me she usually got up at 5:30, had her first class an hour later, and went to bed by half-past ten. She put in eight hours a day in class and study.

As we were on our way to one of the workshops, a volley ball bounced out across the walkway. My young friend knocked it over to me and I volleyed it back across the net. This seemed an enormous joke and they were still laughing about it when we walked on.

There were twenty large precision lathes all in operation in the workshop. One of the lathe operators, quite the prettiest girl I had seen in China, told me she was nineteen and not a student. She was a factory worker who, as she put it, helped teach new students who never had done any mechanical work.

Strains of un-Chinese music grew louder as we went on. A band was tuning up in a wooden shack not far from the workshops. It sounded like a terrific row, everyone seemed to be playing something different. When I appeared in the doorway everything stopped except for the bugler who, with his back to me, played lustily on. They told me they were practicing a number called "The Young Commune Worker." In answer to my query about American jazz, they said emphatically, "Never!"

Loudspeakers blared a message over the campus. It was a report on the accomplishments of students who had gone to work on a commune. I noticed a few couples strolling along hand in hand. Only the other night I had read an account by a recent Canadian visitor who declared that young Chinese regard such displays as "decadent."

As we passed the water tower—like a phony pagoda temple—and circled the lake in the late afternoon sunlight, I brought up to Professor Wang the freedom issue. I told him that one of the things I was concerned about in China was the unanimity of thought, everyone thinking alike, talking alike. Any healthy society must make room for disagreement, and dissent should not be construed as disloyalty.

He hesitated before speaking. "Our society makes room for the man who disagrees as long as he doesn't attack socialism and the government."

"But that's just the point," I said. "There must be some people who disagree, why can't they express themselves?"

"Because this government is what the majority wants."

"Majorities can be wrong. All advance comes from a few who don't like things as they are. After all, *your* revolution was led by dissenters."

"You don't understand. You cannot realize what great changes and improvements have come to us. We know we are being led by those who have our interests at heart. Why should we want to attack them?"

"I don't say you should attack them. But you must acquire the habit of criticizing them. Your leaders today may be wise. But one day they will no longer be living. As you know, unwise people can attain leadership. What if you can't dissent then? This happened in Russia, no one was allowed to criticize Stalin, not even Khrushchev, until after Stalin was dead and many terrible mistakes had been made. Why were people not allowed to point them out?"

"What about *your* country?" he asked. "What about Senator Mc-Carthy and loyalty oaths? Isn't there hypocrisy in all the talk about freedom in the United States?"

So it went, around and around, alongside the lovely lake in the quiet sunlight—not angry or defensive, but our minds never quite meeting because our terms of reference and our vocabulary and concepts were so different. And above all, I did not have behind me the specter of previous degradation, oppression, and hunger. Success brings its own persuasion; and against this enormous fact of China's emergence into self-respect and health and vigor I could see how my talk about intellectual freedoms must appear to these young men as so much chatter, an idle and rather profitless verbal game.

"Come and see China again in a few years' time," Professor Wang told me as he said good-by, and added with a smile, "perhaps you will be convinced then that our system works."

My visit to the university and my discussions there left me with some mixed feelings. But what I did come away with was the picture of those students' faces. This remained more vivid in my mind than anything else. These were faces of happy people.

Never mind the buildings and the surroundings. Look at the human material. There is a vitality and enthusiasm as if life doesn't have enough hours for all that has to be done. Stand in the huge dining hall, like an overgrown armory, without tables or chairs, and watch the crowded little knots standing and eating from bowls which will be rinsed under a tap outside. Forget the drabness and look at these young people, and you will begin to understand China.

"What are you studying, what do you want to be?"

Physics, language teacher, hydroelectric engineer, geologist . . . the answers would come quickly, all stated proudly and directly. How many of them are sons and daughters of peasants, I wonder.

"Where do you want to work?" The answer, in different words, is always the same: "Wherever my country needs me most."

To me this at first seemed naïve and even perhaps a little insincere. But when I heard it many times I began to believe that they indeed meant it. Again the desire for collective advance rather than personal gratification.

I did not know then that I would, before many months, hear another young voice, in a very different country: "Ask not what your country can do for you, but what you can do for your country."

Long Live
the Dancers   23

There is for me a ponderous, heavy-footed quality to the slogan, "mass line in education." One thinks of an army moving over difficult terrain; gradually, by sheer force of numbers and determination, overwhelming the opposition. But China is a land in which there is always another surprise waiting. I thought I had the national education policies fairly well understood and neatly enclosed in my notes, until I visited the Conservatory of Music and the Peking Dance School.

This was like coming across a poem of Keats in the middle of a fifteen-hundred-page census report.

The discovery occurred purely by accident. No one had told me about either of these institutions beforehand.

One evening I happened to have gone to a performance of *Giselle* at a Peking theater. While the dancing was good but relatively undistinguished, the music was exquisite. I could not see the players in the orchestra pit, but kept wondering who they were, whether some group of French or Czech or Russian musicians might be in town whom I had not heard about. I asked a friend sitting by me and he said, "Go and take a look." And during the intermission I did. Not only were the players Chinese, they were all teen-agers! We always think Chinese children younger than they actually are; and these looked like twelve- or thirteen-year-olds, boys in neat white shirts and girls with ribbons in their hair. And here they were, re-creating that dated, stylized nineteenth-century French mood as if they had all just stepped off the Boulevard Saint-Michel.

I learned they were students from the middle school attached to the Peking Conservatory of Music. And I made arrangements as soon as possible to visit it.

Miss Yi, a quiet, rather prim young woman (my first female interpreter) opened the magic casements for me one morning and we stepped through a multicolored gate into the courtyard of the Conservatory. At once we heard a variety of different instruments, tuning up like a forestful of tropical birds at sunrise. The director met us, led us about the buildings. The place was alive with music, swarming with youngsters. We opened doors at random, saw eager-faced girls plucking hesitant notes from their violins or hard at work on piano-fingering exercises. Everywhere groups were practicing together—a string quartet in the corridor, an orchestral section on the stair landing; even in the balcony of the auditorium the woodwinds were having a practice session while the cast of an opera got set for dress rehearsal on the stage down below.

We stood at the back of the auditorium (brand-new, still not completely finished) watching the youngsters on stage. This opera, the director told me, was one the students had composed themselves, and were producing collectively, for their examinations. Girls were splashing paint on stage sets, an amateur electrician kept fussing with the lights, they were raising and lowering the backdrop, just like any college theater in the States. A boy in dark shorts, apparently one of the composers, was making vehement last-minute suggestions to several of the young ladies of the cast.

The title of the opera, I learned, was *Song of Youth*.

Even Caliope must have her facts and figures; and I sat down, after our tour of the premises, with the director.

The study of Western music was practically nil in China; the Conservatory is new since the change of government in 1949. They now have 370 students in the Conservatory and 470 in an attached middle school (high school). There is also a primary school under the Conservatory's direction. These two lower schools, which are open to children with special aptitude, provide, in addition to the regular school curriculum, a musical training which prepares them for entrance into the Conservatory.

As for the Conservatory itself, it has seven major departments:

Composition, Symphony, Conducting, Vocal, Theory and History, Piano, Folk and Chinese Classical Music.

Regardless of the field of specialization, every student spends a considerable amount of time on the folk and Chinese classical studies. There are also requirements in their school curriculum in literature, language, history, science, humanities.

Political instruction, the director told me, is considered an important part of the curriculum here, as in all other schools of China. Each pupil puts in six hours a week. How *political instruction* fits into the training of a musician, the director explained as follows:

In these courses a young person learns how to be a good servant of the people and not to work just for himself. This determination to use one's gifts for the benefit of others is further strengthened by trips made by the students to the factories and communes. They give performances and also share in the work. What kind of work they do would be governed by common sense: piano and violin players are not expected to ruin their hands by heavy work. It is generally considered that music itself is their contribution. Through close contact with workers and peasants, the students learn what kinds of music appeal to the masses. They themselves hear the local folk music. Sometimes students and peasants compete with each other in singing contests. The students also help with musical instruction in local spare-time schools. Sometimes, in this way, fine new talents are discovered.

The visits are reciprocal. Groups of peasants or factory workers are frequently invited to the Conservatory, to attend classes or performances, or to give performances themselves.

All the students in the Conservatory (and almost 80 per cent of those in the middle school) are boarders. And they come from all over China. Entrance requirements are extremely high and competition is stiff. There is no charge for room or tuition. There is a payment of 12 yuan a month ($4.80) for food, but this is covered by the school if the student or his family cannot pay. Ability to pay is not a factor either in selection or retention of students at the Conservatory.

The director agreed with my criticism that the buildings, much older than the school, were not altogether suitable. They are making alterations and additions as rapidly as they can. Equipment seemed to me ample. They have more than three hundred pianos, a large number of these being imported, and several thousand musical instruments, both Western and traditional. What impressed me particularly was their library, which contains 80,000 volumes dealing with music, both theory and history. Also 70,000 recordings of music from all over the world. Some 10,000 of these are European or American; but China is now producing its own Lp's.

In its ten years of operation this Conservatory has already shown some notable results. (There are two other similar schools: one in Shanghai, one in Tientsin.) I mentioned earlier that on the night of my arrival in Peking I heard a thoroughly professional rendition of several selections of Western classical music by a full symphony orchestra. At the Russian Tchaikovsky Competition several years ago the pianist who placed second to the American Van Cliburn was a nineteen-year-old graduate of the Peking Conservatory, Liu Shih-kun. I heard him here in Peking as soloist in the Schumann Memorial Concerto, and there is no question of his excellence.

Even newer than the Conservatory of Music is the Peking School of Dance.

They have three hundred students, equally divided between boys and girls, housed (in this case) in a brand-new building, designed especially for the school. Organization and general curriculum are very similar to those of the Conservatory. Here, too, the pupils are selected by rigorous standards, including local recommendation and examinations. Some 80 per cent of the student body come from families of workers or peasants. Dance students receive substantial extra privileges. Their food rations are almost double the ordinary. Vacation trips home are paid for by the school, and parents visiting from distant areas are put up at the school. Tickets to musical and dance events are free. The rigorous competition makes it fairly certain that the students, once admitted, almost always prove satisfactory and complete their training; and this is highly fortunate, because they told me it costs the state thirteen times as much to train a dancer as it does to train an engineer!

Like the Conservatory, the dance school gives instruction both in Western and Chinese disciplines. One department of the school covers Chinese folk dancing, acrobatics, and theater. The other includes Western ballet, foreign folk dances, and the Chinese *ballet de deux*, which is based on Western classical dance.

I learned from the director that there are schools similar to this one in several cities.

During vacations, he told me, teachers and pupils both go scattering to far areas, in the mountains and villages of remote regions, to find stories and dances of the local people which haven't come to light before. "We are rediscovering our national inheritance in folk art," he said, "and adapting it to the new conditions. But we are anxious to draw from all sources, from our own traditions and from the dance forms of other countries."

As an example of the adaptation of folk material, the director told me of a dance-drama just completed, *The Lotus Lantern*. This was based on an old story, common, with slight variations, to many different regions of China. But it had never before been danced. They worked out choreography based on the traditional patterns of Hopei province, took the main story line as told in Fukien province, but incorporated anecdotes special to other districts. So the old folk story, on the way to being forgotten, becomes a new national property.

After graduation most of the students go directly into performers' groups. But they also continue to teach. And the teachers continue to perform. They would consider it harmful to allow a separation between these two functions.

A beginning dancer draws a monthly salary of one hundred yuan, whether he is in a show or not. The wage goes up when he marries and has a family.

"Do experienced dancers earn a great deal more?" I asked.

Laughing, the director replied, "We are only six years old so we don't have any dancers *that* experienced. The difference in pay is not very great."

I spent many evenings, while I was in China, at performances of all kinds. China is bursting with theatrical, dance, and musical developments and almost every city has its "experimental" drama or dance group. There are more than four hundred and fifty opera schools scattered across the country, teaching traditional opera; and students in all these schools, as in the Conservatory and the School of Dance in Peking, receive room and tuition free.

Generally I found straight dramatic performances quite difficult because of language; and for traditional opera, which is the most popular entertainment form, I have not been able to acquire much taste. But the new developments in ballet, and especially the dance-dramas, I have found very exciting. These are usually based on Chinese folk stories, and they are learning to combine classical Chinese and Western ballet techniques, together with singing, in an extremely interesting way. One particular piece, *Maiden of the Sea*, seemed to me a superb work of art.

For a professional appraisal, however, of Chinese progress in the dance, I turn to an interview in the London *Times* of March 6, 1961, with Miss Mary Skeaping, director of the Royal Swedish Ballet, which had just completed a Chinese tour.

"One of the nicest things for me personally," said Miss Skeaping, "was to meet Tai Ai-lien, whom I had not seen since she studied ballet and modern dance in London during the thirties. . . . Today she is Director of the Peking Dance School and a Deputy to the National People's Congress, which means (imagine!) that the dance has representation in Parliament!

"The Peking Dance School began in 1954 with Russian teachers. Now they have their own Chinese staff. . . . The course lasts for seven years. The ballet dancers have achieved a high standard of technique in the short time since they began. They have assumed the Russian school of dancing completely and it seems to suit them very well. The girls have beautiful, easy back and arm movements and high extensions. The boys perform the showy demi-character type steps brilliantly. Their *pas-de-deux* work is also very good. Among the ballets in the company repertoire is a full-length 'Swan Lake' and 'Le Corsair' which they dance to their own symphony orchestra. . . . Music and dance is very active and interesting in China.

"I saw a beautiful, completely successful, full-length ballet . . . called 'The Woodcutters', produced by the Tientsin Light Opera Theater. It had Western type scenery with a Chinese flavor. . . . The costumes were entirely Chinese and very beautiful. The music combined Western and Chinese instruments in the way they are developing everywhere with great success.

"A fair scene in this ballet included a Chinese circus which was superb, with delightful folk dances. They have wonderful folk dances, and are doing fine work collecting them. Indeed, they are

basing much of their new musical development on this rich folk
tradition and seem likely to reap a big reward before long."

I wrote in my journal, after returning from the visit to the dance
school:

"One of the most delightful experiences I have had in Peking! It
gave me the same *lift* as the Conservatory. Here were children,
eager, healthy, intensely interested, being given what seemed first-
class training. . . . I was particularly struck by a group of teen-age
girls going through their basic skills. They had had about five years'
training. The control, the grace, the 'projection' seemed superb.
They work very hard. The eagerness and a kind of innocent fresh-
ness of these girls was delightful. I asked one girl of twelve to pose
for a photograph, which she did with neither coyness nor shyness.
They carried themselves already like experienced artists, and as a
matter of fact had frequently danced in choruses for performances
of the Peking Ballet.

"But perhaps the most remarkable sight I saw this morning was
a group of boys and girls studying Spanish dances. What gripped my
attention at once was the young instructor; he was twenty-two, Chinese, but Russian-trained. I would have sworn he was Spanish, and
he *was* Spanish in this classroom. By sheer volatility of feeling, he
communicated the Spanishness of these steps to his group of young
Chinese. It was an extraordinary and quite wonderful experience to
see this man live within these traditional movements, and from *inside*, not just by technique.

"The students had not yet quite caught it—perhaps they never
would—so alien, so extravagantly outgoing (for them). But it was
scarcely possible to watch them while the teacher was on stage—
this was an outstanding dancer in any language. . . .

"I felt that here, as at the Conservatory, I had seen something of
the very best of the new China, for me more immediately moving
than the march of tractors off the assembly line. Numerically, of
course, these two schools are small. But the standards are high;
their zest infectious. And the Chinese authorities say that their
aim is eventually to provide the chance of a musical education for
every child in China who shows a gift for it. . . . So, long live
the dancers and singers, on both sides of the great wall!"

Polonius and the Organization Man 24

"From now on your pen will be your weapon. Take as good care of it as a soldier does of his gun. See that your gun is always aimed at the enemy; take care that it never hurts your own comrades."

This piece of advice (according to an article in *Peking Review* for January 13, 1961) had been offered by the party organizer of a Shanghai steel mill to a young steelworker, who, having shown promise as a writer, was about to embark upon the high seas of literature. This was several years ago and the young man took the advice to heart and is now one of China's best-selling novelists. His name is Hu Wan-chun, and I had a long talk with him while I was in Shanghai. But before we come to that, let me note that several centuries earlier another piece of advice was offered to a young man about to set forth on an equally perilous journey: "To thine own self be true," said Polonius to Laertes, "and it must follow, as the night the day, thou canst not then be false to any man."

Here, in few words, is a central precept of the Renaissance which became, in turn, the ethic of the man-of-letters of the Protestant Reformation, and of the "enlightened" revolutions of the eighteenth and nineteenth centuries. Thomas Jefferson would have subscribed to this and so would Walt Whitman; and probably the majority of writers in the Western world of 1961 would be willing to claim it as their own.

It stands in apparently direct opposition to the ethic stated by the Communist organizer.

For Polonius, truth can only be discovered by the individual. There can be no vicar. That which is right is what *my* conscience tells me; that which is true is what *my* reason recognizes. It would be impossible for Polonius to say, "Take care that your pen never hurts your comrades," because he foresees that it may be necessary to deny his comrades. He may be obliged to go to the stake declaring that (in his judgment) the earth does *not* stand at the center of the universe and the Pope, after all, is fallible.

On the other hand, it would have been equally impossible for the Communist organizer to have said to the young writer, Hu Wan-chun, "To thine own self be true . . ." because he does not believe that truth is to be found within "thine own self." A truth, and the discovery of truth, does not come from reliance on dubious subjective feelings but from a study of objective facts. The same issue of *Peking Review* attributes the following comment to Hu Wan-chun himself:

Many people have asked me what I have done to improve my writing techniques and what is the "secret" of my creative writing. I have always answered: technique is important; but what is more important is a proletarian world outlook and mastery of the ideological weapon of Marxism-Leninism.

This sounds forbiddingly sloganistic and dogmatic. It may be noted, however, that by *Marxism-Leninism* the Chinese Communist would understand something like, "*a scientific view of man's existence and history*." Thus truth is to be approached through a study of history and man's response to his environment, which, by definition, can never be complete and which will always appear as the culmination of the efforts of many generations. It cannot be determined individually; but it can be understood and *acknowledged* by the individual. Once he has grasped the driving force and recognized the necessary direction—classless society emerging at last from millennia of class struggle—then he can achieve his own freedom through affiliation; through laboring to speed the advent of the coming synthesis. Here is a purported reconciliation of two generally irreconcilable elements: freedom for the individual, *plus* a theory of historical development, a process which can be delayed but can never be reversed. In this combination of history determined by law and the notion of revolutionary activity in which the individual can participate lies a large part of the enormous world appeal of

Marxism. Dimitrov, on trial, virtually certain of his own execution, still can yell triumphantly from the dock, "The wheel of history slowly moves on to the ultimate, inevitable goal of communism!" That certainly transcends and justifies his fate as an individual. He, too, can go to the stake, if need be; that is unimportant; but, unlike Polonius, he can never deny his comrades without destroying the meaning of his own existence.

To return now to Mr. Hu Wan-chun.

If we take the trouble to recast his words into more familiar terms, deleting the (for us) highly-charged adjective *proletarian*, we come out with this rather formidable statement:

"In creative writing, technique is important; but what is more important is a world outlook based upon a scientific view of man's existence and history."

Even as re-edited, this scarcely would appeal to Polonius, who would defend *individual conscience* against any scientific theory of history; and might even deny the notion of a direction in history altogether. Before we applaud too loudly, however, it will be well to note that modern Westerners may find themselves, in practice, closer to the position of Hu Wan-chun, than to that of Polonius. *To thine own self be true* epitomizes what David Riesman describes as the *inner-directed* man; but Riesman, and many contemporary scholars, regard the *inner-directed* man as a vanishing species, in the United States at least. He is being replaced, they tell us, by the *other-directed*, the *organization*, man.

Mr. Hu Wan-chun, as I can testify from my talk with him, is also an organization man.

I met Hu Wan-chun at the headquarters of the Writers' Association in Shanghai. This was a palatial building with paneled rooms, wide staircases, spacious gardens. It had been, I learned, the private home of a Shanghai capitalist. Did the Writers' Association confiscate the building? I asked. Far from it. They were renting it from the capitalist himself, for sixteen hundred yuan a month.

As for Mr. Hu, he is clearly one of the rising stars among writers. At thirty-one he is rich by Chinese standards. He wears silk shirts, fine new shoes, speaks humbly in an assured sort of way. Mr. Hu's is a veritable Jack London story of success.

Son of a steamboat hand and a maidservant, he went to work when he was thirteen as a laborer in the steel mills. By the time he was twenty-one he was still illiterate, could barely read the daily newspaper. But as an activist in the Shanghai Number 2 steel mill, he was appointed press correspondent, a job which he could carry out only by filing his dispatches verbally with the newspaper reporters. This aroused his determination to master reading and writing.

He began sending out short stories, finally selling one entitled *Repairs at the Rolling Mill,* an account of some workers who gave up their New Year's holiday to get a damaged rolling mill back in operation ahead of schedule. Mr. Hu's fellow workers liked this story, which inspired them to work still harder for socialism. The party organization now pushed Hu Wan-chun forward. He was sent to special cadre-training classes. He was put in touch with established writers. Other stories rolled from under his pen, bearing such titles as *The Man Who Works for an Ideal, On the Way to Work,* and *Red Flag.*

"His work is hugely popular," says *Peking Review,* "not least because of the sure touch in the way he deals with everyday reality. . . . All of Hu's stories have been closely linked with the current political battle. *Key,* which deals with the unmasking of a counter-revolutionary, was written during the campaign to weed out undercover counterrevolutionary elements. *Youth* tells about the dedication of a man's youthful years to the service of his country; it was written to educate our young people in Communist ideals. This topicality has trained Hu to be a rapid writer. During the big leap forward which began in 1958, life in China has moved with exceptional rapidity, and many activities have kept Hu busy; nevertheless, he has squeezed out the time to write eighty-five pieces . . . totaling some 400,000 words. Hu lives the life of his time with an infectious zest. The more stirring life is, the more prolific is his pen."

Mr. Hu told me that he is attached now, as a writer, to the steel mill where he once worked as a laborer. There has been an immense upsurge of writing in China, he said. Nearly every factory has its writing group. Many publish their own magazines. His job (aside from writing about steelworkers himself) is to help the younger writers, to participate with them in discussions and writers' workshops, and to criticize their material.

He is paid, he explained, by the Shanghai Writers' Association. Each member draws a monthly salary of one hundred yuan, more if the family needs it. The money is not regarded as an advance. For a movie scenario dealing with three generations of a steelworker's family, he received thirty-five hundred yuan, which he offered to return to the Writers' Association. They refused it.

This struck me as an extremely interesting organization.

"How does one get to be a member?" I asked.

"By election," Mr. Hu said.

"Election by whom?"

"By the Secretary's Department of the Association."

"And what makes a person eligible?"

"Any writer who has had a piece published is eligible. Membership is not open to amateurs or beginners. But if you publish just one article, provided it has a sound influence on the readers, then you would be acceptable. Some publish as many as two or three books and never become members of the Association."

"I see," I said. "And what if a writer, after he has become a member, writes a book which does not have a sound influence on the readers—is he thrown out?"

Mr. Hu said he was not. No one could be dismissed from the Association. "Some members," he added, "have written only one good piece and nothing of value since, but they are still members. No writer can always be good."

I inquired about royalties and learned that this system is based partly on word count, partly on sales. He cited, by way of example, one of his own novels that ran to 180,000 words. First edition was 20,000 copies, for which he received three thousand yuan. The second printing was 60,000 copies and he received two thousand yuan. The book is still earning royalties. Average first printing, he told me, is 20,000. But the *Song of Youth* (one of China's top sellers) started with a first run of 400,000 copies.

I asked if it were not true that writers were enormously better off than steelworkers.

He agreed that they were.

"There is a move on to reduce the royalty given to writers," he said. "One author recently earned 140,000 yuan for a single novel; it is now thought that writers ought to lower their scale somewhat.

The purpose of writing," he stated, "is not to make money, but to help the people understand what they are working for."

I spent another afternoon with a general secretary of a chapter of the Writers' Union, who came to my hotel in Wuhan. (Some writers' organizations are called "Associations," some "Unions.") The official, Mr. Han Pei-chun, was a somewhat nervous individual who chain-smoked and kept his foot jogging at high speed throughout our two-and-a-half-hour talk. He fanned himself with compulsive haste. I gathered that his job entailed a good deal of pressure; in the United States we would have said he might soon suffer from an ulcer.

"There's so much going on in China," said Mr. Han, "no matter how many writers we had, we couldn't cover it all. There is absolutely no dearth of material, it is bursting all around us every day. We pay the expenses of any member who wants to travel to get local material. Our books are read by workers and peasants and what we write must sound real to them. We must live with the workers and peasants to feel their life and to get the true story, otherwise they would reject what we write.

"Of course, writers have to do their share of political study, too. Before a writer is accepted into the Wuhan Writers' Union, he must have shown himself ready to reflect the ideals of China in his writing. For this, personal experience is not enough. All writers must study Marxism-Leninism and the works of Mao Tse-tung and must raise the level of their political understanding. Only thus," he said, "can they write with more sensation." ("Sensation" was the rendering of the interpreter.)

"Writers must also learn from our culture of old. Everything they write must be acceptable to Chinese readers, must reflect China and the Chinese style. But neither must they neglect their knowledge of other countries."

"What foreign authors do they generally read?"

"Shakespeare," said Mr. Han. "They read a great deal of Shakespeare. And Schiller, Ibsen, Gorki, Turgenev."

"Any contemporary English or American writers?"

"Certainly. Many different ones. Of course, many of our writers have gone through college and would have studied courses in world literature."

As it was clear that Mr. Han was not too well posted on modern Western writing, I offered a question on Chinese folk traditions, which he more readily took up.

"The Writers' Union," he said, "is encouraging our members to go out and discover these traditions for themselves. We want them to scatter into all parts of the country to discover not only the old stories, but the living poets and storytellers of those distant regions. Sometimes members of the Musicians' Union go along with the writers. The musicians transcribe the tunes, and the writers record the words. In this way thousands of ancient songs and ballads are being preserved. We are rediscovering traditional opera, too; that's a most important branch of our work. The people love to see performances of these old operas. But the Kuomintang paid no attention to all this," he added. "Many wonderful things have been lost."

My discussion with Mr. Han ended, I am sorry to record, on a note of disharmony.

I raised the question of the writer's freedom to write as he wished without being bound within the tenets of an official philosophy. Some of the greatest writing, I pointed out, had been in protest against existing conditions. Writers are the conscience of the people and must be free to criticize.

Mr. Han responded at great length, and to start with, at least, we both exercised considerable restraint. His answer, in general terms, went as follows:

"It is difficult for Marxists and non-Marxists to find common ground on this subject. You have your world view, we have ours. Ours is that writers must deal with the world as it is, they must reflect the realities of our time. We in China have come through a vast revolution. The job of writers is to help root up remnants of old ways of thinking. It isn't a question of freedom to 'write as one pleases,' it is a question of expressing the national desire to build a society in which there will be equality between people and in which everyone works for the benefit of all, rather than for himself alone. Such a change cannot take place easily. We have many who still hanker for the old, exploitive days. But if you had known the horror of life in pre-liberation China, you would not now be speaking as you do of 'freedom.' There was no freedom of any kind then. Today there is the freedom to live. And our writers are free to write what they feel, provided they accept the basic concepts of our new society. Why, if you told members of our Writers' Union that they were not free, they would laugh in your face! This is something bourgeois writers cannot understand! The fundamental question remains: *Is their work loved by the masses?*"

I thought I had him there.

"Many great writers were not *popular*," I said. "What of Marx himself? His works were not even read or understood by the masses, let alone loved."

"It is true that Marx was ahead of his time," Mr. Han replied, "but if the masses had been sufficiently educated to read him, they would have understood and loved his works. . . ."

"What suffocates me," I burst out, "is the universal approval, the monolithic unanimity with which everyone talks and thinks in China today. Surely it is the duty of writers to raise the level of intellectual exchange, to inquire, to dissent, to disapprove if need be, not always to speak the acceptable words. . . ."

Our argument continued for a long while, each of us repeating himself, neither one really meeting the thought of the other. It thus ceased to be a discussion, and I will close my account of it here, allowing myself (naturally) the last word.

Mr. Han, to me, personified the weakness of the writer's position in China today. In many ways writers are being encouraged. They are urged to step forward out of the ranks of industrial and commune workers. They are offered financial security, prestige, opportunity for study, even considerable freedom in choice of material. But always the proviso remains in the background, their work must have that certain "sound influence on the readers." And who is to judge the influence? And who is to turn thumbs up or thumbs down when it comes to "electing" new members into this marvelous club which is the Writers' Union? If I were a Chinese writer, I think I would not care to have Mr. Han as arbiter of my destiny. This, despite the fact that I felt him to be honest, devoted to his work, thoroughly efficient—only a little too official, too humorless. And perhaps, like some of the writers Mr. Hu Wan-chun had spoken of, a bit too well paid, at least by contrast with the mass of China's peasants and workers. What he was doing wasn't that *good*; it couldn't have been. . . .

We parted rather huffily. I accompanied the general secretary down to the front door—at least I could say good-by politely—and he climbed into a new copper-green, chauffeur-driven Austin which was waiting at the curb. We shook hands, but between us there was a wide gulf of nonunderstanding.

Mr. Han was a bureaucrat and these are to be found on both sides of the great wall. In his presentation of the writer's role he was faithfully reflecting the official outlook of the government and Communist Party. Thus at the Third Congress of Chinese Literary and Art Workers, held in July when I was in China, the vice-chairman of the All-China Federation of Literature and Art Circles, Chou Yang, set forth the task of artists and writers as follows:

Literary and art workers, in their role as drummers of the times, are using every form of literature and art to give a sharp and prompt reflection of our people's struggle against imperialism, and in defense of our motherland and world peace, and the new people and new things which are constantly appearing on all fronts of construction in our motherland, enthusiastically depicting the growth of the new in the midst of struggles, showing the positive role played by literature and art in close co-ordination with politics. . . .

In a later portion of the same report, Mr. Chou Yang discussed the famous policy set forth by Communist Party Chairman Mao Tse-tung, several years earlier, of letting "a hundred flowers blossom and a hundred schools of thought contend." This had apparently led to certain misunderstandings, which Mr. Chou clarified as follows:

Regarding style, form, genre, and subject matter in art, however, we are for greater variety and encourage originality, while opposing monotony, rigidity, and narrowness. Our principle is the integration of uniformity in political orientation and variety in artistic styles.

And further:

When we let a hundred flowers blossom, poisonous weeds may appear in the guise of fragrant flowers. Therefore, letting a hundred flowers blossom and a hundred schools of thought contend necessarily involve two opposite and interrelated aspects: letting a hundred flowers blossom and eradicating the poisonous weeds.

One of the characteristics of Chinese Communists is that they say exactly what they mean.

No human activity can be judged outside of its historical context. The writers of America, England, France would find the intellectual atmosphere of China today far too uniform, and unbearably suffocating. But our historical moment is not theirs.

Here is a nation emerging from illiteracy; a vast awakened population hungry to find itself in art, writing, and drama, setting out upon a forced march of essential construction. Everything is urgent and must be treated urgently. Action takes top priority. If the dikes are not built, the dams not completed this fall, a million people may die in the floods next spring and drought next summer. This is a stirring period for the Chinese, an epic era; and a war of immense proportions is being fought against poverty, disease, and ignorance. Will the writer pitch in or won't he? He will. He will sit down in the back of his jeep to write the exploits of construction heroes and commune brigade leaders, just as Tom Paine once sat down at a drum head to write, "These are the times that try men's souls. . . ."

Particularly in such times it is well to give credit where credit is due. More classics of Western literature are presently being read in China than at any previous period in history. These are not smuggled in. They are pushed by the government, the school system, the Writers' Union. As Mr. Han himself told me, Chinese writers are reading nineteenth-century European playwrights and novelists. And Shakespeare. "A great deal of Shakespeare," he had said. A list of recent translations from English reveals twelve editions of William Shakespeare, including both sonnets and plays.

Polonius will thus have a chance to speak his piece directly. He may rise up at a conference of the Chinese Writers' Union some day, after the urgency of their crash construction program has eased off a little, to discuss the problems of truth in literature and the writer's responsibility to mankind. Whether he will be welcomed there with the same courteous and impartial attention which we would expect for him at an assembly of, shall we say, the TV

Writers' and Directors' Association of Madison Ave
tion which had best be set aside as, for the time bei
ble.

The Urban Communes 25

In many cities communes adapted to urban condi-
tions have made their appearance. In the beginning this was by no
means a mass movement, as it has been in the countryside, but an
experiment, rather cautiously undertaken.

The Communist Party Resolution adopted on December 10,
1958, approaches the matter in the following terms:

"There are . . . certain differences between city and countryside.
Firstly, city conditions are more complex. . . . Secondly, socialist
ownership by the whole people is already the main form of ownership in the cities . . . therefore the switchover of cities to people's
communes inevitably raises some requirements different from those
in the rural areas. Thirdly, bourgeois ideology is still fairly prevalent
among many of the capitalists and intellectuals in the cities; they
still have misgivings about the establishment of communes, so we
should wait a bit for them. Consequently, we should continue to
make experiments and, generally speaking, should not be in a hurry
to set up people's communes on a large scale in the cities. Particularly in the big cities this work should be postponed except for the
necessary preparatory measures. People's communes should be established on a large scale in the cities only after a rich experience
has been gained and when skeptics and doubters have been convinced."

By June 1960, when I arrived in Peking, there were already more than a thousand urban communes in operation, with a membership of fifty-two million. There seems little doubt that such communes are here to stay.

I visited a number of them in different cities of China and I have selected the Red Flag People's Commune of Shenyang as being fairly typical, in its organization and activities, of the whole group. In size this happens to be relatively small—84,000 members. (I visited a commune in Harbin with 182,000 members.)

I met the director, Mr. Kao Peng-fei in a clean, whitewashed upstairs room. Because of the heat, some bright toweling had been thrown over the leather chairs. There were no pictures of Mao, no slogans, no banners on the walls, which added to its unstandardized, and therefore welcoming, appearance. But it was a poor room nonetheless. The rough boards had just been sprinkled to keep down the dust. One geranium grew in a pot. The lampshade was of brilliant Mexican pink.

Mr. Kao struck me as one of the many eager, professional Communists who form the backbone of the Chinese revolution. He spoke deliberately, thoughtfully, taking his time to think out his answers. There were, as usual, two other persons in the room, who said nothing at all, but they took no notes.

The Red Flag Commune, Mr. Kao told me, was established in September 1958. It had passed through various stages of development and experimentation but everyone believed it to be now on the road to a healthy growth. There were 17,383 member families, 84,375 people. (It is significant that I always have to ask for the total population. This has been true in every commune, they always think in terms of families, not total numbers.)

Mr. Kao proceeded, interrupted by occasional questions from myself, "Many of our familes live in very old houses, forty years old or more. These are very poor and they will have to be pulled down as soon as we can arrange for new buildings.

"Altogether, seventeen workshops belong to the commune, employing 6500 workers, of whom 85 per cent are women. The men work in the larger state-owned factories also situated within the commune area. In our commune workshops, we make 259 different kinds of products. One hundred and fifty are for local, home use (consumer goods, I presume he meant), eighty are parts for the factories, and the rest are for several rural communes outside the city.

"Total value of our production has risen very fast," said Mr. Kao, "as more and more women joined and as our skills increased. In 1959 total production was 18,660,000 yuan ($7½ million). This year our target is 150 million yuan, more than eight times our last year's product. From the figures so far, we believe we will reach this target. The value of our production is determined by standards set by the government, based on national average production costs.

"The Red Flag Commune operates nine primary schools (ages seven to twelve), four middle schools (thirteen to eighteen), and twenty-one spare-time schools for adults. We run thirty-two nurseries and kindergartens of medium size and 130 small nurseries. In all we look after nearly 17,000 children. Of course, we also have our own hospital and many clinics and health stations. Also we have three markets, and 137 dining halls which provide meals for some 49,000 people a day. The rest eat at home, or in state-owned factories where they work."

I asked how he thought the communes had started.

"It seems to us the people's commune system didn't come into being all of a sudden," said Mr. Kao, "but that it came out of the political awareness of the people, out of the kind of economy we have in China." And he quoted from the General Line: "*dwo kwai hao sheng*—more, quicker, better, more economical." The higher level of political understanding, particularly among women during the great leap forward, the excitement and enthusiasm all made it difficult for housewives to sit quietly at home—they all wanted to come out into life and take part. No matter how little they knew or how unskilled they were, they wanted to contribute what they did have.

"So they began to set up little workshops together, in the streets, in people's houses, anywhere there was a spare room. And they began, as we say, 'with empty hands,' that is, without any financial help from the government. Then, of course, because the workers were housewives, something had to be done about the children. They started kindergartens and the nurseries, and then the canteens so the women wouldn't have to cook after they went home.

"At first," Mr. Kao continued, "all this was handled by street committees in the various neighborhoods. But there were many difficulties and it became very complicated, there were so many things going on at once and overlapping one thing over another. At this time we began to hear about the rural communes and some of us went to see them, to see if we could use some of their ideas for our situation in the city. Many of us thought an equivalent movement could be started and we heard this was actually being done in some places. So we went ahead and that's the way it got started here."

I asked, "How much resistance did you encounter?"

He thought for some time before he answered, "I'm not sure one can say there was resistance, although many people doubted whether we could make a success of the idea. What you must realize is that 85 per cent of our members are housewives, women who were very isolated, and rather fed up with household chores. They were eager to start something new which would bring them out into the world more. But there was a lot of fear, too, and people looked down on women's capacities just because they were women, even the women themselves. 'No good can come out of a group of women, they can't do anything!' And we certainly ran into problems because the women had so little experience and didn't know what they could do—or what they couldn't, either. We made many mistakes sometimes because we tried too much, and other times because we didn't try enough.

"You must remember, too, that membership in the communes is *entirely voluntary*." He spoke with great emphasis. "No one was forcing these women to join. So those who weren't sure waited to see what the others would do and how successful it would be. When they were reassured, they applied for membership."

"*Applied?*" I repeated.

"Oh yes; membership is by application. Each new member is discussed beforehand and must be approved by the management committee. You see," Mr. Kao concluded, "if those of us who were starting out had forced or overpersuaded the others to join and then had made a mess of it, what a terrible discouragement that would have been! The last thing we wanted was a group of disgruntled women, they could have ruined the whole project."

I asked, then, if we could set out on a tour of the commune. Our first stop was at what they call a "service station." No, they were not selling oil and gasoline. The Chinese service station is the Chinese commune equivalent to an American shopping center. There was a row of small booths, each offering some particular service. Here was a tinker repairing pots and pans. Next door was an artist hand-lettering notices and posters. Then watch repairs, keys made, the cobbler's; there was a service station (staffed by women who enjoy sewing) for altering or repairing clothing. There was an electric-fan repairer, a laundry, a place where movie tickets could be bought, a bank, a post office. There was also a rental shop where bicycles, tools, electric motors, etc., could be rented by the hour, day, or week. All these services are run on a no-cost, no-profit basis. The women attending them are paid the same wage as those in the workshops. Prices were very low. I asked how much it would cost to patch a small boy's trousers; about ten fen, they said (four cents); to launder a shirt, four fen (one and a half cents); to rent a saw, fifteen fen (six cents) a day.

Farther down the street we came to a machine shop. This was a very simple structure, built, Mr. Kao told me, by the women themselves. None had ever laid brick before, but two old craftsmen from the old people's home had showed them how. (The men were too old to walk around, so sat in chairs directing operations.) Walls seemed a bit out of plumb, doors not very square; but here it was, housing over 150 housewives all hard at work with power machinery, hack saws, drill presses, stamping machines, armature winders. I also noticed two first-rate precision lathes.

Over the clatter of the machines, I shouted, "Who started this?"

Mr. Kao pointed to a red-cheeked woman of about thirty-five, adjusting a drill press. I went over and yelled, "May I ask you some questions?"

She nodded vehemently, wiped her hands on her trousers, and led the way to a window where the din was slightly less.

"What gave you the idea of a machine shop?" I asked.

"Oh, I didn't do it all by myself. There were twelve of us." She waved over to another woman to join us, and the two of them talked, sometimes one, sometimes the other. "It was in 1958 when there was all the talk about everybody pitching in, the great leap forward year. And we wanted to do *something*. So we went to a small bicycle factory nearby and asked if we could make parts for them and they said yes."

"Did any of you have any experience, or money?"

"No. But the factory lent us two hundred yuan, and another factory that makes generators did the same. We needed a stamping machine, and we found where there was one, but not working; it was all broken down. Then the bicycle factory helped us repair it and gave us a few lessons on how to use it. So we started. We worked at first in a shed at the back of my house."

I asked, "What did the neighbors think?"

"Oh, they were very sarcastic. *'Now let's see how these women will do!'* " Both women burst out laughing and one added, "Till the Party heard about us and sent some technical people to help us. From then on it went pretty well. We filled the orders for the bicycle and generator factories and others came in and more and more women wanted to join."

"How many women do you have working now?"

"Four hundred and fifty."

"Four hundred and fifty! Here?"

"Oh no, they don't all work here. We have another workshop we built a little distance away. And, of course, we work two shifts in each place. We only work four or five hours a day, the women have housework to do at home or children to see to. Oh, we feel very confident now. We feel we could do almost anything."

"How much did you turn out last year?"

"Well, it was only in September 1958 we began. And in 1959 we really were just getting under way. We had to take time off to build the workshops, and find the brick and all that."

I tried again. "But how much did you actually produce?"

"Our income?—what we got paid for our products? In 1959 one million, thirty thousand yuan" ($257,000).

"And what do you expect it to be this year?"

"If the whole year keeps on like the first half, ten million yuan" ($4 million).

"Who paid for the machinery?"

"We pay for it, out of our profits." One of the women pointed to a new drill press. "That's paid off completely. The others we're still paying for little by little."

"Did you borrow any money from the government?"

They shook their heads. "We only had the loans from the bicycle and generator factories, four hundred yuan in all" ($160).

"What's the average wage you pay these women?"

"We don't pay them. This is a co-operative. We all get the same wage. Usually, a little over thirty yuan a month" ($12).

"Do you use piece rates or an hourly wage?"

"At first we tried piece rates. It didn't work. Caused lots of trouble and argument. Now it's all hourly."

"How old is your oldest worker?" I asked. "And how old is the youngest?"

"Forty-five. And nineteen."

I thanked them and after a quick handshake they went back to their machines.

Urban communes are now an established and growing feature of Chinese life and one can legitimately ask what effect they are having on the national economy. By altering the status of millions of women, both national productivity and national income have been increased. The output of the urban communes in 1959 was reported as 2 billion yuan ($800 million) and they expected to at least double it in 1960. This is not a large sum in relation to a national productivity of over 241 billion yuan. But this addition to national production, it must be remembered, has been achieved with virtually no capital investment by the state.

The urban communes, like the rural, have been largely self-capitalizing. The cash required to get the workshops going is very small. Built of old brick, often by volunteer labor, the buildings have cost almost nothing; the essential tools with which to get started can be purchased on installments without interest charges; the raw materials, or components for assembly, can be supplied by already-established state-owned factories in the neighborhood. Their main resource, of course, is manpower. But the problem of cash reserves for wages has been solved in many cases by persuading the women to postpone their wage payments until the income begins to come in, the amounts postponed being added to future wages when the workshop is under way.

Thanks to this ability to rely on the workers' co-operation and the over-all let's-do-it-ourselves attitude, very high production returns are obtained with almost no capital outlay. I have never seen its like in any other country in the world.

I was interested to learn when talking to the women in the workshops that the economic theory behind all this was quite well understood by them. A great deal of educational work must have been done to make them accept the postponement of pay and be content with low wages that rise (when they do) so much slower than the increase in production. Not only are millions of former housewives gaining some technical skill, but they are also becoming something of practical economists at the same time.

It is quite true that the monetary incentives are small, and unlike the communes in the countryside, nurseries, kindergartens, and food in the canteens are not free. Nevertheless, millions of women are earning money for the first time; this, in itself, has created problems. Not only are they eating more, but their increased purchasing power has created shortages in consumer goods—watches, cloth, bicycles, even movie and theater tickets. This fact was brought home to me almost as soon as I arrived in Peking, where I noticed a marked increase in the number of women shoppers in the crowded department stores since my previous trip to China. It was the same in other cities. It is claimed that retail sales throughout the country rose from 54.8 billion yuan in 1958 to 63.8 billion in 1959, and by the time I left in 1960, it was estimated that there would be a still sharper rise for that year.

The urban communes have come up against some other problems. One of them is the shortage of administrative personnel. A single commune may have several hundred dining halls, nurseries, and kindergartens; a hundred or more workshops; and, if near the countryside, it may have a sizable agricultural area to administer. Then there are the service stations, clinics, homes for the aged. The directors are often young men and women who have had little training in administration, but are managing with hard work somehow to keep things going.

Economic conflicts arise occasionally between the plans of the central government and the desire of local communes to develop in their own way. The communes find they can sometimes sell products at a higher price to a local user than to the government, and this raises difficulties. The problem of keeping accurate statistical records and financial accounts has also arisen through a shortage of accountants. And, without doubt, there must be many older people who view the changes of family relationships, the communal dining halls, the increasing independence, not only of women but also of children, with great pain and feel that all the "old traditions" of China are being swept aside.

These are largely problems of expansion, growth, and change, not of failure. Further economic problems are quite likely to arise as the communes expand in numbers and their full impact is felt on the national economy.

In his analysis of the urban communes in *Far Eastern Economic Review*, Hong Kong, September 29, 1960, written after a firsthand study in China during 1960, Professor Chao Kuo-chun had this to say:

. . . The facts that membership in a commune is voluntary, and that the pace in setting up communes in many cities has been gradual, help to ease the difficulties.

. . . But from the impressions I gathered during the visits to the communes (such as the busy activities at the workshops, systematic plans explained to me by the street committees, and the confidence shown by the commune leaders), it would not surprise me if this new form of social organization steadily progresses in China.

It would not surprise me, either.

China ☆ Kaleidoscope 3

Notes from My Journal and Letters

Letter to Elena   August 10

The Chinese are extraordinarily unself-conscious with each other. I have told you this before, but I am repeatedly struck by how much like members of a large family they are.

Yesterday on the train—it was very hot—the two men who were sharing my compartment took off their trousers and sat comfortably in their underpants, and I did the same. Very sensible and comfortable. I had a momentary shudder thinking of what would happen to me if I took my trousers off while traveling on the Southern Pacific! This morning I shared the washroom with a young woman. We smiled good morning to each other and went on with our respective tooth-brushings and washing without concern.

This sense of being among a family has its sad side, too. I feel, however friendly they are, that I am still on the *outside*. As when staying with a large and affectionate family, they can do everything to make one feel at home, but one is never one of them. I think a Westerner could be in China for years, perhaps all his life, but would never escape the sense that he is suspended between two worlds, never able really to enter and become part of the stream of Chinese life.

The Sad Story of Lizzy

One Sunday afternoon in Shenyang I wandered to the sports ground and watched a local track meet, the athletes of Shenyang against a neighboring city. I sat down for a while next to a school-boy of about twelve or fourteen, with a Red Pioneer scarf round his neck. After a few moments he summoned up enough courage to ask me in very hesitant words, "You speak the English?" I said yes, and we got on fine. He was in his second year of English at middle school. He had a pile of his schoolbooks with him and he fished out his English-language textbook, and later I bought a copy of the same book from a local bookseller.

I studied the book. I expected to find a tirade against the wicked imperialists. But that word isn't mentioned. It takes the children through the months, the seasons, the days of the week, and has several simple and harmless little stories about ping-pong matches; catching sparrows; and the new Yangtze bridge. This was too good to last. Toward the end of the book, (Lesson 35) comes the story of Lizzy. Lizzy was a poor English girl of twelve who lived in a big city in the north of England. Lizzy led a sad life:

Every morning Lizzy went to work in a cotton factory. The workshop was dark and noisy. The air was hot. Little Lizzy was afraid of the big machines. And noise and the hot smell of the room made her ill.

In the afternoon Lizzy went to school. Miss Brown, the school-teacher, did not like her because she was poor. Very often Miss Brown punished her and made her stand in class. She did not know how hard Lizzy studied. She did not understand how tired Lizzy felt. She did not help her.

Lizzy loved to work, but she hated the factory. She loved to study, but she hated the school and Miss Brown.

Today many children in capitalist countries are like Lizzy. They are poor and miserable.

Quite good, but about eighty years out of date.

Enemies and Friends

The Chinese, Pearl Buck once said, make the finest of friends and the most terrible of enemies.

I think she is right; and this says so much.

Égalité

Assumptions of our superiority lie deep. Today, Yen and I were talking together in the hotel lobby and a visitor, rather upper class and just out from Europe, came up. "I wonder," he said, "whether your man could help me a moment?" I felt Yen stiffen. He was not "my man," he was Yen Chao-hua, citizen of the new China. I caught his eye and winked, and he relaxed.

This is an *egalitarian* society. You feel it everywhere. I watched some soldiers at drill one hot day. They were smart as could be, officers barking orders. Then drill ended and all, officers and men, raced each other to the tubs of fruit juice. No priorities.

Every foreign country here entertains on its "national day" and last week one of these receptions was held in this hotel. I was standing near Chou En-lai and I watched while a waitress with a large tray of drinks came up and offered one to the Prime Minister. They stood chatting together as easily and naturally as could be, the girl without a trace of shyness or servility. With respect, of course; but the respect, I felt, was both ways.

It was probably easier to maintain this sense of equality and comradeship when they were guerrillas in the mountains; more difficult now as this country becomes an elaborately organized modern state. But they are trying. It is a pretty well-established rule that everyone in authority must spend at least one month a year in the lowest rank of the organization of which he might be the head. The director of the steel company I visited told me he had just finished a month's work as a puddler. All officers, generals, even the chief of staff, spend one month a year in the ranks as ordinary GI's. I asked about this; it struck me as being a little theoretical and phony, and that the other privates would probably make it pretty easy for him.

Not a bit, I was told. No special privileges. The point being that it gives the GI's a chance to see whether the general running their show is the kind of man they can trust. *They* are inspecting *him* for a change!

The other day I was with Yen in a taxi, and the driver seemed puzzled about the way, and I didn't think he was driving very well either. I asked Yen whether he was a new driver. "No," Yen said, "he isn't ordinarily a taxi driver. He's in the taxi administration office." This was one of the bosses, doing his month's stint.

Cultural Shock

I talked with an English businessman today in the hotel. He had just arrived and he was very unhappy. Never having been to China before, he was suffering from what I believe psychologists call "cultural shock." Many Westerners feel this when they first come to China, especially the lone traveler.

I remember, on my first trip in 1957, feeling for several days painfully bewildered, disoriented, unmoored; all I wanted to do was to run away. A Swiss radio man I met in Hong Kong told me he was driven nearly mad with loneliness and misery when he first arrived in China. The disorientation comes, I believe, from suddenly finding oneself in a totally alien environment, with no point of contact with anything in one's normal life.

Added to this is the sense of being precipitated into complete illiteracy. Between you and the swirling crowds around you there is a total gap in communication. Street signs mean nothing. You cannot ask for the simplest necessities. Even the name of your hotel (if you can remember it at all) is beyond your ability to pronounce in a way that would be recognizable to anyone else. I remember being impressed (while in this state of initial bewilderment) with absurdly irrelevant things: a half-obscured sign above a shop written in *English*; a bath fixture with an American trademark. Even a French clock in a shop window, I recall, gave me an obscure comfort.

So I didn't deride this Englishman's misery. Instead I took him for a walk and showed him the Imperial Palace. But he wasn't very interested. In the park we sat on the ground sipping tea and he told me about Huddersfield, where he was born, and how he didn't think much of this Chinese tea; it wasn't nearly as good as the tea they have in Huddersfield.

The Inside Change

Today, Ku (my interpreter) and I were having lunch together at the Shung Lung restaurant near the Tungan Market. We talked about some of the changes that have taken place in China—I was thinking especially of the disappearance of tipping, begging, stealing.

The absence of beggars, Ku told me, was easy to explain, everyone now has work so there's no need to beg. Those who are sick and cannot work are looked after. As for tipping, this is now a country that tries to share everything, he said. (The English would call it a "fair-shares-for-all" country.) The slices may not be very large but everyone believes he's getting more or less an equal share of the pie. So there are no longer rich people who can buy extra attention or flattery by tipping. And apart from this, though Ku did not put it into these words, accepting handouts would injure their pride.

But the lack of stealing? That puzzles me. Like everyone else who comes to China, I have grown careless about my possessions. I come back to my room to find I left money strewn over the desk; I never bother to lock my door, though in this hotel there are keys, which is more than can be said of the place I stayed in three years ago. The wife of one of the British Embassy officials told me the other day how she had some jewelry stolen on a visit to Hong Kong simply because she had forgotten that people elsewhere lock up valuables. I asked Ku how the regime established this moral sense, what fearful penalties are imposed on those who do steal.

He hesitated. He was obviously puzzled how he was going to explain it. "I don't think these changes have come because of laws. You can't change people by passing laws. We have laws, of course, against stealing and so does every country. And, don't think stealing doesn't happen, because it does, although not very often. I think your question shows that you haven't really understood the Chinese revolution. The change inside people that now makes stealing rare—well, that change *is* the revolution; that is what the revolution is, and what it did to us. We can't think of stealing from others any more than we would steal from our own family." And then Ku made a little gesture with his hands which conveyed much more vividly than any words how impossible it was to explain this to someone who had not been through it.

Forlorn

(A poem found on a factory wall newspaper)

> The leadership is too careless
> of my well-being; comrades
> are not in the least polite to me.
> In my work group all
> simply criticize me! Who then
> can I say is close to me?

Letter to Elena   July 11

This evening I've been to Wu's house—I mentioned him to you some time back. He's the chap who studied in England and then went to the University of Chicago. His family was rather upper crust before the Communists came and he must have had quite a time adjusting.

I've seen Wu once or twice since I first met him and have always enjoyed meeting him. He's youngish—under forty is my guess—very learned, and is something important in one of the government departments, though what he actually does he never lets on. They asked me to dinner, but I wasn't sure how much this would strain their food situation (this reminded me of wartime England), so I had dinner at the hotel and went after, taking along a bottle of *mao tai* for good cheer.

It was a lovely evening, though still very hot. We sat on wicker chairs in their little courtyard unshelling salted peanuts and sipping *mao tai* and fanning ourselves. Mrs. Wu called to the two girls to come out of the house to greet me, which they did very demurely —I almost expected them to curtsy as in a Victorian drawing room

—and then they went off to bed and Mrs. Wu left with them. Wu and I didn't talk much, just sat fanning ourselves and helping ourselves to the *mao tai.* I was glad. I've been talking too much lately, and been too much talked to.

All I wanted to do this evening was to sit and watch the great lazy moon creep over Peking. Wu is companionable and sensitive. He has a thin, intense face, the face of a scholar, serious in repose but quickly responsive. The Chinese are comfortable to be silent with—they don't feel they have to talk. I was quite content to watch the silhouette of the curved roof with its little goblins perched along the rim as the moon rose behind it. The courtyard, the graceful roof-line, the golden moon, the *mao tai*—it was almost too Chinese. But then Wu spoiled it all. He began about America. The same old record. I have heard it a thousand times already. Why does America do this? Why does America do that? American imperialism. . . . He went on and on. The thought of America *preys* on the Chinese so.

Wu disappointed me. I expected something a little more perceptive from him. He has a subtle and sophisticated intelligence and I usually find I can really *communicate* with him. He's lived in the West long enough to know our idiom of thinking. But here he was giving me the same old rehash like any junior Party member who had never been outside his village.

"Oh, for God's sake, Wu!" I said, "you talk and talk about America but you know you aren't really saying anything. You people seem to know only what's wrong with America. You know the latest crime statistics down to the last child murderer. You probably know exactly how many drunks there are in Los Angeles. You know all about our juvenile crime and how we cheat each other and all about Little Rock. . . ." I spoke sharply.

I told him what he was saying might all be true, but add it all up and it still doesn't spell America. And it was my turn to go on and on, partly out of irritation and disappointment, partly out of a sudden ache of nostalgia. And a homesickness for you and Anne was mixed up in this too.

When I finished Wu didn't say anything for a while and then he said, "I don't think you realize why we feel as we do; and I think you should."

I felt we would get into a deeper and even more self-defeating

wrangle so I didn't go on with it and in a little while I left. Wu
wanted to walk with me to Wang Fu Street where I could catch
the trolley bus back to Hatamen, near the hotel, but I said I'd
rather walk by myself, which was unkind. He came to the doorway
to say good-by. He is rather slender and he stood there blinking
through his glasses. He suddenly seemed touching and vulnerable.
I felt (as I always feel when I have been cross with a Chinese)
that I had been crude and something of a bully. I wanted to say
something to put it right, but didn't know how, so I said good-by
and went off. I found my way through the maze of *hutungs*. Quite
deserted now, all the children indoors and asleep. I didn't take the
trolley but walked home. There was a line from *Family Reunion*
that kept running in my head (I may not have it right): "Something important should have come of this conversation." And it
should, but it didn't.

P.S. Next Morning

I've just sent a note round to Wu's house. "I am sorry about
last night. I was defensive and irritable. Sometimes one needs to
talk; sometimes for the sake of one's sanity one needs to be silent.
Our needs last night just didn't coincide! I shall be leaving Peking
soon. Can we meet again before I go?"

*

I never had an answer to my note.

But during the next few days one sentence of Wu's kept recurring to me: "I don't think you realize why we feel as we do and
I think you should."

He was right. Wu tried to tell me something and I shut him off.
If I was to try to understand China I should be less argumentative,
more ready to listen. Though I did not see Wu again (I learned
he had left Peking) there were others. From then on I kept notes.
I made a file of the newspaper articles and clippings (mostly American) that were sometimes thrust into my hands. Those who (like
Wu) had been educated in America, and Chinese historians, were
especially anxious to explain the Chinese position; and sensing that
I was willing to listen, they often spoke at great length. Some were

passionately angry, some were legalistic, as if they were speaking from a lawyer's brief, some were jeering, and some spoke with restraint; and further comments came to me in letters after I returned to America. From this mass of material I have written what might be called "The Chinese Case." I have tried to represent as clearly as I can what the Chinese feel about America and why. And this case forms the next part of this book.

PART SIX ☆

The Chinese Case 26

We believe, Mr. Greene, you came to our country in order to understand us. Many come already convinced that anything to do with communism is evil. They see what they want to see. They are appalled at our poverty, our backwardness, and all that is ugly and mean in our country. They are quick to notice our mistakes. They will carry back with them what they came with, for where in the world cannot a visitor find unpleasant and unworthy things if that is what he is looking for? And others, thoughtless people, idealists, come disposed to see only what is good. They have an idealized picture of the new China in their minds, and they are in some ways more difficult to deal with than the others, for when they can no longer pretend to themselves that everything in China is wonderful, they turn on us bitterly and reject everything because we disappointed them.

We want neither to be prejudged nor idealized. We would like to be seen as we are—a people trying, and with great effort, to lift ourselves from a state of poverty and feudalism into a modern nation with equal opportunities for all.

The lines of communication between China and America are now so tenuous that they hardly exist at all. We read with amazement what is said about us by writers living in Hong Kong who have never been here—never, at least, to the new China, which bears so little resemblance to the old—or by China "experts" sitting in New York or Washington. We do not think that any writer can comment with understanding upon a gigantic social revolution such as ours without seeing it himself. That is why our government offered visas to American correspondents a few years ago and invited them to come and see for themselves what we are trying to do. But what happened? Your State Department immediately announced that they would not be allowed to come. And since then many eminent American citizens and some of their most trusted political leaders, even the wife of one of America's greatest presidents, were told they must not travel to China. Why this reluctance on the part of the American government to allow its citizens to see for themselves? Is it possibly a fear that some of the myths about us might be dispelled?

All we ask of our visitors is that they come ready to report honestly whatever they find. Is that so much to ask? But let these writers always bear in mind that no country can be understood except within the context of its own historical development. They will not find parallels here for many of the social or political institutions that you have developed in America or England, but that does not mean that those we have developed are not better for our own needs.

The improvement of relations between China and the United States is essential if there is to be a way for all of us to continue to live peacefully on this earth. And it is for this reason that we here in China feel it necessary to expose to the world the real nature of American policy, which prevents this necessary improvement. This policy in its most belligerent form has been in existence since the day we formed our government in 1949. But it was, long before that, based on exploitation and assumptions of superiority which deeply wounded the self-respect of our people.

We have read reports of a television program broadcast in London by the BBC. This was the interview you had with Premier Chou En-lai. As you must know, in England this interview was followed by a discussion in which an American correspondent took part. Presumably he was invited to present the "American view." He appeared puzzled as to why China should feel unfriendly to the United States.

"We never tried so hard to help another country as we did China," he told the British audience, "and therefore, when China suddenly turns against us and becomes hostile to us, we find it a little difficult to understand."

When Americans say, as they often do, with a look of innocence, "We haven't done anything to China," we can only answer, "*Look at history.*"

Let us recall that when the West "opened up" China (as your historians say), the Chinese society was the oldest in the world. It was a feudal society, and as such an oppressive one, but it is quite wrong to think, as many Westerners do, that through the centuries China was constantly in turmoil, always being pulled apart by factions, war lords, and civil wars. Cut off from other countries, China enjoyed long periods of peace. Isolated by poor communications, most of the local needs were met by local craftsmen. There was little money and there was little need for it and among the people there was a general dedication to a humane regard for the needs of others. Confucianism influenced our people greatly and though it arrested needed reforms, it taught them a universal sense of mutual responsibility. From across the years our poets and artists speak to us of our culture moving from generation to generation, from century to century.

Change, it is true, had to come to China; it was long overdue. But the change should have been our change, accomplished our way, not yours. Into our society, for purposes of commercial plunder, with an unbounding certainty of its moral superiority, the West brought strife and great misery to our people.

When your Western traders first came to China it was not at our invitation; we were not eager for it but were prepared to engage in foreign trade if your merchants would obey our laws. In our commerce with the West at this time we were the suppliers of tea, silk, and fine porcelains, but there was little that China required from the outside world and the Europeans had to pay in silver for what they bought. The British, however, found something else to make up for their not inexhaustible supplies of silver. From their recently subjugated colony of India, they brought in opium, a drug banned by the Emperor in 1729 and which, since then, was little known in China.

British shipments of opium from India began arriving in 1781, and it was not long before this trade had become highly lucrative. By 1800 our Emperor attempted to reinforce the prohibition and penalties for its importation were strengthened. However, profits now were so great that it became impossible to prevent corruption and smuggling at all levels; the trade continued to grow. In 1800, 280,000 pounds of opium were imported into China. By 1838 this had risen to 5,600,000 pounds.

Although the bulk of the opium trade was in British hands, Americans were also involved. Turkish opium was carried to China in American vessels, and, just as in the case of the British, the profits made in opium served as the foundation for some of the large American trading organizations that later dominated the foreign commerce of China.

By 1839 the Chinese government, aghast at the physical and economic effects of the opium trade on the people, made another desperate effort to suppress the trade. An Imperial Commissioner, Lin Tse-hsu, was sent to Canton. By this time even the British superintendent of trade in China, Captain Elliot, had written to his fellow countrymen in Canton saying that "this course of traffic was rapidly staining the British character with deep disgrace." On June 3, more than 20,000 chests of opium, on orders of the Imperial Commissioner, were publicly destroyed in Canton. This led to aggression, and in 1840 the British declared war. Thus began the first Opium War, which lasted for two years.

The result of this war, which ended in our defeat, was the humiliating Treaty of Nanking. Under its terms the Chinese government had to pay a large indemnity for the opium seized; the port cities of Canton, Foochow, Amoy, Ningpo, and Shanghai, occupied by foreign troops, were to be opened to British trade and residents were exempted from Chinese law. We had to give up our island of Hong Kong. This was the first of the humiliating "Unequal Treaties," imposing conditions which no country would ever have dared to offer a vanquished European nation.

Perhaps the cruelest of all the conditions imposed on us by this treaty was that the Chinese government was prevented from ever levying more than a 5 per cent import tax on foreign goods. This opened up our country to a flood of cheap manufactured articles and prevented the development of our own industries. Countless thousands of our artisans and small traders were brought to ruin and starvation by this decree.

This, then, was our introduction to a century of exploitation by the "civilized" and "Christian" nations of the West. We submitted because we had to, for we were not a military power. But do you not suppose that our sense of justice was outraged?

China, still embittered after this defeat by the British, was forced to cede even wider extraterritorial privileges to America under the Treaty of Wanghsia and additional special rights for American ships on China's internal waterways. But the British were not to be outdone. Under the "most-favored-nation clause" they immediately claimed the extra benefits extorted by the Americans.

In 1853 the British, Americans, and French took over control of the Chinese customs. In 1856 a dispute about a flag (a dispute in which we still think we were in the right) was made the excuse by the British and the French to declare war on us again. Once more we were defeated; once more we were required to pay a war indemnity. Under the Tientsin Treaties which followed, both the opium trade and missionary activities were legalized and the foreign control of our customs was made perpetual. Under this treaty foreign powers were permitted to export our very people to their colonial territories for use as cheap labor. When the Chinese Court, shocked by the harshness of the conditions, delayed ratification, the war was resumed and Western forces occupied Peking, looting and burning the famous Yuan Ming Yuan Summer Palace and committing barbarous outrages against our defenseless people. As the nineteenth century drew to a close, the Western powers grabbed further territorial footholds. It became a veritable scramble. In 1897 Germany seized the naval port of Tsingtao; in 1898 she took the Shantung peninsula. Three weeks after this treaty was signed Tsarist Russia forced a lease on the naval base of Port Arthur and the commercial port of Dairen. Within five days Britain appropriated the naval base of Weihaiwei and a few weeks after that France seized the South China bay of Kwangchowwan. "Spheres of influence" were assumed by each of the powers.

And what about America? Did she protest? Did she attempt to curb the rapacity of her allies? Did she condemn the wanton sacking of Peking? No protests, no condemnations. In 1899 she pronounced the famous "Open Door" policy. This policy did not in any way dispute the advantages wrested from China by the others, all that this policy required was that the commerce within each "sphere of influence" be equally open to all. While able to assume a pose of "not wanting any of China's territory," America was able to reap all the financial and commercial advantages gained by the other nations by force. "Hitch-hiking imperialism" one of your writers has called it!

How readily some Americans see themselves playing the heroic and magnanimous role in history—how rarely do they know the real facts! When our people, provoked beyond endurance, rose up in what is known to you as the "Boxer Rebellion" in 1901, a further infamous treaty was imposed upon us; foreign troops (including the 15th United States Infantry Regiment) were stationed in our capital, the Chinese were excluded from parts of the city, and another huge indemnity was levied on our people.

But if there was even a small amount of good will that survived the exploitation of a century, it was finally dissipated by the support by successive American governments of Chiang Kai-shek. Do Americans not realize with what hatred we recall those last dreadful years of Chiang's regime? Do they not know of the countless thousands killed or tortured by Chiang's secret police? Or of the fortunes made by his politicians while our people everywhere were starving? Can they not realize that this persistent support of a man who was inflicting the most gross injuries on his own people convinced us that American policy was designed in no way for our benefit but to prevent us from controlling our own country? In spite of countless official reports, articles by reputable American reporters, eyewitness accounts, documented proof of his cruelty and corruption, Washington has persisted to this day in supporting Chiang with money, with arms, and with all the moral support that she can muster.

*

The first and central issue which divides the United States and China and prevents any lasting settlement is the issue of Taiwan. Over this the United States government has thrown a cloud of confusion and complexity. Finding themselves in a politically hopeless and embarrassing position, politicians and writers jumble facts, raise political issues which do not pertain, rewrite history, and hide their own previous statements from public view. But the facts themselves are quite simple. Let us outline them without feeling. Let us segregate the myths from reality.

The Myth: Taiwan was never part of China.

The Reality:

> 607 A.D. (1344 years ago) The Sui dynasty Emperor sent an official to administer Taiwan.
>
> 1360. During the Yuan dynasty Taiwan was governed as part of Fukien province.
>
> 1624. The Dutch (and for a while the Portuguese) occupied portions of the island.
>
> 1662. The Dutch were driven out by the Chinese.
>
> 1684. Taiwan's status was raised to that of Prefecture.
>
> 1885. Taiwan became a province.
>
> 1895. Taiwan was ceded to Japan after China's defeat in the Sino-Japanese war.
>
> 1943. In the Cairo Declaration, Britain and the United States agreed that "all territories Japan has stolen from the Chinese such as Manchuria, Formosa and the Pescadores shall be restored to the Republic of China."
>
> 1945. (July 26) The Potsdam Declaration confirmed that "the terms of the Cairo Declaration shall be carried out."
>
> 1945. (August 30) The Chinese government proclaimed Chinese sovereignty over Taiwan.
>
> 1945. (October 25) The Japanese Governor formally handed back Taiwan to China.

The Myth: That the Taiwanese are "not really Chinese."

The Reality: More than 90 per cent of the eight million odd people who were residents of Taiwan belong to the Han (Chinese) nationality. In addition there are about 200,000 Kaoshan people living in Taiwan. Like the forty or more other national minorities on the mainland, the Kaoshans are a member of China's big family of nationalities. To say that the residents of Taiwan are not Chinese is as absurd as to say that the residents of the United States are not Americans because the Indians were the original inhabitants!

The Myth: That the Taiwan people never "really wanted to rejoin the mainland."

The Reality: In an official memorandum (April 18, 1947) the United States ambassador to China, Leighton Stuart, had this to say:

"The Formosan Chinese greeted the surrender of Japanese authority to the Chinese with immense enthusiasm on October 25, 1945. After fifty years under Japanese control . . . they welcomed a return to China, which they had idealized as the 'Mother Country.'"

and again:

"Japanese rule had sharpened their sense of Chinese nationality and race. . . . Formosans have been ambitious to see Taiwan become a model province of China . . . proud of their race and nationality, proud to be taking part in the National Reconstruction."

The Myth: That the United States has never conceded that Taiwan was a province of China.

The Reality: On January 5, 1950, the United States Secretary of State announced:

"The Chinese have administered Formosa for four years. Neither the United States nor any other ally ever questioned the authority of that occupation. When Formosa was made a province of China nobody raised any lawyer's doubts about that. That was regarded as in accordance with the commitments. The United States is not going to quibble about the integrity of the position. That is where we stand."

The Myth: That the United States never promised not to interfere in the Chinese civil war.

The Reality: On January 5, 1950, President Truman said:

"The United States had no predatory designs on Formosa or any other Chinese territory. The United States has no desire to obtain special rights or privileges or to establish military bases on Formosa. . . . The United States Government will not pursue a course which will lead to involvement in the civil conflict in China. Similarly, the United States will not provide military aid and advice to the Chinese forces on Formosa."

The Myth: That the existence of a Communist government on the mainland gives the United States a moral right to disregard previous pledges.

The Reality: The United States Secretary of State on January 6, 1950, declared (after the establishment of the Communist government):

"The world must believe that we stand for principle and that we are honorable and decent people and that we do not put forward words, as propagandists do in other countries, to serve their advantage, only to throw them overboard when some change in events makes the position difficult for us."

and again, five weeks later (February 9, 1950):

"Taiwan has been included into China as a province since 1945. For the United States Government at this date, to seek to establish a non-Chinese administration on Formosa, either through SCAP or a United Nations or Far East Commission-sponsored plebiscite, would be almost universally interpreted throughout Asia as an attempt by this Government to separate Formosa from China in violation of its pledges and contrary to its long-standing policy of respecting the territorial integrity of China."

> *The Myth: That to allow Taiwan to fall into the hands of the Communists would seriously endanger the military security of the United States.*

> *The Reality:* In a State Department Policy Information Paper, written in 1949 and presented to the Senate Committee on Armed Services and the Committee on Foreign Relations in June, 1951, it was stated categorically:

"Formosa has no special military significance. It is only approximately 100 miles off the China coast. . . . China has never been a sea power and the island has no special strategic advantage to the Communist armed forces."

In other words, the return of Taiwan is a *political*, not a *military* issue.

> *The Myth: That Chiang Kai-shek still plans to launch a successful return to the mainland from Taiwan.*

> *The Reality:* No one really believes this any more, not even Chiang's own people. As early as October 5, 1958, a Taiwan military spokesman reported to the London *Observer*:

"We haven't seriously considered invading the mainland for at least five years now. We have to keep up the pretence, of course, largely for domestic consumption—a matter of morale and discipline."

We wonder whether the taxpayers of the United States realize how much it costs to keep up this pretense. In the authoritative *Foreign Affairs Review* of Washington of April, 1958 (with which Allen W.

Dulles, the head of the CIA, is connected as a member of the Editorial Advisory Board), a report from Taiwan stated:

"Chiang Kai-shek maintains about 800 generals and admirals on full pay waiting for commands, a skeleton officialdom for the provinces, and the Central Government of China."

And all to "keep up morale and discipline"!

The Myth: That the United States government is seeking only a "peaceful solution" to the problems in the Far East.

The Reality: The scene: the subcommittee of the Committee on Appropriations, House of Representatives, Washington.

The date: January 26, 1954, seven months after the end of the Korean War.

Representative Frederick R. Coudert: "Did I correctly understand you to say that the heart of the present policy towards China and Formosa is that there is to be kept alive a constant threat of military action vis-à-vis Red China in the hope that at some point there will be an internal breakdown?"

Mr. Walter S. Robertson, Assistant Secretary of State for Far Eastern Affairs: "Yes, sir. That is my conception."

Coudert: "In other words, a cold war waged under the leadership of the United States, with constant threat of attack against Red China, led by Formosa and other Far Eastern groups, and militarily backed by the United States?"

Robertson: "Yes . . ."

Coudert: "Fundamentally, does that not mean that the United States is undertaking to maintain for an indefinite period of years American dominance in the Far East?"

Robertson: "Yes. Exactly."

We have referred to the State Department Policy Information Paper of 1949. It is a very remarkable document. It is worth careful study. One of the most interesting parts of the document is where the State Department excellently argues against the very policy that was subsequently pursued, and forecasts what the consequences of following such a policy must be.

". . . Sending in troops [into Formosa], supplying arms, dispatching naval units or taking similar action would:

(a)   Accomplish no material good for China or its Nationalist regime;

(b)   Involve the United States in a long-term venture producing at best a bristling stalemate, and at worst possible involvement in open warfare;

(c)   Subject the United States to a violent propaganda barrage and to reaction against our 'militarism, imperialism and interference' even from friendly peoples, and particularly from Chinese, who would be turned against us anew;

(d)   Eminently suit the purposes of the USSR which would like to see us 'substantiate' its propaganda, dissipate our energies and weaken effectiveness of our policies generally by such action."

What sort of regime on Taiwan is it that the U.S. government is supporting? A well-documented characterization of the Kuomintang may be found in another publication by the State Department, which we believe is not widely known to the American public. We refer to the report by Ambassador Leighton Stuart on massacres of Taiwanese by Kuomintang forces, contained in the White Paper on United States Relations with China published in 1949.

Taiwan had greeted its reunion with mainland China after Japanese surrender with "immense enthusiasm." The islanders were, however, quickly disillusioned. They found themselves virtually excluded from all government posts. These were awarded to Chiang's friends from the mainland. Once again it was the old Kuomintang story of nepotism and corruption. Smuggling and official black-marketeering were widespread. The economy declined. Health services broke down. Cholera epidemics occurred for the first time in thirty years.

Resentment against Chiang's regime became more and more intense. On February 27, 1947, a crowd of some two thousand Taiwanese, in protest at the fatal beating of a woman cigarette vendor by Chiang's police (for selling "untaxed cigarettes"), marched "in orderly fashion" to the Governor's office, where they wished to submit a petition. Without warning a machine gun opened fire on the crowd and a number of the people were killed. This unprovoked shooting was the signal for a citywide outburst of anger. American officials on Taiwan reported that though there was rioting and protesting, the people refrained from looting. Nor were they armed. The next few days there was general disorder. Buses filled with squads of government troops armed with machine guns swept through the streets firing indiscriminately. The military were evidently trying to frighten the public into obedience. In one incident observed by American officials a long burst of machine-gun fire swept a crowd without warning, felling at least 123.

On March 8, General Chang Wu-tao made the following categorical statement: "The demands for political reform are very proper. The Central Government [Chiang's government] will not dispatch troops to Taiwan. I can risk my life to guarantee that the Central Government will not take any military actions against Taiwan." This statement was made when the speaker must have known that Kuomintang troops in great numbers were about to land. After dark that same night Chiang's troops began to disembark and for the next nine days troops poured in from the mainland to Taiwan.

"Beginning March 9th," continues the United States White Paper, "there was widespread and indiscriminate killing. Soldiers were seen bayonetting coolies with no apparent provocation . . . soldiers were seen to rob passersby. An old man protesting the removal of a woman from his house was cut down . . . anyone thought to be trying to hide or run was shot down. Looting began wherever the soldiers saw something desirable . . . a systematic search for middle school (high school) students was begun . . . students were beheaded. . . . Many bodies began to float into the inner harbor at Keelung. . . . In rural areas . . . mounted machine gun patrols were observed shooting at random in village streets. Manhunts were observed being conducted through the hills." Established critics of the government, middle-school students, teachers, lawyers were seized and executed. "The continuing presence of fresh bodies in Keelung Harbor and other evidence indicate that the eliminating of the informed opposition is continuing. . . . It is reported at Tapai that although shots and screams in the night have become less frequent they continue. . . ."

We have given this brief account of the terrible massacre in Tai-

wan because we think that you and others in America have never
realized the real nature of Chiang Kai-shek's government. The sequence of events in Taiwan, first the bleeding of the economy by
Chiang's officials and then the mass executions of those who dared
to rise up in protest, came as no surprise at all to the millions who
for years suffered under his terrible regime on the mainland, a
regime sustained and supported by the American government.
When America supports the Chiang Kai-shek regime as representing "free China," it discredits her name throughout Asia.

Even the most naïve of Chiang's followers must today realize
that no amount of money, guns, or planes will ever set Chiang back
on the mainland into a position of power. The accumulated hatred
of more than six hundred million Chinese has swept this tiny
remnant from the stage of history. This remnant is irrelevant. It
is on the mainland and not in Taiwan that history is being written
and lived, and the little gang on Taiwan will one day be as completely forgotten as the band of Royalist refugees who fled America
to Canada at the time of your revolution.

When some Americans ask how many people the Communists
in China have "executed," do they ever show any curiosity about
the millions of dead, wounded, and murdered in the civil war on
the mainland, the direct result of American aid to Chiang? Does
anybody wonder how long the fighting was prolonged after VJ Day
because of the billions of dollars in aid, military and civil, which
were handed to the Kuomintang? A few voices were raised from
time to time about the American taxpayers' pouring money down
a rathole; but has there been one public figure of first stature who
has asked how many Chinese were killed because of the shipments
of guns, of planes, of tanks that Washington sent to China between
1945 and 1949?

Even now the aid continues. American planes piloted by Kuomintang officers have bombed our cities from Taiwan, where, but for
this aid, Chiang Kai-shek would have long since been removed.
Your government may have succeeded in keeping "free China" in
the United Nations, but it has at the same time succeeded in earning the contempt and hatred of the Chinese people.

The "Taiwan problem" is a problem of America's own making.
If wiser decisions reached earlier regarding "noninterference" in

China's civil war had been adhered to, Taiwan would now be peacefully and happily a part of the mainland of China. By sending the
Seventh Fleet to intervene in our civil war, American policies have
kept alive political problems which would have found their natural
historical solution. There would now be no embarrassing pretense
that Chiang Kai-shek's clique "represents" China at the United Nations. The United States would not today be committed to a lost
cause. By financing and arming the remnants of Chiang's discred-
ited regime America has only multiplied her own difficulties and
insured her own future humiliation. The Seventh Fleet is still today
enabling Chiang to harass our coastal shipping, interfere with
peaceful commerce, and even sink our civilian ships. And for what
compensating advantages?

Your Mr. O. E. Clubb, who served for twenty years as an official
in the United States Foreign Service in Asia, was Consul General
in Peking, and later became the head of the Office of Chinese Affairs in your State Department, had this to say in an article printed
in 1957:

> The United States' political position on "the China question" is
> crumbling, for it was built on sand. . . . Through our own policy . . .
> we have been entrapped and isolated on the China coast. Never be-
> fore in our history have we joined vital interests to so barren and ill-
> omened a cause as that of Generalissimo Chiang Kai-shek. Our China
> policy has poisoned our Asian relations for years; now we discover that
> it has brought us to a position vis-à-vis China from which we can neither
> advance nor retreat with profit.

We believe that when the American people learn the facts they
will insist that past errors be corrected and that steps be taken to
bring their government's policy in line with realities. As long as
your leaders and your public opinion veto any gesture of reconciliation, any correction of historic error, no settlement between us
seems likely. But we are a patient people and time is on our side.
We are willing to wait until some new generation of Americans are
prepared to sit down with us as equals. We will not talk with those
who try to "negotiate from strength," or attempt to intimidate us
with guns of their fleet. Do not expect us to talk under the shadow
of missiles trained on our cities from a dozen bases. Do not speak
to us in tones which imply that you are very nearly perfect and

that we are almost wholly malevolent. But we are ready to sit down with you at any time as equals and discuss our problems like men.

*

While the Western press has been rather silent on the background of the Taiwanese dispute, there has been a great deal written about "Chinese aggression"—first in Korea, more recently in Tibet, India, and Laos.

With respect to Korea, the facts, as we Chinese record them, are the following: Fighting in Korea started on June 25, 1950. No Chinese forces were involved at the time. Indeed, the Indian ambassador to Peking, Mr. K. N. Pannikar, reported in his book *In Two Chinas*, "that United Nations intervention in Korea caused no particular reaction in China. . . . During the first three months of the Korean War, there was hardly any noticeable military activity. . . ."

Upon the outbreak of hostilities in Korea that June, the American Seventh Fleet was ordered to "protect" Taiwan, and has been so engaged ever since, thus providing Chiang Kai-shek with a shield from the shelter of which he has carried on an endless series of raids and nuisance attacks against coastal shipping and against the mainland. Deployment of the Seventh Fleet constituted a direct intervention by the United States in the Chinese civil war. Had it not been for this intervention, the civil war might have ended in that summer of 1950—with the removal of Chiang from his last foothold on Chinese soil. This in turn would have terminated Chiang's claim to a seat in the United Nations.

In October 1950, American forces began their drive north to the 38th Parallel, which had been established by the Allies after Japan's surrender as the dividing line between North and South Korea. Certain American generals spoke publicly of going all the way to the "Manchurian border."

On October 2, Premier Chou En-lai called in the Indian Ambassador to inform him that "If the Americans crossed the 38th Parallel, China would be forced to intervene in Korea." Mr. Pannikar records how he then asked Premier Chou whether China would intervene if only the South Koreans crossed. The Premier was emphatic: The South Koreans did not matter, but American intrusion into North Korea would encounter Chinese resistance.

This warning was passed on to the British Minister in Peking, and was relayed to Washington. It was ignored. There were many who believed the Chinese government was bluffing. The 38th Parallel was crossed and a week later Chinese troops entered North Korea.

We do not believe that any other nation could have stood by and watched the encroachment of an obviously hostile army—whose government was supporting our chief enemy on Taiwan—to its very border.

For ten years the Western nations in the UN refused to discuss China's credentials because (so went the argument) the People's Republic of China had been an aggressor in the Korean War and was therefore not eligible for the UN.

That myth has now been shattered by a report prepared by the Rand Corporation, who were commissioned by the United States Air Force to make a dispassionate examination of why China entered the Korean War.

The Toronto *Globe and Mail* on February 22, 1961, commented editorially on the Rand Corporation report: "General of the United States Army Douglas MacArthur . . . Far East commander of the United Nations forces . . . wanted to cross the Yalu into China and crush the Communist armies. . . . This week the general once more bewailed the cruel fate that stopped him. . . . It [the Rand Corporation report] claims that China neither participated in planning the initial North Korean aggression nor intervened later as the result of Russian pressure but was 'rationally motivated' when it moved its armies into Korea after apparently ignoring the first three months of war there. The Rand Corporation study concludes that the Korean War provides an instructive warning on the dangers of a limited war exploding into a thermonuclear war. . . . China intervened because it assumed from belligerent statements issuing from General MacArthur's headquarters in Tokyo that he intended to invade China. . . . General MacArthur this week reaffirmed that this was his intention and that it remains an unfulfilled ambition."

So much for China's "aggression" in the Korean War.

Regarding Tibet, it ought to be made clear, first of all, that Tibet has been, until very recently, one of the most isolated and backward regions of the world. A system of serfdom actually prevailed there until it was abolished by the Chinese government in 1959. The so-called "Tibetan independence movement" was in fact a counter-revolutionary action, led by groups of feudal landlords and religious aristocrats, with assistance from outside. Even Western sources never estimated more than 20,000 were involved. Out of a total population of 1,200,000 living in Tibet itself (there are almost three million Tibetans living in other parts of China) this does not sound like mass support.

Let us also add this: one of the first acts of the Chinese government after liberation of Tibet in 1951 was to prohibit *mutilation*: it was still the custom there to gouge out eyes, cut off ears, and employ similar brutal punishments. The only hospitals in Tibet are those that have been built by the People's Republic, the only secular schools were begun after liberation, and peonage and the medieval system of land-tenure were abolished, as reported by the London *Times* of June 28, 1958.

As in the case of Taiwan, no question about Tibet being part of China was ever raised officially until recently. Until it became convenient to charge China with "foreign aggression," it has been accepted both by international law and by immemorial custom that Tibet was part of China. From as long ago as the thirteenth century we have records showing that Kublai Khan appointed the Grand Lama of Tibet; the British recognized Chinese suzerainty in 1792; and during Chiang Kai-shek's rule Washington would not admit a trade delegation from Tibet until it had obtained visas from the Kuomintang government. It is significant that when the Dalai Lama, after his "flight" to India, appealed to the great powers to bring the case of Chinese "aggression" before the United Nations, no great power would take the initiative. The reason? That under international law there was no case of aggression.

We have been accused, too, of aggression in Laos. In the summer of 1959 the United States, in apparently great alarm, called an emergency session of the United Nations Security Council to consider the "foreign aggression" against this small country. The United Nations sent an international commission to investigate the charges on the spot. The Commission reported no evidence of aggression; that no foreign troops had crossed the border. In 1960 the same wild charges were repeated, and again quietly dropped for lack of evidence. There never has been any proof of Chinese soldiers in Laos because there never were any. However, a report in the New York *Herald Tribune* from Vientiane on October 5, 1960, revealed that American soldiers disguised as civilians were secretly training the Royal Laotian army.

As for India, it is true that our relations are not as cordial as they were some years ago. But we do not feel that we are to blame for this. Premier Chou En-lai discussed this matter with you [see the Appendix for the transcript of the author's TV interview with Chou En-lai], as he did with Edgar Snow [*Look* magazine, January 31, 1961]. We know that we have been called "aggressive" and "intransigent" in connection with this border dispute yet we are sitting down with the Indian government and attempting to negotiate the demarcation of a border some thousands of miles in length which has never been precisely agreed upon in the long and peaceful history of China and India. In a similar situation we reached an amicable solution with the Burmese government. We are confident that in the course of time a just settlement for both India and ourselves can be found.

[In the course of a conversation I had with Mr. Nehru in 1959 it was clear that he felt the issue had been exaggerated for political reasons and that a settlement with China was possible. This attitude was confirmed by L. M. Morris of the *Christian Science Monitor,* who in an article on January 28, 1961, reported that Mr. Nehru ". . . surprisingly dismissed the Communist China invasion of India's borders by first saying he felt it had petered out, and secondly by stating that 'up there' there are only mountains and a couple of small villages."]

We who are so frequently accused of "aggression" have often been victims of it ourselves. We believe we know it when we see it. We know that American planes at the disposal of Chiang Kai-shek bombed our cities after liberation and continued to fly arms to remnants of the Kuomintang forces on the mainland. We know that American U-2's have flown over our land. We know that weapons have been dropped to counterrevolutionary forces in Tibet.

On December 15, 1960, the *Christian Science Monitor's* correspondent in New Delhi reported that Prime Minister Nehru "has expressed the belief that some of the air violations of India's northeast frontier about which India has made several protests to Communist China may be due to overflights by United States planes. . . . New Indian radar devices have been plotting the course of marauders at a height of more than 60,000 feet and as far as New Delhi knows, Communist China lacks aircraft flying at such heights." The same correspondent also stated: "The fact that several incoming Tibetan refugees have been found to carry United States arms leads to the supposition that some United States planes may have been engaged in dropping arms to help the still simmering Tibetan revolt against Chinese overlordship. . . . Unless doubts are cleared up both Peking and Indian Communists have another perfect opportunity to make U-2 type of propaganda.

Needless to say, this interview was ignored by the rest of the American press.

*

Which brings us to the question: Is it China or the United States that is the aggressive country?

Item: How many military bases is America maintaining on foreign soil? Hundreds. And China? Not one.

Item: America has a navy larger than all the other navies of the world combined. China's navy? Negligible.

Item: America today spends six million dollars *every hour* on military armaments. America spends in just sixteen days what China spends on her military requirements in the whole year.

Item: America has a stockpile of H-bombs with an explosive force of 96,000 megatons or *45 million times the force that was exploded at Hiroshima.* Mr. Leo Goodman, who is the atomic advisor to the United Automobile Workers, gave this figure to the Annual Conference of the American Association of the United Nations in March 1960. Dr. David Inglis, physicist at the U.S. government's Argonne Laboratory, who was present said, "I think you are 30 per cent low." Taking this lower figure, what does this mean in terms that are more imaginable? That the United States today has stockpiled in its arsenals the equivalent of thirty-two one-ton bombs of high explosive *for every man, woman, and child in the entire world.*

Item: America spends 56.4 per cent of its national budget on current military expenses, *excluding* the billions of dollars she gives to arm her allies. The Chinese spend 8.3 per cent.

Item: In dollar equivalents America spends $47 billion; China spends $2.3 billion. For every man, woman, and child America spends $260 annually on current military expenses; China spends $3.50.

Item: The proportion of America's national budget that she spends on military expenditures increases year by year. In China the proportion *decreases* year by year. The average annual expenditure on military defense during China's first Five-Year Plan was 17 per cent. Today (1960) it is down to 8.3 per cent.

Item: *Ten times* more money is spent in America on its current military expenditures than for the combined expenditures on social security, education, health, and welfare. China spends 50 per cent *more* on these items than on military expenditures.

Item: It was understood that both sides would withdraw their troops from Korea. Today (and your leaders have acknowledged this) not a single Chinese soldier remains on Korean soil. The American troops have not been withdrawn from South Korea. Today they number tens of thousands, and the airfields in South Korea have recently been enlarged.

With these facts before us, which of our two countries would appear the more "warlike"?

*

Americans do not like being called an "imperialist" power. They believe we are stretching words beyond their accepted meaning. "Point out to us," your leaders say, "a single people that America is ruling as a colonial power; show us one country that America is threatening to seize."

In our view colonialism is only one aspect of imperialism and though the United States may not "rule" as a colonial power, she nevertheless effectively dominates and controls other countries by her financial and commercial power. Americans should understand that we use the word *imperialism* as a symbol, a kind of shorthand description, of the control of one power by another. Let us not split hairs over words, let us look at the facts. European colonialism, deeply damaging though it was, was at least open, it was admitted, even gloried in. The worst feature of American imperialism is its *secrecy*. Its actions throughout the world are flagrant, but they are largely hidden from the ordinary people at home. American commercial imperialism operates without public control or check. It is politically irresponsible.

A dozen or twenty men may meet in New York and their decision can mean that 10,000 workers in Bolivia or Venezuela or in the Philippines are thrown out of work and their familes starve. But how can they seek redress? Who in America speaks for them? Who even knows? How can these workers, many of whom cannot even read, understand the intricacies of finance and world markets, the return on invested capital, and the many subtle considerations that led to their predicament? Who can explain to these workers how a few men five thousand miles away can exercise such a terrible power over their simple lives? Who in American public life, in Congress or out, feels called upon to challenge decisions based on exclusive commercial interests?

The American government, far from challenging these unrestricted powers, feels that its duty lies in protecting them. Without the American people being aware of it the full weight of American diplomacy is directed toward propping up in these backward countries the men who can best serve American financial interests. Look at the leaders whom your government has supported! Why else has it supported them? Why Franco? Why Syngman Rhee? Why Batista? Why Chiang? Why Perez Jimenez in Venezuela? Why Boun Oum in Laos? Why Pinilla in Colombia? All dictators. All your men. All "good" men from the point of view of your commercial interests, but all hated as oppressors by their own people.

The recent revolution in Cuba sent a wave of apprehension through financial and government circles in the United States. Reaction was harsh. Diplomatic relations were cut off. How many Americans realized why there was a revolution? How many Americans knew, before Castro shouted it from the rooftops, that 40 per cent of Cuba's productive land was held by American interests? And 90 per cent of her electricity supply? Almost all her oil resources? Fifty per cent of her railroads? Eighty per cent of her telephone system? How many Americans knew that the American government was supplying the arms and the bombs and the airplanes with which Batista fired on his own people? Your government told you that he was "against communism" and therefore must be a good man! And because those in financial power were behind him, he was recognized by your government after a blatantly corrupt election, within eleven days!

Are you so naïve as to imagine this is not taking place elsewhere? And not only in the backward countries! An intricate network of commercial and financial control has been spread across the world. What name would you have us give American actions other than imperialism? Being kept so much in ignorance of what is done in their name, it naturally comes as a shock to most Americans to hear that their country is thought of as imperialist even by their allies. As the London *Observer*, a paper by no means unfriendly to the United States, wrote on July 10, 1960:

"The crisis in the relations between Cuba and the United States underlines a paradox which pains and surprises most Americans; that the United States which sees itself as the precursor of colonial freedom is widely regarded abroad as an imperialist, even a colonial, power. . . .

"In Latin America it has too often behaved as an Imperialist Power itself. The Monroe Doctrine . . . was obviously motivated by anti-colonial altruism, but it did not stop the United States from feeling free to intervene itself in Latin American affairs. This intervention started in Mexico with the occupation of Texas, formerly a State of the Mexican Union, and continued with the foundation of the Republic of Panama, formerly a Province of Colombia; the invasion of Mexico shortly before the outbreak of World War One; the occupation by the U.S. Marines during the war of Nicaragua, the Dominican Republic, Cuba and Haiti; and finally the overthrow of an elected Guatemalan Government in 1954.

"Though officially Cubans have been free from colonial domination for nearly sixty years, in fact they have been tied to the United States as Iraq and Egypt were to Britain. And their pride very naturally resents this. . . .

"Britain, over Suez, learned the hard way that being tough with proud people no longer pays."

America, it seems, still has that lesson to learn.

*

For the past twelve years China has lived under constant military threat. A network of installations keep American planes, missiles and rockets zeroed-in twenty-four hours a day on our major population centers. Quemoy is almost as close to our shores as Alcatraz is to the Golden Gate. Almost within shouting distance. How would the people of San Francisco, the leaders in Washington, react if on that island were guns and missiles in hostile hands? In Japan, in Okinawa, in South Korea, in Taiwan (in Laos, too, if she had her way), America has huge military establishments. Riding close to our shores as a constant harassment and interference to our coastal shipping is the Seventh Fleet, armed with nuclear weapons. Your ships encroach into our waters and your planes fly over our territory.

Can you not, just for a moment, make the effort of imagination to reverse our roles? When the Russians offered to assist Cuba with arms, there was immediate talk in your press about a "Soviet base" being established in Cuba. Did we hear you respond in "measured tones"? What happened then to the "temperance" of language which you demand of us under infinitely greater provocation? You yourselves have a powerful naval base in Cuba, but a wave of indignation and fear swept your country at the thought of the Soviet Union having one there too, "within a hundred miles" of America! If a mere rumor of a Russian base in Cuba can so excite and enrage your public, how would they respond, we wonder, if a hostile power held bases in Mexico, in Canada, in Hawaii, in Bermuda? If a hostile navy encroached constantly on your coastal waters and hostile planes were flying over your cities?

Your leaders, of course, tell you that your huge array of armaments are needed to preserve your "way of life." Americans believe that their country stands for tolerance and decency and for the essential equality of all men; they see themselves as the supporters of the underdog against the arbitrary powers of wealth and prestige. Your way of life apparently is so precious that the future of mankind must be jeopardized to protect it. But who in his right senses can now think of America as standing for the underprivileged? Where does she uphold the weak against the strong? America stands for power and wealth. Instead of fighting privilege, she protects it. Is it to America that the ordinary people of Africa, of Latin America, of Asia look for help in their struggle against tyrants? How can they, when more often than not it is America that supplies weapons to their oppressors?

That something is profoundly ailing in your society you yourselves know. Deep in the national consciousness there appears to be a growing conviction that America has lost her way. Your lawlessness has gone beyond all lengths; your jails are full, your courts are overworked; from your own records we learn that 5,500 of your juveniles are arrested every twenty-four hours; 55 per cent of your hospital beds are used for the mentally ill; your syphilis rate (according to your own medical reports) has increased by 200 per cent in the past two years—and half the new cases are young people between the ages of fifteen and nineteen. A country that spends more on drink than education, more on advertising than on health, must indeed ask itself: What has gone wrong?

The speeches and writing of your more thoughtful men are full of serious self-searching. "I am concerned, desperately concerned," said your Mr. Adlai Stevenson in a speech in 1959, "about our mainspring. That it has run down, we know. But is it broken beyond repair?"

We can give Mr. Stevenson an unexpectedly reassuring answer. No nation's "main-spring" is broken beyond repair. We do not believe that history is just a jumble of accidents. We think the rise and fall of nations, the health and sickness of societies, are susceptible to rational understanding and improvement if the laws that govern these changes are understood. The basic direction of American society can be reversed as soon as the real reasons of your country's predicament are understood by the masses of the people.

To us it seems self-evident that your competitive economic system (the system you so greatly extol) was bound eventually to bring about precisely the social results you now deplore. It is a self-destroying system. By the force of its own inner logic the system becomes a jungle in which every man is compelled to seek his own gain even if it be at the expense of his fellows—or of the society's as a whole. One analysis that Marx makes and which you reject (usually, we suspect, without ever really reading it) is that when once commodity production becomes the central focus of man's existence, all other preoccupations will be subordinated to it. Marx makes sense to us because we see his general laws working out in history. You, for instance, have become a "business-obsessed" society.

That your system has produced enormous wealth we cannot and

do not wish to deny. But at what cost of suffering to others? With what exploitation of people in a less advanced stage? With what a ruthless plundering of your own resources? And in your own society, it is wealth that has been achieved by denying other values which we hold too dear to sacrifice. With you the individual is the unit. With us it is the group, the family, the village, the co-operative, the association of friends working together for a common end. Without this sense of interrelatedness and comradeship we believe there can be no happiness, only a restless striving for personal success. Where there are no stable human relationships, no reverence for the past, where there is no respect for excellence, no discipline, no deep feeling contact with the great rhythms of nature, but only an insatiable desire to exploit nature for financial profit—there, we think, there can be no true harmony. Within the terms of your competitive system you measure the degree of civilization by material wealth; we measure civilization by the quality of our relationship with our fellow men. It is relationship and not the possession of things which in the end provides all that is most dear and precious in life.

And hating so much in their own life but unable to express it, caught within a system which compels them to deny so much in themselves that is tender and trusting, it surely isn't surprising that many Americans have to express their hatred elsewhere, outside of themselves—against "communism," against "China." Is it really communism they hate? Is it China? For indeed what do they know of China? They see China and communism only through the distorting lenses of their own frustrations. As long as people assume that their system is fundamentally sound, while every day there is mounting evidence that something is very wrong with it, it is utterly unavoidable that they will continue to find an external enemy that must be the cause of their predicaments.

We in China look across the oceans and see people in different stages of their historical development. We see some still in feudal conditions, or as colonial subjects. We see some societies suffering (as America is suffering) from the contradictions of advanced capitalism. But with the people in these countries we feel a sense of common humanity. When we shout our defiance at American imperialist policies in Asia, it is not the people of America we shout at. We cannot any more "reject" the people of America than we could "reject" ourselves—though we reject with all that is in us the corrupting influence of their public philosophies.

This has led some of your writers to suggest that we are trying to "divide" the American people from their government. We are not so naïve as they suppose. What seems to us clear is that American imperialist policies abroad and the inner decay of American life at home are part of a single process. They are problems related to this specific period of American history, they are developments following historic imperatives, but they are not rooted in the particular "character" of the American people. Historic processes can be retarded or hastened. We will continue to shout our defiance at America's imperialist policies and we will continue to feel a democratic relatedness to the people of America. And in this we see no contradiction at all.

*

The rest of the world, we can assure you, has grown weary of America's moral admonitions, her holier-than-thou attitude. Standing far above the pressures of hunger and poverty, she preaches to the world as to how we should all behave. We watch the creeping degradation of American life and listen to her sermons. A nation with the highest crime rate in the world talks to us about "respect for law"; the nation with one of the highest rates of drunkenness tells us to be sober; the nation with the highest divorce rate preaches to the world about "sanctity of the home"; the nation that has the largest navy the world has ever seen and has piled up the equivalent of 32 tons of high explosives for every man, woman, and child on earth talks to us about not being "warlike"; the nation which is in perpetual racial crisis with its Negro population, and a hundred years after the abolition of slavery has still not found it in its heart to deal with colored peoples on a basis of equality, talks tirelessly to the world on the virtues of democracy; a nation renowned for the extent of corruption among its public officials gives us homilies about good citizenship! It is enough to make a cat laugh!

Wake up Americans! Come off your moral high horse and join the people of the world. You are no better than the rest of us. All of us are part good, part bad; part self-seeking, part generous. China has foolish, passionate, bigoted people just as you do. We are not saints. We make mistakes. But we are trying not to pretend to ourselves, so that here in China today it isn't any longer considered un-dignified to say, "We made a mistake—let's try something else." And if some of us do pretend, and in our enthusiasm give larger figures of production than are true (as we did two years ago with our grain figures), we publicly correct the figures when we find this out. But you, in your ivory tower, encased in your moral rectitude and your poses and pretenses, you feel you dare not admit mistakes, or the whole sham front will collapse. You make a historical error as you did with Taiwan, and though you know it's an error and is leading you every year into greater and greater difficulties, you cannot say (as the British have learned to do), "It is time for our withdrawal," and do it with dignity and good feeling. You cling to your false positions and your false allies just as you cling to your H-bombs and missiles because that's all the "security" you know. You cling to an economic system that is inwardly and outwardly bringing you to ruin because you dare not make a change. You cling to your super highways and super cars and super kitchen gadgets and super tran-quilizer pills and tell yourselves, "This is the life!" because you can-not face the full extent of your inner impoverishment. Wake up, Americans, before you do yourselves and all of us irreparable harm.

In China we are extremely poor compared to you, but we are enjoying life. We are enjoying ourselves as we have never enjoyed ourselves before! We work hard, perhaps too hard. We get tired, we don't have much to eat, though no one starves, and when we have bad harvests we get even less—but we are as excited as school-children. And we are busy—as your pioneers were busy—not making money, but building colleges and schools and hospitals; we volun-teer by thousands at weekends or vacation time to help farmers make dams and bridges and new irrigation ditches. We are learning something new every day; millions of us are learning how to read and write for the first time in our lives; we are studying to be doctors and physicists and geologists and engineers and dancers and poets.

We are the oldest country in the world, but we are much younger than you are. We are like you were when you started America, still able to thrill to new ideas. And we are not alone. We feel we are moving with history. Africa is waking up, Latin America is waking up, Asia is waking up—and we are all working harder and with greater zest than we have ever done before. But you do not thrill any more, you Americans! You have lost your capacity to believe.

What visions stir your hearts? What new horizons move your children? And how will history judge between us? We who are trying to bring health and education and morality and cleanliness and joy to our old country—and you who stand on the side lines and sneer?

China ☆

Kaleidoscope 4

Notes from My Journal and Letters

Continuity

In 1958 Mao Tse-tung said, "China's six hundred million people are first of all poor, and secondly, 'blank.' That may seem like a bad thing, but it is really a good thing. Poor people want change, want to do things, want revolution. A clean sheet of paper has no blotches and so the newest and most beautiful words can be written on it, the newest and most beautiful pictures can be painted on it."

Almost 2500 years ago, Lao-tzu, speaking of Tao, the "Way," said, "The Way is like an empty vessel. . . ." And, "We turn clay to make a vessel, but it is on the space where there is nothing that the usefulness of the vessel depends. . . . Just as we take advantage of what is, we should recognize the usefulness of what is not."

Peking, Taipei, and Quemoy

Chinese are Chinese, whether they are on Taiwan or the mainland. Their civil war is imposed upon a much older and deeper conflict, against the foreign powers. Chiang accepts U.S. help, not because he has the slightest sympathy with American democracy, but because he has to.

Mao's government and Chiang's are agreed on two things: that Tibet is part, and has always been a part, of China; and that Taiwan must never, under any circumstances, be detached from China. The United States would like to solve her Taiwan predicament by encouraging a "Two Chinas" policy; the great stumbling block in her way is that this policy is rejected by *all* Chinese, Nationalists and Communists alike.

In June 1960 Lei Chen, a newspaperman on Taiwan, announced he was forming an opposition party; Chiang Kai-shek responded by promptly putting him into jail for sedition. Those familiar with the ways of Chiang saw it as just one of his old methods of handling opponents. And, of course, it was partly that. But my reading of the incident is this: Chiang jailed Lei Chen not so much as a political opponent, but because he suspected that Lei was being groomed by the U.S. State Department as a possible leader who would be amenable to the Two Chinas policy. To Chiang, this was an immediate threat; once this policy was openly formulated and received the full weight of American official support, it could mean an end to his rule.

I sometimes suspect that on this question of two Chinas, however bitterly they distrust each other on other issues, there is more understanding between the Chiang group and the Peking government than we realize. We look on, utterly baffled, by the on-again, off-again shelling of Quemoy from the mainland, often with loudspeaker announcements to inform the islanders where the next day's shells will be aimed so that they can get out of the way. This is *not*, we feel, the way to fight a serious civil war!

The clue to this puzzle can again be found in the essential unity of the two Chinese groups on the question of two Chinas. The United States has, it is generally understood, for a long time been urging Chiang to withdraw the very heavy military contingents he has been holding in Quemoy and Matsu. Both Chiang and the Peking government probably consider that a withdrawal of these troops might well be the first step in a compromise which Washington would welcome—the evacuation of Quemoy and Matsu (as being of "no military significance") in return for an "Independent Formosa." This neither side will allow. So Quemoy and Matsu must be made to appear by no means of military insignificance. And, anyhow, how could Chiang be expected to withdraw under fire? Would that not be interpreted everywhere as defeat? So the shelling on alternate days goes on; the Chinese chess game is played, and Washington remains bewildered and frustrated!

Letter to Elena   August 16

. . . This is an uncomfortable country to be in in some ways. I find I am constantly confronted with *myself*. Krishnamurti once said the real value of relationships is that they can act as a mirror to oneself. This whole country is a mirror. When I get annoyed here the Chinese never respond with annoyance, they respond by being solicitous and helpful, which makes one feel as if one had acted like a little child. They have a rare gift of letting one sit with one's anger, and I am always left feeling rather ashamed of myself and boorish. Another thing I notice, especially when I am tired and am not getting my way about something, that my voice takes on that damned supercilious English tone, the voice of someone who unconsciously feels he should be specially treated. Other things I notice here about myself that I wouldn't even *see* at home. I find myself automatically leaving my heaviest bag, knowing it will be carried by someone else. This comes from years of expecting someone to be around to do the donkey work. I think if I lived here I would have a hell of a job rooting some of this superior-status assumption out of me.

And perhaps *that's* at the bottom of this self-criticism business. China was confronted, even to a greater degree than England, with people who were extraordinarily conscious of their *status*. An upper-class Chinese must at first have found it inordinately difficult to adjust himself to a society that was deliberately and consciously setting out to be egalitarian. I hate to think of the criticism meetings I would have had to go through! And perhaps the Chinese are right that it can only be done through constant reminders by interested, friendly, and determined comrades.

Though the Chinese I meet never respond to anger with anger, this doesn't mean that their feelings are not hurt. I had a good example of this with Yen at the time he was taking me to the hospital to have my foot dressed. I was in pain and hadn't slept; and I was irritated that he and the doctor were having a conversation which Yen was not translating. I asked three times, but they just went on talking. I finally said, very irritably, "For God's sake, Yen, the whole point of your being here is to translate for me . . ." and so on, in a very who's-paying-you-anyway tone of voice.

Yen didn't say anything, but I could feel that he was hurt. The next day he didn't turn up—they sent someone else to interpret for me—and the *next* day. The third day he came but was rather aloof. I said, "Yen, let me practice a little self-criticism. I was annoyed and spoke impatiently with you the other day and I think now it was without cause. I wish to apologize."

From that moment we got on fine again.

I am coming to see what they are trying to say when they talk about getting rid of the "last vestiges of feudalism." That phrase can hit close to home.

Do-It-Yourself Country

For a people with no technical background, the Chinese peasants seem to be taking to mechanics like ducks to water. They are extraordinarily confident that they can do *anything*. This has led to some heartbreaks. At one commune they showed me where they had originally placed a dam for a water catchment, but the water seeped underneath and washed the whole thing away. Thousands of man-hours wasted. But they went to work immediately and put it in another place which held.

I came across a typical example of this readiness to make anything, in a rural commune in Hopei province. I found one workshop in the commune turning out transformers, the kind you see slung on high-tension poles. This seemed such an unlikely product for a rural commune to be making that I asked how it all started.

It seemed a long-distance power line was built across the commune land; and the management committee, all excited, bought electric pumps, saws, grinders, etc. But when they asked the linesmen to hook them up, they learned there were no transformers available. The commune would have to wait its turn, six months or more. The committee didn't think much of this, particularly in the year of the great leap forward. So they sent one of their members into town to borrow an electrical handbook from a technical library. For nights they pored over this manual, trying to understand how a transformer works; then they went ahead and made one, using old wire and pipes and odds and ends they picked up or bought secondhand. The power engineers came out to see it. (Inspectors aren't as fussy in China as ours would be, and do-it-yourself efforts like this one are thoroughly approved of.) It didn't look like much of a transformer but they hooked it up, and it worked. When the story got around, a number of neighboring communes in the same fix put in orders. By this time the Party, having got word of this example of local initiative, sent down a man with blueprints. From then on, the commune was in the transformer-making business. And there I saw their previous week's output awaiting shipment, stacked up in the yard with ducks and chickens pecking around them.

Cost of Entertainments

I have gone a great deal to concerts, drama, and ballet, here in Peking. Tickets are cheap and very much in demand. One yuan (forty cents) will usually buy the best seat in the house. I have gone to performances in the park concert halls for as little as fifteen fen (six cents). Today I stopped in at an exhibit of contemporary painting. The ticket was three fen (1.2 cents) for the public and two fen (0.8 cent) for students. I asked the girl selling tickets what would happen if a sudent who couldn't afford even two fen came. She said, "I'd pay for him myself!"

The Militia

The women's militia brigade of this hotel has a drill in the quiet side street outside my window at six in the morning, twice a week. Each woman has a rifle, and a man is trying to train them in the rudiments of close-order drill. They are dressed in ordinary work trousers. At first they were a pretty ragged group, and quite giggly.

"*Yi! Er! San! Sih!*" (One! Two! Three! Four!), the instructor would yell, but they couldn't keep step at all. And the rifles slung over their shoulders got mixed up too. That was some weeks ago. But what a difference today! Smart; no giggles. They fling themselves to the ground, up again, down again; and their marching is precise.

All over China young men and women are training in the militia, millions and millions of them. I have seen them outside factories, in the fields, at colleges—everywhere. It makes me think a little of what America must have been like after the revolution, when the citizens insisted on a constitutional guarantee of the right to bear arms.

The *Sunday Times* of June 12 came in from London a few days ago with Montgomery's article and I was interested to read what he made of all this militia training. This is what he wrote:

"All fit persons between the ages of 18 and 25 have to serve. These militia units are the 'Ming-Bing,' the people's soldiers.

"I inspected the militia unit of a factory in Canton which made electric torches. It was an amazing parade of men *and* women, all armed with rifles or tommy guns; there was an anti-aircraft section manned entirely by women; a signal section of men and women; and a medical section.

"This militia organization covers the country, and in the event of a foreign invasion of China the invading army would have a very poor time, indeed it would be engulfed by the Ming-Bing. I have always said that the *second* rule of war is not to go fighting with your land armies in China, and what I saw of the Ming-Bing proves the correctness of that rule. I was once asked what is the *first* rule of war, and I replied without any hesitation, 'Don't march on Moscow.'"

These are armies of civilians—a home-guard, we would call them in England. I have seen the peasants in the communes drilling or at target practice in the evening after work; each man and woman drills twice a week, I think, but this probably varies. Sometimes I have seen the peasants strolling home after drill carrying their rifles with them.

For years we have read in the Western press that China's people are "slaves" awaiting the opportunity to revolt. But here they are being armed by their government! It is unlikely, I think, that a regime which was uncertain of popular support, would set about arming its peasants and workers.

Foreign Aid

A dispatch from Delhi today reported that the Planning Commission there had announced that steel and grain targets for India's second Five-Year Plan (April 1956–March 1961) will not be realized. The target for finished steel was 4.3 million tons but the government now expects production to reach only 2.6 million; grain was set for 80.5 million tons; this now is expected to be 75 million. The same dispatch quotes the *Times of India* as saying that agriculture "has remained almost stagnant."

These are *low* figures. India has almost two-thirds the population of China but is producing proportionately far less. Chinese steel production in 1960 was over seven times the production in India; and China's grain production (in spite of climatic disasters) was two and a half times greater than that in India.

I know the attitude in the West is that India is going slower because she is accomplishing her revolution through a politically democratic process, more gradually, more humanely. But when we move from political theory to the mathematics of human survival, we face the fact that a Chinese child today has better health, better food, better work prospects, more education, and greater security than an Indian child, despite the fact that Britain left India with a more advanced industrial base and more extensive communications than China had when the present regime took over.

Walter Lippmann, whose judgment I often greatly respect, has stated (in *The Communist World and Ours*):

"The Communists are expanding in Asia because they are demonstrating a way, at present the only obviously effective way, of raising quickly the power and standard of living of a backward people. The only convincing answer to that must be a demonstration by the non-Communist nations that there is another and more humane way of overcoming the immemorial poverty and weakness of the Asian peoples.

"This demonstration can best be made in India, and there is little doubt in my mind that if we and our Western partners would underwrite and assure the success of India's development it would make a world of difference. . . . India is the key country. . . . To make a showplace of a small island like Formosa . . . is a good thing to do. But it is not very convincing. . . . If there is any other way of meeting the Communist challenge in Asia, I have not heard of it."

I think, however, that Lippmann has missed a crucially important point: aid by itself can do very little to help a country if other conditions are not present as well. Let us look at the simple arithmetic of aid to India. Not long ago three eminent bankers, members of the World Bank, were asked to report on the needs of India and Pakistan. They suggested that these two nations required about 8.5 billion dollars in aid from the West to carry them through their next five-year development plans. Per head of population, this amounts to scarcely more than a penny a day. I do not believe that aid on this scale—or any scale, for that matter—is really getting to the heart of the matter.

Chinese advances have *not* been dependent on foreign assistance, nor on coercion, for that doesn't work either. Russian aid (almost all of which was paid for by China) has amounted to less than one-tenth of a cent a day per capita of population. The vital factor is not money from abroad, but the *latent labor power in the people themselves*.

It appears to me that if backward countries rely on programs that are Western-inspired and which do not come out of the genius and will of the indigenous people themselves, they are certain to fail. India's problems will be solved only when she discovers ways of releasing the tremendous creative powers of her people that are at present lying unused. It seems to me India's real revolution lies before her. She is hanging on precariously to political and economic concepts which are more Western than Indian; she should not look to Russia or China any more than she should look to the West. She must look to *herself*, discover the sources of her own energies within herself, find an *Indian* political and economic system that makes sense to the Indian people—then, and only then, I think, will foreign money and technical assistance really help her on her way.

Reflex

At the Swiss National Day reception, Chou En-lai made an unexpected pronouncement. It was generally thought that a Central Committee meeting was in progress at the time. Chou arrived well after the reception had started. He made a speech in which he brought up once again the Chinese suggestion of a Pacific peace plan, to include the United States and all countries bordering the Pacific Ocean, the purpose of which would be to make the Pacific a zone free of all nuclear tests. It was a dramatic proposal.

Clare McDermott was the only Western correspondent present; Ullmann of Agence France Presse was away; *Hsinhua* was unprepared and it took them some hours to get the story on the wires. McDermott rushed immediately to the Central Telegraph Office and filed his story to London, a clear beat of several hours for Reuters.

Within minutes the message must have been relayed to the United States. Only an hour or two later the "Voice of America" announced the official response. A spokesman for the State Department had already dismissed Chou's proposal as "nothing but propaganda."

Who made this evaluation? Who sat down and pondered what was behind the suggestion? What its implications were? How sincerely or otherwise it was put forward? It was a Chinese proposal, and therefore automatically had to be rejected.

Some European governments huffed and puffed a little at the rapidity of Washington's rejection of a suggestion that might have had some interesting nuances. But the damage was done. Those here who have been advocating a hard line against the United States have been given more ammunition.

Calisthenics

On long train journeys, at the first stop in the mornings (usually between six and eight o'clock), some of the passengers tumble out for their morning setting-up exercises on the platform. From loud-speakers strung along the light poles come music and instructions. I usually join in.

We sometimes make a motley display: portly businessmen from Shanghai, professors thin and bespectacled, students, the girls from the train crew, soldiers, children—there we all are. "Bend *down*, one, two, three, four; swing *sideways*, one, two, three, four; stretch hands above the head, one, two, three, four," comes the voice above the music.

Farther down the platform there are usually some older men who scorn these newfangled Swedish calisthenics. They, with deliberate slow-motion movements, with rapt and inward concentration, go slowly, beautifully, through motions of *tai chi chwan*, the traditional Chinese form of physical and mental training. No one looks at them. It is a very common sight, in towns, in the park, out on the streets in the early morning, to see these older men (and sometimes younger ones, too) performing these ritual movements. If I were here longer I would take instructions.

As for the Swedish drill, I'm for that too. After a fitful night on the train it limbers up the old joints.

PART SEVEN

Public Health
and the Mass Line   27

There cannot be the slightest doubt that China, during the past eleven years, has achieved enormous advances in public health. As early as 1957 nine distinguished British doctors visited China. They reported that while some formidable problems still remain to be conquered, the Chinese claim many outstanding achievements:

Item: "Between 1949 and 1957, 860 new hospitals were built (averaging 350 beds)" i.e., one hospital was completed somewhere in China every *three-and-a-half days*.

> Report by F. Avery Jones, M.D., FRCP,
> *British Medical Journal,*
> November 9, 1957.

Item: On the care of the mother: "In some ways, of course, the Chinese are giving a lead. . . . Five to seven antenatal examinations are done. . . . Maternal mortality in 1956 was said to be only 0.3 per 1000 live births in this district [Peking] and 0.28 in Shanghai . . . the rate in England and Wales in 1955 was 0.54."

> Report by T. F. Fox, M.A., M.D., FRCP,
> *The Lancet*
> November 9, 16 and 23, 1957.

Item: Since 1957 the maternal mortality rate in Peking has been still further lowered to 0.26 per 1000.

> Reported to me by Madame Li Teh-chuan,
> Chinese Minister of Health,
> August 1960.

Item: The Child: "Infant mortality is said to have fallen in Peking from 117 per 1000 births in 1949 to 37 in 1956. . . . In one area where work has been intense it has come down to 22. . . . Shanghai figures were 31 in 1956—not so much higher than the English figure of about 25."

> Reported by Dr. Fox.

Item: "China has apparently been free of cholera since 1949 and from smallpox since 1950. In Peking relapsing fever has disappeared and typhus has almost done so. . . . This epidemiological transformation of huge Eastern cities . . . required intelligent organization of medical resources . . . and no small scientific competence."

> Reported by Dr. Fox.

Item: "In some of the more densely populated areas considerable success has already been achieved in the control of gastro-intestinal diseases such as typhoid and bacillary and amoebic dysentery, together with many of the common worm infections. . . . The standard of hygiene reached already is . . . most impressive."

> Reported by Professor Brian Maegraith,
> Dean of the Liverpool School
> of Tropical Medicine, and
> formerly Dean of the Faculty
> of Medicine at Oxford, in
> *The New Scientist,*
> December 5, 1957.

I am not a doctor or an authority on public health and for this reason I am quoting extensively from the reports by the British doctors who went to China specifically to study medical developments. I, myself, visited many hospitals in China—I received treatment in some of them—and I cannot but record the astonishing contrast between these hospitals in China with those I have seen in other parts of Asia, the Middle East, Latin America, and Africa.

The findings by men eminently qualified to form judgments confirm and validate the conditions I myself saw in China.

"The cleanliness was impressive, with complete absence of litter and filth, and practically no flies," wrote Dr. F. Avery Jones of England's Central Middlesex Hospital. "Many litter boxes were to be seen, particularly in the parks. Even the mules had dung sacks under their tails to prevent them soiling the streets. The eradication of flies had been the result of a national campaign and had proved an important contribution towards the public health."

Professor Brian Maegraith reported: "The successful control of flies, the litterless streets, and fanatical household cleanliness are having a profound effect on the spread of gastro-intestinal infections, especially in children, in whom, we were told, bacillary dysentery is much less common than it was.

"How has this been done? How for instance, can a notoriously dirty city be tidied up? The answer lies in the will of the people, who must be persuaded that it is worthwhile making their dwelling places clean and keeping them that way. The public cooperation demanded in such an exercise is immense, and the Government has been remarkably successful in achieving it. This may have been easier in a totalitarian state than elsewhere, and there was probably some element of compulsion needed to persuade the population to clear away hundreds of thousands of tons of dirt and litter from the streets and to swat flies and trench maggots until the insect population was brought under control. Nevertheless, the Chinese man-in-the-street is essentially practical, and no amount of cajoling without a good leavening of common sense and social persuasion could have given him his present passionate belief in hygiene.

". . . In vast rural districts . . . interim measures leading to conservation of night soil are already in operation and are helping considerably to limit further the spread of intestinal diseases. Perhaps this is nowhere more important than in communities like those living huddled together in sampans along the banks of the Pearl River, for even the casual stranger to Canton must be impressed with the early morning parade of decorated family pots awaiting collection of night soil, which, not so long ago, would have been cast freely into the swirling yellow waters."

While the doctors of this British group naturally concentrated each on his own specialty, they expressed general agreement in their reports that the major advances have been achieved through broad-scale campaigns involving the people at a grass-roots level.

Dr. T. F. Fox, editor of the British medical publication, *The Lancet*, had this to say about a "street committee" which he visited in Shanghai:

". . . I want to introduce you to the chairman of a street committee. He is a small, worn man in early middle-age—a pedicab driver. . . . His committee looks after a section of a district, and it is the representative body for about a thousand families—say 5,000 people. Its three functions are (1) to administer welfare services, (2) to explain the policy of the Government, and (3) to reflect and transmit the opinion of the residents. The chairman, at any rate, seems to think of himself as chiefly representing his people, rather than authority. If the dustbins of his area are not cleared as usual at 5:00–6:00 A.M., the city office responsible will hear of it very soon.

"As the medical authorities see it, the main function of the health group of a street committee is to 'carry out the directives' of the city health office as regards sanitation, immunization, and health propaganda generally. Having such close contact with people in their homes, they are in the front line of the patriotic health campaign; and in Shanghai, the health office has in the past few years given no fewer than 50,000 such voluntary workers the elementary training they need as campaigners.

"The slum we visited was pretty frightful . . . but it was under hygienic control. . . ."

An example of such a grass-roots campaign in the rural areas was presented by Professor Maegraith, the tropical-diseases specialist, in his description of the drive to "liquidate" schistosomiasis, a hideous tropical parasitic infection, for centuries a scourge of South China:

"It is endemic in twelve of the major food-producing provinces irrigated by the waters of the Yangtze and the rivers to the South. A recent survey disclosed that something over 11 million of the inhabitants of this great granary are suffering from the crippling physical and economic effects of the disease. Transmission . . . depends on contamination of water with human faeces containing the eggs of the worm. Active larvae hatch from the eggs and invade certain snails, and from these other larvae are eventually discharged, which in turn infect the farmer by penetrating his skin when he is exposed to the water of the canals, creeks and irrigation ditches in which he spends his working life. [Symptoms of the infection in human beings include debilitation and enormous swelling of the abdomen.] The chain of transmission could be broken by preventing contamination of water by faeces . . . by destroying the larval forms or by killing the host snails. In theory, control sounds easy. In practice it is extremely difficult and requires exceptional organization and the all-out cooperation of the people exposed to risk. The Chinese have achieved both.

"A lay committee was formed directly under the Communist Party to coordinate the attack, and each province was provided with its own central organization below which subsidiary units for the districts, towns and villages are now being formed. All methods of control, from treatment of infected persons to destruction of snails, are carried out by these units, in which approximately 70,000 workers are already engaged.

"To ensure the cooperation of the mass of the people concerned, intensive propaganda is being directed at the farmers with the intention of making them appreciate the economic and social dangers of the disease. . . . Village news sheets, posters, cinemas, radio talks, group meetings and discussions are all being used to this end. Since the disease is the vital concern of the whole community, it has been decided that the community should help as much as possible in its control, and this principle is being brought into effect everywhere. For instance, the practical business of killing snails is not executed, as in other countries, by experts from outside, but by teams selected from the local farmers, who . . . take over the work in their own villages and paddy fields.

"I saw this scheme working in the outskirts of Shanghai. The banks of the canals and streams in the villages were being slowly scorched by flame throwers. Beyond the villages, the ditches and paddy fields were being cleared by arsenical spraying. These simple procedures were estimated to kill about 80 per cent of the snails during the summer.

"In the winter, the surviving snails burrow into the mud near the water line. Ditching this mud and packing it in the fields above kills most of them in a few months. . . .

"One further method of control which goes on all the time, illustrates the degree of general cooperation obtained. Until artificial fertilizers can be developed on a big enough scale, human excreta remains the cheapest and most valuable manure. Fortunately the dangerous schistosome eggs do not live long if left in faeces without contact with water. Storage thus renders the material noninfective. Thanks to skillful propaganda, this essential conservation of night soil is becoming an economic and social fact. Each family now has its own privy, a portable, gaily-colored pot. Every morning, the contents are poured into large communal earthenware containers, which are sealed when full and left for the appropriate time necessary for the ammonia generated to kill the eggs, after which the faeces are safe for use in the fields. The collection of family night soil is assured by paying the family for it *pro-rata*, so many cents a day per person, according to age. This scheme is also being used for the control of water pollution by fishermen, for each boat now has its own collecting pot, which is regarded as a regular source of income."

The reports by these medical people graphically describe what might be called the "First Five-Year Plan" approach to public health. The pace has not slowed since 1957, when these positive accounts were made. For example, Dr. Jones reported 860 new hospitals, averaging 350 beds, between 1949 and 1957. By 1960 another 161 hospitals, each with several medical departments and qualified doctors and nurses in attendance, had been added. This over-all figure of 929 new hospitals since 1949, of course, does not include the thousands of small hospitals, clinics, and maternity homes that have been introduced throughout the countryside.

Lacking doctors, lacking hospitals and clinics, lacking many of the more complicated medications which are easily available in the Western world, the Chinese government carried out nationwide immunization programs and selected those diseases which can be effectively attacked by simple methods of sanitation and prevention, upon which to concentrate its first efforts. This was sensible in any case because these diseases happen to be the great mass killers and debilitators—gastro-intestinal infections, parasitic infections, malaria, venereal disease, and the common diseases of children.

Regarding the plans to combat malaria, Professor Maegraith wrote: "The general campaign is similar in many respects to that in operation against schistosomiasis. . . . The magnitude of the social problems it presents can be judged by the population at risk, which is estimated at somewhere between 300 and 350 million. The ultimate aim is eradication. . . . This is to be achieved in 1969."

With respect to schistosomiasis, considerable progress had been made by the summer of 1960, according to information I received from health officials in South China, but the disease was a long way from being "liquidated." However, farther north in communes I visited in the Yangtze Valley, in an area where schistosomiasis had previously been fairly common, I learned that no new cases had been diagnosed during the past two years.

Perhaps one of the most spectacular public-health victories achieved by the new regime has been the virtual wiping out of venereal disease. I visited in all ten hospitals in China—city and country, old and new. In each one I asked about the incidence of syphilis. In each it drew a similar response: "None for two years," "None for a long time," etc. Wassermann tests are required from both partners before a marriage certificate is granted.

I met, while I was in Peking, a most remarkable man, an American of Syrian descent, Dr. George Hatem, who came to China in the early thirties—a resident, in fact, of such long standing that he is usually known here by his Chinese name, Ma Hai-teh. He is one of the few Westerners to have lived with the Communist Eighth Route Army during their years in Yenan in the first decade of the civil war.

Dr. Ma works at the Research Institute of the Academy of Medicine in Peking, specializing in skin and venereal diseases. I found him vigorous and highly informed, with yet a trace of the accent of North Carolina, where he had lived as a young man.

We had dinner together one day before I left Peking for the Northeast, but it was from others that I learned about Dr. Ma's remarkable medical achievements and these were confirmed from various sources. It appears that in the past five years only four fresh cases of syphilis have been diagnosed in Peking, a city of four million people. Two of the four cases involved a man and his wife who had come in from an outlying province. One was a baby, born to a woman previously infected, who had neglected her pregnancy blood test. Thus only one of the four represented an actual new case in Peking. At a 1960 conference of venereologists from the large cities, all cases reported for Peking, Shanghai, Tientsin, Shenyang, Hankow, Sian, Chungking, and Canton totaled only twenty-eight. "The problem of fresh cases in the cities is finished," Dr. Ma said in a recent report.

Most venereal disease work is now in distant areas, among the national minorities. The doctors go out to clean up localities where there still remains some infection—and to obtain specimens for slides at medical schools. At the Research Institute in Peking, most graduates during the past five years have never seen an active case of syphilis or gonorrhea. Dr. Ma reported that in his last three trips to Inner Mongolia, which used to be a sinkhole of venereal disease, he had not found a single case.

He attributes these seemingly extraordinary results to the following:

The end of the Kuomintang armies with their camp followers and their bevies of officers' concubines.

The closing down in 1950 of all houses of prostitution. Organized prostitution is today nonexistent.

And finally, *health education*—the fact that the vast masses of the Chinese population had become involved in the national health campaigns.

The methods which had been used in the rural areas in the fight against venereal disease were described to me. A check list of symptoms was drawn up and posted in every village store, every co-operative headquarters, every community center, throughout the country. "If you remember you ever had any of these symptoms," the posters announced, "go to the clinic and get a blood test." And the slogan was: "We don't want to take syphilis into communism. Let's get rid of it now!"

Peasants know their fellow villagers very well. And there was probably many a case of someone who didn't quite wish to remember being jogged by a friend or neighbor: "Didn't you have this trouble when you used to go around with so-and-so; or when you used to visit the whorehouse?"

Later, I was told, as facilities improved, doctors were able to provide blood tests for every suspected case. The great thing was to get the people to understand the problem, then give them the techniques. That's really what is meant by the "mass line" that one always hears about in China.

I was under the erroneous impression that with the arrival of the antibiotics, venereal disease was virtually eliminated in the United States until I read an editorial in the December 1960 issue of *Today's Health*, published by the American Medical Association. Here I learned that the U.S. Public Health Service reported that one million new gonorrhea cases are developing every year; that syphilis has increased over 200 per cent in a period of three years; that there is an appalling increase in syphilis in the larger cities—New Orleans showing an increase of 818 per cent since 1955, San Francisco 591 per cent, Washington, D.C., 280 per cent —and that teen-agers are among the primary victims of the resurgence of venereal disease. More than half of the new VD cases are in the fifteen- to twenty-four-year group. The Communicable Disease Center also found, the editorial states, that more females are being infected today at the age of high-school graduation than at any other age.

On my return to the United States I related this account of the virtual elimination of venereal disease in China to a doctor of some eminence in California, expecting a snort of disbelief. Instead, he said, "We in America could do the same in six months if we really applied our knowledge and resources to it."

Madame Minister 28

"Take your jacket off," she said, "feel at home—like your countrymen made me feel at home in England!"

This was how my interview with Madame Li Teh-chuan started. Madame Li is Minister of Health, in charge of the national medical program since 1949.

In my hotel immediately afterward I wrote the following account of the interview in my journal:

I have just returned from the most enjoyable, confusing, lively, frustrating interview I have had in China.

An official was waiting for me at the entrance of the Ministry of Health and took me to the main building across a garden court. On the second floor at the top of the stairs were standing Madame Li and a Vice-Minister of Health whose name I never recorded. She greeted me warmly in very fair English and took me to a pleasant reception room, flowers on the table, sun pouring through the windows.

After the tea was poured I waited for Madame Li to give me the accustomed "briefing" but she said, "Go ahead, go ahead—ask me some questions."

I began by asking her to give me a picture of the over-all development of medical services that had taken place in China.

Madame Li: The total number of hospital beds available in 1949 was 60,000 in 171 hospitals; today our latest figures are 467,000 beds in about 1200 hospitals. Still far too few. But I'm talking now only of well-equipped hospitals with various departments, fully trained doctors, and a trained nursing staff. In addition we have hospitals and maternity homes at the county level—6000 of them; and at a still lower level we have 200,000 health clinics in the rural communes.

F. G.: How many doctors are you training today?

Madame Li: I'll have those figures immediately.

She sent out one of the young aides, who returned with a list as follows:

1. *Higher Medical Colleges*

Total graduated in twenty years before liberation	9,499
Number graduated in 1949	1,314
Number graduated in 1959	14,849
Total graduated in ten years	48,474

This is 510 per cent more than were graduated in twenty pre-liberation years.

2. *"Secondary" Medical Schools*
(Doctors receive four-year course but are not fully qualified.)

Total graduated in twenty years before liberation	41,437
Number graduated in 1949	3,803
Number graduated in 1959	50,155
Number graduated in ten years	181,263

This is 437.4 per cent higher than were graduated in twenty pre-liberation years.

I next asked Madame Li about infant mortality.

She was off! Speaking fast, sometimes in English, more often than not in Chinese, with Yen trying his best to keep up. . . .

Madame Li as she spoke was leaning forward, hands on knees. She has black hair, swept back; glasses; she wore a blue skirt, white blouse, strong shoes. Her hands are those of a peasant, strong and capable. She reminded me of some of the vital pioneering women of the West—Elizabeth Fry in England, Jane Addams of Hull House in America. Jane Addams and Madame Li would, I think, have understood each other perfectly.

"The greatest cause of infant mortality in the past was due to tetanus infection and old-fashioned methods. Another reason was that in the minds of the women there was something shameful about pregnancy, and they attempted to hide their condition. Also there was a measure of shame attached to having their babies delivered by a man doctor."

She had, she told me, a very special, personal interest in this question of infant birth and care. She had spent a great deal of time in the countryside. She had seen and talked to the midwives, and found them eager to learn new methods.

The state today, she went on to tell me, makes every effort to see that mothers are delivered in a hospital or maternity center. She feels the psychological state of a mother is as important as the actual medical care. Good equipment is important, of course, but the attitude of a mother toward childbirth is equally so. She is now studying very hard to get a real insight into the current psychological attitudes prevailing among the people in the country.

In the cities maternal mortality is low; in the countryside—especially in the remote regions of Inner Mongolia, Sinkiang—where communications are bad, it is higher. She estimated the national average rate of maternal mortality as .26 per thousand.

We then had a lively discussion about the causes of mental ill-health. I said it was the number-one socio-medical problem in the United States; that the incidence in China was undoubtedly lower, but that we had heard of some developments here, especially regarding a new treatment for schizophrenia.

The Minister replied that mental health was largely dependent upon the relationships between human beings. She had visited the United States for two years: "There was far too much that was overstimulating there; night and day it would go on—crash, crash, noise and pressure—no tranquillity is possible there. Living is insecure, which leads to anxiety. Undoubtedly in China there are some mental cases handed down from the old society and a few cases that are new for a variety of reasons. But our society is paying the greatest possible care to the security of livelihood of everyone and the healthy relationship between people."

The Vice-Minister then broke in and said, "Mental ill-health is a social disease often brought on by economic insecurity. A number of people get mentally ill through anxiety. Who is it that gets mentally ill? Stockholders, speculators, and so on—this anxiety is an important factor in causing mental illness. We are not in a position to say there is no mental illness, but as our economy expands and we move ever closer to real socialism, we will eliminate even the little we have."

F. G.: There are surely factors more important than economic anxiety. We have learned, for instance, that the primary cause of mental illness is the lack of real affection which a child receives in his early life, but which might reveal itself only many years later. . . .

Madame Li (breaking in): I want to tell you an experience of my own during the anti-Japanese war, when I worked with the Children's Health Protection Committee. Many fathers were killed in this war and their children had become beggars, because the mothers were unable to look after them, having to go to work to earn. This was in 1938. We took 20,000 of these children and took care of them in institutions and public-welfare centers and I haven't heard of a single case of mental illness in any one of them. Other people can take the place of mothers and fathers.

Vice-Minister: Consideration and love to children is important and so is physical and mental care; and this depends a great deal on the child's education. We think it is very important to give children humane care, adequate nourishment, and plenty of physical exercise. Some in your Western countries who have no economic insecurity have mental illness, so we agree there are other causes than that.

Madame Li: I will tell you something of my own experience. During these last few years I have been very happy—I wish I were a child again so that I could go on enjoying life longer, and to have the fun the children get now. . . .

This account is far more orderly than it really was. I interjected here with a question about population increase. What was the official figure? I had heard estimates ranging between 2 per cent and 3.5 per cent.

Even a simple factual question like this gave rise to a flood of talk, sometimes both Ministers talking at once, one often breaking in again before the first translation had been completed; often the Minister would turn and talk to me in English while Yen was still translating—utter confusion. That is why this interview was both enjoyable and frustrating; enjoyable because here were two highly competent, humorous, extroverted, jovial, and friendly people. But frustrating because here, at the very pinnacle of the public-health program, were two people who had it in their power to give me all the statistics I required, but not doing so. *Not* because they were hiding anything from me—why should they?—but because statistics are so boring compared to the vivid stories of improvement, personal anecdotes, chit-chat, enthusiastic references to the Chinese recovery, etc. They are too human, too spontaneous to think that *figures* can be of interest. I felt over and over again during this interview that by bringing the conversation back to a factual statistical level I was a little boorish. They must have felt as one would telling an exciting adventure story to someone who kept asking us about the blood pressure of the young man or the calorie intake of the heroine.

But it was exciting to see their excitement. The health story of China is one of fantastic success. Children who ten years ago would be scratching for food on garbage dumps, eating grass, dying by tens of thousands through malnutrition, are now among the healthiest children in Asia. Smallpox licked, tetanus licked, venereal disease licked, cholera licked, maternal mortality down to Western levels; schistosomiasis, a terrible scourge in China, being tackled, the streets cleaned up; a public highly health conscious, universal immunization programs, flies "liquidated," slums cleaned up and under hygienic control, hospitals built by the hundreds; streets, hotels, trains, public buildings, schools, as clean as our own. The greatest transformation, probably, in the history of public health!

And realizing I was not getting an answer to my question on population increase, I tried another tack and asked the Minister about the official birth control policy.

"We have no *moral* objection to birth control. To women in a weak condition, women who shouldn't have any more children or who do not want any more children, we give birth control advice. Otherwise, people who want children have as many as they want. It is entirely and absolutely up to the family. There are two main considerations: the protection of the woman's health and the health of the children."

Turning to me suddenly, Madame Li asked, "How many children do you have?"

"One," I said.

"Pooh, shame on you. I have five, the Vice-Minister has four. I wish I had more."

Again it is the *personal*, the immediate, that matters.

I tried once more to get the figure on population increase.

Vice-Minister: Yes, yes, we will try and find the figure. Somewhere around 10,000,000 a year, more or less. (Again the noninterest in the population growth as a problem. Here, just as in the agricultural department, the figures that we know and worry about are just not known offhand, and are not considered very important.)

F. G.: Are there any signs of exhaustion among your population? They work harder than any people I have ever seen. I notice they sleep in buses coming back from work. I have seen men lie down on the sidewalk, put their caps under their cheeks for a pillow, and go to sleep. Are you not pushing your people too hard?

Madame Li: Yes, there were periods when we worked too hard and there are still some cases of exhaustion. We have given this quite special attention. The national policy now is no workday to be longer than eight hours, six days a week. There may be exceptions such as during harvest time, but these are quite temporary and unavoidable as all farmers know. The general rule today is an eight-hour maximum day, two hours of study, eight hours of sleep —and six hours for recreation, doing nothing or whatever one wants. We are very aware of this problem. We are encouraging wherever we can the development of reading circles, drama groups, individual creativity through painting and music, and in this way people can learn while they are also relaxing.

Vice-Minister: Our problem is really one of urging people not to work too hard, rather than to urge them to work harder. That is difficult for Westerners to believe, but it happens to be true. The collective socialist enthusiasm for getting on with all the things that need doing, the socialist construction of the country, has been so great that we have had to devise ways through propaganda to teach people not to overdo it, but to give themselves plenty of time to relax and sleep.

I asked two questions about fall-out. First, are tests made to see to what extent food and milk are being contaminated in China through fall-out of Strontium 90, etc.? Second, sooner or later China will have her own bomb and what are those who have opposed all tests to say to China when she contributes *her* share of contamination?

This started another avalanche of talk from both at once, more confusion. I finally got the general drift: that this country is opposed to all nuclear weapons (no mention was made of possible Chinese weapons), that they are very conscious of the genetic consequences of excessive radiation dosage, that it is less dangerous to small children here as milk is not part of the Chinese diet.

Madame Li: Our children, all of them above ten years old, know very well about the bombs on Hiroshima and Nagasaki and the horrors of war. They sing little songs about this. So from the youngest children to adults we are *all* against H- and A-bomb tests.

F. G.: What is the Chinese suicide rate? (A guffaw from the Minister.)

Madame Li: What should *we* want to commit suicide for?

I press this. Another flood of talk. (I *like* this, I'm dealing with people, not calculating machines, but it is difficult for me as a reporter!)

Vice-Minister: We are now "walking on two legs." That means we are using both skilled and less skilled doctors; full education and spare-time education. We are using all our human resources. This means that we are trying to eliminate unhappiness. Of course, there is some. But this is a socialist country and the relationship between our people is a good one. There is great *hope* in this country and a great sense of *purpose*, and those are not conditions that lead to a high suicide rate. I think the number of suicides must be infinitesimal, certainly far too small ever to appear on any of the returns we compile here.

F. G.: What is the expenditure from the national budget that is devoted to public health?

Madame Li: We will look that up for you. It is the second highest of the social expenditures, it comes after the expenditure on education.

(I received this figure later: 1.6 billion yuan ($640 million) was spent by the state for medical purposes in 1960. This does not include provincial or local expenditures.)

Vice-Minister: Expenditure on public health falls into two sections: 1) the facilities provided by the Department of Health, and 2) the facilities provided by the factories and other enterprises. When any factory is built now, a clinic and a hospital *must* be built as an integral part of that factory, though it needn't be right at the same site. This is for the factories above county level. In rural areas each residential district must set up a clinic; the size varies according to the need, but it must provide hospital care and an out-patient department. This means that virtually every Chinese is covered by some medical service wherever he may live.

F. G.: Madame Li, you were once closely associated with the Christian church. Are you still a Christian?

Madame Li: That's a very good question and I want to answer it. I was born of very poor peasant parents, neither of them could read or write. They were ignorant, but they were Christian. I was baptized when I was three months old. My parents couldn't afford to send me to school but they did send me to a missionary school. Missionary schools were divided, there was one kind for the richer people and another kind for the poorer. I went to the poorer one. The food was very bad. We used to sing [and here the Minister sang lustily], Do Ray Me . . . Me Ray Do.

The work at this poor school was done by the students—part

work, part study. I washed clothes, my own and others'. I cleaned up the yard, too, and that sort of thing.

Then I went to college at the expense of the mission school, they would pay for some of us on condition we would pay it back. After I left college I worked for five years getting the equivalent of twenty-four yuan a month, and half of this I paid back to the mission school until it was all paid off. I paid back not only the tuition but the interest on the loan as well.

At that time I believed in Jesus, because he was the son of a carpenter. "There is a nest for the birds, a lair for the wolves, but the son of man hath nowhere to lay his head." . . . I may not have got that right, but you know the quotation. That's why I loved Jesus. As you may know, my late husband, Feng Yu-hsiang, was known abroad as the "Christian general." At that time I loved Christianity. Later on I got an understanding of Marx and Lenin. I saw the USSR. I wanted to help improve the conditions of the people, but everywhere I saw the way in which the landlords were making improvement impossible. I saw that it was the Party that seemed really concerned with the welfare of the ordinary people.

The discussion having lasted over two hours, and knowing how busy these Ministers must be, I felt it was time for me to leave. They insisted on coming down to the street to see me to the car. We walked through the gardens—part of the Ministry had been a private house belonging to the uncle of Henry Pu-yi, the last Emperor—and I climbed into my car. The two Ministers remained standing in the road, waving, as I drove off.

A remarkable interview with a remarkable woman.

"Walking on Two Legs"

One sip is worth 10,000 words.

Somehow I had picked up a nasty variety of foot-infection while I was in Peking, and found myself, one disenchanted morning, in company with my interpreter headed for the hospital, not as a VIP, but as a rather anxious patient. For ten days I had been on anti-biotics and sleeping pills. Today, with a foot twice its normal size, they were to decide what further action was called for.

My journal for that day reads as follows:

I sat for half an hour in line downstairs outside the surgery clinic. It reminded me of some of the older London hospitals, the cracked paint, the exposed pipes everywhere, the people crowding the benches waiting their turn.

Alongside me was a Young Pioneer, red scarf round his neck, short pants, keen-looking. Little by little in the hot passage his head drooped and finally I felt it resting against my arm.

On another bench a father with a small girl and younger boy waited while the wife was being attended inside. I watched the endless delight he seemed to take in his children as he played with them, letting them thump him playfully on the chest, letting the boy go through his pockets. No one took much notice of their antics; I think they would have been "hushed" in England or America. The little fellow, perhaps he was all of three, crawled under the bench and tugged away at a loose bracket. But no one minded.

Down the line was a young tough whose injured forearms were bandaged together to keep him from moving them too much. An old, old lady with bound feet with that wise and patient look so many elderly Chinese have. Then, a mother who held an infant and showed her neighbors where the child had a skin disease which was causing his wailing. To comfort him she lifted her blouse and nursed him. A woman, with a four- or five-year-old, who paced up and down the corridor. She wore a pretty skirt and matching red shoes, carried a neat shopping bag. She was unmistakably middle-class. I looked at her a moment wondering whether she really was Chinese. I made room for her beside me and we spoke in English for a few minutes before she was called in. She reminded me so much of England, the ladies one sees nowadays waiting in line at a public hospital who find everything quite awful, wishing they could afford a private doctor and not mix with the hoipolloi.

There is no aura of "authority" about doctors in China. They don't appear to be much different from their clients and there is a definite lack of putting on airs. But I learned from Yen that doctors enjoy high social respect, which is not necessarily translated into their pay checks. He doubted whether many doctors earned more than 150 yuan a month, a senior surgeon perhaps as much as 200. "But they have a great opportunity to serve the people," Mr. Yen said.

My foot ached outrageously and I agreed with him.

My turn having come round, I was ushered into the examining room.

Dr. Wang, after some careful probing, decided minor surgery was necessary. He got on the telephone, told me there would be another short wait because an emergency had just come in, but it would not take long. Meanwhile I was sent off in a wheel chair to a dressing room where I was given a quite attractive pair of blue pajama trousers and a striped institutional-type top. I am a tall man and must have appeared rather ridiculous in a pair of pajamas made for the average Chinese.

The fourth floor was in great contrast to the sub-basement. No little boys peeking through dividing screens, no babies crying. Everything quiet. Orderlies were moving anesthetic equipment about. The nurses wore masks and close-fitting white caps.

Dr. Wang turned me over to the surgeon, Dr. Wu, slight and young-looking, but as I learned later, one of their most experienced surgeons. He spoke English well. He and his assistant wheeled me into an operating room. I should think this one is chiefly used for small affairs like mine, although it had all the lights, instruments in cases, and other gadgets in case they were required.

Lying on the operating table, I could see through the window the sloping roofs of the hospital, one of the eaves leaning so close to the window that the little animals on the green glazed tile seemed almost to be looking in.

Dr. Wu and his assistant examined the foot with great care. They discussed it, checked my pain reactions. Dr. Wu then told me they would freeze the foot, make an incision, and clear the abscess. He didn't know how deep he would have to go. I would feel some pain, he told me, but not for long; then I would notice an immediate diminishing of the pressure which had caused so much discomfort. He was in no hurry. Sterile instruments were brought in under a steaming cloth. Two nurses in masks stood by. Dr. Wu's hands were delicate and deft and I felt completely confident of his skill.

I felt a number of jabs, and I am sorry to say emitted a few groans and ouches, all the while telling myself that it was incumbent on me to set a good example of Western fortitude in the teeth of pain. However, I was sweating like a Turk in a steam bath before the doctor finally said, "That's all. It's all over."

I should have asked Dr. Wu a few professional questions: How long had he been practicing? Did he have a specialty within the field of surgery? Was he a member of the Chinese Medical Association? Where was he trained? Instead, I just watched him swab and bandage. What I wanted most was to get along back to the hotel and lay me down with a good shot of Chinese brandy.

The inquiring reporter could wait for another day.

The field of medicine in China has had its share of ideological struggle since 1949. At first there was a tendency to discard completely traditional practices as feudal and nonscientific. Then, there were other "theoreticians" who insisted that Western medicine was "capitalistic" and urged strict adherence to "socialist" (Russian) medical practice and theory.

While this "great debate" raged, however, emphasis in training much-needed medical personnel continued to be on Western methodology, "capitalist" and "socialist." In 1956, though, the whistle was blown and both sides stopped short. All aspects of Western medicine were to be considered. In an address before a group of intellectuals, Lu Ting-yi, head of the propaganda department of the Central Committee, suggested that in general "we borrow everything worthwhile the capitalists have devised in the field of science and technology." At the same time the need to incorporate the best features of traditional medicine was stressed.

Although the bulk of China's new doctors are being trained in Western methods, the present trend indicates an integration of the traditional and the Western. Thus, traditional practitioners are urged to acquire some Western learning, and vice versa.

For us in the West, one of the peculiarities of Chinese medicine is this dual acceptance of Western and traditional practice.

The traditional includes a bewildering variety of herbs and medications; muscular massage; control of pain through induced relaxation; and acupuncture, a technique which allegedly relieves pain and other symptoms by means of a fine needle thrust deeply into the tissue.

The position of the Chinese Western-trained doctors is that since traditional methods unquestionably cure patients, there must be something good in them and therefore they merit study. They point out that many drugs on the shelves of a modern pharmacy have been included for centuries in the traditional Chinese pharmacopoeia. Ephedrine (derived from the Chinese herb *ma-huang*) is only one of the most recent examples.

In all the hospitals and clinics I visited, both in the cities and in the communes, I was told that Western and traditional doctors work closely together. A patient may choose either variety he wishes; and one school of physicians frequently refers patients to the other school. In my own case, for example, when I returned on the day after surgery to have the dressings changed, I complained of muscular cramps in the calf and thigh, and was sent over by Dr. Wu to the "traditional" department.

There I received a good old traditional Swedish massage, and very comforting it was, too. On another occasion, when I was visiting a hospital in Chengchow, I asked one of the traditional doctors to try an acupuncture on my arm, which he did readily enough. Since I was not feeling any pain to begin with, I could scarcely determine how much it might have cured. But at least it didn't cause any pain. And the insertion of an inch or two of needle into the flesh provides an experience sufficiently dramatic so that I feel confident it would take my mind off whatever anxieties might be troubling me.

Written records show that acupuncture dates back to the Sung Dynasty, A.D. 1000. The needles are manufactured from a silver-steel alloy and range in length from three-eighths of an inch to three and a half inches.

The general theory seems to be that the stimulation of key nerve centers, often some distance from the area of ailment, can result in a partial or complete cure of certain types of disorders, chiefly motor and digestive. Treatment of deaf mutes is traditionally done in this manner.

How effective, or ineffective, all this is I am unable to answer. It continues to be practiced and delved into by both styles of doctors in China. They believe it has merit.

There was, apparently, sufficient evidence that Chinese traditional medicine obtains, under certain conditions, striking therapeutic results, for the government to set up an institute for a full-scale investigation to determine what scientific basis for it there might be. This is a long-term inquiry and its reports are not expected for some time.

Here in Peking, as well as in some of the commune clinics I visited, Western doctors tried to convince me that appendicitis was now being handled by traditional methods. When I pressed for chapter and verse, it turned out that persistent or acute cases are still being sent into surgery just as they would be in Chicago or London.

Dr. Fox, in his article in *The Lancet*, writes: "How much importance Chinese 'modern' doctors really attach to traditional medicine is not quite clear. Cooperation has been ordained and it is easily made to sound sensible. . . .

"The more cynical among us [he is referring to the visiting group of English doctors] could not but note the convenience of being able to refer one's less rewarding patients to an alternative system of medicine, which makes full use of the scientific arts."

There are other, and I think even more compelling, reasons.

China had in 1960 a little more than 200,000 doctors trained in Western medicine—this included those with "secondary" training—in a population of 700 million inhabitants. But there were 400,000 traditional doctors, more or less. Obviously the vast majority of Chinese, particularly those out in the country, if they ever received a doctor's care at all would have to receive it from one of the traditionalists.

Had the government attacked this group, it would only have created widespread opposition. To include them *in*, to grant them acceptance and status, thus bringing them into co-operation with, and to some extent under the direction of, the Western doctors, was a thoroughly sensible compromise. I learned that traditional doctors in many areas were being taught sterile techniques and were carrying out government programs of vaccination and immunization.

I remember, as I remembered a good many times during my trip through China, what the Vice-Minister of Health had said to me on the occasion of my visit to the Health Ministry: "We are now 'walking on two legs.' That means we are using both skilled and less skilled doctors; full education and spare-time education. We are using all our human resources."

The Misfits 30

It takes two sides to make a revolution, any revolution, and one side loses. Thus every revolutionary upheaval must leave behind masses of uprooted and disoriented persons. From these come the forces of active opposition if there is to be any. And from these come the inevitable *émigrés*, loyalists, refugees. The Chinese civil war was a bitter thirty-year struggle, combined with seven years of a war of national liberation against the Japanese. The residue of social dislocation is correspondingly vast. The *losers* of China's revolution could be divided into three categories:

1. Top leaders of the Kuomintang, many of whom had amassed huge fortunes. Some of these—for example, the Chiangs, Kungs, Soongs, Chens—left China even before the Communists had completed their victory. The wealth they took with them ran into the hundreds of millions. The Associated Press, on August 13, 1949, reported that the United States had frozen 500 million dollars deposited by Chinese citizens in American banks to prevent the new Peking government from getting its hands on it. The amount of similar funds in Europe and South America has never been made public.

2. A second major group among the losers were the landlords. It has been estimated there were twenty million landlords in China. With the coming to power of Mao Tse-tung, they lost all their holdings, except a plot of land for each one to work himself. Many of these were "rich" only in relation to the poverty of the bulk of the population. They could not have fled even if they had wished. During the first years they probably thought Communist rule was only a passing phase; and that the Kuomintang forces, as they had done in the thirties in sections of South China, would return.

Besides the loss of their land, many landlords suffered more severe penalties. Probably thousands were tried for various crimes, particularly in connection with the Japanese war, when landowners frequently sided with the invaders and were used by the Japanese. And there were those who had taken advantage of periods of calamity to extort the last remaining plots of ground, tools, and even children from peasants made desperate by starvation. How many were tried and condemned, and whether justly or unjustly, and how many were killed without trial it would be impossible to estimate. But the price was not always death. Some were deprived of the rights of citizenship for several years; others were denied admittance into the developing co-operatives or communes.

3. The third group among the losers were those elements of the middle-class professionals, businessmen, and intellectuals who were not able to come to terms with the new regime. These groups, for the most part, were not among those who had fought actively on the side of Chiang Kai-shek. They had been caught in between, unable to identify with either side. They had shared neither the misery of the peasants nor the age-old privileges of the wealthy. Many, particularly young people, as the Kuomintang disintegrated during

its final years through corruption and chaos, had thrown in their lot with the revolution. These were writers, actors, students, teachers, and some Christians.

But others remained on the fence. They could neither support the revolution nor reject it. Living largely in the coastal cities, they had developed a sense of inferiority about their country and its people. They felt that progress could only be *Western* progress, and above all, American. They would display a certain esteem for China's ancient culture; but for anything of contemporary China, they felt only shame.

These groups from among the intellectuals and the middle class, during the ten years since the end of the revolution, have fared considerably better than the ex-landlords. Opportunities on a scale never before dreamed of have opened up for their children. Still, there remain, I am sure, considerable numbers of the older ones who have not adjusted and probably never will. How many, I have no way of telling; but I would not be surprised if there were several million, perhaps 1 or 2 per cent of the population. With the exception of the handful who may find their way out of China to Taiwan or to overcrowded Hong Kong, for the most part these people are living out their lives as outsiders in their own land, misfits in a world they are no longer able to comprehend.

Their lot is a deeply tragic one; history has left them stranded. They are not likely to play any very effective role, either in China or outside of it.

I ran across a few of them, altogether by accident, during my travels. A glimpse of their stories is revealing.

There was a young man I sat beside at a concert one night in Shenyang. He spoke English and we chatted. As we were parting, I said, "Look in and see me if you have time." Which, unexpectedly, he did. For an hour we sat in my room and talked. He said he was a Christian. He hoped I would write objectively about China; and added, "I mean *really*, not just what they tell you." I pricked up my ears. "How much do people believe of what they say?" I asked.

"Most believe every word. Some only some. Some none at all. We go along. It's no good spoiling your career before you've begun."

He was eager to talk. During that discussion we covered many topics: the monolithic similarity of all public speeches; the food situation, which was very tight in the cities then; the Party committee in control of every undertaking; the question of dissent.

"The real penalty of being named a rightist," he said, "is public ostracism. Sometimes even to the point where shopkeepers will not sell to such a person." He estimated that in a free election only 50 per cent of the people would approve the new regime.

I asked him about sexual codes.

He said there was some sexual relationship among unmarried young people and this was not morally disapproved of. Extramarital relations were not held against a man if it were known, unless his political views happened to be suspect as well. "The correct political attitude is more important than your sexual morals."

A wife might complain of her husband's political outlook at a Party meeting (or vice versa) but this would be largely for outside consumption. Their relationship at home would not be changed. He thought a good deal of this was political hypocrisy.

He seemed to me an earnest, intelligent individual, rather Western, rather liberal, still attempting to respond within the framework of his religious conditioning. He would be more at home in Europe than in China, and is hungering for some greater degree of individualism. Not caught up by the collective élan, he finds himself an outsider, and that must be painful indeed. But he was by no means a counterrevolutionary.

I asked him, "What do you think is the alternative to the present regime?"

Here he paused. This clearly was the crux of his predicament. In his answer lay the tragedy of his life.

"I don't think there is one. This regime, historically, was inevitable."

"What is your personal hope?"

"That it may change in time. Russia has changed. That's my only hope."

There was another man, thirty-five I should say, who started a conversation with me as I sat on a park bench in Shanghai. Our first meeting was brief. We talked about a number of things, none of them particularly interesting. I didn't take to him too much; I felt that at any minute he was going to try to sell me something.

When he asked whether he could come to my hotel to see me again, I hesitated, but I said "all right," and we fixed a time.

At the second meeting we talked quite a long time. For what it's worth, I record the gist of our conversation.

I started by asking him how freely people could travel in China today.

"Foreign travel is out, of course. Even if I saved up my money for ten years, I wouldn't have enough. And if I did, I wouldn't be allowed. Before, Chinese of my family's status often went abroad; now there's no chance. But I think it's important that young people see the world and so can judge things for themselves. For a while I had a chance of seeing foreign magazines, this gave me a picture of what the outside world is."

"What restrictions on travel *inside* China?"

"No actual restrictions, no travel permits or anything like that, but there are many difficulties which make travel complicated. And of course, there's always the money problem."

"What sort of difficulties?"

"You have to arrange your rations; and immediately you arrive at a place you have to notify the street committee where you are to be. And the authorities can come and ask you how long you are to be there, what you are planning to do, why did you come, and even suggest that you return to your own town sooner than you had wanted to. Accommodation is a difficulty, too. There are so few hotels or small inns."

"Tell me about the political meetings you have to attend."

"There are two kinds. First, the regular meetings held once or twice a week for political discussion. I have to go twice a week, and the meetings last from two to four hours. We read sections of Mao's writings and discuss them under the tutorship of a Party member."

"Is it a *real* discussion?"

"No one would be foolish enough to *question* anything fundamentally. We might ask for some passage to be explained technically, or say we don't quite understand how this fits in with that . . . not as a criticism but merely wanting enlightenment. It's very boring, but I have to do it. The other kind are the criticism and self-criticism meetings. They are held more rarely and are much more drastic. During the anti-rightist campaign they were held frequently but now my group doesn't have more than one every month or even two months. What happens is that if in your group of four or five it has been determined that you are the one that they will concentrate on, the others are told beforehand. When the meeting starts everyone says some of the things that they have done wrong, but when this has gone round the circle they will then come back to you and concentrate on *you*. It is very important for everyone to be able to say something bad about you, so you hear all the things that everyone can think up to say. You cannot get out of it by just admitting it, even if you *mean* it and quite genuinely see that what they are saying is right; you are still made to think it over and discuss it further and go over it."

"What is the purpose of this criticism?"

"To eradicate any of the old feelings, especially in those of us who had money and family position. It is a way the Party controls opposition. They don't have to discipline you, your associates do. It saves the Party a great deal of trouble."

"What is the result of this criticism on the one who is being criticized?"

"It is humiliating, of course, and very painful; and it makes you feel that the only way to get on is to lose your old courteous ways and begin criticizing others, and in this way you might avoid being the target yourself."

"Have you ever been the target?"

"No, but I have to join in and criticize the others."

"Don't you all begin to feel that it's something of a game, a play, that you have to go through but that doesn't mean very much?"

"That might be true of some, but for most people, they believe in the system and the Party enough so that these criticisms are taken very seriously."

"What do you think the system should be?"

"I don't know, but I think this country is more restrictive than Russia was twenty years ago. And things are tightening. We used to see a few Western movies but we hardly ever see them now. We used to be able to read translations of contemporary American and British authors but we hardly ever see them on the shelves any more. Formerly we could read foreign books, criticize and praise them; now it seems that almost *all* Western books are bad; *all* Western films are bad. We are more cut off from the world than we used to be."

"Do you believe one reason might be that this government genuinely fears there is a likelihood of invasion, and that it is preparing the people for it?"

"Yes, I believe that is true. The government is more militant, more all-the-time denouncing America. I think it is preparing to meet what it considers an inevitable conflict between East and West. We see reports about America strengthening her forces in Asia, especially around China, and what can we think?"

"Should America get out of Taiwan?"

"Of course. The Kuomintang was very bad. Even intellectuals, non-Communists, were so disgusted that they felt *anything* would be better than that. The Kuomintang is responsible for everything. It was their rottenness that made this government inevitable. You would not believe what I have seen in my youth, the disregard for the people, the cruelty and arrogance of that gang. Chiang Kai-shek is responsible for millions of deaths, people who starved because his officials were too corrupt, people he had shot.

"I wish that many young Americans could come here and that many of us could go there. I think it's very important for us to know America. But that can't happen until everything is changed."

"What are you going to do?"

"Do? There's nothing to do but go along with it."

From an acquaintance who was not at all an opponent, but a supporter of the regime, I gained a picture of the difficulties in adjustment encountered by a Chinese intellectual acclimated to Western ways.

Tsu Shou-cheng had returned to Shanghai from ten years in the United States only eight months previously. The authorities, he said, had been understanding of his problems. Realizing he was accustomed to a high living standard (he had been earning $800 a month in Chicago), they first put him up in a hotel, then found him a pleasant four-room flat. They also paid his fare out from San Francisco. He is now engaged in research in the ceramics industry, he was a ceramics engineer in America. He doesn't want to go back. The country is basically on the right lines, he believes; and as for the talk about freedom or lack of freedom, he feels that is all meaningless until a society can really stand on its own feet, until people are secure in their basic wants.

He said, "Whether a man coming back to China after ten years in America can adjust here depends on what he really wants from life. As you advance toward middle age, you realize that your time on earth is limited. So what do you wish to do with it? If your aims are merely personal, then it would be best to stay in America. If you want to feel you are part of a great movement that is trying to do something for the good of others, then return to China."

He has periods of nostalgia, he told me, for the easy, pleasant life of America; but feels his place is here with his own people. He insisted that living in China today calls for a fundamental readjustment of values, a drastic re-examination of one's own motives.

"The real revolution," he said, "is in the people." But he had had a rough time finding the key to all this. He felt the easiest way to grasp what was going on, was to consider it as a "religious" movement, directed not toward personal salvation, but toward a common advance. The results of this, the improvements he found in China after ten years away, were staggering.

Let me conclude this chapter with a word on Hong Kong refugees.

The picture that has been painted in Western reports is of a stream of desperate people, fleeing under cover of darkness, at the risk of their lives, across a heavily fortified frontier, from slavery to freedom. The theme has been embroidered endlessly in news dispatches on "mass executions" and "slave-labor communes," datelined Hong Kong.

Actually the facts are rather different.

Certainly there are refugees in Hong Kong, large numbers of them, who come from one or another of the various groups of losers discussed above. But it is important to place the refugee problem in the context of a realistic picture of Hong Kong and its relation to the mainland.

First of all, there is little necessity for people to sneak across the border "at the risk of their lives" because the frontier is practically open. Trains to the border run frequently; small boats ply back and forth; there is a constant flow of people from China to Hong Kong and from Hong Kong to China. For example, in February of this year, a CBS-TV news report quoted a British border official as saying that "a thousand to fifteen hundred Chinese a day go to China [*from* Hong Kong] to visit relatives: they pass quite freely; their papers are accepted by Red China."

Second, it is important to remember that Hong Kong is a *Chinese* city. It is ruled by the British, and 99 per cent of the population are Chinese. And Hong Kong bears the same relationship to adjacent areas of mainland China that a metropolis always bears to the agricultural hinterland. The city imports food from the country and the country people migrate to the city looking for jobs, just as young people from "downstate" go to Chicago to work in the factories. This has been true for centuries, except that before 1949 they were called *migrants* or *temporary residents*, rather than refugees. The Chinese in Hong Kong even today do not call the newcomers "refugees."

Finally, it is important to keep the size of this migration in proportion. China has a population close on 700 million, some of whom were obviously the losers in the revolution. Many of them suffered deeply and wanted to get out, just as there were considerable numbers of Empire Royalists, the losers in the American Revolution, who became "refugees" in Canada.

For the Chinese losers Hong Kong constitutes virtually the only port of exit; and for most of them it is a route that leads to no place else. Once in Hong Kong they must stay there or return, as many do. A few reach America or Taiwan. Long before 1949 there was a steady migration from both China and other parts of Asia to Hong Kong. The population of Hong Kong today is, roughly, three million. In 1949 it was 1,700,000. In eleven years, therefore, the island's population has increased by 1,300,000. But Hong Kong, like every other place, has a *natural* increase of population which in 1960 was estimated as no less than 60,000 per year.

When all these facts are balanced out, it appears that there has been an average inflow into Hong Kong *from all countries* of an average of about 70,000 a year, which represents *one-hundredth of one per cent* of the Chinese population.

Across the border, as I have said, stream many hundreds every day in both directions, and accurate figures are difficult to come by. Even the estimates of the numbers going into China every day for visits to relatives and friends vary considerably. Among those who come to Hong Kong from China there are undoubtedly many genuine refugees: those who have either detested the life there and find it too restrictive, active counterrevolutionaries, or those who are being sought, perhaps for nonpolitical crimes, by the Chinese police. But the figures, in popular imagination, have I think been greatly exaggerated.

No one would want to minimize the hardship or the extent of the human suffering implied by this migration to Hong Kong, nor the accute problem that it created for the tiny island which had to find accomodation for these newcomers. But from an account by the Hong Kong government we can see another and more hopeful side of the picture:

At first the endless lines of immigrants were regarded with pardonable misgiving. Overcrowded Hong Kong could well do without people who obviously would become a burden on its already strained resources.

These fears were quickly proved unfounded, however. Many of the Chinese were not refugees in the accepted sense. They had capital and they brought it with them. The rest showed traditional Chinese characteristics—a strong desire to find work, make money and be independent of everybody.

The Wealthy and the Wise   31

There is a widespread belief in the West that all the rich people of China, the former owners of businesses, for instance, as well as the intellectuals and scholars, even if they outwardly support it, must be secretly opposed to the Peking regime. I think this is a mistaken conception.

I had talks with several intellectuals—professors, heads of university departments, elderly scholars engaged in historical research—and I am convinced that their support of the government is genuine and not a clever bit of acting. They might on this aspect or that express sharp criticism but their basic acceptance and the reasons they gave for it appeared to me full-hearted and honest. And that seems to be true, also, of the middle class, although I met only a very few of these. There was one extended talk, however, that I had with a man who had once owned a large textile mill in Shanghai.

I was staying in Hangchow and was planning to leave the following day by train for Canton; this involved an overnight journey. I wanted, at the last minute, to bring my journey forward by a day. A train was due shortly—it was coming from Shanghai and had already left there—and I was told there were no tickets available for this train. But I took a chance and went with my bags to the station, hoping that the conductor would be able to find me, if not a sleeper, at least a seat on the train. As it turned out, there was one place available in a sleeping compartment which I shared with a Mr. Wang.

I relate these circumstances of my catching the train because others afterward have said that "quite obviously" Mr. Wang (whose conversation I am about to relate) was planted on the train specifically so that he could fill me with propaganda. This was quite impossible, for he had already boarded the train in Shanghai before I decided to catch it at Hangchow.

Mr. Wang spoke English fluently. He was on his way to Hong Kong for a two-week vacation. He was clearly a man of wealth. His shirts were of silk, and he had cuff links of star sapphires; his clothes were probably Hong Kong made. We had this long journey together, and enjoyed each other's company and had a good many congenial beers.

I asked him to tell me what happened when the Communists took over Shanghai, and this in outline was his story:

Shanghai suffered total demoralization during the last few months of Chiang's regime. Business had virtually come to a stop.

Inflation made money valueless. So almost everyone was in favor
of change—anything, they felt, was better than what was going on.
The strong "defense" of Shanghai—before Chiang, himself, left for
Canton he had ordered the city to "fight to the last man"—simply
petered out. The few pillboxes the army had built around the city
were soon overrun and large segments of the army deserted to the
Communists, including many officers. Everyone knew by that time
the game was up, so why lose one's life in a hopeless cause?

"But what happened to you, I mean those of you who owned
large undertakings?"

"Nothing at first. The Communists supported us. They confiscated immediately the holdings of the key Kuomintang officials, but
as for us, they needed us, they wanted the mills and factories to
keep going and they helped us do it. A political party was formed
and sponsored by the Communists, the capitalist party. This was
all written into the constitution; it says there that the positive sides
of capitalist industry which are beneficial should be retained. But,
of course, from the beginning it was made clear to us that this was
just temporary, that sooner or later the government would take over
our enterprises."

[I looked this up afterward. Article 10, dealing with this, reads in
part: "The state protects the right of capitalists to own means of
production and other capital according to law.

"The policy of the state toward capitalist industry and commerce
is to use, restrict, and transform them. The state makes use of the
positive sides of capitalist industry and commerce which are beneficial to national welfare and the people's livelihood, encourages
and guides their transformation into various forms of state-capitalist
economy, gradually replacing capitalist ownership with ownership
by the whole people."]

"We worked, of course, under strict regulation," Mr. Wang continued, "and eventually the state decided step by step to take over
legal ownership of our undertakings. The transfer was gradual, but
the plans were precise. There was no room for argument."

"What was their deal?"

"It was this. The capital value of our undertakings would be mutually agreed upon. They were prepared to pay us 5 per cent of this
value each year up to ten years. It was simple and forthright; and it
was also a take-it-or-leave-it proposition. Most of us took it, there

seemed to be nothing else to do. Some wouldn't, they left for Hong Kong or Taiwan, where probably they had salted away some funds earlier. I stayed."

"How has it worked out?"

"For me? Fine. They will pay me the final installment in a few years. I invested the money—it comes to a great deal—in the People's Bank and am drawing good interest on it. In addition I earn four hundred yuan a month as manager of the factory I once owned. In my life it has made very little difference. I even live in the same apartment as I did before. I don't have the worries I used to have!"

"And what happens to the money in the bank when you die?"

"Oh, my family gets it. Under the constitution there is the right to inherit family property."

"One last question," I said. "What do you call yourself?"

He laughed cheerfully. "Do you know what we call ourselves? We call ourselves 'Communist capitalists!' "

And that, I thought, was as good a description as any.

Here was self-interest at work. It was a straight business deal that the Communists offered, more sensible than running these men out of town or executing them. It was a no-nonsense plan that benefited both sides. They had clearly learned something from the Russians, who were left after their revolution with no people of managerial skill and had to start painfully from scratch.

But the intellectuals?

There is a general impression in the West that the scholars and intellectuals have suffered greatly under the new regime. Forgotten are the executions and assassinations of writers and professors by Chiang Kai-shek in the thirties and forties. The assassination of Professor Wen Yi-tuo in Kunming in 1946 was one that received some note in the Western press at the time; the full list, running into the hundreds, has always been known in China. In the final desperate years many intellectuals were forced underground, others fled to Hong Kong. In the latter case there were wholesale returns following Chiang's defeat in 1949.

With the exception of a handful, the leading writers, artists, scholars, poets, scientists, philosophers, and religious leaders not only welcomed the new government, they have continued actively to support it. A number who had been living abroad returned to

China after the government was already entrenched. Lao Sheh, author of the best-selling novel *Rickshaw Boy* came back from America, where he had been a guest of the United States Information Service.

A few have had their difficulties, some have been dismissed from their positions. Two well-known members of China's literati, Hu Feng and Ting Ling, are examples of intellectuals who were dismissed from the Writers' Union for political reasons. Hu Feng was a well-known literary critic and Ting Ling a famous woman novelist. Submitted to severe public criticism, both fell out of favor, but neither was imprisoned.

In the case of Hu Feng, in 1955 his two-hundred-page protest calling for the abolition of the Writers' Union and plea for taking cultural affairs out of the hands of the government was published as a supplement to China's leading literary magazine, *Literature and Art*.

It would be quite wrong, I believe, to assume that the intellectuals of China just go along. They continue to play a vital role in the life of the nation. Dr. Joseph Needham, whose reputation as a Sinologist and student of Chinese science is second to none in the West, and a personal friend of innumerable scholars in China before 1949, after his 1958 visit reported how much less ideological pressures were influencing their work or lives than he had expected.

The names of the intellectuals who remained in China and are wholeheartedly supporting the regime read almost like a roll of honor: Feng Yu-lan, philosopher; Fei Shiao-tung, sociologist; Mao Tun, Tsao Yu, and Pa Chin, novelists; Kuo Mo-jo, historian and academician; Ai Ching, poet; Li Ssu-kuan, head of the Ministry of Geology; Tao Meng-ho, President of the Academia Sinica; Y. T. Wu and T. C. Chao, leaders of the Protestant church.

The list of eminent intellectuals—scholars and scientists—could be extended almost indefinitely. With rare exceptions, such as Dr. Hu Shih, who left China before the Kuomintang debacle, there is scarcely a single ranking intellectual of world reputation who has not found a useful place for himself in China.

Professor C. P. Fitzgerald addresses himself to this point in his book, *Revolution in China*, which was described by the London *Times* as "the most important contribution that has so far appeared

on the nature and behaviour of the Chinese People's Republic."
This is what Professor Fitzgerald says:

"It is . . . difficult for the West to believe that the Chinese people can have voluntarily accepted Communism. It is hard to credit
the free support given to a regime which denies freedom to some
and only hands out a very qualified freedom to others. And yet
there is no real doubt that the new system has obtained the support
of the people, has satisfied the aspirations of the literates, and has
won to itself the devotion of the men of religious temperament.

"The military success of the Communists would have been in
itself insufficient to secure the new regime had it not been accompanied by a conversion which has aligned the great majority of intellectuals behind the Communist movement."

Nevertheless it is probable that the initial alliance between the
Communist Party and non-Marxist intellectuals soon became a
somewhat cautious one on both sides—the intellectuals were thank-
ful that Chiang's repressive measures and his indiscriminate purges
in the universities had come to an end and they were ready to give
the new regime full support in its agricultural and industrial reforms, but they must have looked with some dismay on the reten-
tion of political power by a single party—with all the restrictions
on freedom that that would imply. To the Communists, on the
other hand, the non-Marxist intellectuals must have appeared too
deeply conditioned by bourgeois ideas of individualism ever to be
fully trusted.

Pressure on the intellectuals to become aware of their "mistaken
attitudes" continued until 1956. They were expected to undergo
intensive political study to overcome their ideological "inferiority."
The Communist Party undoubtedly hoped that a sincere change
of outlook, a sort of religious conversion, would bring the intellectuals full heartedly to their side.

In 1956 Mr. Chou En-lai called for more support for intellectuals
and less suspicion of them. And this was followed up in 1957 by
Mao's famous "Hundred Flowers" speech in which he declared that
ideological differences could not be expected to disappear all at
once and that they could only be resolved by free discussion. In
this speech the people of China were invited to criticize the Com-

munist Party's conduct of the revolution. It received an overwhelming response. It lasted just one month.

It became clear that some of China's intellectuals refused to limit themselves to a criticism of the workings of the system, but condemned the system itself. They were accused of rightism and some were sent to the country to work among the peasants to learn the real meaning of the revolution.

It was immediately assumed in the West that the "Hundred Flowers" speech had been merely a trick to catch the discontented ones. I, personally, do not believe that this was so, nor do others who have followed this episode closely. A most interesting analysis of this speech and its consequences by Mr. John Gray was broadcast by the BBC in England and subsequently printed in the *Listener* of March 9, 1961. Mr. Gray is a lecturer at the School of Asian Studies at London University. This is what he said: "The 'Hundred Flowers' movement can be regarded as one of a series of attempts to keep open the channels of communication between Party and people which Mr. Mao has been making since 1942. The reaction in which it ended is more than adequately accounted for by the fact that the criticisms were unexpectedly radical, that the critics clearly had Hungary in mind, that they showed that they had forgotten none of their western bourgeois prejudices, and, finally, that the revisionism which they represented had become—as a result of events in Eastern Europe—a threat to the unity of the Communist bloc, on the solidarity of which China feels that her safety depends. The only surprising thing about that reaction was its mildness; a year later, most of the principal victims were at liberty and had been restored to some, though not all, of their positions."

The French writer and poet Claude Roy, who was also seeking clues as to why China's intellectuals had in such large measure given their allegiance to the Communists, records the following interview in his book, *Into China* with the author of *A History of Chinese Philosophy*, which is regarded by Western scholars as the definitive work on Chinese philosophy.

"Professor Feng Yu-lan is an old Chinese gentleman of between 60 and 70, with long thin classic goatee and extraordinarily fine and expressive hands.

" 'Have you spent all your life at the Tsing Hua University in Peking?' I asked.

" 'No, I took my philosophy degree in 1924 at Columbia University and my doctorate at Princeton in 1946. I taught Chinese philosophy in the States. . . . I was offered a permanent chair but preferred to return to China in spite of the civil war.'

" 'Were you interfered with or persecuted by the Kuomintang government?'

" 'No. Like many intellectuals I adopted a passive but rather distant attitude towards the Kuomintang. I felt that I was keeping aloof from politics. . . .'

" 'Weren't you tempted to leave China after the liberation?'

" 'No, but I prepared to follow the course of events with all my powers of criticism. Out of curiosity I asked permission to participate in the land reform in the country districts and in this way I made contact with the people as I had never done before. I was extremely impressed by the technique of criticism and self-criticism practiced by my Marxist colleagues. Before leaving for the front, two of my students, both Communists, discussed their ideas with me for two days. When they left, I was so interested by all I had seen and heard that I wrote an essay on self-criticism from the philosophical point of view. One of my friends then pointed out that I was trying to lecture academically on self-criticism but not to practice it myself. I was forced to admit that was right. . . .

" 'I am definitely convinced today that the goal of philosophy should be the modification of men and the world. I have resumed the study of Chinese philosophy in the light of this principle and on the basis of a total union between practice and theory, between thought and action. I have just finished a work in which I outline the epistemological evolution of Chinese thought through Confucius, the Moists, Taoist idealism and the School of Laws down to modern times.'

"[After speaking of this work] Professor Feng took a book from his shelves and read me a few lines of Wang Yang-ming (a philosopher of the Ming dynasty, who lived from 1472 to 1528): 'It is not necessarily difficult to know but it is certainly difficult to act. The most difficult then should be our preliminary preoccupation, and this same preoccupation will be difficult at the outset. Knowledge depends on action for its fruits, but action does not necessarily depend on knowledge to be effective. Action, however, always leads to knowledge, whereas knowledge does not necessarily lead to action.'

"'Philosophers like . . . Wang Yang-ming were misunderstood or unknown even in China. I think that it would be of the greatest interest both here and in the West to rediscover them and to see their ideas being realized at last in contemporary Marxism,' and Professor Feng added: 'Tell my friends and colleagues in America and in the West that there is no mystery about my intellectual evolution. There is a Christian saying: "For the tree is known by its fruit." I have tasted the fruit of the New China and I wanted to know the roots of the tree which produced it. That is the entire story of my "self-criticism".' "

I recall, too, in this connection, an evening I spent with a historian, a man who came from a wealthy and distinguished family, educated at Oxford. He was a scholar to his fingertips.

I had arrived at his house a little earlier than he. His wife greeted me and he appeared a few moments later, looking rather drawn and tired. We sat for a while quietly sipping tea and eating small cakes.

I asked him if he was ever involved in any of the political meetings I had heard so much about.

"Oh yes," he said, "we have meetings every week. We are all, whatever our work, members of some group. We meet and exchange ideas about our work."

"Aren't these meetings a fearful *bore?*"

He smiled. "It depends on who you *are*. A pedicab driver, I think, will look forward with real eagerness to his political meetings. After all, reading is still difficult for most of them; it's a chance to be read to and meet and talk. An occasion for them, a weekly social gathering. And they learn a good deal about the society they are living in."

"And you?"

"Well, yes, it often becomes tedious for us; and I find it especially aggravating when I am in the middle of some intensive work. But more often than not, the discussion is what we make it. If we are dull, the meeting is dull. And of course, some of these meetings are self-criticism or mutual criticism and they are never dull!"

"Tell me about them."

"I do not think you can understand the workings of this new

society unless you realize the profound effect these criticism meetings have had on the people, on all of us. From the earliest days these meetings have been an integral part of the Communist technique for the remolding of this country. Tonight, that's why I was late, we had a criticism meeting; it's part of a campaign that my research group is involved in just now to rectify mistakes in our work. Sometimes during these campaigns we might have to meet almost every night. What's happening in this campaign is that we are going through and evaluating both our research and our teaching work. We are attached to a university and we bring up mistakes that we think the university is making; they might bring up mistakes they think we are making. It's like an elaborate postmortem. Every mistake is discussed very seriously. [He looked across at me and smiled.] Oh, we are very, very solemn about all this; and we usually find that the mistake was because of some error of thinking by some person who will then have to be helped to reach an understanding of the failings that led to the mistake."

"Would he ever get fired?"

"No. Dismissal is very rare. It's the last, most drastic step, and we consider it a collective failure. Now, it will be a little different in a university, but if I were in a bank, shall we say, and I were constantly making mistakes, or always in disputes with my colleagues, I would first be reprimanded by my immediate superior. If that didn't help, I would be asked to attend a mutual-criticism meeting. One or two other people in my group (mutual-criticism meetings are usually not larger than five or six, never more than ten) would have prepared suggestions as to how I could be helped. A whole evening might be spent in discussing my difficulties. You must remember that criticism today is considered *helping*. We do not regard it as hostile, as you might. And if the meeting is properly conducted, I would be made to feel that the motive was really to help me, and not by any means to injure me or to lower my self-respect. Of course, there are some who resist even so; and then a big criticism meeting would be called, and that would be a very grueling experience. But only after these successive steps had been taken, and only if they had failed to improve the situation, would dismissal or transfer be felt justified."

"To me," I said, "all this sounds frightful! I would rather be fired."

"I can understand that. I felt at first as you do. I suffered intensely. Perhaps I was too Westernized, too remote and aloof. But do you know, I have come to believe that they are on the right track. The end result of these criticism meetings is therapeutic. They break down the wall of pretensions and defenses we build around ourselves. You cannot go on pretending and putting up a bluff after you have been through two or three of these meetings with your immediate associates! And we are never really very hard on the 'victim,' for we've been through it all ourselves."

"They sound like group-therapy sessions to me," I said.

"Not really, but they have some of the same effects, and go through the same cycles. At first when a group meets, the members are strangers and distrustful; and then as these meetings progress the members bring up all kinds of hidden hostilities that they have for each other. But that stage passes, too. And at the end of it all, you find you are working among people who really know each other and have become a group of intimate friends. The meetings are a conscious attempt to break down our pretenses and protectiveness. When I look back on my life I am not sorry that things have turned out as they have. My wife and I work too hard, and we often are too tired; and if you looked into our kitchen you would see how little there really is to eat. We both nearly always eat at work, you see, except on special occasions. But I think I am being honest when I tell you I am really *happier* now than I was before. I get twinges, of course. There's much in the old life that was more comfortable, and we were greatly respected and looked up to . . . but the fact is that I go to work every day quite happily because I am going to be among friends, real friends, not just professional colleagues.

"There are others, of course, who haven't really gone along; they resist this whole idea; they never will break down the shell of ego-defensiveness; they do their work, they join in, but never really feel one with the group, because basically they want to feel superior to the group; and anyone who wants to feel superior to a group in China today is a very lonely person."

China has long been known as the "land of famine." Before 1949, Americans were all too familiar with appeals for Chinese famine relief. For centuries the twin plague of flood and drought wreaked havoc upon the Chinese people; in the public mind this and a huge population were the sole causes of recurring famine in China.

Scarcely if at all, was it recognized that the nature of Chinese society was the main contributing factor. Feudal and backward, China lacked the necessary machinery to subdue the ravages of nature in such a huge area. A completely inadequate transport system prevented the movement of food to stricken areas, even though a surplus might exist elsewhere.

Under the Kuomintang, corruption and warlordism were further contributing factors. Detailed accounts have been published in the West of relief supplies and funds from abroad finding their way to the black market and into official pockets, while hundreds of thousands were reduced to eating bark and grass. It will be recalled that former Mayor of New York Fiorello La Guardia resigned his post as China UNRRA director in 1947 for precisely this reason.

One of the monumental changes which has come to China under the new government has been the launching of the huge complex of flood control, water conservation, and forestation projects, which, helped by the extension of railways and highways, has diminished the hazards of flood and drought. Measures previously unheard of, such as transporting flood-evicted peasants to areas where planting can be done while inundated lands are drained, have been carried out.

While I was traveling in China during 1960, I saw many signs both of the excessive rainfall and the extreme drought which had afflicted the country during the first half of the year. In some areas there had been no rain for more than two hundred days, in others there were disastrous summer typhoons—eighteen hit the Northeast coast alone. Westerners who had known China in the old days told me that 1960's drought, following the poor harvest of the previous year, at one time would have meant death for millions.

By the end of 1960, after my return to the United States, reports of the agricultural "disaster" in China were familiar headlines. The London *Times* of December 30 described weather conditions in China as "something not merely worse than in any year since the present government came to power in 1949 but worse possibly than anything China has experienced in this century. Certainly the succession of rainless days in north China last winter and spring was longer than that which led to China's last major famine in Honan province in 1943 . . . [when] it is estimated two million people perished. . . ." [The 1942 famine carried over into 1943.]

Despite sensational headlines in our press of "famine," "bungling," "mismanagement," there was no documentation of mass starvation, or of hordes of refugees and beggars as in former times. In my opinion there could be no repetition of the famine of 1942 and this belief was shared by Western observers with whom I spoke while I was in Peking. The work already done on flood control and water conservation has enormously cushioned the impact of adverse weather conditions. Beyond that, the Chinese will do exactly what we do when the Missouri River floods—send in relief supplies from outside. And the government, for the first time in Chinese history, is capable of doing so. It has the railways and the trucks. Due to its immensely strengthened international trading position it has the foreign exchange. During the autumn and winter of 1960–61, the commercial pages of Western newspapers were reporting large Chinese purchases of grain from Australia, Canada, France, the Sudan, and Burma. And these were not charity handouts to aid the "starving Chinese." They were paid for in cash.

Any assessment of the adverse weather conditions of 1959 and 1960 on China's economy must differentiate between short-term changes of emphasis and long-term policies. The greater emphasis placed on agriculture in 1961 does not mean that the nation's basic objectives—the simultaneous and proportionate development of agriculture and light, medium, and heavy industry—have been abandoned; as the Chinese put it, they intend to "walk on two legs."

When the Communists came to power in 1949 both industry and agriculture were appallingly backward; industry made up a minute proportion of the national economy. The new government felt it necessary to plan for a more rapid growth of industry than agriculture in order to form the necessary base for the development of the entire economy. But the Chinese envisioned an eventual narrowing of the gap between the two, not by slowing down industrial expansion but by speeding up agricultural growth.

In 1958 Chinese economists were explaining the importance of agricultural growth as a vital cog in a rapid and proportionate economic advance. The importance of agriculture in supplying industry with raw materials is now being emphasized, as is the fact that China's peasantry offers industry the largest home market in the world. For some time to come agriculture will continue to be a major source of capital accumulation, as well as an important means of obtaining foreign exchange.

China's unprecedented high rate of economic growth has been possible, according to the Chinese, because agricultural development was carried out simultaneously with the swift expansion of industry. Statistics reveal a highly significant fact: the yearly increase in industrial production has been influenced by the preceding year's agricultural output. For example, in 1952 the agricultural rise was 15.3 per cent, and in 1953 the industrial rise was 30.2 per cent. After the great leap forward in 1958, the ratio was 25 per cent and 66 per cent. In 1959 agricultural production rose 16.7 per cent and industry followed with a 39.3 per cent increase.

Contrary to reports common in the United States, the communes, which originally grew out of the nationwide movement for irrigation and land reclamation, and the development of industry in the countryside, have not only proved their ability to meet the natural disasters of 1960, but are said by Peking to be the key factor in the drive to expand agricultural production in 1961, to help overcome the losses in 1960.

Nevertheless, there are enormous problems facing Chinese agriculture. This was acknowledged by the authorities while I was in China, and continues to be. They are written about and talked about in the press and on the radio, and discussed in meetings on a national scale. These problems are:

1) The immense demands of Chinese agriculture on industrial resources. The Chinese estimate that to fulfill their agricultural program several million tractors will be required. In 1960 there were only about 100,000; these were being turned out at about 20,000 annually. It is estimated that millions of tons of industrially-produced fertilizer are needed annually, while output in 1959 was less than one and a half million.

2) An insufficiently developed statistical system whereby production and distribution can be competently planned and carried out.

3) Lack of adequate storage facilities. Although there have been years of abundant crops in the past ten years, food supplies have been lost through deterioration. Also, refrigeration in China is far from sufficient.

4) The general increase in the standard of living, which has enormously enhanced the pressure of demand on agriculture. This is not Peking propaganda. Anyone who has ever seen or read about the China of ten years ago knows this to be a fact as far as more than 90 per cent of the people are concerned—this is especially true of the nation's half billion peasants, who consume a greater share of what they produce than at any time in China's history. I am, after seeing records and talking to peasants in many parts of the country, fully convinced that this is so.

With perhaps only half of her land potential being used and still in the first stages of mechanized agriculture, China's food production and consumption have shown a steep increase in the last decade. The Chinese view their food difficulties in late 1960 and early 1961 as a temporary setback. While the government was alerting the population to the need for temporary over-all belt-tightening, preparations on an immense scale were being made to insure an adequate harvest for 1961.

It is commonly held that China, with its 700 million people, is tremendously overpopulated. The annual birth rate of about 2 per cent is often cited as conclusive evidence of the impossibility of China ever supplying its people with enough to eat. The Chinese do not agree. In fact, on this subject they seem curiously unperturbed; the bogy of Malthus and his contemporaries holds no terrors.

Some years ago William Vogt, a widely read writer, stated in his book *Road to Survival*: ". . . There is little hope that the world will escape the horror of extensive famines in China during the next few years. But from the world point of view, these may be not only desirable, but indispensable."

One of the more knowledgeable and wiser of the prophets of doom is Aldous Huxley. When he looks to the future he speaks in tones of almost unmitigated despair:

Human numbers are now increasing more rapidly than at any time in the history of the species . . . every four years mankind adds to its numbers the equivalent of the present population of the United States, every eight-and-a-half the equivalent of the present population of India. . . . It took sixteen centuries for the population of the earth to double. At the present rate it will double in less than half a century. . . . In parts of Asia and in most of Central and South America populations are increasing so fast that they will double themselves in little more than twenty years. . . . Overpopulation leads to economic insecurity and social unrest. . . . It is a pretty safe bet that, twenty years from now, all the world's overpopulated and underdeveloped countries will be under some form of totalitarian rule. . . . If overpopulation should drive the underdeveloped countries into totalitarianism, and if these new dictatorships should ally themselves with Russia, then the military position of the United States would become less secure and the preparation for defense and retaliation would have to be intensified. But liberty, as we all know, cannot flourish in a country that is permanently on a war footing, or even a near-war footing. Permanent crisis justifies permanent control of everybody and everything by the agencies of the central government. And permanent crisis is what we have to expect in a world in which overpopulation is producing a state of things, in which dictatorship under Communist auspices becomes almost inevitable.

And what, when I presented this view to Chinese agricultural experts and economists, was the general tenor of their reply? It could, I think, be fairly summarized this way:

1. The world is confronted with a staggering paradox. The peasant countries—where nearly everyone is engaged in growing food—

are the hungry countries. The *industrial* countries—in which only 10 or 20 per cent of the population are occupied in growing food—have ample food. The United States has a rate of population increase greater than that of India; it is the greatest industrial nation; and it has on its hands an agricultural explosion and a food surplus so great that it doesn't know what to do with it. In some nonindustrialized countries it takes ten men growing food to feed one non-food-growing man. In New Zealand, where agriculture is highly advanced, one man growing food can feed forty who are not growing food.

2. For thousands of years, with sickle and wooden plow, the average time needed to produce one hundred pounds of wheat was three hours. Today, with modern equipment, it takes less than two minutes, including the time taken to make the plows and harvesters. At the end of the Middle Ages a cow produced four hundred litres of milk a year; today in a modern agricultural country a cow produces nearly four thousand litres. Indian cows today still produce only one-tenth of the European average.

3. Seventy per cent of the world's food-growing families are still using wooden plows or hoes—and this alone is a cause of primal poverty. Only 2 per cent of the agricultural families of the world possess tractors or motor plows. It is this handful that have caused the agricultural revolution.

4. The present-day world average of agricultural land is approximately 3.3 billion acres. This could, by irrigation, forest clearance, and drainage, readily be doubled. With modern farming techniques the world's food production could be increased by five to seven times. This with our present knowledge. And what new discoveries lie in store for mankind?

5. As for Huxley's fear that overpopulation will lead to an intensification of war preparations, the Chinese would say this: That he is still thinking in terms of the nineteenth century. The greatest obstacles to the full development of food production in the underdeveloped countries are the superstitions, the religious taboos, the dull passivity, the lack of hope, and, above all, the class exploitation that is present in feudal or colonial territories. No real advance can be made without a fundamental change in a social system. There can be no significant release of human energies without such a change. And, as this would inevitably be one toward a socialist,

planned economy, this makes archaic the notions of international rivalries envisaged by Huxley. He assumes military rivalry because he is still thinking in terms of mutually exploiting, mutually competitive capitalistic nationalities.

As far as the Chinese are concerned, I found no agricultural expert or economist who did not talk to me in terms of *optimism* about their agricultural potential and they never question its ability to take care of a much larger population than the country at present is sustaining.

China today is still using less than one-half of the two million square kilometers of her potentially cultivatable land.

In the past ten years, while the average rate of population increase has been about 2 per cent, the rate of increase of grain has been well over four times this rate. The peak year for grain production prior to the new regime was in 1936 when 150 million tons were produced. When the new government came to power in 1949 this had sunk to 113 million tons. By the beginning of the First Five-Year Plan in 1953 production was 167 million tons; by 1958 production had risen to 250 million tons (final corrected figures) and despite the climatic calamities 1960 production was probably not much less than in 1957. India with a population nearly two-thirds that of China is expecting a 1961 grain production of less than 75 million tons.

I have traveled I don't know how many thousands of miles across China, north and south and to its center, by land and air. I have seen something of this vast country. Most of us have a picture of a China teeming with people. Like many of the images we have it is based on a partial truth. Not many of us realize, I think, that at least half of this huge land has less than fifteen persons to the square kilometer—a "rich" country like Holland has several hundred! Or that west of Lanchow (the equivalent of Chicago on the map of the United States) there is no city with even half a million people. Much of this empty western space could be used if modern techniques of water conservation and irrigation were applied.

I did not, until I traveled in China, fully appreciate the tremendously wide disparities in population densities that exist, even in the Yangtze Valley, China's traditional "Rice Bowl." I came away from China with the powerful impression that much of China is waiting to be settled and developed just as was the American West a century ago. And that given a rational and planned approach, the solution of the abnormal distribution of China's population lies in something more than trying to convince half a billion peasants to practice birth control.

One official in the Ministry of Agriculture with whom I discussed population and food production was confident that new, and as yet unimagined, methods of producing food would make the anxiety shown by Westerners seem quite foolish. He showed me a copy of an editorial which had appeared in the London *Daily Mail* on September 2, about three weeks before our meeting. The editorial was a comment on a conference of British agricultural experts in Cardiff and this man obviously shared its sentiments:

Traditional methods of food production are still far from being fully exploited. Beyond them are newer methods, and after them again are the miracles wrought by biochemistry. To begin with our own small island: there are still seventeen million acres of completely undeveloped countryside lying on the hills. Think of the immensities there must be elsewhere. Outside the West, most agriculture is primitive, inefficient, and on the wrong lines. Fertilizers and other techniques could double food production in less than a generation. But it would not stop there. Many countries have recorded individual yields of five tons of food an acre. This should be possible nearly everywhere. The human race is in sight of a very high standard of living and unlimited leisure. Unless we all go mad the best is yet to be.

The arguments put forward by this official and others I found attractive and compelling; they spring from an essentially optimistic outlook on life itself. But I must admit that some doubts remain. As I brought up in my discussion later with Premier Chou En-lai, I still feel that eventually there is a limit to the amount of food that any country can grow and when that limit is reached, for sheer survival population will have to be curtailed or other territories be plundered. Even this, to me unanswerable, logic does not dismay them. As one Chinese said to me, "The time when we exhaust the possibilities of increasing our food supply is very far distant and we needn't worry about that yet. When the time comes that the population of China should be stabilized, we shall by then have new ways. . . ."

China through the Eyes of Others

Except in Peking one is not likely to run across many foreigners in China today. However, in the nation's capital, almost every country in the world is represented, except, of course, America: official delegations and advisers from the Soviet bloc, European, Asian, African, and Cuban diplomats and businessmen, "peace delegates" from all parts of the globe, students from several score of countries, and a handful of resident Westerners who work for the Chinese government.

These people have opinions, ranging from high optimism to crushing pessimism, on what is taking place in China. I have met a fair sampling of them; I've chatted with some and engaged in extended talks with others. Most of my contacts were with foreigners (Europeans and Asians) who have been here for at least a year or more, either on business or in the service of their governments.

The following are some of the thoughts and observations they expressed to me, as I recorded them in my notebook:

Englishman: The leaders, especially Mao, are not motivated by desire for personal glory. They are basically modest men. The cult of Mao does not spring from a growing self-importance on his part. The government remains as always a group government; the policy of establishing Mao as the father figure of the nation was probably a consciously arrived at, politically sophisticated decision taken collectively by the politburo for reasons of sound necessity. The Chinese have traditionally looked to a man as a leader, rather than an impersonal "government."

Indian: China's attitude toward India underwent a change in the summer and fall of 1958, at the time of the great leap forward. The Chinese, filled with self-confidence, saw themselves playing a new role in international affairs, achieving great power status under their own steam. Also, they felt the Indian government was drifting to the right, and saw Nehru in his declining years more and more a prisoner of the right.

As to the border dispute, China genuinely believes she has a legal case. We, of course, feel we have a case too. The reality probably lies somewhere between. The border has never been settled between our two countries and we are trying to sit down and reach an agreement. The Chinese demands are such that, even if our government were willing, it would not be acceptable in terms of Indian public opinion.

Wife of European Diplomat: This is the only country she has ever been to where she leaves her jewelry lying on her dressing table, and never even thinks of it.

Another wife: "I hate these people. They stare at me so. I feel their silence and curiosity expresses hostility. I hate going out of the compound. I try to go out as seldom as possible. When I have to go to the hairdresser I drive out and rush back as quickly as possible."

Five minutes later she was telling me, "You people who come here for just a few months, how can you expect to get to know these people? You need to live here as we do."

Burmese: "The most impressive thing about China is her self-reliance. She is a nation pulling herself up through her own efforts. She wants to reach the time when she is not dependent on any outside help."

Indonesian: "The Chinese government is making a real effort to settle its dispute with Indonesia on the question of the Overseas Chinese and their dual nationality. This is partly because China cannot afford to have too many disputes with Asian countries."

East European (oil expert): Gave the Chinese credit for a remarkable industrial development, but he personally was finding life here difficult; the Chinese were very much lacking in initiative, too reliant on the foreign expert, too ready to copy. Until 1959, he said, they were extremely anxious about their lack of petroleum resources. However, within the past year vast and hitherto unsuspected oil fields have been uncovered. He now believes China will be one of the great petroleum-producing countries of the world.

West European (recently returned from trip to hinterlands): He listed his outstanding impressions: Massive unity of the people. Self-confidence of the government, which knows it has the allegiance of the people. Improved material conditions. The enthusiastic youth are the base of the society. A real danger of China withdrawing from the world, excluding the world, reverting to her traditional isolation; at heart disliking other peoples. A tremendous desire to become independent of everyone. Pride of a strong nation, which doesn't want charity, even from the Russians. A nation where people have great ignorance of the outside world they shun, caught in stereotyped images of the West, particularly the United States, while the leaders themselves are very highly informed.

Pole: China was, in some ways, fortunate to have a hard time in 1960 on a number of fronts, especially her crops. This has helped to correct various mistakes and to bring their agricultural planning back to a basis of reality. Mao has said that they must "turn calamity into good fortune and disaster into luck."

All this has tested the durability of the commune, which, basically, this man feels convinced, is the best system for China. As a result of the setbacks, a new approach to the communes was being taken. The trend will be toward more individual freedom and initiative. Mao's 1959 tour of the communes and his analysis has been largely responsible for this shift.

There is very little individual decision-making even at the highest level. Mao himself invariably seeks the opinions of many before making his pronouncements.

There is a strange contrast to be found in the Chinese government's dealings at home and abroad. At home they have shown an extraordinarily keen sense of what their people want, how to talk to them; they really understand their own people and how to handle them. Here they have shown wisdom and flexibility. In their dealings with other countries they sometimes lose this "feel," sometimes act clumsily and with a very un-Chinese lack of deftness. He thought they have shown cleverness in dealing with the United States, however; they have refused to be provoked into military action against American forces around Quemoy and Taiwan. The Chinese have allowed America to stew in its own predicament without giving any excuse for military retaliation. The Indian dispute they handled badly and lost far more friends in Asia than they need have done.

The Chinese, after years of suffering from the arrogance of foreigners, are touchy. They won't let themselves feel humiliated by American policies re the UN etc., but they have built up an "overcompensation." A single word of criticism in an otherwise friendly article by a foreigner will sometimes damn the writer as not understanding and objective. This is not an intellectual reaction, but an emotional one.

Although they do not show it outwardly, the Chinese become exasperated with what they call Western obtuseness and the tendency to talk in meaningless clichés. For example, in the middle of an explanation of the details of medical benefits for women workers —pregnancy, leave with pay, and so on—a Western visitor will say, "That's all very fine but what about *freedom?*"

Russian: (While I was in China, reports in the American and European papers of a Sino-Soviet split were becoming frequent. More and more talk was being heard in Western circles in Peking. The Chinese and the Russians were saying nothing. On one of my trips I had an English-speaking Soviet technician for a train companion. This man had been in China once before, in 1956. From all I could gather, because of the nature of his work and his contacts, this man seemed well qualified to deal with the range of subjects we discussed.)

On the split: "We are aware of the rumors about Chinese and Soviet differences of approach and emphasis toward the Western powers. It should be clear that both the Chinese and ourselves are united in our fundamental hostility to the foreign policies of the Western bloc led by the United States; we are agreed the United States is the greatest single barrier to world peace and progress.

"As to differences, they are not as serious as the West likes to make out. If we don't have differences we are said to be rigid and monolithic, if we do we are said to be splitting.

"The conditions confronting China and the Soviet Union vis-à-vis the United States are not the same. The Americans have had to accept the Soviet Union as an equal power, while they do not yet have to do so with China. For example, the United States is actually occupying Chinese territory in Taiwan. This is an act it could not attempt with regard to us. China's only recourse is to be outspoken and militant in speech.

"If there is one single piece of advice I would give Americans it is that China should be dealt with on an equal basis. The greatest mistake in American foreign policy is her treatment of the Chinese as a lesser power." (He was very emphatic about this.)

Taiwan: "This is the outstanding issue preventing any normalization of Sino-American relations. There are two possibilities for resolving the impasse, internal revolt against Chiang Kai-shek, or American withdrawal. The former is unlikely, although it would be well to bear in mind the violent expression of anti-American feeling during the riots in Taipei two years ago.

"The answer for the United States is to face reality and withdraw, leaving the Chinese to settle the civil war. This would not necessarily be brought about militarily. By making such a move the United States position in the eyes of Asians, who do not look at Chiang as a symbol of freedom, would be improved. Moreover, it would avoid ultimate mortification for the United States.

"On the matter of Taiwan, there is complete agreement with the Chinese, as Premier Khrushchev has often stated. This means 100 per cent military support in the event of any American military action against China over the island."

Technicians: "Recent accounts of a sudden mass withdrawal of our technical experts from China are highly exaggerated. The governments concerned did not make any statement about the matter so as not to give it undue importance.

"The total number of Russian technicians who have come from Russia to China since 1950 is only something over 10,000. The peak was between 1955 and 1958, when there were more than 5000. At present there are less than 1000, which is about the average for the ten years. As perhaps is natural, there have been some purely technical disputes, and some of our engineers feel the equipment we have supplied is sometimes overworked. But, this has no political significance. The Chinese are now taking over all of the normal engineering functions. It is only in very advanced techniques that China still needs our help, which we are very ready to give."

Nuclear Physics: "In the field of nuclear physics we have helped set up the Chinese Institute. We have also helped in constructing a cyclotron. China now has four. Many Chinese are studying in the Soviet Institute of Nuclear Physics, and the Vice-Director there is a Chinese."

Uneasiness: "Regarding speculation in some quarters of Soviet uneasiness over the unexpected rapidity of China's industrial advance, this is Western wishful thinking. The Russians, far from being apprehensive, welcome it. The stronger the socialist world becomes the better domestically and in terms of world peace.

"The Chinese are the first to admit that they have learned much from us. Unlike the Soviet Union, they have not had to build their industrial base without friends."

Recognition: "We have always felt that it is only a matter of time before China obtains her seat in the United Nations. Each year brings it closer.

"As for American recognition, it took sixteen years in our case and the delay did us no harm. The Chinese are in no hurry, and it is not harming them, either."

Knowledgeable West European Diplomat: Had some views on Chinese-Russian relations. Says Russians fundamentally dislike the Chinese, and the East Europeans do also. This is not true of the East Germans, however, whose rather close tie with the Chinese gives them some status in Europe and a little power which they can exert against the Russians. East Germany is now second to the Russians in trade with China.

One of the things some of these Europeans dislike about the Chinese, for example, is that a sample order will be given which the Chinese then copy. Recently, a technician from an East European country arrived to inspect some machinery that had been installed by his organization; he was asked to inspect precisely similar machinery made by the Chinese as well. He refused.

He estimates the Chinese will have the Bomb "any time and certainly by 1962," and will achieve it without Russian help. Russia, he said, is showing signs of hanging back a little in its aid, delaying deliveries, retarding orders. They probably think China is moving too fast.

On the matter of a Sino-Soviet split he felt that where there is so much smoke there must be fire. However, he did not see a major break in the foreseeable future and felt that any Western policy based on such an occurrence would be wholly unrealistic. He also felt that some people in America were more concerned with making a strong case rather than understanding a matter which is highly subtle.

He agreed that serious differences developed at the meeting of Communist parties in Bucharest in the spring of 1960. The Chinese were said to have had varying but minority support on different issues. Some of the differences revolved around the following:

1. *War:* The Russians say the socialist bloc is now powerful enough to prevent war. The Chinese reportedly argue that the imperialists can still bring about a war at any place and time of their choosing. The Chinese position is that war can be prevented only if the socialist bloc gains strength and wins over new adherents in the colonial world, and if the anticolonial revolutions continue. The Chinese look to America's *actions*, not her *words*, and they have seen nothing in her actions which would suggest the country is moving from a war to a peace footing.

2. *Colonial Revolution:* Chinese hold to a variant of the old permanent-revolution theory, namely that colonial revolutions must either go forward to socialism or slide back into some form of liberal capitalism. This premise is viewed as the basis for China's attitude toward India, a country increasingly oriented toward Western capitalism. The Russians do not agree with this thesis, particularly with regard to India. In fact, there is reason to believe that it is a serious error for the Chinese to press their border differences with India. The best thing to do is to leave such things in abeyance, the Russians contend.

3. *World Situation:* The Chinese believe Lenin's definition that this is still an era of imperialism, war, and revolution. The Russians hold that this dictum must be modified and brought into line with a major change in the world situation, namely, the rise of a

group of socialist powers which now plays a decisive role on the world scene.

4. *Road to Socialism:* Russians now feel the world situation is such that different countries will proceed to socialism in different ways, including the possibility of parliamentary elections. The Chinese position adheres to the more traditional presentation of the revolutionary road to socialism.

Whatever the final outcome, this man thought that at present China was ready to carry the burden of any difficulties rather than transfer it to the senior member of the "Communist Club," as he put it. This is in line with the Chinese belief that the greater loyalty always includes and supersedes the lesser. Just as it is taken for granted in China that no leader will pursue his own career at the expense of the nation, so no divergences with the Russians are deemed as important as the unity of the world Communist camp.

(Following the Bucharest meeting, an effort to resolve differences was made at the eighty-one-nation gathering in Moscow early in December 1960. Although the Chinese were reported to have strenuously argued their position, they accepted the final statement—the 20,000-word Moscow Declaration, which largely reflected the Russian position.)

He was critical of the Edward Crankshaw article appearing in the *Observer* of June 19. He said it was an example of an analysis trying to make a case for the contention that the Chinese adhere to the line of the "inevitability of a third world war." (Referring to a speech by Chairman Liu Shao-chi at a banquet on June 3, for a visiting Albanian official, Crankshaw reported that Liu "called for persistent struggles against the United States 'to isolate it to the greatest extent.'")

He then showed me the complete text of Liu's speech, in English, pointing out that what immediately followed Crankshaw's quote read: "Only thus is it possible to force the United States imperialists to sit down and enter into negotiations with us, put off and even stop their plan for launching a new war, and provide a reliable guarantee for world peace."

He pointed out that the writer had chosen to quote the last seven words of a sixty-eight-word sentence from a paragraph of more than three hundred words, to convey an almost opposite meaning to what Liu intended. This sort of reporting, he thought, was a grave disservice to the West.

PART EIGHT ☆

"Water in Our Hands" 34

All China is intensely conscious of the problem of water because on water depends both the industrial and agricultural future of the country. The use of water power is understood by *everyone*, from schoolchildren who make model dams, and commune brigades which back up small streams in order to drive their home-made generators, to the engineers planning vast hydroelectric and river-control projects, comparable in scale to our TVA.

China has too much water in the south (though in the past most of it was lost through flood runoff) and too little in the north, particularly the Northwest. The planners are talking of long-range schemes for diverting some of the great rivers, or channeling part of their flow, into the semi-arid northern regions. But that is for the future. The most immediate problem was to check the floods which for centuries had ravaged China's two greatest food-producing areas, the Yellow and Yangtze basins; and at the same time, to realize the potential hydroelectric power for mechanization of their farms and for general industrial development.

I selected the Sanmen Gorge Dam in Honan province for a visit, not because it is the largest, but because its construction was furthest advanced of all the really big projects.

It was late at night when I arrived at Hui Shin Station, closest point on the railroad to Sanmen Gorge. It had been raining heavily. The sky was black, starless; and the station building, which showed

half-finished concrete walls, was surrounded by wallows of mud and
pools of water in which the lighted windows of the train appeared
in fragmentary reflection between gusts of wind. Beyond the station there was no light to be seen in any direction. I was glad someone from the hotel had come down to meet me.

We piled into a Russian-built jeep, gunned out axle-deep in mud,
slewing half sideways down a steep grade.

To my surprise, we came out on a hard-surfaced road where an
ordinary sedan was waiting, into which we transferred for the rest
of the ride to the hotel. The hotel, like the station, was only half
finished; everything here was brand-new. My room had a bathroom, but most of the plumbing apparatus was lying outside in the
hallway, not yet installed.

In the morning when I woke, the sun was shining.

We took off at 7:30 sharp in a Russian car for the thirty-five-kilo-
meter trip to Sanmen Gorge. As we drove out to the highway, I
saw there was a good deal more to the town than I had perceived
the night before. Rows of new buildings, movies, theaters, offices,
playgrounds. Originally a village of three thousand, the chauffeur
told me, it had grown since the project began in 1957 to sixty thousand.

The road to Sanmen Dam had taken six months to build; and
as we rolled up over long, well-graded curves, I saw that it was
taking us into some of the most remarkable country I had seen in
China. The green hills of central China climbed higher and higher.
There were no rocks, almost no trees. The soil appeared to be a
mixture of sand and yellow clay and everywhere the hills had been
terraced, step by step, up these enormously steep slopes; in some
places the terrace walls had to be higher than the breadth of the
terraces they supported.

Now and again, coming suddenly over a high ridge, we would
catch a glimpse of the hills stretching off far into the distance, endlessly looped and contoured by those terrace walls. God, what
labor! It was the work of centuries. And the terraces, as far as the
eye could see, bright green with young wheat.

"Look, there!" The driver pointed.

Far below us I caught a glimpse, deep among those tumbled
hills, of the bend of a great river. It was yellow-brown like the earth
and looked peaceful and sluggish enough at that distance. And all

this under a China-blue sky with clouds driving on the wind and their shadows racing across the terraced landscapes.

It was only when we reached the dam itself that I saw there was nothing sluggish about the Yellow River. The main body of the river came thundering out through the spillway in roils of brown foam.

There is always, for me, an intense excitement in the sight of a great engineering work. I have felt this at Grand Coulee and at Boulder and I felt it now as we stepped from the car by the engineers' shanties, looking out over the Sanmen Dam. The construction seemed largely complete. Crews were still at work along the top, finishing the floodgates and the roadway. Containers of concrete sailed out by high cable line from a mixing plant on the opposite bank. These were taken off by huge cranes along the top of the dam and dumped into the square section forms. It was an impressive sight.

The chief engineer, Mr. Jiou Yi-ning, stepped out of his shanty to greet me. He would give me a general outline of the project from this viewpoint, and later one of the junior engineers could take me on a tour of the work.

"The Yellow River," said Mr. Jiou, "follows a course from Chinghai province and flows through nine provinces till it reaches the ocean above Shanghai. Its total length is forty-eight hundred kilometers. The drainage basin is arid country with an average rainfall of only forty millimeters per year. But these rains are concentrated into a very short period, and consequently there is a great variation in the rate of flow. The yearly average varies from 160 to 1330 cubic meters per second. But in some years it falls lower, or rises much higher. An absolute maximum," Mr. Jiou continued, "which has perhaps occurred only once or twice in history, would be 35,500 cubic meters per second. This is the figure we have reckoned with in our construction of the Sanmen Gorge Dam.

"Here at Sanmen is where the stream comes down from the high country and runs out into the coastal plains, which are wide, but low. Over the centuries, silt carried from the hills has raised the level of the river bottom till for long stretches it is higher than the surrounding country. The people, to protect themselves, have been constantly building dikes so that now the Yellow River flows through a raised trough across some of the most heavily populated sections of China. There are eighty million people who live in the floodlands of the Yellow River. When very heavy rains have fallen in the hills, the river has broken its dikes; and our historical records show that this has occurred fifteen hundred times during the past three thousand years. The river actually has changed its course twenty-six times. This river," said Mr. Jiou, "has been the scourge of China. But we have tamed it at last.

"The worst disaster of recent times was in 1938 when the Kuomintang broke the dikes in an attempt to halt the Japanese advance. Insufficient warning was given the peasants and there were no plans for evacuation. The area flooded was greater than the engineers had anticipated. The result was that twelve and a half million people were made homeless and 890,000 lost their lives."

"By whose estimate was that?" I asked.

"By the estimate of the Kuomintang, made immediately afterward.

"For thousands of years," Mr. Jiou went on, "our people have been struggling against this river. But they had no proper means. Later, under the Kuomintang, the social system made any fundamental planning impossible. It was only after liberation that plans could be made and carried through. The first stage was that of strengthening the dikes on the lower course. During the past ten years there has been no flood damage downstream. But even so, an unusual runoff might have broken the dikes, and this remained always a danger until the second stage could be put into effect.

"The second stage," he concluded, "is the Sanmen Dam." He waved his hand across the view before us.

"When will it be finished?" I asked.

"We closed the gates last spring. To this extent, it is already complete so far as controlling the river is concerned. The generators which still need to be installed will be in operation by the end of the year. That is a year ahead of our schedule."

Then he turned me over to one of his assistants and I spent the morning touring the project. We visited the concrete plant and the gravel quarry; had a look into the interior galleries; descended long sets of ladders through a forest of bamboo staging to see the partially completed powerhouse and the enormous penstocks, each one twenty-two feet in diameter. The eight turbine generators, my guide informed me, have been manufactured in the Soviet Union and are presently in shipment. They will make possible the industrialization of the central Yellow River Valley. Minimum flow required to keep these generators turning will be 250 cubic meters per second for each one. The lake already filling up behind the dam will have storage capacity of 35,400 million cubic meters and this water will be put to work not only for power generation, but for irrigation as well. The great basin of the Yellow River has suffered almost as grievously from drought as from flood. The dam, with its storage lake, will regularize the flow, making possible effective irrigation of some 40 million mu (6,667,000 acres) of potentially rich agricultural land lower down. The young engineer added that it will also be feasible, then, to maintain a predetermined channel depth below the dam so that ships of 500 tons displacement will be able to come inland as far as Sanmen. In addition, they anticipate raising fine harvests of fish (he was not speaking of sportsfishing) in the new reservoir.

In anybody's language Sanmen is a big project. Its height of 348 feet compares with 550 feet for Grand Coulee. (Both are gravity dams, therefore comparable.) Sanmen has a base of 312 feet while Grand Coulee has a base of 500 feet but will hold more water than Grand Coulee and Boulder combined. Grand Coulee is capable of irrigating about one million acres. The Chinese claim that Sanmen will make possible the effective irrigation of about six and a half million acres. Grand Coulee took slightly less than eight years to build. Sanmen will be completed in a little less than four.

Perhaps an American superintendent might not be satisfied with the finish of the concrete. The form panels were of rough planking rather than plywood and the junction lines did not run true. Obviously they considered this a minor matter. I saw the compressed-air vibrators they were using and noticed that no aggregate was exposed on the surface. Safety precautions were minimal. The stagings were all of wooden poles lashed with cord and the ramps and catwalks were frequently innocent of any guard rails. Very, very few accidents, the assistant engineer assured me, but I could not get any figures. Heavy construction everywhere has its accident rate; I can offer no comparison.

It seemed to me that with the tremendous burden of sand and topsoil carried by the stream, the consequent silting up of the storage lake must eventually become a problem. All this, I was told, had been taken into consideration. The master plan calls for one other large dam comparable to Sanmen and for forty-six smaller reservoirs on the headwaters which will convert the fall of the river into a series of controlled steps. They call it the "stepladder" plan. Much of the silt will thus settle out hundreds of miles upstream. This, combined with forestation and erosion control, will reduce silting of the power-dam lakes to a negligible factor. The same difficulties exist, undoubtedly, for all river-development projects. I have heard the problem of silt discussed in the United States, particularly in relation to the Colorado River and Boulder Dam.

I imagine Mr. Jiou's assistant would have hurried me back and forth, his hand under my elbow, pointing and explaining, all that day and the next day, too. But I had to be back at Hui Shin Station by midafternoon to catch the train which would take me down the valley to Chengchow and Wuhan.

As we returned to the car at the engineer's shanty, Mr. Jiou himself came out to bid me farewell.

"Whatever they tell you there downstream," he said, laughing, "remember you have seen here at Sanmen the key to the Yellow River Basin. From here we will check the floods. From here we will send water for irrigation. From here will come the electric power for lights and workshops. And this is only the beginning. They have already started some projects on the Yangtze River which will make this one look like a toy. . . ."

I stopped the car to take some last photographs from above, where the road enters the project area. An archway spans the road just here, and on it were characters written boldly. I asked my interpreter what they said:

> Conquer the Yellow River!
> Command it to make way
> And the mountains shall bow to us.
> Harness the river to rock
> And we will hold the water in our hands!

In the Valley
of the Yangtze

The Northeast may be the most important industrial area in China, but there are others where industry is rapidly expanding. Wuhan, a vital river port southwest of Nanking on the Yangtze River, has become a major industrial city. The constuction of a huge integrated iron-and-steel works a few years ago has made this the steel center of central China.

After Anshan in the Northeast, Wuhan is destined to become China's number-two steel base. The transport hub for nine provinces, it is close to rich iron ore in Tayeh; not far off are limestone, dolomite, and coking coal. From this industrial site in central China, it is expected products will be made available to large sections of the country.

Located where the Yangtze meets its northern tributary, the Han River, this tri-city (Hankow, Wuchang, and Hanyang) was finally linked when the Yangtze Bridge was finished in 1957. Like so many Chinese cities, Wuhan was once staked out by Western powers, into six foreign concessions. There is still a big clock here and its chimes remind one of Big Ben in London.

Wuhan and its surrounding area has been ravaged throughout recorded history by the Yangtze overflowing its banks. In 1931 flood waters reached a record height of ninety-two feet. Dikes burst and the three cities and countryside were submerged for months. Nearly a million people were victims, more than half of them losing their homes, many their lives.

In the summer of 1954 both the Yangtze and Han rivers overflowed, reaching a height of more than ninety-eight feet. Unlike the past, the government carried out emergency measures. An army was mobilized—peasants, workers, soldiers, office personnel, students, working around the clock to reinforce the dikes. Boats, barges, freight trains, trucks were pressed into service to haul 60 million tons of earth, tree trunks, pumps, equipment, food, and medical supplies. Wuhan was saved from disaster only after a three-month seige. Doctors and nurses poured into the area to combat any threat of epidemic. Victims from the inundated countryside were evacuated.

July 31

This afternoon I saw the Wuhan Heavy Machine Tools Plant. The chief products are vertical lathes, planers, drillers, and steam hammers. The minimum weight of tools turned out here is twenty tons, the maximum four hundred tons. The average weight of the lathes is one hundred tons.

I was told by Mr. Kuo Ming-nan, a worker and editor of the plant newspaper who showed me about, that only 20 per cent of the equipment was Russian or East European. The rest, he claimed, was all Chinese. Mr. Kuo was somewhat misleading, from all I could gather. All the really important machinery was Russian or East German. Perhaps, if one counted every small tool, the 80 per cent made-in-China figure would be correct. Nevertheless, I felt that he could have been more frank.

One of the features which struck me is the technical training school affiliated with the factory. This is not uncommon in China, but here I stopped long enough to get some sort of picture. In addition to the seventy-five hundred plant workers there are one thousand in the school.

This kind of training program is an attempt, with a minimum expenditure of time, to speed up the process of getting the skilled workers China needs so desperately. This particular school offers an intensive two-year course emphasizing machine-tool building techniques.

For the students—most of whom have had some high school—tuition, room, food, and incidental expenses are paid by the factory. The school has its own experimental shop where students learn at machines they will later operate. The average age is twenty, and 18 per cent of the enrollment is made up by women. Upon completion of the course, students are given examinations, and depending on the results are assigned to factories throughout the area.

Someone once said China is an old country turned young. I am often reminded of this wherever I go. Perhaps it is because Chinese always look younger than they are in our eyes. But one does not have to be in China very long to be aware of its youth. So many of them are found in factories, at jobs where we would expect to encounter veterans, who seem to know this is it, there are no horizons.

Whatever the factory lacked in terms of the general slickness and tidiness one finds back home, it more than made up for in the outlook of its preponderantly youthful workers. One fellow, age nineteen, had recently completed his course at the technical school. His father was a doctor and he hopes to become a senior engineer one day. Meanwhile, he seemed to be having the time of his life at his precision lathe.

One of the girls, who said she was twenty but looked about seventeen, was the daughter of peasants. She had received a year's technical training somewhere else, but had really learned everything she knew on the job. She was checking notches in a shaft—it had to be true to three-thousandths of a millimeter—and using a special form of gauge I had never seen. Her grin and general cheerfulness attest that these kids like working here, and it is hardly a wonder that they are grateful to a regime that has enabled them to do this, at no financial cost to themselves.

How long this youthful enthusiasm will endure I don't know. Several years of doing the same job—most of them will not become senior engineers—even in China could bring on a different attitude. Right now, though, they are not thinking along such lines.

Letter to Elena August 1

When I got up this morning the sun had only just got over the horizon and there was a mist over the Yangtze. It was a quite wonderful experience sitting on this boat pushing through the misty air while above hung the faint outlines of the hills. It was exquisitely like an old Chinese painting. I sat on deck caught in the beauty of the morning. Now and again the tattered sail of some junk would be seen, and once, almost too perfectly placed, a lone bird flew across the river ahead of the boat. Then, the inevitable shrill voice over the loudspeaker telling the ship to "arise and shine," followed by equally piercing Chinese music. Later in the day I surreptitiously switched off the loudspeaker in the lounge, nobody said a word and I don't think anyone even missed it.

This was a sudden idea, to go to Nanking by boat instead of train. It loses me half a day in Nanking but it will be worth it. I caught the boat last night at midnight in Wuhan and have had all day on it, and then tomorrow soon after dawn we will put in at Nanking. I had hoped it would provide some chance of getting some good movies, but it's been a washout from that point of view. The river is so wide, several miles in places, that there is nothing to be seen beyond a thin line of green above the mud-brown water. And sometimes beyond, lifting in the haze, the outlines of some distant mountains. We have put in here and there at small river ports, but the rather fussy ship's "police," a young man in T shirt and shorts and bare legs, insisted it was against regulations to photograph the ports, so that was that. Stills are O.K. It's the movie camera that raises their suspicions.

But I wouldn't have missed today for anything. Firstly, it's given me a day of laziness and rest, just sitting on the so-called deck letting the breeze blow through my hair, sitting in a half doze watching China float by. Secondly, with a spurt of effort after lunch this afternoon I finished my notes.

It's been hot, hot so that one's eyeballs pop; and damp. Wuhan was the worst. I went through a machine-tools factory there and later had a long discussion about modern Chinese writing with the secretary of the Wuhan Writers' Union; and I think I got hotter in the discussion than I did at the factory. All Wuhan was sleeping in the streets. I went for a walk in the late evening (and got myself lost—took me a time to retrace my steps) and everywhere the people had brought their bedding down to the street and were lying there, scattered over the sidewalks and into the streets themselves, thousands and thousands of them.

There are about twenty of us traveling "second class," there is no first. It means being less crowded than the hundred or so on the lower deck. I'm sharing a small cabin with a youngster in his twenties. He's from Chungking and there is practically no verbal communication; he speaks something I've never heard before, and I'm sure he's never heard my outlandish speech! Small and lithe, he is extraordinarily neat; the Chinese have an almost compulsive neatness. He comes and goes quietly in his black cloth shoes.

We are all sitting around, mostly without shirts, cooling off as the day wears on. A small baby is crawling along the floor, watched lovingly and cooingly by an old amah.

Some of the people are playing Chinese chess. In a few minutes another man in blue shorts and a damp T shirt, who is the steward, will with a great flourish lay a single table in this room. He will put a cloth on it—rather stained, it doesn't come out often. He will do all this and then come over and with a jerk of his thumb indicate that "food's on." All this is special, for the foreigner. I'm the only one, of course. I'll have a warm beer with my lunch if there's one left.

As I write, several people are standing by me in rapt attention; a typewriter is a rarity in China and they stand and watch me by the hour. Now the baby has crawled over to my legs and I have stopped for a few moments to pick him up and coo over him like everyone else does, and gently smack his little bare bottom. While I eat, several of the people will pull chairs over and stare. I don't mind this curiosity, it is so candid and so obviously good-natured, although I know it worries some foreigners.

Among these people in "second class" are some fine-looking youngsters—such alive, keen faces. Students, I think, going down to Shanghai; and among them some girls having the outing of their lives on this boat.

A huge basin has just been brought into this lounge and the baby is to have its bath in public. I think I have at last hit on the single most pervasive characteristic of the Chinese people; they are utterly *unself-conscious* with each other. They are like a great family together. No one minds what you do or don't do, or what you wear, or how you look, or if you've shaved. The only thing they are reticent about is a show of affection in public; they don't kiss in front of others and sometimes don't even hold hands. That is all a private matter. Everything else, well—who cares? Their bodily functions they are careful to do by themselves, although little children are given complete freedom in this. But with these few exceptions, and rather good ones, the Chinese act in public just as they do when they are with their intimate friends and don't put on a show at all. Breast-feeding is nothing to be hidden; that has to do with the children and where they are concerned anything goes.

At lunch the T-shirted steward marched in brandishing *my* tablecloth, stains and all. Just as I thought, he chose the table right in the geometric center of the room. The service—fork, knife, spoon, and plate—are courtesy of the U.S. Navy.

There is a belief in China that no European can possibly eat a meal without bread, though the Chinese don't eat it in the form we do. Even if the rest of the meal is strictly Chinese, they will go to any lengths to provide it. I don't know where the steward gets it but at every meal he turns up with two hunks of very thick bread; it's almost uneatable it's so dry and coarse but I try to get some down in order not to hurt his feelings. Today I thought jam might help so I asked for it in my best Chinese. I thought my pronunciation must have baffled him, for he stayed away a long time. Just as I was finishing, he turned up, his pock-marked face wreathed in a smile, with a small unlabeled and rather dented tin of stawberry jam. It must have been a relic of URRA days back in 1946.

Ah-h-h! the cool evening air is beginning. The sun is down at last. I shall sit outside now and let the air dry out my shirt. I shall sit and watch China slide by in the evening light. This has been a wonderful restful day, I feel so well again. And what puts me in good spirits too is that I can at last put the whole weight of my body on my foot and feel no pain. It is really cured.

Later. The cook outdid himself tonight! Decided to give me a European meal complete with French fried potatoes. I wish they wouldn't, but they love to show they can. And the bread was fried. The meat was a kind of chicken—must have had a pretty rough life, that hen. Then tomatoes and raw onions. Well, wonders never cease. I washed the whole thing down with a beer, warm; then the finishing touch, what they call English tea or red tea, in a cup. Bless his heart. He really tried to make me feel at home.

Nanking, August 2

I write this on the train to Shanghai, a six-hour journey. Summer south of the Yangtze reminds me of Washington, humid and oppressive.

Windows wide-open, curtains flapping like mad, and mats on the seats to keep one less sticky. Thanks to the rain it is cooler this evening.

The chief reason for my Nanking visit turned out to be a dud. The prison, reputed to be the best in China, was not having me today. Later in the week, yes, but not today. I insisted, pointing out that I had been promised this visit in Peking. Yes, they were aware of this, but there was nobody available to take me around.

I became irritated. Somewhat petulantly I hinted that perhaps they did not want me to see the prison. I insisted that people in Peking, the seat of the national government, had told me I could. Didn't this mean anything?

Always, always, in China they seem to get in the last word. I have never shown irritation in this country without feeling afterward most profoundly ashamed. Why? Because of their nonresponse, their imperturbable kindness, which merely makes one feel as if one has acted like a child.

Chinese courtesy is proverbial. My first experience of it when I went through the countryside on my last trip is repeated everywhere again. The Chinese will argue strongly with me about American policy, but never does this become a personal issue which would undermine their innate courtesy to me as a guest. In Peking, during an "anti-American rally," in the midst of all the shouted slogans and clenched fists, I was asked where I was from. "America," I said. Immediately grins and handshakes and applause from those immediately around us for "our American friend."

A Quick Look at Shanghai 36

My hotel in Shanghai caters chiefly to Overseas Chinese who are visiting China, or coming home to stay. For the latter this hotel serves as a "staging area" until they find permanent quarters in Shanghai or move on to jobs elsewhere. Most of the guests are from Southeast Asia, but some come from Europe, and I am told that several are returnees from the United States.

The building is in the Western style, with large rooms and excellent service. Meals are Chinese or European. From my seventh-story window I look out over an expanse of lawns, trees, flowers; and off to the right is the Museum of Natural History. All this was once the famous Shanghai Race Course. Now it is the People's Park.

Nanking Road, where my hotel is, remains Shanghai's most thriving shopping district. Night and day, Nanking Road is crowded with people, bicycles, and buses; and already some of the tiny new two-horsepower, four-seater taxiettes—it is hoped they will in time replace the pedicabs—are beginning to appear. About a mile south from the hotel is the Bund, the famous quayside along the muddy Hwangpu River. Just this way from the bridge crossing Soochow Creek, opposite the British Consulate Compound, is Garden Park, where, as my interpreter hastened to inform me, used to be posted the never-to-be-forgotten, never-to-be-forgiven sign: "No dogs or Chinamen admitted."

Shanghai, when I came here three years ago, had seemed stagnant and drab. But on the present trip, nowhere was I so struck by the rapid change as here in this city. Shanghai is booming; her streets are crowded, her stores bustling. New "satellite towns" in the surrounding countryside have made possible demolition of slum sections which, as I can well believe from what I saw myself, used to be among the most terrible in the world.

Shanghai, in 1960, has again become one of the world's great ports, her docks are handling more cargo than ever before in the city's history.

Compared to Paris, Rome, or Peking, this is not an ancient city. Marco Polo, on his travels, would never have heard of it, since it was no more than a fishing village at the time. By the end of the Ming dynasty, as a result of the construction of the Grand Canal, which linked the city to Peking, and its network of smaller canals, Shanghai was becoming the trade center for the lower Yangtze Valley. But the city's period of rapid growth came after 1842, when it was designated a "treaty" port following China's defeat in the Opium War. Concessions and rights of "extraterritoriality" were granted to the victorious Europeans. Shanghai became the main "open door" for the West into China.

The city grew during the following century into a commercial and industrial center. Nearly 80 per cent of its industries (chiefly textiles) were foreign-owned. The hungry overpopulated countryside of the Yangtze Valley fed Shanghai's mills and factories. By the time of the First World War, Shanghai was China's largest city. Its working class supported the revolution initiated by Sun Yat-sen. When, in 1927, two years after Sun's death, the revolutionary armies under Chiang Kai-shek approached Shanghai in the great "northern drive" to unify China, Shanghai's workers, then under Communist leadership, seized the city and opened the gates to Chiang's forces —as André Malraux has vividly described in his novel *Man's Fate*.

It was at this point, immediately after the occupation of Shanghai, that Chiang broke with the Communists. Shanghai trade unions were dissolved, twelve thousand workers, supposedly Communists, were executed in three weeks, and another fifty thousand imprisoned or put to death within the year. By a curious stroke of fate Chou En-lai, who had helped plan the rising of the workers, was one of the few Communist leaders to escape from Shanghai.

For the next ten years Shanghai (the Chinese section of the city, that is) was ruled by the Kuomintang government of China. In 1937 it was taken by the Japanese, who held it till the end of

the Second World War. Then, for a brief period, once more under
Kuomintang control, Shanghai regained its old position as the financial center of China, and as the "wickedest city in the world." It
was also called the "least Chinese of cities," and on the surface this
was true. The great hotels, the waterfront skyscrapers along the
Bund, which housed the Hong Kong–Shanghai Bank, Butterfield
and Swire, Jardine's, the American-owned telephone and power
companies, and a host of other American or European firms, all
gave it the appearance of a Western metropolis. Every public utility
in this largest of Chinese cities was foreign-owned.

By 1949 the wheel of fortune had turned full circle. The victorious Communist armies of General Chen Yi (now Foreign Minister), amply supplied with American trucks and matériel, marched
into Shanghai. How much of it was captured or how much was purchased from Chiang's officialdom nobody knows.

That was eleven years ago; yet something of the Western atmosphere still remains. Shanghai is the only city in China today
where one sees advertisements for cosmetics. The elevator girls in
the hotels wear lipstick, the waitresses have their hair waved.
Women here are more style-conscious than anywhere else in China.
They show off their hairdos, flowered jackets, and contour-fitted
slacks; and for a visiting Westerner, at least, they are a true delight
to look at. Some of the department stores even have fashion pa-
rades! At a cosmetics counter on Nanking Road I counted thirty-
eight brands of perfume, twenty-eight facial soaps, ten different
shades of lipstick.

Nevertheless, the atmosphere of the new China—the sense of the
importance of being earnest, the emphasis on study and production
—is dominant. And one sees the same contrasts of old and new
as in other Chinese cities: the housing project rising from the ancient slum; human beings dragging overloaded carts, and fleets of
diesel trucks; ramshackle sheds serving as factories, and up-to-date
plants that cover acres of ground.

In Shanghai, a city in the past notorious for its filth and its slums,
I asked to visit the worst slum in the city. The worst, they told
me, had been torn down, several years before; but there were still
some nearly as bad.

What the *worst* would have been like in the old days I dread to imagine. The one I did visit was like the bad parts of Marseilles or Mexico City, except that here it was a *clean* slum. The hovels, the lean-to sheds were miserable enough, there were dark corners and narrow lanes; but no stench, no refuse lying about. And the people were not badly dressed. It was drizzling, but in spite of the rain a crowd of curious children followed wherever I went; every one of them looked adequately nourished. (Nowhere in China did I see signs of undernourishment in children.) From the appearance of these people it was apparent that they were not here because they were poorer than others in the city, or because they were out of work. Actually they were employed at the same kinds of jobs as those who live in the brand-new housing projects. But Shanghai was not built in a day, and its reconstruction will not be done in a day either. The people were waiting their turn. It was, if I may put it this way, a *hopeful* slum, and this was something entirely new in my experience.

I later met the chairman of the neighborhood committee, who told me there were twenty thousand people living in this district. Bad as it looked now, it had, apparently, been far worse. During the last years of the Kuomintang the people had suffered terribly from unemployment and inflation. Most of them were pedicab drivers, peddlers, existing at best on the very margin. Next to starvation, their great fears were: *Rain*. The area had no drainage. A heavy rain flooded the houses and converted the streets and house floors into mud which took weeks to dry. *Fire*. Roofs were almost all of thatch. No one had electricity. If they used lights or cook-stoves at all, these were kerosene. Between 1942 and 1946 three disastrous fires swept the neighborhood, causing many deaths. *Wind*. Summer windstorms, occasional typhoons, would carry away roofs, flip up the flimsy walls like card houses.

There was, then, no sanitation of any kind. There were no latrines, no running water. Drinking water came from roadside ditches and in these were washed everything from cooking pots to night-soil containers. Cholera, typhoid, dysentery, TB were perennial killers.

Ninety per cent of the population had been illiterate.

That was the situation as it had been. Since 1949 there had been improvements, many improvements, the committee chairman told

me. He pointed proudly to the fresh-water taps which stood at intervals along the narrow alleys. Garbage collection and disposal of
night soil are now taken care of daily. But by far the greatest improvement, the chairman said, was in the economic conditions.
Some of the people still are pedicab drivers; the others now held
regular jobs in the new factories and workshops. No one went hungry. There was no fear of inflation.

"Every family in this neighborhood can now afford to eat," the
chairman said.

Health, and the level of education, too, had risen since the old
days. Cholera, typhoid, dysentery, were virtually gone. There was
a hospital in the neighborhood, several clinics. All children received
immunization shots. And the children were going to school. As
for the adults, the chairman estimated 90 per cent had now passed
their literacy tests.

At the end of my visit, as I was taking my leave of the chairman
and the various others who had come with us to the neighborhood
committee room, an old man stepped forward, gave me a tooth-
less grin, and spoke a few words. My interpreter told me, "This old
man says they all hope you will come again and see for yourself
how things have changed here, the next time you are in Shanghai."

I told him I certainly intended to.

I had also intended to visit some of the urban developments already completed—the *satellite* cities in the outskirts, where self-
contained communities are being constructed, with their own markets, schools, theaters, their own industries, and their own sources
of food supply from the rural communes nearby.

But my stay in Shanghai was cut short.

Upon my return to the hotel after my visit to the slum neighborhood I found a message from the local office of the Ministry
of Foreign Affairs that they must see me at once "on a very serious
matter." I was alarmed. Certain that I was in a jam of some sort,
I racked my brain trying to imagine what I had done wrong. I
must have stepped on somebody's toes without realizing it. The
Writers' Union man in Wuhan, with whom I had the run-in over
freedom of conscience? Had he reported me? It seemed quite possible.

So be it. I shrugged my shoulders and went on over to the Ministry. A bright-eyed young woman at the reception desk greeted

me, "Oh Mr. Greene, we are so glad to see you!" Then a higher official hurried out, grasped me by the hand.

"Mr. Greene," he cried, "we have a message for you from Premier Chou En-lai. He wishes you to know that if you care to return to Peking, he will be glad to see you for an extended talk, and that, if you wish, part of the interview can be filmed for television. It would be best, I think, to return to Peking as soon as possible."

The Foreign Office man was very enthusiastic. He shook my hand several times, repeating, "Congratulations, Mr. Greene, congatulations!"

"Will you send word to the Premier," I asked, "that I will catch the next train to Peking?"

An Interview
with Chou En-lai 37

I had prepared my questions on the train, and on arrival in Peking, hurried to the Ministry of Information. The Shanghai message was confirmed. Mr. Kang Mao-chao, Deputy Director, told me the ground rules. Mr. Chou En-lai wished the questions in advance. Part of the interview could be filmed for TV; the remainder would be a direct discussion afterward. I was free to submit any questions I liked, but the Premier would prefer that I not ask personal questions. He would be speaking officially, not personally. Further, I must agree that the interview, whenever released, would be broadcast in its entirety, without cuts. I agreed to this.

I gave Mr. Kang my list of questions. They were, I thought, the key issues that any thoughtful Westerner would have liked to raise regarding China's policies. Many implied a critical attitude. Mr. Kang, after reading them with close attention, suggested there were too many to be properly answered in a half-hour TV interview. If I would choose eleven or twelve which I considered particularly suitable for an international audience, the others could be taken up during the nonfilmed portion of the discussion.

I did so. He then asked what technical arrangements I would propose? This was the first TV interview with a top official ever photographed in China. They wished it to be of technical excellence. My proposals were simple: three cameras with first-class cameramen. A beautiful, and typical, Chinese setting. An experienced sound engineer and topnotch interpreter. None of these presented any problem. I stopped at the cable office on my way back to the hotel and sent off messages to England, Canada, and the United States.

Then nothing happened. One week passed, then another. I phoned the Ministry. No news. I decided that the project was off. The Premier had changed his mind; they didn't like the questions. The Indian ambassador tried to cheer me up: "If they said you were going to have an interview, you will have one." I didn't believe him. In fact, I was on the point of making arrangements for my departure when, at a reception in the Great Hall of People, I had my first official reassurance, and this came from the Premier himself. He walked across to speak to me. Chou En-lai speaks very little English and for once he had no English interpreter with him. I had no interpreter either. We stumbled, both of us, trying to cross a no-man's land of noncommunication. Then at last I made out the words: "Excuse delay—few days, few days. . . ."

So it was on again—the great Felix Greene scoop. I was elated; and I sat out another seven-day week with no word.

Almost three weeks after I had rushed back breathless from Shanghai, I received a phone call one morning at 8:15. It was Mr. Kang, who told me he had heard from the Premier at four o'clock that very morning, instructing him to schedule the interview for noon. What about technical arrangements? I asked. Everything had been in readiness for many days. I put on my best suit and waited for the car from the Ministry to call for me.

The cause of the long delay, was, I believe, the gravity with which the Chinese government viewed the occasion. No such interview had ever before been granted in China. Here was an official pronouncement to be made, by one of their highest officials, which would be heard by people in many countries of the world. The questions I had offered touched all the most sensitive points of Chinese foreign relations.

At quarter to twelve, guided by Mrs. Chen of the Ministry of Information, I entered the Great Hall of the People. One of the reception rooms—the Kiangsu Room, she told me—had been equipped as a TV studio. Mrs. Chen and I waited in an adjacent chamber where a young woman brought us tea and damp towels, softly scented. Precisely at noon I was ushered down wide carpeted passages to the Kiangsu Room. The doors stood open and as we approached, I could see the cameras, and camera tracks laid over the carpets, a profusion of wires and brilliant lights.

There, Madame Kung Peng, was waiting. While she greeted me, I heard the cameras begin to whir; saw them follow us as we walked together across the wide hall to where Mr. Chou En-lai was seated. He rose, shook hands, beckoned me to a seat beside him. Then, without pause, without opportunity for rehearsal or voice balance or light-meter check, the interview was on. I thanked the Premier for agreeing to see me and answer my questions. As I had many questions, could I begin at once?

"*Shih*" (yes), he said.

During the long translations of Premier Chou's replies (they were afterward dubbed over his voice) I had ample opportunity to look around me. This was the most orderly, and certainly the most beautiful, "studio" I had ever had the luck to work in. It was a vast, high-ceilinged room, at least eighty feet long. A single carpet covered the entire floor, magnificent, with its central floral design, though this was now intertwined and partially obscured by tracks and electric wires.

Two cameramen stood beside each camera, the sound engineer sat at his controls; a still photographer from *Hsinhua* moved silently over the thick carpeting; and beyond the batteries of lights, motionless around the room, sat the top officials of the Prime Minister's office, the Ministry of Foreign Affairs.

It was all enormously impressive.

As TV shows go, however, the interview, I am afraid, left much to be desired. It was neither lively nor brisk. I had hoped the Premier's wit and warmth, which are immediately apparent in any personal exchange, would come through. But the occasion was too serious. Despite my previous request that he speak without notes, this was not done. He was reading his answers, which was understandable, for the issues were too important, but unfortunate.

All in all it went smoothly. The technical quality—sound, photography, interpretation, and later, the dubbing—was excellent.

After the televised portion of the interview (the text of which is included in the Appendix) we shook hands again while flashlights popped, then moved into another magnificent hall where armchairs upholstered in blue silk were drawn up to a tea table. The Premier glanced at the chairs and said he didn't care for that kind, I suppose because of their being the type one sinks half a yard into, like a very soft bed. When I suggested we bring up another chair, he laughed, and waved me to a seat.

We proceeded with the remainder of the list. I was able to go back and question some of the answers the Premier had given in the filmed part of my interview. I had questions on communes, questions on intellectual freedom, questions on their plans for increasing the supply of consumer goods. All of these the Premier answered at great length, though he had not previously seen these questions.

Only at the end, as we were saying good-by, did our exchange slip into a less formal pattern, and we stood for quite a while talking together. We had been talking about the Warsaw talks, then (and still) going on from time to time between American and Chinese ambassadors in Poland.

"Why are you so worried?" Premier Chou En-lai said to me, smiling. "All your questions are *worried* questions. These Warsaw talks are proceeding, things move forward little by little. There have been over a hundred talks at Warsaw."

"Yes, but what's been accomplished?" I asked.

"They are going on, *that's* the main point. Just as the Korean armistice talks went on, for over two years, and they accomplished the armistice in the end." And as this was being translated, he broke in, in English. "How old are you?" he asked.

"Fifty-one," I told him.

"Well, I'm much older than that and I'm not worried. So why should you be?"

I said that perhaps we are more impatient, that we need quicker results than the Chinese.

"No, no," he said, "you are British—the British have a long historical perspective too."

"But even the British don't have four thousand years of history behind them," I said. And Chou En-lai laughed and held out his hand and we said good-by again.

It had often occurred to me while in China that the confidence in the future that one senses everywhere among her people springs from a consciousness of age, of having met wars and invasions and disasters of all kinds through many centuries and survived them all. China has the confidence of immortality.

And Chou En-lai, I felt, having delivered the official views of his government, was taking this opportunity for a personal word, through me, to those whom I would speak to in the West: *What are you all so worried about?* China has been here four thousand years, and China will be here a great many years longer. That is the reality you are dealing with. You and I, as individuals, are of no great importance.

POSTSCRIPT

No one can come away from a visit to China today without being impressed, even overwhelmed, by the experience. It is impossible not to feel while one is there that one is witnessing one of the great episodes of history and that all our futures are bound to be influenced by it.

Throughout my stay in China, as during my visit there in 1957, I had an extraordinary impression that China was drawing on resources latent within her for a long time and was moving forward very rapidly to a great future. With her vast manpower, the industriousness and intelligence of her people, and the aptitude they are showing in mastering technological processes, it is quite possible that our children, or theirs, may see China regain the position of world leadership that she held before for so many centuries.

The advances achieved by the Chinese people in the past eleven years have been too well-documented to be denied. But questions at once come to mind. The material advances may have been great, but at what human cost have they been achieved? At what loss of human dignity? With what denial of human freedom?

But on whose standards are we to judge and make an answer?

If China's advances are well-documented, so are the conditions of the past.

"I knew Shanghai when it was the gayest city in the Far East [wrote Richard Hughes of the London *Sunday Times*]—gay, that is, if you were a foreigner or a Chinese millionaire. But there were corpses in the street every night, 20,000 died a year from hunger, cold and exposure. And there were swarms of beggars. And the childish street walkers. And the sweating rickshaw coolies, with a professional life expectancy of eight years if they didn't smoke too much opium. . . .

"Now no one goes hungry in Shanghai. . . .

"So arises the dilemma. Who can strike the balance between freedom from starvation for the majority against freedom of thought for the minority? The comparison, one must keep repeating, is not the China of today with the Western world of today, but the China of today with the China of yesterday."

A French correspondent, Robert Guillain, though a sharp critic of life in China today, gives us the same reminder:

"Before, it was appalling—that truth predominated over every other. Poverty, corruption, inefficiency, misery, contempt for the people and for the commonweal, these were the elements which made up the most wretched nation on earth. And I knew China then."

It is difficult for us who stand so far above the corroding effects of poverty to understand that some peoples' conception of human dignity is very different from our own. Not much dignity is possible when life is dominated by the most basic and elemental anxieties. The values of free thought seem remote and irrelevant to those whose history is being written in the language of sheer physical survival.

When a Chinese worker or peasant says he is freer today than he has ever been in his life, he means it. And he sounds as if he means it. Perhaps he doesn't mean it in our way, for he has never known the particular forms of political and social freedom which have been the product of our own historical past and which are the fruit of our relative physical security.

A Chinese uses the word freedom in a very personal, down-to-earth, nontheoretical sense. He is not talking about abstractions but experience. He means that he at last is free to eat, and not to starve; he is free of the landlord and moneylender; he is free to learn to read and write; he is free to develop skills and to exercise talents which would otherwise have remained hidden; he is free to send his childen to school, and when they are ill there is a doctor who can help to make them well; he is free to look at the future with hope and not with despair. For him these are all *new* freedoms. And it's not such a bad list!

As for dignity, I think it is very probable that the forty million people of minority races in China who for the first time are enjoying complete political and social equality with all others, would say their dignity has been enhanced, not lessened. The Marriage Law, which is printed in the Appendix, released the women of China from the miseries of a very degrading feudal system. I would like to see someone ask one of the young women of China today if she feels her human dignity has been infringed!

This book is about China, but by implication, it is also about ourselves. I cannot promise that on this one point or another some error may not be found, and cannot be sure, of course, though my checking was careful, that on this fact or that I may not have been deliberately misled. But I do not believe you can fake a whole country, and I think in all significant respects this book presents a fair and honest account of what is going on in China today. If this is so, or if only half the facts that I have presented, or even one-tenth of them, are true, then it becomes clear that the American people have been most seriously misinformed. I have in one chapter shown the contrast between the reports about the communes as presented to American readers and the reports which appeared in the press of other Western nations. If that is the case with respect to the communes, it is equally the case in regard to most other Chinese developments.

A nation which allows itself to be deluded to this extent is on a dangerous path.

It is not that true reports about China never appear in our press. They do, along with many untrue ones. But by selection, even true reports may convey a false impression. Ugly and brutal things happen in all human communities and I am not suggesting that they do not happen in China, too. But think for a moment what a distorted image of American life readers in another country would receive if the only news they ever heard about America was what was discreditable, if they read only accounts of our crime, our corruption, our juvenile murders, our racial segregation.

What is happening in China today is far livelier, far richer in content, far more successful, than we have been permitted to learn. It is inconceivable to me that ordinary Americans would not welcome and support the vast improvements that have been made, in the health of children, in education, in the general level of cleanliness and morality, in the care of old people; or the devoted restoration of historical buildings, the encouragement given to artists, the support of traditional handicrafts, the new developments in drama, dance, and music. Of all this we know virtually nothing.

To this extent at least, this book may help to redress a balance.

Nor is it realized, I think, the extent to which the Chinese people support their present leadership. The Chinese Communist revolution was not a sudden one. It did not flare up; it burned slowly as a peat fire burns and the source of the flame was always deep in the Chinese soil. For this reason, it was unquenchable.

Our ignorance of what is going on in China has its counterpart in our political attitudes, our decision to have nothing to do with China, and our determination to perpetuate the fantasy that Chiang Kai-shek is the real leader of the Chinese people. Our present China policy is ripe for debate, for discussion on the widest possible scale. Both political parties are involved in our present policy, both have supported it in the past, but there is, I believe, a growing sense that it is a policy which no longer serves our best interests, for it is essentially based on unrealities.

". . . We have wandered lonely in a cloud of self-deception and wishful thinking [wrote C. R. Sulzberger, foreign affairs expert of the *New York Times*, in his book *What's Wrong with U.S. Foreign Policy?*]. Contrary to our own diplomatic traditions and all good sense we have refused to recognize the Peiping regime. . . . We imposed an embargo and an economic blockade. . . . The only consequence of this was to force the Chinese more closely into Moscow's arms."

Mr. Walter Lippmann, of the New York *Herald Tribune*, has repeatedly criticized China policy based on the "untruth that the real government of China is in Formosa." He described U.S. relations with Chiang Kai-shek as, "a classic example—the most far-reaching in our history—of an entangling alliance. Far from it being, as the official apologists say, indispensable to our prestige and influence, this entangling alliance is an enormous liability which, if it does not entangle us in war, is losing us surely and steadily the respect and confidence of our friends."

I share this view. I believe our present policy of hostility toward China and friendship toward Chiang Kai-shek is a mistaken and detrimental one. It has brought us to an impasse which permits us no initiative for action, and offers no compensating advantages. Rarely has history afforded such an example of a nation of first magnitude self-entrapped into a predicament where it can do nothing but wait upon events. It is very easy, I know, to be wise after the fact, and I claim no special gift of insight, but looking back from today's perspective it is surely possible to trace with increasing clarity the mistakes which one by one led us to this dead end.

The refusal by the State Department in 1956 to allow our correspondents into China when the Chinese government offered them visas without strings I think was possibly one of the most tragic of many diplomatic errors, for it has ever since clouded the issue of the exchange of correspondents and so contributed to the present prevailing ignorance about China. Now, when we may want to send our correspondents, we may find it impossible, for China now says that more fundamental issues must be settled first.

Our relations with China have too often been irrational and clouded by emotion. Like the unfolding of a Greek tragedy, initial errors led to others and were then still further compounded; indefensible positions were rationalized and made the basis of "moral obligations"; myths took the place of reality; until today we find ourselves with no strategic alternative to a policy of military opposition and economic boycott toward 700 million Asian people.

Our China policy—or more accurately, our lack of policy—will, it seems certain to me, involve us in ever-increasing difficulty and embarrassment. We are out of phase with our closest allies. And how will we act, vis-à-vis a China we do not recognize, when she is seated (probably against our opposition) in the United Nations? Or if we succeed by one means or another in continuing to keep her out, what will happen to disarmament and to world inspection plans, which must depend, for their effectiveness, upon China's participation? The Chinese government has made clear that it will *not* come into the United Nations if the Chiang Kai-shek group continues to be represented there.

But one day, perhaps by persuasion of our allies, the United States may find it to her best interests no longer to oppose China's entry into the United Nations. Whether this happens tomorrow or in ten years' time, such a change will necessarily appear as an American diplomatic defeat, for it will require abandonment of that guardianship of Chiang which we have so frequently justified on grounds of "moral obligation."

Has the history of diplomacy ever shown a great nation involved in such a web of mutually contradictory commitments?

And to make matters worse, the web is largely of our own making.

The easing of the present tension between the United States and China is surely essential if the peace of our world is to be preserved. I do not believe that this tragically bitter enmity is likely to be resolved by any sudden "bright" solution; and still less will it disappear as a result of clever maneuvers aimed at putting the other side to disadvantage in debate. No single measure will substantially alter the situation—the exchange of correspondents, for example, or relaxing the trade embargo, though both of these would appear to me sensible steps. And least of all are we likely to find a solution through the much-discussed "Two Chinas" policy, which would attempt to make Taiwan an independent country. For the Chinese consider (and with compelling historical reason) that Taiwan is part of China and any such "solution" would only further embitter the Chinese people and would only consolidate and in no way ease the tensions that exist at present.

I believe that America's relations with China can no longer be seen as an issue by itself, in isolation. For it is, at bottom, the consequence of America's world policy. At some future time the United States and China will once again enter into practical and common-sense relations. That is bound to be. But before this can occur, we will, I think, have to undertake a deep and searching examination of what our world policy *is*, and when all is said and done we must make up our minds what kind of a world we wish it to be. The grand language of military threat and moral crusade on which we rely so heavily today may turn out to be irrelevant to our necessities and to the world's hopes.

Understanding starts with a wish to understand. It is difficult to assess what is happening in China today and easy to be deluded by our fears and prejudices; and China must be understood within the context of China's history. Understanding, sanity, and perhaps human survival, too, can be sought only by looking at facts, not by ignoring them.

APPENDIX 1
Language Reform

Among the real problems confronting the Chinese people as they move into the modern world is the complexity of their language, written and spoken.

Unlike our own language, Chinese has no alphabet. Written Chinese was originally ideographs, or pictures, of the object denoted; and though these ideographs, known as characters, today are no longer recognizable as such, they are a cumbersome way of expression.

With our alphabet of twenty-six symbols we can make tens of thousands of words with comparative ease; in Chinese each word requires its own character to be laboriously memorized. Many of them are highly complex. The word for "I" in Chinese requires seven strokes. "Salt" calls for no less than twenty-four. The Chinese have estimated, for example, that it takes a child at least two years longer to master the rudiments of reading and writing in China than it does his counterpart in a country where an alphabet is used.

The handicaps of written Chinese are obvious. Typewriters in China —there are very few—need several hundred keys; typesetting of books, magazines and newspapers is enormously complicated; telegrams have to be encoded and decoded with each character given a four-number code; and the work required to learn even a minimum of one thousand to fifteen hundred characters—enough to be able to read a newspaper —is extremely arduous. A scholar is required to know characters in the thousands. Experts are divided on the total number of characters in the language—between forty and fifty thousand.

Another complication that confronts the Chinese is the great variety of their dialects. Although more than 70 per cent of the people speak various forms of *pu tong hua* (known in the West as Mandarin), the remainder speak dialects quite different from this, as well as different from each other. While the written language is the same throughout the country, the dialects often are so different that people from one area cannot understand those from another. For example, "Mandarin" pronunciation for cabbage, *bai tsai,* is pronounced *bak choi* in Cantonese. Wu dialect, which is spoken in and around Chekiang province and Shanghai, pronounces the word for foreigner, *na ge ning,* in "Mandarin" it is *wai gwo ren.*

Many urban Chinese speak "Mandarin" and one other dialect, and it is not uncommon to hear a conversation going on between two people in two "languages." It is also not uncommon, as I have witnessed, to see men from different areas trying to communicate by writing out a word in mid-air, or one dipping a chopstick into the soysauce and making himself understood on a restaurant table.

The complicated task of language reform was tackled almost immediately after the present government came to power. A committee for reforming the Chinese written language was set up. There were three main objectives: 1) to simplify the written characters; 2) to popularize *pu tong hua* (meaning "common speech"); 3) to draw up and put into practice a scheme for a Chinese phonetic alphabet to annotate the characters by sound symbols.

The task has not been finished, but a start has been made. Five hundred and forty-four of the most common characters have been abbreviated. Before this simplification these 544 characters averaged sixteen strokes each, now the average is eight. To popularize the "common speech," it is being taught in all public schools and emphasized in films and radio; this in itself necessitated the teaching of thousands of teachers throughout the country who had never spoken it. Dialects are not interfered with—many children in China today grow up learning both their local dialect and the "common speech." However, it is believed that in the course of time the "common speech" will be the spoken language all over China.

After much trial and error a written alphabet based on Latin symbols has been adopted. An impression has been gained abroad that the Chinese are scrapping their written language in favor of this. It is not the case. The chief purpose of the Latinized alphabet is to make the language easier to learn by helping to annotate the characters phonetically and transcribing the "common speech." It is also being used to help unify pronunciation.

Scholars abroad have deplored the effect the adoption of these reforms may have on the ancient art of Chinese calligraphy. It is not intended that this art will be affected, although calligraphers in China are encouraged to use the abbreviated forms of the characters. Chinese language authorities apparently recognize that language is a living thing, that it must grow naturally, and that no one can arbitrarily determine what changes the future may bring.

Speaking of the future of the Chinese written language, Chou Enlai declared in January 1958:

We all agree that they [Chinese characters] have made immortal contributions to history. As to whether or not they will remain permanently unchanged, whether they will change on the basis of their original forms, or whether they will be replaced by a phonetic language . . . we need not draw a hasty conclusion. Any language is, however, subject to change, as evidenced by the changes of the characters in the past. There will be changes in the future. We can also say that there will be a day when the languages—written and spoken—of the different peoples of the world will gradually become one and the same. . . . This is a good and not a bad anticipation. . . . On the question of the future of the Chinese language, there may be various views. We can bring them out for discussion and debate.

APPENDIX 2

Food Rationing

There is no over-all food ration applied. Rations vary from area to area. This is partly because of differences in eating habits.

North Chinese eat far less rice than southerners, but they eat more wheat and millet. There are areas where almost no rice is eaten. Moslem people eat more meat, especially mutton. Some sections grow more food in proportion to their population than others. For example, Szechuan province grows more food than it uses and thus exports it to other areas.

While there are no established national standards, there are "norms" which give a general rule of thumb. An office worker, under this general average, would be given thirty pounds of grain per month; an ordinary factory worker would get forty, while those engaged in exceptionally heavy work would get fifty or more. That is, when it is available.

By the autumn of 1960, while I still was in China, these norms were considerably reduced because of the accumulative effects of the poor 1959–60 harvests. One feature of the Chinese rationing system—many Westerners may find it difficult to believe—is that people are asked to set their own "norms" according to their eating habits. People realize, of course, that to claim more than is really needed means someone else goes with less; but it is another application of the "trust the people" principle I have found to be astonishingly true here.

While it is impossible to reach a quantitative national picture of the rationing system, some priority principles are applied generally. Workers involved in exceptionally heavy work (steelworkers, coal miners, etc.), children, and pregnant and nursing mothers get top priority; ordinary workers come next; intellectuals, students, sedentary workers are next in about that order. The lowest on the list are housewives (unless they are pregnant or nursing their babies), the street hawkers and shopkeepers. Artists, actors, and performers; students at the dance and theater schools, and writers get extra rations of meat and edible oil and are in many ways the most favored group of all, but they represent, of course, a very small proportion of the population.

Cities, generally, are worse off for food than the countryside in times of national shortage, but at other times have a generally higher per capita consumption. From June 1960 on, when already it was clear that China would be facing a period of acute food shortage, the city people were being urged to plant vegetables on every available plot of ground. Outside my hotel a rough corner of yard covered with brick and rubble was tackled one afternoon by a crowd of youngsters, who in a few hours had transformed it into a neat vegetable garden. Medical students and nurses from the hospital just opposite the Shin Chiao Hotel dug up and planted another small area. The vegetables when they started to grow in this plot seemed pretty sickly until one day a group of medical students doused them with antibug powder and before I left it was a fairly thriving plot of Chinese cabbage.

In all cities I visited even the small strips of earth that sometimes run between the street and sidewalk were being dug and planted in vegetables. In some cities pipelines with faucet stands at intervals were run in as an aid to these efforts. The vegetable plots were all in the open and unguarded; the vegetables could easily have been stolen at night. One man at the Ministry of Foreign Affairs told me he and his wife had planted onions in their window boxes instead of flowers.

Such efforts, of course, could only slightly alleviate the effects of the poor harvests. In early 1961 a doctor who had recently been in China wrote me of evidence of malnutrition in the cities—though not among the children. Peking and Canton were hard hit. Although information about daily calorie intake was hard to come by, my doctor friend estimated that in the cities, steelworkers were getting 3000 daily, ordinary workers 2500, students 2000, and housewives 1500 or less. This friend, who spent many years in China before 1949 and has been back to China several times since, noted that there was no famine. The situation was tight, rationing strict, but no starvation.

APPENDIX 3
The Marriage Law

More than any other single act, the Marriage Law of May 1950 revolutionized the social structure of China. In one step immemorial feudal customs were made illegal.

Great care was taken with the wording of the law. It had to be simple, so that all could understand, and exact, so that there would be no ambiguity of intention. Under discussion even before the new regime formally took power in October 1949, a draft of the law was formulated by the legal division of the Communist Party in association with women's organizations. Before and after October, forums and discussions were held with numerous groups; the draft was sent for examination to groups on the local level, and many changes were made. It took months of discussions and revision before the draft was finally approved by the national government.

The nature of marriage in China before the Marriage Law is described by Teng Ying-chao, Vice-Chairman of the All-China Democratic Women's Federation:

A special feature of the feudal marriage system in China was that marriages were arbitrarily arranged by parents and forced on their children. Marriage was a sort of bargain. Girls were usually betrothed in their early childhood by arrangement of their parents, who would receive money and gifts as a betrothal or marriage present. Not only was this kind of marriage not free, it was also contracted on the basis of the idea of the superiority of men over women. Many were the victims of this system; many were the unhappy couples forced to share the same roof while their hearts were far apart. This was one of the forms of oppression suffered by the whole people, but women were its special victims. They were required to "follow their husbands no matter what their lot," as the saying went. Under the patriarchal system of old China a woman was required to wear widow's weeds for the rest of her life when her husband died . . . "to die faithful to one husband and not to remarry." A woman divorced by her husband was an object of social contempt.

An old Chinese saying like "a wife married is like a pony bought; I'll ride her and whip her as I like" vividly describes the position of women in old China. They were not only denied political and economic rights and held in servitude but were also stripped of the right even to manage daily domestic affairs. At home their husbands could and did beat them and curse them, and their parents-in-law were free to insult them with impunity. The sufferings endured by luckless daughters-in-law were proverbial. Such miseries resulted in unhappy family life, filled with sorrow and hatred. And this in turn had its direct adverse effects on the physical and mental health of the younger generation.

In the struggle against these evils the women of China learned through bitter personal experience that the feudal marriage system, deeply rooted in the past, and the feudal outlook of men toward marriage and women, were inseparable from the whole system of feudalism in China.

The aim of the Marriage Law was to totally uproot this ancient marriage system. Traditionally there was no such thing as freedom of marriage either in law or in practice. During the Kuomintang regime there was legal provision for freedom of marriage. It was not carried out in practice except in the upper circles of society. For most Chinese it was a freedom that existed only on paper. In the same way freedom of divorce was largely a theoretical freedom for the provision was surrounded with so many qualifications that it was hardly ever applied. In rural areas the freedom of divorce was unthinkable. In areas where feudal attitudes were most deeply rooted women who applied for divorce were sometimes put to death.

Polygamy in China was fairly widespread among the upper classes in the form of concubinage, and adultery was either recognized or tolerated by law. The Kuomintang made some attempts to prohibit concubinage but never succeeded.

A nationwide educational campaign was instituted following the promulgation of the Marriage Law. In general, this Magna Charta of women's rights in China was widely supported, especially in the cities and towns where, through the newly formed women's federations, the educational groundwork had been laid. Nevertheless, what was being attempted was a gigantic effort to overthrow deep-rooted traditions and there was some opposition, particularly in the more remote rural regions.

The abolition of any form of slavery always finds some who resist their new freedom and the women of China were no exception. Despite its initial success, progress in carrying out the new law was uneven, and in some places there was real difficulty in persuading the women that the new law was to their benefit. (There had to be a complete halt for a time in certain sections.) But the educational campaign continued and in almost all areas the population gradually learned that the change was desirable. As the Chinese put it, "step by step" it moved forward.

In 1953 the government, reassured by its general acceptance, launched a final drive to close the remaining gaps, and a new program of education was carried out. Today, the new position of women is accepted by a great majority of the Chinese, including many of the men who had earlier reservations. However, it is undeniable that some of the old attitudes crop up from time to time, as shown in the divorce case described in Part 5, Chapter 19.

Because this law—which gave civil rights to women—had such a profound effect on the lives of hundreds of millions, it is printed here in full. It is an example of the simplicity and directness of language that marks much of present-day Chinese law.

THE MARRIAGE LAW OF THE PEOPLE'S REPUBLIC OF CHINA

General Principles 1

ARTICLE 1

The feudal marriage system, which is based on arbitrary and compulsory arrangements and the superiority of man over woman and ignores the children's interests, shall be abolished.

The New-Democratic marriage system, which is based on the free choice of partners, on monogamy, on equal rights for both sexes, and on the protection of the lawful interests of women and children, shall be put into effect.

ARTICLE   2

Bigamy, concubinage, child betrothal, interference with the remarriage of widows, and the exaction of money or gifts in connection with marriages, shall be prohibited.

The Marriage Contract   2

ARTICLE   3

Marriage shall be based upon the complete willingness of the two parties. Neither party shall use compulsion and no third party shall be allowed to interfere.

ARTICLE   4

A marriage can be contracted only after the man has reached twenty years of age and the woman eighteen years of age.

ARTICLE   5

No man or woman shall be allowed to marry in any of the following instances:

a) Where the man and woman are lineal relatives by blood or where the man and woman are brother and sister born of the same parents or where the man and woman are half-brother and half-sister. The question of prohibiting marriage between collateral relatives by blood (up to the fifth degree of relationship) is to be determined by custom.

b) Where one party, because of certain physical defects, is sexually impotent.

c) Where one party is suffering from venereal disease, mental disorder, leprosy, or any other disease which is regarded by medical science as rendering a person unfit for marriage.

ARTICLE   6

In order to contract a marriage, both the man and the woman shall register in person with the people's government of the district of *hsiang* in which they reside. If the marriage is found to be in conformity with the provisions of this Law, the local people's government shall, without delay, issue marriage certificates.

If the marriage is not found to be in conformity with the provisions of this Law, registration shall not be granted.

Rights and Duties of Husband and Wife 3

ARTICLE 7

Husband and wife are companions living together and shall enjoy equal status in the home.

ARTICLE 8

Husband and wife are in duty bound to love, respect, assist, and look after each other, to live in harmony, to engage in productive work, to care for the children, and to strive jointly for the welfare of the family and for the building up of the new society.

ARTICLE 9

Both husband and wife shall have the rights to free choice of occupation and free participation in work or in social activities.

ARTICLE 10

Both husband and wife shall have equal rights in the possession and management of family property.

ARTICLE 11

Both husband and wife shall have the right to use his or her own family name.

ARTICLE 12

Both husband and wife shall have the right to inherit each other's property.

Relations between Parents and Children 4

ARTICLE 13

Parents have the duty to rear and to educate their children; the children have the duty to support and to assist their parents. Neither the parents nor the children shall maltreat or desert one another.

The foregoing provision also applies to foster-parents and foster-children. Infanticide by drowning and similar criminal acts are strictly prohibited.

ARTICLE 14

Parents and children shall have the right to inherit one another's property.

ARTICLE 15

Children born out of wedlock shall enjoy the same rights as children born in lawful wedlock. No person shall be allowed to harm or discriminate against them.

Where the paternity of a child born out of wedlock is legally established by the mother of the child or by other witnesses or by other material evidence, the identified father must bear the whole or part of the cost of maintenance and education of the child until the age of eighteen.

With the consent of the mother, the natural father may have custody of the child.

With regard to the maintenance of a child born out of wedlock, in case its mother marries, the provisions of Article 22 shall apply.

ARTICLE 16

Husband or wife shall not maltreat or discriminate against children born of a previous marriage.

Divorce 5

ARTICLE 17

Divorce shall be granted when husband and wife both desire it. In the event of either the husband or the wife alone insisting upon divorce, it may be granted only when mediation by the district people's government and the judicial organ has failed to bring about a reconciliation.

In cases where divorce is desired by both husband and wife, both parties shall register with the district people's government in order to obtain divorce certificates. The district people's government, after establishing that divorce is desired by both parties and that appropriate measures have been taken for the care of the children and property, shall issue the divorce certificates without delay.

When only one party insists on divorce, the district people's government may try to effect a reconciliation. If such mediation fails, it shall, without delay, refer the case to the county or municipal people's court for decision. The district people's government shall not attempt to prevent or to obstruct either party from appealing to the county or municipal people's court which must, in the first instance, try to bring about a reconciliation between the parties. In case such mediation fails, the court shall render a verdict without delay.

In the case where, after divorce, both husband and wife desire the resumption of marital relations, they shall apply to the district people's government for a registration of remarriage. The district people's government shall accept such a registration and issue certificates of remarriage.

ARTICLE 18

The husband shall not apply for a divorce when his wife is with child. He may apply for divorce only one year after the birth of the child. In the case of a woman applying for divorce, this restriction does not apply.

ARTICLE 19

The consent of a member of the revolutionary army on active service who maintains correspondence with his or her family must first be obtained before his or her spouse can apply for divorce.

Divorce may be granted to the spouse of a member of the revolutionary army who does not correspond with his or her family for a subsequent period of two years from the date of the promulgation of this Law. Divorce may also be granted to the spouse of a member of the revolutionary army who had not maintained correspondence with his or her family for over two years prior to the promulgation of this Law and who fails to correspond with his or her family for a further period of one year subsequent to the promulgation of the present Law.

Maintenance and Education of Children after Divorce 6

ARTICLE 20

The blood ties between parents and children do not end with divorce of the parents. No matter whether the father or mother acts as guardian of the children, they still remain the children of both parties.

After divorce, both parents still have the duty to support and educate their children.

After divorce, the guiding principle is to allow the mother to have custody of a baby still being breast fed. After the weaning of the child, if a dispute arises between the two parties over the guardianship and an agreement cannot be reached, the people's court shall render a decision in accordance with the interests of the child.

ARTICLE 21

If, after divorce, the mother is given custody of a child, the father shall be responsible for the whole or part of the necessary cost of the maintenance and education of the child. Both parties shall reach an agreement regarding the amount and the duration of such maintenance and education. In the case where the two parties fail to reach an agreement, the people's court shall render a decision.

Payment may be made in cash, in kind, or by tilling land allocated to the child.

Such agreement reached between parents or a decision rendered by the people's court in connection with the maintenance and education of a child shall not prevent the child from requesting either parent to increase the amount decided upon by agreement or by judicial decision.

ARTICLE 22

In the case where a divorced woman remarries and her husband is willing to pay the whole or part of the cost of maintaining and educating the child or children by her former husband, the father of the child or children is entitled to have such cost of maintenance and education reduced or to be exempted from bearing such cost in accordance with the circumstances.

Property and Maintenance after Divorce 7

ARTICLE 23

In case of divorce, the wife shall retain such property as belonged to her prior to her marriage. The disposal of other family properties shall be subject to agreement between the two parties. In cases where agreement cannot be reached, the people's court shall render a decision after taking into consideration the actual state of the family property, the interests of the wife and the child or children, and the principle of benefiting the development of production.

In cases where the property allocated to the wife and her child or children is sufficient for the maintenance and education of the child or children, the husband may be exempted from bearing further maintenance and education costs.

ARTICLE 24

After divorce, debts incurred during the period of their married life together shall be paid out of the property jointly acquired by husband and wife during this period. In cases where no such property has been acquired or in cases where such property is insufficient to pay off such debts, the husband shall be held responsible for paying these debts. Debts incurred separately by the husband or wife shall be paid off by the party responsible.

ARTICLE 25

After divorce, if one party has not remarried and has maintenance difficulties, the other party shall render assistance. Both parties shall work out an agreement with regard to the method and duration of such assistance; in case an agreement cannot be reached, the people's court shall render a decision.

Bylaws 8

ARTICLE 26

Persons violating this Law shall be punished in accordance with law. In cases where interference with the freedom of marriage has caused death or injury, the person guilty of such interference shall bear responsibility for the crime before the law.

ARTICLE 27

This Law shall come into force from the date of its promulgation. In regions inhabited by national minorities, the people's government (or the Military and Administrative Committee) of the Greater Administrative Area or the provincial people's government may enact certain modifications or supplementary articles in conformity with the actual conditions prevailing among national minorities in regard to marriage. But such measures must be submitted to the Government Administration Council for ratification before enforcement.

APPENDIX 4
Text of TV Interview
with Premier Chou En-lai

GREENE: Mr. Chou En-lai, may I thank you first for this opportunity of asking you some of the questions about your country and its policies which are concerning many thoughtful people in the West. As I have a good many questions in my mind and our time is rather short, may I plunge right in?

PREMIER CHOU: Yes. Please go ahead.

Question 1: I have seen many things while traveling through this country which give me the impression that China is strenuously preparing to defend herself. Does this mean that the Chinese government feels that war with the United States is a probability?

Answer: The Chinese people do not want war with the United States. The Chinese people have always wanted to be friends with the American people. We wish to build up our own country in a peaceful environment. We believe that the American people, too, do not want war with China. The U.S. government, however, has all along pursued a policy of aggression against China. The United States has occupied China's territory, Taiwan, and set up many military bases and guided-missile bases in regions close to China. It seeks in this way to form a military encirclement of China. The United States has carried out endless military provocations and war threats against China. Since September 1958, U.S. aircraft and warships have intruded into China's air space and territorial waters over a hundred times. Moreover, the United States has time and again staged large-scale military maneuvres in the Far East with China as the hypothetical enemy. It has stepped up the rearming of Japan and concluded a treaty of military alliance with Japan, thus threatening the security of China, the Soviet Union, and the Southeast Asian countries. Confronted with these war threats, the Chinese people cannot but be constantly on guard and strengthen their power to defend themselves. The greater our power for self-defense, the harder it will be for the United States to carry out military adventures. We believe that so long as the people of China and the United States, as well as the peace-loving people throughout the world, work together, it is possible to prevent the U.S. government from launching a war of aggression against China.

Question 2: It would seem that no fundamental improvement in the relations between China and the United States is possible while the issue of Taiwan (or Formosa as we call it) remains unresolved. Am I right?

Answer: You are right. So long as the United States continues to occupy Taiwan, there can be no basic improvement in the relations between China and the United States. Supposing Long Island in the United States were occupied by another country, could the United States improve its relations with that country? The Chinese government has always stood for the settlement of international disputes through negotiations, without resorting to the use or threat of force. It is even willing to sit down and talk with the U.S. government which has invaded and occupied China's territory, Taiwan. The Chinese–United States ambassadorial talks were started on China's initiative. But, as the United States government persists in occupying Taiwan by force, the talks have dragged out for five years, through a hundred sessions, without results so far.

Question 3: Are there any conceivable arrangements regarding Taiwan under which China would be prepared to consider a compromise?

Answer: Taiwan is an inalienable part of China's territory. This is a historical fact. The Cairo and the Potsdam Declarations, both signed by the U.S. government, confirm that Taiwan is Chinese territory. After the Japanese surrender, Taiwan was formally restored to China on October 25, 1945, and was taken over and administered by the then Chinese government. Liberation of the mainland of China is purely China's internal affair in which no foreign country can interfere. The question now is that the U.S. government is occupying China's territory, Taiwan, with its armed forces and blocking the Chinese government from exercising its sovereignty in Taiwan. There is only one way to settle this question. The U.S. government must agree to withdraw all its armed forces from Taiwan and the Taiwan Straits.

For quite some time now, the U.S. government has been scheming to create "two Chinas." In this regard, both the Republican and the Democratic Parties in the United States have the same policy. The United States seeks to set up what they call an "independent state"

of Taiwan, or a "Sino-Formosan nation," or to conduct what they call
a "plebiscite" in Taiwan, or even to place Taiwan "under trusteeship,"
and so on. All this is aimed at dismembering Chinese territory, violating
China's sovereign rights and legalizing the seizure of Taiwan by the
United States. All the Chinese people, including those on Taiwan, are
firmly opposed to these schemes; even those members of the Chiang
Kai-shek clique who have the slightest concern for the national interest
don't approve of them.

Question 4:   Both sides seem to have taken and reaffirmed policies
which seem irreconcilable, both are deeply committed. Do you consider
that your recent proposal for a Pacific nonaggression pact which would
include the United States might form the basis of some agreement
which would end the present impasse between the United States and
China?

Answer: China has always advocated peaceful coexistence among
nations with different social systems. Proceeding from this principle of
peaceful coexistence, the Chinese government recently again proposed
that the countries of Asia and those bordering on the Pacific, including
the United States, should conclude a peace pact of mutual nonaggression and turn this whole area into an area free of nuclear weapons.
This proposal by the Chinese government has won wide support from
world public opinion. It also won a warm response in the general resolution adopted by the Sixth World Conference against Atomic and
Hydrogen Bombs and for Total Disarmament held in Tokyo not long
ago. But, the proposal was hurriedly rejected by the U.S. State Department. This shows that the U.S. government is afraid of peace; it
is afraid that it will no longer be able to make use of tension to control
its military bases in Asia and the Pacific region, and that the puppets
it has reared in many countries in this region will all collapse like Syngman Rhee and Kishi. This also shows that the allegations of United
States officials and certain newspapers to the effect that "China is belligerent," that "China rejects peaceful coexistence between countries
of different social systems," that "China wants to start a war to advance the world revolution," and so forth are all groundless slanders.
The Chinese government's proposal is not only in the interest of the
people of China and the United States, but it is also in the interest
of the people of other Asian countries and those bordering on the Pacific. The Chinese people will work tirelessly over a long period of
time, together with the peoples of these countries, to bring this proposal to fruition.

Question 5: I want to ask a few questions about Russia if I may. There have been reports lately of a divergence between China and the Soviet Union, especially in regard to this policy of "peaceful coexistence." Do you have any comments to make about these reports?

Answer: China has always stood for peaceful coexistence among nations with different social systems. This has also been the consistent stand of the Soviet Union and the other socialist states. There is no divergence on this. As early as in 1954, China initiated jointly with India and Burma the Five Principles of peaceful coexistence. They are: mutual respect for aggression, noninterference in each other's internal affairs, equality and mutual benefit and peaceful coexistence. At the Bandung Conference in 1955, China, together with other Asian and African countries, formulated the Five Principles of peaceful coexistence. China has established peaceful and friendly relations with many Asian and African countries as well as a number of European countries, and has now established formal diplomatic relations with Cuba. In the past two years and more, China has signed treaties of friendship and mutual nonaggression or treaties of peace and friendship with Yemen, Burma, Nepal, and Afghanistan. The facts show that China has consistently pursued a policy of peaceful coexistence, and that China's stand has never changed. If other countries, the United States included, also cherish the same desire, China is of course willing to co-exist peacefully with them on the basis of the Five Principles. But the imperialist countries, particularly the United States, persist in the policies of positions of strength and the cold war. They, and particularly the United States, have imposed embargoes, carried out subversive activities, military provocations, and war threats against the socialist countries, thereby gravely jeopardizing world peace. Such policies are against the common interest of the people in the United States and throughout the world. Only by concerting their efforts and struggling persistently to expose and resist these policies of the U.S. government can the people of the whole world possibly prevent the U.S. government from launching an aggressive war. Only by so doing can they possibly force the U.S. government to enter into earnest negotiations on disarmament and the prohibition of nuclear weapons, and compel it to agree to abolish its military bases on foreign soil and disband its aggressive military alliances. And only thus can our wish for peaceful coexistence with the United States possibly be realized.

Question 6: China, though lagging behind the Soviet Union in technology, is potentially more powerful in natural resources and, of course, in population. Some Westerners think that Russia is already becoming apprehensive of the rapidly growing industrial and military power of China. Have you anything to say about this?

Answer: The socialist camp headed by the Soviet Union is today more powerful than ever before. The recent safe return to the earth of the second spaceship launched by the Soviet Union proves that the Soviet Union is far ahead of the United States in science and technology. The Chinese people are overjoyed at this brilliant achievement of the Soviet people.

As for China, there is no need to deny that we are still backward economically and culturally. We are making efforts to lift ourselves quickly out of this backwardness, striving to catch up with or surpass Britain in the output of the main industrial products in about ten years. The rapid progress of China's socialist construction adds to the strength of the socialist camp. It is therefore something that the peoples of the other socialist countries are glad to see.

The relationship between socialist countries is a brand-new type of fraternal relationship between nations. The socialist countries cannot possibly be apprehensive of each other. Their common interest is to help and support each other for a common upsurge in their national economy and continuously raise the material and cultural standards of their own peoples. The solidarity among all the countries of the socialist camp is unbreakable. What is more, the solidarity between the two great countries, China and the Soviet Union, is the bulwark of the defense of world peace. What the imperialists and all reactionaries fear the most is the solidarity of the socialist countries. They seek by every means to sow discord and break up this solidarity. But they will never succeed in these despicable designs. In case the imperialist countries delude themselves into thinking that there is a chance to start some military adventure against the socialist countries, then, I would like to reaffirm now what the Chinese government has repeatedly declared in the past, namely: The socialist camp is one integral whole; a provocation against any socialist country is a provocation against China, and in that event we would never sit idly by.

Question 7: Have you any comments to make about the border dispute between China and India and the present discussions that are taking place between the two countries?

Answer: China has undelimited boundaries with many neighboring countries in Southeast Asia. This is a question inherited from history. The Chinese government has always held that in accordance with the Five Principles of peaceful coexistence, settlements fair and reasonable to both sides should be sought through friendly consultations in a spirit of mutual understanding and mutual accommodation, and that pending an over-all settlement of the boundary questions, the *status quo* should be maintained and not altered by one-sided action, let alone by force. The boundary questions between China and Burma, and between China and Nepal could be and were settled precisely because both sides adopted such an attitude. If the Indian government had taken a similar attitude, the boundary question between China and India could have been settled. But, it is regrettable that the Indian government not only wants to hold onto a big piece of territory which belonged to China, but has brought up new territorial demands against China. What is more, Indian troops provoked armed clashes on the border. At the same time, an anti-China campaign was launched by forces in India who tried to use disputes with foreign countries for political aims at home. All this has brought about tension between China and India for a while.

In order to seek various ways to a reasonable settlement of the boundary question, I went to Delhi in April this year to meet with Prime Minister Nehru. In spite of very great efforts on our part, the Indian side failed to respond accordingly. At present, Chinese and Indian officials are holding meetings. I hope they will achieve positive results.

The traditional friendship of the 1000 million people of China and India is a profound one. We are confident that the Indian people, like the Chinese people, hope that the boundary question between the two countries will be speedily settled. With continued sincerity and confidence as before, the Chinese government will go on working tirelessly for a fair and reasonable settlement of the Sino-Indian boundary question.

Question 8: In regard to Japan, does the constitution of the new Japanese government give any grounds for hope of an improvement in Chinese-Japanese relations?

Answer: This will depend on what attitude the new Japanese government adopts toward China. We are willing to work for the normalization of Sino-Japanese relations in accordance with the Five Principles of peaceful coexistence. We have seen the Japanese people giving strong expression to the same desire. Provided the new Japanese government no longer pursues a policy of hostility to China, as did the Kishi government, provided it no longer trails behind the United States in manufacturing "two Chinas," and that it no longer obstructs and sabotages the normalization of Sino-Japanese relations, the relations between the two countries can be improved. But up to now we have seen no positive moves on the part of the Ikeda cabinet toward improving

Sino-Japanese relations. On the contrary, the Ikeda cabinet still sticks to the Japan-U.S. treaty of military alliance which is aimed at aggression against China and the Soviet Union and threatening the Southeast Asian countries, and it continues to revive the forces of Japanese militarism. That's exactly why the Japanese people's struggle for independence, democracy, peace, and neutrality continues to develop. The Chinese people give sincere sympathy and support to their just struggle.

Question 9: Some Westerners maintain that China is extremely anxious to become a member of the United Nations—that is, for the Peking government to be accepted as the rightful representative of the Chinese people. Others believe that your government is quite content to leave things as they are for the present, as the exclusion from the United Nations provides what may be called a legitimate grievance, very useful for propaganda purposes, especially against the United States. Have you anything to say about these speculations?

Answer: China is a member of the United Nations in the first place. Indeed, it is one of the founding members of the United Nations together with the Soviet Union, the United States, Britain, and France. The question is now that the U.S. government, controlling the United Nations, is forcibly keeping there the Chiang Kai-shek clique, which was cast aside long ago by the Chinese people. China's seat in the United Nations is thus usurped, and the People's Republic of China, with its 650 million people, is deprived of its legitimate rights in the United Nations. The Chinese people firmly oppose this line of action of the U.S. government. If the U.S. government fails to change it, the United States and not China will be more and more isolated; and the prestige of the United Nations and not China's international status will suffer more and more. The United Nations must expel the Chiang Kai-shek clique and restore China's legitimate rights. Otherwise, it will be impossible for China to have anything to do with the United Nations.

Question 10: I have two questions to ask you about population, which I can put into one. China's population today is nearly 700 million and is growing at the rate of twelve to fourteen million a year or (to make it more vivid) at the rate of about 1700 every hour. So my first question is this. Why is the Chinese government making less effort to popularize the use of birth control than it did in say a few years ago? While it is true that China over the past ten years has increased her agricultural production at a higher rate than the rate of increase of her population, there is surely a definite limit to the extent to which any country can increase its food supply. So my second question is: What will happen when China reaches that limit? Will she not then be impelled either to drastically reduce her birth rate or to forcibly expand her territories?

Answer: China is the most populous country in the world, but its density of population is only about seventy persons per square kilometer, much lower than that of Britain, Japan, or India. Education on planned parenthood was and continues to be carried on in China mainly to protect the health of mothers and provide favorable conditions for bringing up children, not because of so-called "population pressure." China's population is increasing at an annual rate of about 2 per cent. In absolute figures, it means an increase of over ten million each year, which is indeed a considerable number. It is not such a great number, however, when you consider the natural conditions of China with its vast territory and rich resources. It seems even less like a large number considering the manpower needed in our long-range, large-scale construction and development programs.

China's cultivated area is only a little over a million square kilometers, which is about one-ninth of the total area of the country. After long-term efforts at land reclamation, the cultivated area can be gradually enlarged to over two million square kilometers. So the question of scarcity of arable land will not arise at all.

What is even more important, the rate of increase of our grain output is higher than the rate of increase of our population. Our production of manufactured goods for daily use is increasing at an even faster rate. During the ten years from 1949 to 1959 the average annual rate of increase of the population was 2 per cent, while that of grain output was 9.8 per cent. That is to say, grain output increased at a rate more than four times that of the population. Our industrial production has been developing even more rapidly, with output of articles of daily use increasing by over 10 per cent every year. As we take various steps to modernize our agriculture, our yields per unit area will greatly rise, in addition to which, the cultivated area will be gradually enlarged. So grain output will continue to increase at a faster rate than population, and there can be no question of a grain shortage because of population growth.

You seem to think that a country carries on expansion because of overpopulation. We disagree with this view. Before the First World War, Britain had a population of forty-five million, which was not a large figure. Yet Britain for a long time had a colonial empire on which, it was said, "the sun never set." The United States has an area slightly smaller than China and a population less than one-third of China's.

Yet the military bases of the United States are spread out all over the globe, and it maintains as many as 1.5 million troops on foreign soil. China, on the other hand, in spite of its enormous population, has not a single soldier, let alone a military base, on foreign territory. So you can see that whether a country carries on expansion or not is not decided by the size of its population, but by its social system.

Being a socialist country, China cannot, must not, and need not seize a single inch of foreign territory under any circumstances. The Chinese people in the past suffered greatly from imperialist aggression. We know very well that an aggressor can only end in defeat. He has no other fate in store. We have boundless sympathy for all peoples who were or are subjected to imperialist and colonialist oppression. We resolutely support the Asian, African, and Latin American peoples in their just struggle against imperialism and colonialism, to win and preserve their national independence. We are willing to make common efforts together with the people of other countries to oppose imperialist aggression and safeguard world peace.

GREENE: I have many other questions I would like to ask you, but unfortunately our time has run out. May I thank you again, on behalf of people in many countries for your readiness to answer the many important questions I have put to you.

APPENDIX 5
List of Government Officers

1. *People's Republic of China*

Chairman of Republic	Liu Shao-chi
Vice-Chairmen of Republic	Soong Ching-ling (Madame Sun Yat-sen)
	Tung Pi-wu

National People's Congress

Chairman of NPC Standing Committee	Chu Teh
	Li Chi-shen
	Lo Jung-huan
	Shen Chun-ju
	Kuo Mo-jo
	Huang Yen-pei
	Peng Chen
	Li Wei-han
	Chen Shu-tung
	Dalai Lama
	Saifudin
	Cheng Chien
	Panchen Lama
	Ho Hsiang-ning
	Liu Po-cheng
Secretary General NPC Standing Committee	Hsieh Chueh-tsai
Chief Procurator	Chang Ting-cheng

State Council 1 premier, 16 vice-premiers, 39 ministers and chairmen of commissions, 1 secretary-general

Premier	Chou En-lai
Vice-Premiers	Chen Yun
	Marshal Lin Piao
	Marshal Peng Teh-huai
	Teng Hsiao-ping
	Teng Tzu-hui
	Marshal Ho Lung
	Marshal Chen Yi
	Ulanfu
	Li Fu-chun
	Li Hsien-nien
	Marshal Nieh Jung-chen
	Po Yi-po
	Tan Chen-lin
	Lu Ting-yi
	Lo Jui-ching
	Hsi Chung-hsun

MINISTERS and Chairmen of Commissions

Internal Affairs	Chien Ying
Foreign Affairs	Marshal Chen Yi
Defense Affairs	Marshal Lin Piao
Public Security	Lo Jui-ching
State Capital Construction Commission	Chen Yun
State Planning Commission	Li Fu-chun
State Economic Commission	Po Yi-po
Scientific and Technological Commission	Marshal Nieh Jung-chen
Finance	Li Hsien-nien
Food	Sha Chien-li
Commerce	Yao Yi-lin
Foreign Trade	Yeh Chi-chuang
Aquatic Products	Hsu Teh-heng
Metallurgical Industry	Wang Ho-shou
Chemical Industry	Peng Tao
Machine Building 1st ministry	Tuan Chun-yi
Machine Building 2nd ministry	Liu Chien
Machine Building 3rd ministry	Chang Lien-kuei
Petroleum Industry	Yu Chiu-li
Coal Industry	Chang Lin-chih
Geology	Li Su-kwang
Building	Liu Hsiu-feng
Textile Industry	Chiang Kuang-nai
Light Industry	Li Chu-chen
Railways	Teng Tai-yuan
Communications	Wang Shou-tao
Posts and Telecommunications	Chu Hsueh-fan
Agriculture	Liao Lu-yen
Land Reclamation	Wang Chen
Forestry	Liu Wen-hui
Water Conservation and Electric Power	Fu Tso-yi
Labor	Ma Wen-jui
Culture	Shen Yen-ping (Mao Tun)
Education	Yang Hsiu-feng
Public Health	Li Teh-chuan
Physical Culture and Sports Commission	Marshal Ho Lung
Nationalities Affairs Commission	Ulanfu
Overseas Chinese Affairs Commission	Liao Cheng-chih
Committee for Cultural Relations with Foreign Countries	Chang Hsi-jo
Secretary-General of State Council	Hsi Chung-hsun

2. *The Communist Party of China*

Chairman of Central Committee	Mao Tse-tung
Vice-Chairmen	Liu Shao-chi
	Chou En-lai
	Chu Teh
	Chen Yun
	Lin Piao
Secretary-General	Teng Hsiao-ping
Political Bureau (Politbureau) Normally 20	Mao Tse-tung
	Liu Shao-chi
	Chou En-lai
	Chu Teh
	Chen Yun
	Lin Piao
	Teng Hsiao-ping

The above are the Standing Committee of the Political Bureau.

Tung Pi-wu
Peng Chen
Lo Jung-huan
Chen Yi
Li Fu-chun
Peng Teh-huai
Liu Po-cheng
Ho Lung
Li Hsien-nien
Ko Ching-shih
Li Ching-chuan
Tan Chen-lin

Politbureau alternate members	Ulanfu
	Chang Wen-tien
	Lu Ting-yi
	Chen Po-ta
	Kang Sheng
	Po Yi-po

Secretariat (9)   Teng Hsiao-ping
                                         Peng Chen
                                         Wang Chia-hsiang
                                         Tan Chen-lin
                                         Tan Cheng
                                         Huang Ko-cheng
                                         Li Hsueh-feng
                                         Li Hsien-nien

Alternate Secretariat   Liu Lan-tao
                                         Yang Shang-kun
                                         Hu Chiao-mu

APPENDIX 6
Population

By 1952 it became clear that the Chinese government would require accurate population statistics, partly because of the impending general election of deputies to the National People's Congress and partly because preparations were being made to launch the First Five-Year Plan. Using the 1939 Soviet census as a model, therefore, the State Statistical Administration developed in 1952 a huge organizational plan for taking the first census, and the decision to take the census on June 30, 1953, was widely publicized in the papers and on the radio.

For six months two and a half million students, schoolteachers, civil servants, and others were mobilized and trained as census takers. The initial results were announced in June 1954. As a check, a sample survey was subsequently carried out in 343 counties in twenty-three provinces, five cities, and one autonomous region. The check was said to have covered more than 52 million persons or 9 per cent of the total population. As a result of this check the final figures were slightly modified and the official total population of China (excluding Taiwan) was declared to be 582,603,417.

I am greatly indebted for my information regarding the 1953 census in China to a most scholarly and interesting book entitled *Studies on the Population of China 1368–1953*, by Dr. Ho Ping-ti. This will for long, I think, remain the definitive work concerning China's population. Though in Dr. Ho's view the census was not without some flaws, it was planned with great care and the results are likely to be closer to the truth than any previous Chinese population figures.

There is some doubt about how quickly China's population is increasing. This can only be fully determined when the next census is taken. When I was in China in 1957 the figure generally accepted was 2.2 per cent per annum. Further studies apparently indicated it was closer to 2.0 per cent per annum. Premier Chou En-lai used the 2.0 per cent figure in the course of my television interview with him.

With the 1953 census as a base, and using the 2.0 per cent figure as the annual average increase, China's population on December 31, 1961, will be 689,329,559. Including Taiwan (somewhat over ten million) the population at the time will have reached close to 700 million; excluding Taiwan, China's population will pass the 700 million mark during 1962.

On December 31, 1961, the population of China (excluding Taiwan) will be increasing at the rate of 13,786,591 per year or about 1,574 *per hour*.

To put these figures in their world setting, the population of the world on December 31, 1961, will be approximately 2,996,450,000, increasing at an estimated rate of 1.65 per cent according to UN estimates or 49,441,425 per year; or approximately 5,644 every hour.

APPENDIX 7
TV and Radio in China

China first began making TV sets, on a limited scale, in 1958. In September 1960 two stations were in operation, in Peking and Shanghai. Daily programs—popular science, sports, opera and theater, children's programs—usually lasted two to three hours, and special public events brought the average total transmission time to around twenty-five hours a week. There were then only 12,700 receiving sets in the entire country. These were nearly all for public use: set up in parks with benches for viewers, some in railway stations, hotels, and other public places.

As with all statistics in China, these figures were soon out of date. Before the end of 1960 new stations in Tientsin, Harbin, Shenyang, Changchun, and Canton were operating. All in all, there were twenty-nine stations and relay centers throughout the country, with sixteen stations still in the experimental stage.

The receiving sets I saw in Peking were fourteen- to eighteen-inch sets, made in Shanghai. The number of sets manufactured will undoubtedly move up.

A spare-time "TV University," was instituted in March 1960 by the Peking station. By the end of the year nearly nine thousand worker-students had taken courses. Mathematics, physics, and chemistry are given to students of upper high-school level, and preparatory courses are taken by those of middle high-school level.

Radio stations are numerous. Every large city has one or more stations. (Peking stations broadcast altogether a total of seventy hours a day.) The number of receiving sets is small, however, for such a large population: four and a half million in September 1960. Public loudspeakers bring the listening audience to a larger figure than is suggested by the number of radio sets. Many commune workshops, I noticed, were assembling sets on an assembly-line basis and it is likely that the total number of sets will be reaching high figures quite soon. Almost all rural communes have their own "radio" stations: usually the public loudspeakers in different villages in the commune being linked by line; and in a few cases by low-powered transmitters. All long-distance trains have not only a record player but a central radio receiving set with a loudspeaker in all compartments.

Radio Peking broadcasts on various short-wave frequencies all over the world twenty-four hours a day. The total transmission time on Radio Peking (International) is over 133 hours each day. The equipment, studios, tape recorders, etc., which I saw there were quite up-to-date.

BIBLIOGRAPHY

I. Books
II. Periodicals, Pamphlets, and Documents

Bibliography I—Books

Barnett, A. Doak, *Communist China and Asia*, New York: Harper and Bros. (Council on Foreign Relations), 1960.

Belden, Jack, *China Shakes the World*, New York: Harper and Bros., 1949.

Bodde, Derk, *China's Cultural Tradition*, New York: Rinehart and Co., 1957. (Source Problems in World Civilization.)

Boorman, Howard L., Eckstein, Alexander, *et al.*, *Moscow-Peking Axis*, New York: Harper and Bros. (Council on Foreign Relations), 1957.

Cameron, James, *Mandarin Red*, New York: Rinehart and Co., 1955.

Chao Kuo-chun, *Agrarian Policies of Mainland China* (1949–1956), Cambridge, Mass.: Harvard University Press, 1957.

Clark, Gerald, *Impatient Giant: Red China Today*, London: W. H. Allen, 1960.

De Beauvoir, Simone, *The Long March*, Cleveland: World Publishing Co., 1958.

De Riencourt, Amaury, *The Soul of China*, New York: Coward-McCann (with the Foreign Policy Research Institute of the University of Pennsylvania), 1958.

De Segonzas, A., *Visa for Peking*, London: William Heinemann, 1956.

Faure, Edgar, *The Serpent and the Tortoise*, New York: St. Martin's Press, 1958.

Fei Shiao-tung and Chang Chih-i, *Earthbound China: A Study of the*

Social Life of a Chinese County Seat, New York: Frederick A. Preager, 1945.

Feng Yu-lan, *A History of Chinese Philosophy*, Princeton, Princeton University Press, 1952.

Fitzgerald, C. P., *Revolution in China*, London: The Cresset Press, 1952.

—— *Flood Tide in China*, London: The Cresset Press, 1958.

Gale, G. S., *No Flies in China*, London: George Allen and Unwin, 1955.

Granet, Marcel, *Chinese Civilization*, New York: Meridian Books, 1958.

Guillain, Robert, *600 Million Chinese*, New York: Criterion Books, 1957.

Harrer, Heinrich, *Seven Years in Tibet*, London: Pan Books, 1956.

Ho Ping-ti, *Studies on the Population of China, 1368–1953*, Cambridge, Mass.: Harvard University Press, 1959. (Harvard East Asian Studies 4.)

Hughes, T. J., and Luard, D. E. T., *The Economic Development of Communist China, 1949–1958*, London: Oxford University Press, 1959.

Isaacs, Harold R., *Scratches on Our Minds*, New York: John Day Co., 1958.

Levenson, Joseph R., *Confucian China and Its Modern Fate*, Berkeley and Los Angeles: University of California Press, 1958.

Lippmann, Walter, *The Communist World and Ours*, London: Hamish Hamilton, 1959.

Mao Tse-tung, *Selected Works of Mao Tse-tung*, Vols. 1–4, London: Lawrence and Wishart, 1956.

Needham, Joseph (research assistant Wang Ling), *Science and Civilization in China*, Vols. I and II, Cambridge: Cambridge University Press, 1954 and 1956.

Pannikar, K. M., *In Two Chinas: Memoirs of a Diplomat*, London: George Allen and Unwin, 1955.

Payne, Robert, *Chungking Diary*, London: William Heinemann, 1945.

Peck, Graham, *Two Kinds of Time*, Boston: Houghton Mifflin Co., 1950.

Peking Opera, Peking: New World Press, 1957.

Prawdin, Michael, *The Mongol Empire*, London: George Allen and Unwin, 1953.

Rostow, W. W., *The Prospects of Communist China*, London: Chapman and Hall, 1954.

Roy, Claude, *Into China*, London: McKibbon & Kee, 1955.

Snow, Edgar, *Random Notes on Red China* (1936–1945), Cambridge, Mass.: Harvard University Press, 1957.

Sues, Ilona Ralf, *Shark's Fins and Millet*, Boston: Little Brown and Company, 1944.

Sulzberger, C. R., *What's Wrong with U.S. Foreign Policy?* New York: Harcourt Brace, 1959.

United States Relations with China, Department of State Publication 3573, Far Eastern Series 30, Division of Publications, Office of Public Affairs, 1949.

Wales, Nym, *Red Dust*, Stanford: Stanford University Press, 1952.

Waley, Arthur, *Analects of Confucius*, London: George Allen and Unwin, 1949.

Wollaston, Nicholas, *China in the Morning*, London: Jonathan Cape, 1960.

Bibliography II—Periodicals, Pamphlets, and Documents

Foreign Affairs, Vol. 36, No. 3 (April 1958), Lancaster, Pa.: Council on Foreign Relations.

Greene, Felix, *What's Really Happening in China?* San Francisco: City Lights Books, 1959.

The Agrarian Reform Law of the People's Republic of China, Peking: Foreign Languages Press, 1959.

Brown, Harrison, and Real, James, *Community of Fear*, Santa Barbara, Calif.: Center for the Study of Democratic Institutions (Fund for the Republic, Inc.), 1960.

What's Going On in China, American Friends Service Committee, 1959.

International Affairs, Vol. 36, No. 3, Oxford: July 1960.

Die Weltwocke, Zurich, Switzerland, September 6, 1958.

Mineral Trade Notes (*Rich Mineral Resources Spur Communist China's Bid for Industrial Power*), U.S. Department of the Interior, Bureau of Mines, Special Supplement No. 59, Washington, D.C., March 1960.

"Red China's Hidden Capital of Science," by J. Tuzo Wilson, *Saturday Review*, November 8, 1959.

Chinese Trade and Economic News Letter, September 1958, British Council for the Promotion of International Trade, 15 Hanover Square, London, W.1, England.

"China's Economic Growth," by Professor Charles Bettelheim, of the Sorbonne, Paris, *The Economic Weekly,* Bombay, India, November 22, 29, December 6, 13, 1958.

Chinese Trade and Economic News Letter, February 1959.

Chinese Trade and Economic News Letter, June 1958.

Article on Chinese Agriculture by Chou Pei-yuan, *Bulletin of the Atomic Scientists,* October 1958.

"Chinese Agriculture," by René Dumont, Professor of Comparative Agriculture at the Agronomic Institute, Paris, in *Le Monde,* Paris, October 12, 1958.

Article by the Editor of Reuters, *New York Times,* February 27, 1958.

New Republic, January 5, 1959.

"The Chinese are 'liquidating' their disease problems," by Dr. Brian Maegraith, *The New Scientist,* London, December 5, 1957.

"Visit to China," by F. Avery Jones, M.D., F.R.C.P., *British Medical Journal,* November 9, 1957.

"The New China—Some Medical Impressions," by T. F. Fox, M.A., M.D., F.R.C.P., *The Lancet,* London, November 9, 16, 23, 1957.

"A Letter from Peking," by Dr. Joshua Horn, F.R.C.S., published by Britain-China Friendship Association, London, 1959.

"Party Resolutions on Questions Concerning People's Communes," December 10, 1958, *Hsinhua* News Agency, London.

Article by R. H. S. Crossman, M.P., *New Statesman,* London, January 10, 1959.

"China May Soon Be *the* World Power," by Edward B. Jolliffe, *MacLean's Magazine,* November 22, 1958.

"The Challenge of China," by James Muir, Souvenir Edition of the *Royal Bank Magazine,* Royal Bank of Canada, October 1958; also in *Congressional Record,* July 15, 1959.

Memorandum to American Diplomatic Missions setting forth official reasons for non-recognition of China, State Department, August 1958.

"China and the Cold War," by Michael Lindsay (Lord Lindsay), Melbourne, the University Press.

Statement on China adopted by the Fifth World Order Conference, Cleveland, Ohio, November 18–21, 1958; convened by the Department of International Affairs of the National Council of the Churches of Christ in the U.S.A.

"Contemporary China and the Chinese," *The Annals of the American Academy of Political and Social Science*, January 1959.

Department of State, Public Affairs Area—Policy Advisory Staff (Special Guidance No. 28, December 23, 1949).

"The China Impasse," by Li Thian-hok, *Foreign Affairs*, April 1958.

Far Eastern Economic Review, Yearbook, 1961, Hong Kong.